First World War
and Army of Occupation
War Diary
France, Belgium and Germany

52 DIVISION
156 Infantry Brigade
Headquarters
1 April 1918 - 31 March 1919

WO95/2897/1

The Naval & Military Press Ltd
www.nmarchive.com
Published in association with The National Archives

Published by

The Naval & Military Press Ltd

Unit 10 Ridgewood Industrial Park,

Uckfield, East Sussex,

TN22 5QE England

Tel: +44 (0) 1825 749494

www.naval-military-press.com

www.nmarchive.com

This diary has been reprinted in facsimile from the original. Any imperfections are inevitably reproduced and the quality may fall short of modern type and cartographic standards.

© **Crown Copyright**
Images reproduced by permission of The National Archives, London, England, 2015.

Contents

Document type	Place/Title	Date From	Date To
Heading	WO95/2897-1		
Heading	52nd Division 156th Infy Bde Bde Headquarters Apr 1918-Mar 1919		
Heading	52nd Division B.H.Q 156th Infantry Brigade April 1918		
Heading	War Diary 156th Infantry Brigade Volume XXXV April 1918		
War Diary	Surafend	01/04/1918	03/04/1918
War Diary	Kantara	04/04/1918	04/04/1918
War Diary	Alexandria	05/04/1918	05/04/1918
War Diary	Alexandria Egypt	06/04/1918	12/04/1918
War Diary	At Sea	12/04/1918	16/04/1918
War Diary	Marseilles	17/04/1918	17/04/1918
War Diary	En Route By Train	18/04/1918	20/04/1918
War Diary	St Firmin	20/04/1918	25/04/1918
War Diary	Wizernes	25/04/1918	26/04/1918
War Diary	Mametz	27/04/1918	30/04/1918
Miscellaneous	156th Infantry Brigade Administrative Instruction No.6	01/04/1918	01/04/1918
Miscellaneous	4th Royal Scots 7th Sco Rifles	22/04/1918	22/04/1918
Miscellaneous	156th Infantry Brigade Administrative Instruction No.1	24/04/1918	24/04/1918
Miscellaneous	Time Table		
Miscellaneous	Administrative Instructions No.1		
Operation(al) Order(s)	156th Inf. Brigade Order No. 33	25/04/1918	25/04/1918
Miscellaneous	Effective Strength 156th Infantry Brigade	30/04/1918	30/04/1918
Heading	War Diary Of 156th Infantry Brigade For May 1918 Vol XXXVI		
War Diary	Mametz	01/05/1918	07/05/1918
War Diary	Neuville St Vaast	08/05/1918	08/05/1918
War Diary	Mont St Eloi	09/05/1918	14/05/1918
War Diary	Willerval Section	15/05/1918	31/05/1918
Miscellaneous	Provisional Defence Scheme		
Operation(al) Order(s)	156th Infantry Brigade Order No. 30	21/05/1918	21/05/1918
Diagram etc	Diagram		
Miscellaneous	Allotment Of Training Grounds		
Operation(al) Order(s)	156th Inf. Bde Order No. 34	05/05/1918	05/05/1918
Miscellaneous	Time Table		
Miscellaneous	Warning Order	13/05/1918	13/05/1918
Operation(al) Order(s)	156th Inf. Brigade Order No 35	14/05/1918	14/05/1918
Miscellaneous	Disposition of Troops in Right (Willerval) Section	14/05/1918	14/05/1918
Diagram etc	Diagram		
Heading	War Diary Of 156th Infantry Brigade For June 1918 Volume XXXVII		
War Diary	Willerval Section	01/06/1918	01/06/1918
War Diary	Mont. St. Eloi	02/06/1918	11/06/1918
War Diary	S 27b.0.5	12/06/1918	12/06/1918
War Diary	Chaudiere Section	12/06/1918	28/06/1918
War Diary	Mont St Eloi	29/06/1918	30/06/1918
Miscellaneous	Report Of Day Patrol 1/7th Royal Scots	01/06/1918	01/06/1918
Operation(al) Order(s)	156th Inf Brigade Order No. 38	07/06/1918	07/06/1918
Miscellaneous	156th Infantry Brigade Administrative Orders No.4	07/06/1918	07/06/1918

Miscellaneous	Action Of Reserve Brigade		
Operation(al) Order(s)	156th Infantry Brigade Order No. 39	16/06/1918	16/06/1918
Operation(al) Order(s)	156th Infantry Brigade Order No. 40	25/06/1918	25/06/1918
Miscellaneous	BM1/71/1 VIII		
Miscellaneous	Tactical Description Of The Section		
Miscellaneous	Organisation Of The Area For Defence		
Miscellaneous	Plan For The Conduct Of The Defence		
Miscellaneous	Appendix 1 Probable Enemy Action.		
Miscellaneous	Appendix II Organisation of Anti-Aircraft Defence.		
Miscellaneous	Appendix III Action Of Artillery And Trench Mortars		
Map	Map		
Diagram etc	Communications 156 Infy Bde		
Map	Map		
Miscellaneous	4th Royal Scots 7th Sco Rifles	28/06/1918	28/06/1918
Miscellaneous	156th Inf. Bde. Left Section Defence Scheme	28/06/1918	28/06/1918
Operation(al) Order(s)	156th Infantry Brigade Order No. 41	27/06/1918	27/06/1918
Miscellaneous	War Diary Appendix		
Heading	War Diary Of 156th Infantry Brigade 1st To 31st July 1918 Volume XXXVIII		
War Diary	Mont St Eloi	01/07/1918	08/07/1918
War Diary	Right Section (H.S.T.6.C.6.5)	09/07/1918	16/07/1918
War Diary	Right Section	17/07/1918	21/07/1918
War Diary	St Eloy	22/07/1918	22/07/1918
War Diary	Barlin	23/07/1918	30/07/1918
War Diary	Ecoivres Chateau Meurice	31/07/1918	31/07/1918
Miscellaneous	G.O.C. 4th Royal Scots.	29/06/1918	29/06/1918
Miscellaneous	BM 96	29/06/1918	29/06/1918
Miscellaneous	156th Infantry Brigade Order No. 42	06/07/1918	06/07/1918
Operation(al) Order(s)	156th Infantry Brigade Order No. 42	06/07/1918	06/07/1918
Miscellaneous	Administrative Orders No.6	06/07/1918	06/07/1918
Operation(al) Order(s)	156th Infantry Brigade Order No. 43.	14/07/1918	14/07/1918
Miscellaneous	Administrative Order No. 7	14/07/1918	14/07/1918
Operation(al) Order(s)	156th Infantry Brigade Order No. 44	20/07/1918	20/07/1918
Miscellaneous	March Table		
Miscellaneous	Issued With 156th Infantry Brigade Order No. 44.		
Miscellaneous	Ref. Map Sheet 44 B.1/40.000	23/07/1918	23/07/1918
Miscellaneous	4th Royal Scots 7th Sco. Rifles		
Operation(al) Order(s)	156th Infantry Brigade Order No. 45	21/07/1918	21/07/1918
Operation(al) Order(s)	156th Infantry Brigade Order No. 37	31/05/1918	31/05/1918
Miscellaneous	Amendment To 156th Inf. Brigade Order No. 39	01/06/1918	01/06/1918
Miscellaneous	War Diary Appendix Casualties May 1918		
Miscellaneous	War Diary Appendix Effective Strength		
Operation(al) Order(s)	156th Infantry Brigade Order No. 45	29/07/1918	29/07/1918
Operation(al) Order(s)	156th Infantry Brigade Order No. 47	30/07/1918	30/07/1918
Miscellaneous	March Table		
Miscellaneous	Table "A"	30/07/1918	30/07/1918
Operation(al) Order(s)	156th Infantry Brigade Order No. 48	31/07/1918	31/07/1918
Miscellaneous	156th Infantry Brigade		
Miscellaneous	War Diary Appendix XIV		
Heading	War Diary A.D.P.S Canadian Forces August 1st-31st 1918 Officer A.Gs Office at The Base		
Heading	HQ 156 Infy Bde Vol 5 Agst 18		
Heading	War Diary Of 156th Infantry Brigade 1st To 31st August 1918 Volume XXXIX		
War Diary	B.20.b.2.6.	01/08/1918	16/08/1918
War Diary	Chateau Berles D14b57	16/08/1918	20/08/1918

War Diary	Berneville	21/08/1918	22/08/1918
War Diary	Blairville Quarries	23/08/1918	25/08/1918
War Diary	T.1.b.1.5	26/08/1918	26/08/1918
War Diary	N 34.A.6.8	27/08/1918	27/08/1918
War Diary	N.36.D.6.8	28/08/1918	28/08/1918
War Diary	S 5.B.6.8	28/08/1918	31/08/1918
Operation(al) Order(s)	Operation Order No. 1 156th Infantry Brigade	22/08/1918	22/08/1918
Miscellaneous	Casualties First Phase		
Miscellaneous	War Material Captured First Phase 22/28 August 1918		
Map	Map		
Miscellaneous	War Diary August 1918 Appendix I		
Miscellaneous	Gavrelle Section	06/08/1918	06/08/1918
Miscellaneous	Gavrelle Section Intelligence Summary No.7	07/08/1918	07/08/1918
Miscellaneous	Gavrelle Section Intelligence Summary No.8	08/08/1918	08/08/1918
Miscellaneous	Gavrelle Section Intelligence Summary No.9	09/08/1918	09/08/1918
Miscellaneous	Gavrelle Section Intelligence Summary No.10	10/08/1918	10/08/1918
Miscellaneous	Gavrelle Section Intelligence Summary No.11 for 24 hours ending 6 am 11-8-18	11/08/1918	11/08/1918
Miscellaneous	Gavrelle Section Intelligence Summary No.12	12/08/1918	12/08/1918
Miscellaneous	Gavrelle Section Intelligence Summary No.13 for Period 6 am 12/8/18 to 6 am 13/8/18	13/08/1918	13/08/1918
Miscellaneous	Gavrelle Section Intelligence Summary No.14 for Period 6 am 13/8/18 to 6 am 14/8/18	14/08/1918	14/08/1918
Miscellaneous	Gavrelle Section Intelligence Summary No.15	15/08/1918	15/08/1918
Operation(al) Order(s)	156 Infy Bde Order No. 53	31/08/1918	31/08/1918
Miscellaneous	War Diary Appendices 156th Inf Bde		
Miscellaneous	War Diary App. IX		
Miscellaneous	Report On Operations Of 156th Infantry Brigade. 20th-28th August 1918 (both days inclusive)		
Operation(al) Order(s)	156th Infantry Brigade Order No. 40	08/08/1918	08/08/1918
Miscellaneous	4th Royal Scots	09/08/1918	09/08/1918
Miscellaneous	O.C. 4th Royal Scots	10/08/1918	10/08/1918
Operation(al) Order(s)	156th. Infantry Brigade Order No. 10	14/08/1918	14/08/1918
Operation(al) Order(s)	156th. Infantry Brigade Order No. 83	14/08/1918	14/08/1918
Operation(al) Order(s)	156th. Infantry Brigade Order No. 52	15/08/1918	15/08/1918
Miscellaneous	Relief Table		
Map	Map		
Map	France		
Heading	52 Div 156th Bde (inf) Sept 18		
Miscellaneous	Hdqrs 52nd Division	16/10/1918	16/10/1918
Heading	War Diary Of 156th Infantry Brigade 1st To 30th September 1918 Vol 6		
War Diary	U.7.c.9.5	01/09/1918	01/09/1918
War Diary	U.20.a.96	02/09/1918	02/09/1918
War Diary	V.30d53	03/09/1918	03/09/1918
War Diary	D 1a.35	04/09/1918	06/09/1918
War Diary	B3c36	07/09/1918	15/09/1918
War Diary	C.6b48	16/09/1918	20/09/1918
War Diary	D.15.b.6.7. H.Q Moeuvres Sector	21/09/1918	23/09/1918
War Diary	Bde H.Q D.7.a.83	24/09/1918	26/09/1918
War Diary	H.Q E19.a.2.9	27/09/1918	30/09/1918
Operation(al) Order(s)	156th Infantry Brigade Order No. 54	01/09/1918	01/09/1918
Miscellaneous	Diary Of Operation		
Map	Map		
Miscellaneous	Attached App II		
Miscellaneous	A Form Messages And Signals.		

Type	Description	Date From	Date To
Miscellaneous	A Form Messages And Signals. Attd App II		
Operation(al) Order(s)	156th Infantry Brigade Order No. 57	26/09/1918	26/09/1918
Miscellaneous	Addendum To 156th Inf Brigade Order No. 57	26/09/1918	26/09/1918
Miscellaneous	O.C. 1/7th Sec. Rifles	26/09/1918	26/09/1918
Miscellaneous	Report On Operations Of 156th Infantry Brigade	12/09/1918	12/09/1918
Miscellaneous	Casualties Second Phase	01/09/1918	01/09/1918
Miscellaneous	War Material Captured Second Phase		
Miscellaneous	Lessons Learned During Operations	13/09/1918	13/09/1918
Operation(al) Order(s)	156th Infantry Brigade Order No. 52	14/09/1918	14/09/1918
Miscellaneous	156th Infantry Brigade Administrative Instructions No 11	15/09/1918	15/09/1918
Miscellaneous	156th Infantry Brigade		
Miscellaneous	156th Infantry Brigade Casualties September 1918		
Miscellaneous	Division-XVII Corps	17/09/1918	17/09/1918
Diagram etc	Diagram		
Miscellaneous	4th Royal Scots	07/09/1918	07/09/1918
Miscellaneous	A Form Messages And Signals.		
Operation(al) Order(s)	156th Inf Bde Order No 56	20/09/1918	20/09/1918
Miscellaneous	Report On Operations Of 156th Infantry Brigade	30/09/1918	30/09/1918
Miscellaneous	A Form Messages And Signals.		
Miscellaneous	Appendix XI Instruction No. 1 To attack entered in Divisional Order No. 150		
Miscellaneous	156th Infantry Brigade Administrative Instructions No.23	20/09/1918	20/09/1918
Operation(al) Order(s)	156th Infantry Brigade Order No. 27	21/09/1918	21/09/1918
Miscellaneous	Addendum To 156th Inf. Brigade Order No. 57	26/09/1918	26/09/1918
Miscellaneous	Account Of Operations Of 156th Infantry Brigade	30/09/1918	30/09/1918
Map	France		
Miscellaneous	Attached App XIV		
Map	Map		
Heading	War Diary Of 156th Infantry Brigade 1st To 31st October 1918 Volume XLI		
War Diary	E.19.a.3.9	01/10/1918	01/10/1918
War Diary	Cantaing	02/10/1918	06/10/1918
War Diary	Louverval	07/10/1918	07/10/1918
War Diary	Izel-Lez Hameau	08/10/1918	18/10/1918
War Diary	Chateau De La Haie	19/10/1918	19/10/1918
War Diary	Billy-Montigny	20/10/1918	20/10/1918
War Diary	Auby	21/10/1918	24/10/1918
War Diary	Coutiches	25/10/1918	27/10/1918
War Diary	Mont Du Proy	28/10/1918	31/10/1918
Operation(al) Order(s)	156th Infantry Brigade Order No. 58	01/10/1918	01/10/1918
Miscellaneous	March Table		
Miscellaneous	A Form Messages And Signals		
Operation(al) Order(s)	156th Infantry Brigade Order No. 59	06/10/1918	06/10/1918
Miscellaneous	March Table Issued With 156th Bde. Order No. 59		
Miscellaneous	O.C. 4th Royal Scots	09/10/1918	09/10/1918
Operation(al) Order(s)	156th Infantry Brigade Order No. 60	18/10/1918	18/10/1918
Miscellaneous	March Table Issued With 156th Infantry Brigade Order No. 60		
Operation(al) Order(s)	156th Infantry Brigade Order No. 61	19/10/1918	19/10/1918
Miscellaneous	March Table Issued With 156th Inf Brigade Order No. 61.		
Operation(al) Order(s)	156th Infantry Brigade Order No. 62	20/10/1918	20/10/1918
Miscellaneous	March Table Issued With 156th Infantry Brigade Order No. 65		

Miscellaneous	4th Royal Scots	22/10/1918	22/10/1918
Miscellaneous	Table "A"		
Miscellaneous	Load Table Light Trench Mortar Battery		
Miscellaneous	4th Royal Scots	22/10/1918	22/10/1918
Operation(al) Order(s)	156th Infantry Brigade Order No. 63	23/10/1918	23/10/1918
Miscellaneous	March Table		
Miscellaneous	O.C. 4th Royal Scots	24/10/1918	24/10/1918
Operation(al) Order(s)	156th Infantry Brigade Order No. 64	26/10/1918	26/10/1918
Miscellaneous	March Table		
Operation(al) Order(s)	To All Recipients Of 156th Inf. Bde. Order No. 65	28/10/1918	28/10/1918
Operation(al) Order(s)	156th Infantry Brigade Order No. 65	28/10/1918	28/10/1918
Map	Map		
Miscellaneous	Reference Sketch On Back		
Miscellaneous	156th Infantry Brigade Effective Strength		
Miscellaneous	156th Infantry Brigade Casualties October 1918		
Heading	War Diary Of 156th Infantry Brigade From 1st To 30th November 1918		
War Diary	Mont De Proy	01/11/1918	08/11/1918
War Diary	Hergnies	09/11/1918	09/11/1918
War Diary	Blaton	10/11/1918	10/11/1918
War Diary	Herchies	11/11/1918	27/11/1918
War Diary	Lombise	28/11/1918	30/11/1918
Operation(al) Order(s)	156th Infantry Brigade Order No. 65	02/11/1918	02/11/1918
Operation(al) Order(s)	156th Infantry Brigade Order No. 66	31/10/1918	31/10/1918
Miscellaneous	O.C., 7th Sco. Rifles 412th Field Co. R.E	01/11/1918	01/11/1918
Diagram etc	Diagram		
Miscellaneous	412th Field Coy. R.E "B" Coy. 52nd.	05/11/1918	05/11/1918
Miscellaneous	4th, Royal Scots	05/11/1918	05/11/1918
Miscellaneous	156th Infantry Brigade Effective		
Miscellaneous	156th Infantry Brigade Casualties December 1918		
Miscellaneous	O.C., 4th Royal Scots	05/11/1918	05/11/1918
Miscellaneous	4th Royal Scots	05/11/1918	05/11/1918
Miscellaneous	4th Royal Scots	07/11/1918	07/11/1918
Miscellaneous	156th Infantry Brigade Effective Strength		
Miscellaneous	156th Infantry Brigade Casualties November 1918		
Operation(al) Order(s)	156th Infantry Brigade Order No. 69	08/11/1918	08/11/1918
Miscellaneous	March Table		
Operation(al) Order(s)	156th Infantry Brigade Order No. 70	09/11/1918	09/11/1918
Miscellaneous	March Table To Accompany Brigade Order No. 70		
Miscellaneous	A Form Messages And Signals		
Miscellaneous	Report On Operations Of 156th Infantry Brigade For The Period	17/11/1918	17/11/1918
Miscellaneous	4th Royal Scots	19/11/1918	19/11/1918
Heading	War Diary Of 156th Infantry Brigade From 1st To 31st December 1918		
War Diary	Lombise	01/12/1918	31/12/1918
Miscellaneous	4th Royal Scots	14/12/1918	14/12/1918
Miscellaneous	G.O.C., 156th Inf. Bde	13/12/1918	13/12/1918
Miscellaneous	4th. Royal Scots	21/12/1918	21/12/1918
Heading	War Diary Of 156th Infantry Brigade From 1st To 31st January 1919		
War Diary	Lombise	01/01/1919	31/01/1919
Miscellaneous	156th Infantry Brigade Strength		
Heading	War Diary Of 156th Infantry Brigade 1st To 28th February 1919 Volume XLV		
War Diary	Lombise Belgium	01/02/1919	28/02/1919

Miscellaneous	War Diary Jany 1919 Effective Strength of 156th Infantry Brigade		
Heading	War Diary Of 156th Infantry Brigade From 1st To 31st March 1919 Volume XLVI		
War Diary	Lombise Belgium	01/03/1919	17/03/1919
War Diary	Soignies Belgium	17/03/1919	31/03/1919
Operation(al) Order(s)	156th Infantry Brigade Order No. 71.	15/03/1919	15/03/1919

W005/2887 (1)

W005/2887 (1)

52ND DIVISION
156TH INFY BDE

BDE HEADQUARTERS
APR 1918 — MAR 1919

52nd Division.

Sailed from EGYPT 11.4.18 for Western Front.
Disembarked MARSEILLES 17.4.18.

B. H. Q.

156th INFANTRY BRIGADE;;; APRIL 1918.

Confidential

—(ORIGINAL)—
WAR DIARY

156th. INFANTRY BRIGADE.

VOLUME XXXV

APRIL. 1918.

Vol 1

156TH INFANTRY BRIGADE. WAR DIARY OR INTELLIGENCE SUMMARY.

Army Form C. 2118.

APRIL. 1918.

PAGE ONE
Summary of Events and Information

Place	Date	Hour	Summary of Events and Information	Remarks and references to Appendices
SURAFEND	1		The Brigade in Bivouac area. Preparatory arrangements now being carried out for move. Odmmishabie instructns. No. 6. issued to all concerned. Brig. General A.N. Leggett D.S.O. returned from short leave and resumed command. Capt. D. Bruce DSO. M.C. returned from home leave & resumed duties as Staff Captain. The Commander in Chief visited Brigade Headquarters to say Good Bye to	APPENDIX I
"	2		Brigadier General Commanding, and asked Brig. General to convey best wishes to all ranks of the 156th Brigade. 412th Coy. R.E. entrained at LUDD for KANTARA. Representatives from units in Brigade group proceeded yesterday and today by train from LUDD to adjust financial matters of units concerned befor embarkation. Tents and Bivouacs and various stores returned to ORDNANCE. All horses and other animals and all vehicles returned.	
"	3		The Brigade group – less artillery – entrained at LUDD in five trains at 3-hour intervals, commencing at 0851. Lt. Col. J.M. Findlay having gone to hospital as a result of a riding accident, Major G.R.V. Nunn-Fore M.C. took over command of 1/8th Scottish Rifles, Major C.H.J. Metcalf, Bedfordshire Regiment, reported for duty as Brigade Major vice Capt. H.E. Elliot 1/4 Royal Scots. N. Sayer. Sussex Yeomanry	

Army Form C. 2118.

156TH INFANTRY BRIGADE WAR DIARY or INTELLIGENCE SUMMARY

APRIL 1918.

PAGE TWO

Place	Date	Hour	Summary of Events and Information	Remarks and references to Appendices
KANTARA	4		Trains reached KANTARA at intervals during the day. A halt took place on reaching KANTARA EAST, Troops detrained and had a meal. After an interval of about three hours during which all base kits were collected units entrained again at KANTARA WEST, and five trains proceeded at intervals as before, bound for ALEXANDRIA. Weather good.	WBCH
ALEXANDRIA	5		Trains conveying Brigade units arrived at GABARRI DOCKS at intervals during the day, the first train arriving at 6 a.m. Troops detrained immediately and embarkation took place, the units embarking on two steamers. S.S. "LEASOWE CASTLE" (J. Holl, MASTER) conveyed Brigade Hdqrs. 1/4th Royal Scots, 1/7th Royal Scots, and 1/7th Scottish Rifles. Major General J. Hill, D.S.O. Commdg. 52nd Division, also travelled on this ship. Brig. General A.N. Leggett D.S.O. was in command of the troops, with Capt. W. Robertson 7th Royal Scots as Adjutant and Capt. W. Robertson 7th Royal Scots as Quartermaster. S.S. "CANBERRA" (J. Douton, MASTER) conveyed 1/8th Sco. Rifles, 156th M.G. Coy. 156th Light Trench Mortar Battery, 1/1st Lowland Field Ambulance, and various R.A.M.C. details. Major J.R.V. Nunsifore M.C. Commdg. 1/6th S.R. was O.C. Troops, with Capt. E.R. Boyd 1/8th S.R. as Adjutant and Lt Greenwalaw 1/8th S.R. as Quartermaster.	WBCH

2Lt D.W. Watson

155th INFANTRY BRIGADE.   **APRIL. 1918.**

WAR DIARY
or
INTELLIGENCE SUMMARY
Summary of Events and Information

Army Form C. 2118.

PAGE THREE

Place	Date	Hour	Summary of Events and Information	Remarks and references to Appendices
ALEXANDRIA EGYPT.	6th to 10th		The embarkation of all units being complete, S.S. "LEASOWE CASTLE" and S.S. "CANBERRA" moved, on the afternoon of the 6th, from quayside to the middle of the harbour, where they were moored. No leave ashore was granted. Both steamers were crowded, but initial difficulties in accommodation and commissariat were largely overcome before sailing. The time was spent in resting and cleaning up after the railway journey, practice alarms on emergency stations, practice in manning boats and rafts. Bathing parades by boats to the breakwater, and rowing in small native boats round the harbour helped to vary the monotony. The various submarine guards, boat sentries, deck sentries, and other duties were detailed and the wearing and care of lifebelts were practised and explained to all ranks. During this period the other Brigades (155th and 157th) were arriving and detraining and embarking, and by the evening of the 10th the convoy was ready to put to sea. Before sailing, Brig. Genl. A.H. Leggett D.S.O. read to the assembled officers messages of thanks and good wishes which G.O.C. Division had received from the Commander in Chief Egypt. By order E.S. Bulfin, C.B. D.S.O. Commdg. XXIst Corps.	

Army Form C. 2118.

156TH INFANTRY BRIGADE.

WAR DIARY
or
INTELLIGENCE SUMMARY.
(Erase heading not required.)

APRIL. 1918.

PAGE FOUR

Place	Date	Hour	Summary of Events and Information	Remarks and references to Appendices
ALEXANDRIA EGYPT.	11	2 pm	The 52nd Division Convoy sailed, escorted by Japanese destroyers. Until clear of the swept channel, aeroplanes and motor patrol boats also assisted. The weather was calm but dull and the visibility low. The ships in the convoy were INDARA, OMRAH, KAISER-I-HIND, CALEDONIA, CANBERRA, LEASOWE CASTLE.	
			All ranks stood to on emergency stations till 5.30 pm. At dusk every port hole and window has to be darkened over, and no smoking is allowed on deck after dark, the result being that not a speck of light remains to indicate the position of our ship to any enemy. Sufficient orderly officers are detailed for duty by night to enforce strictly all the orders issued.	
	12th		The weather fortunately favoured the convoy, and during the first two days out was comparatively calm. Later there was a considerable swell, but not rough enough to cause any discomfort to the majority of the troops, but sufficiently rough to make the operations of enemy submarines more difficult.	
AT SEA	to		The convoy steered a 3 ÿ zog course throughout and the order in which the ships moved was constantly changing.	

Army Form C. 2118.

WAR DIARY
or
INTELLIGENCE SUMMARY.

(Erase heading not required)

15th Infantry Brigade

April 1918.

Instructions regarding War Diaries and Intelligence Summaries are contained in F. S. Regs., Part II. and the Staff Manual respectively. Title pages will be prepared in manuscript.

Place	Date	Hour	Summary of Events and Information	Remarks and references to Appendices
AT SEA	16th		At 10 a.m. daily the O.C. Troops inspected the ship, and once per day an alarm was sounded to practise the men in getting quickly to their stations. The time taken was gradually reduced to four minutes. During the voyage lectures were given by the Brigade Major on "Conditions in France". Parades were held under Battalion arrangements and special attention was given to Gas Drill. Considering the crowded conditions below decks, the health of the men was good. The conduct of the troops during the voyage was very satisfactory. On the 16th the weather became hazy, and observations became more difficult in consequence.	[signature]

156TH INFANTRY BRIGADE WAR DIARY

INTELLIGENCE SUMMARY

APRIL 1918.

Army Form C. 2118.

(PAGE SIX)

Place	Date	Hour	Summary of Events and Information	Remarks and references to Appendices
MARSEILLES	17	9 a.m.	After a voyage of 5 days 19 hours, the convoy reached MARSEILLES this morning in calm weather, and all the ships were at once berthed in the docks. No enemy craft were sighted during the voyage and every ship reached port safely. The good weather, which had been experienced during the voyage, broke down, and disembarkation, which commenced immediately, took place in a downpour of rain. Orders were received to entrain forthwith by Battalions.	
EN ROUTE BY TRAIN.	18 19 20		For nearly three days the Brigade travelled slowly up through France. The "halte repas" were few and at long distances apart, and consequently the feeding arrangements for the men were rather unsatisfactory. The climate seemed very cold after Palestine, especially by night, and whenever possible hot tea was served at the halts. The first train carried Bde. Hdqrs and the 1/7th Bn. The Royal Scots, and travelling via CETTE, ORLEANS, VERSAILLES, reached NOYELLES-(ABBEVILLE 1/100,000) at 6 a.m. on the morning of the 20th, and the other trains arrived at intervals of a few hours through the day.	

WAR DIARY or INTELLIGENCE SUMMARY

156th INFANTRY BRIGADE

APRIL 1918

Army Form C. 2118.

PAGE SEVEN

Place	Date	Hour	Summary of Events and Information	Remarks and references to Appendices
ST. FIRMIN.	20		M. Lieut DEVALS, French Army, was attached to Brigade as Interpreter. On detraining at NOYELLES units marched to billeting areas situated on the north of the mouth of the RIVER SOMME, and were allotted to villages as follows (Ref ABBEVILLE 1/100,000)	
			Brigade Headquarters, 7th Sco. Rifles, 156th T.M. Battery - ST. FIRMIN	
			4th Royal Scots — RUE	
			7th Royal Scots — ST. QUENTIN.	
			8th Sco. Rifles — BOUT des CROCS.	
			The troops were quartered in farm buildings and officers in the farm houses and cottages. Considerable difficulty was experienced in billeting owing to the fact that the Brigade is much stronger than the average Infantry Bde in France.	
			The billets at RUE proved to be unsuitable and the 7th Royal Scots	8/S/C/1
			camped in a field adjoining the Chateau on the south of the town.	8/S/C/1
—"—	21		The day was spent in resting and cleaning up after the long railway journey. The Brig. General Commdg. visited the units billets.	
—"—	22		Cleaning up, parades, and inspections.	
			B.M. No 3. issued to units. (Re TRAINING)	8/S/C/1
			All units drew horses and transport animals & vehicles at ABBEVILLE. (APPENDIX III)	

156th INFANTRY BRIGADE WAR DIARY or INTELLIGENCE SUMMARY

Army Form C. 2118.

APRIL 1918.

(PAGE EIGHT)

Place	Date	Hour	Summary of Events and Information	Remarks and references to Appendices
ST.FIRMIN	23.		Issue of clothing &c. Parades and inspections of Box Respirators. Preliminary orders received for move to take place on 25th.	
—"—	24		Administrative Instructions No 1 issued to units — (Ref. move) Administrative Instructions No 1a issued to units —	(APPENDIX III) (APPENDIX IV)
—"—	25		The Brigade left RUE Station in six trains, the first including Brigade Headqrs, leaving at 8.44 a.m. The route was via ETAPLES, MONTREUIL, ST. POL, LILLERS to WIZERNES (Ref. map HAZEBROUCK 5a, 1/100000) where detrainment took place at 5.30 p.m. Orders had been received for the Brigade to move into billets in neighbouring villages, and the Brigade Headqrs moved into HALLINES, two miles West of WIZERNES. The 1/4th Royal Scots arrived at 7.30 p.m. and marched to QUELMES where billets were allotted to the Bn. Before the third train arrived, fresh orders were received, to the effect that the Brigade would move by road tomorrow. The B.G.C. decided that the other Battalions would not move to Billets on detraining, but would Bivouac in fields adjoining WIZERNES Station. Brigade Order No B3.	(APPENDIX V)

WAR DIARY

156TH INFANTRY BRIGADE

APRIL, 1918.

INTELLIGENCE SUMMARY.
(PAGE NINE)

Place	Date	Hour	Summary of Events and Information	Remarks and references to Appendices
WIZERNES	25 (cont)		was accordingly issued, the 1/7Z Royal Scots conforming, in addition to the Battalions named. All six trains arrived during the night 25/26/4/	
—"—	26		After breakfast the Battalions moved off separately by road via HELFAUT, HEURINGHEM, ECQUES to new Billet Area situated near MAMETZ (Ref. FRANCE 1/40,000 Sheet 36a.) and were accommodated as follows. Brigade Headquarters. 1/7Z R. Scots, party 1/7Z. Sco. Rifles. — MAMETZ. 1/4Z Royal Scots — REBECQ. L.T.M. Battery + party 1/8Z. S.R. GLOMENGHSN. 1/7Z Sco. Rifles — RINCQ. The Brigade is now in the 1st. ARMY. — XI. Corps. Corps HQrs are at ROQUETOIRE and Division HQrs will shortly open at AIRE. The billeting area is far better than the last one and units were soon settled in their new quarters.	
MAMETZ	27		Brig. General Commanding and Brigade Major visited units. As most of the Land is under crops, it is difficult to find training areas.	
—"—	28		Capt. Allcott, Gas Officer from the 1st Army has been today attached to the Brigade to advise and superintend Anti Gas Training, and today delivered the first of a series of lectures to officers and N.C.O's on the subject.	

Army Form C. 2118.

156th INFANTRY BRIGADE.

WAR DIARY
or
INTELLIGENCE SUMMARY.

APRIL 1918.

(PAGE TEN)

Place	Date	Hour	Summary of Events and Information	Remarks and references to Appendices
MAMETZ	29		Units carried out route marches and gas respirator training. The attached gas officer superintended gas test, all ranks of 2 Battalions being passed through a Gas Chamber, wearing Small Box Respirators.	JJS C/-
--	30		Major General John Hill C.B. D.S.O. Commdg. 52nd Division visited Bde. Headqrs. and accompanied by the Brig. General Commanding, attended Lecture delivered to the Brigade (in two parties) by Lt Colonel Campbell of the Army Gymnastic and Bayonet Fighting Staff on "The Spirit of the Bayonet". The Lecture was listened to with great interest by the men, and at the close Colonel Campbell was duly thanked. An expert Bayonet Fighting Instructor has been attached to the Brigade today. Gas Chamber Tests were continued and the remainder of the Brigade passed through Gas. Effective Strength of Brigade, today's date, Casualty Return. -- nil.	JJS C/- (APPENDIX VI) (APPENDIX VII)

OM Monteagle Lt/Col.
Brigade Major.
156th Infantry Brigade.

SECRET.   *War Diary April 1918*   COPY No. 20

156th Infantry Brigade Administrative Instructions No. 6.

APPENDIX 1

2nd April 1918.

1. BAGGAGE and EQUIPMENT.
(i) Nine camels per Battalion will be drawn at 0530 tomorrow and loaded with stores. They will be ready to move off from Bde. Supply Dump at 0645 under Q.M.S. of Bde. Camel Section. One mounted orderly per Battalion will be sent.
　　The camels will be unloaded by Battalion Guards at Railway Siding.

(ii) Two G.S. Wagons per Battalion
　　One   do.   for M.G. Coy.
　　One   do   for L.T.M. Battery,
will report to units at 0800, and will take stores to units' dumps at Railway Siding. They will be loaded as quickly as possible as they are proceeding for rations.
　　One mounted orderly per Battalion, and one (one) for M.G. Coy and L.T.M. Battery, will be sent.
　　The camels will be unloaded as quickly as possible by units' Guards at Railway Siding.

(iii) All baggage, less what can be taken on camels detailed below for move of units will be sent to the Railway Siding early tomorrow.

2. S.A.A., GRENADES, STOKES SHELLS and VERY LIGHTS.
Camels will be drawn at 0630 tomorrow from "D" Section, and will be loaded with all ammunition, less pouch, L.G. Magazine and M.G. Belt S.A.A.
　　The convoy will assemble at Bde. Supply Dump at 0730 under an Officer to be detailed by O.C., 1/4th Royal Scots.
　　The B.T.O. will detail a N.C.O. and 10 men mounted to accompany this convoy.
　　The number of camels to be drawn will be wired to units and the Camel Officer to-night.
　　The ammunition will be handed to D.A.C., RAMLEH.

3. RATIONS.
Two days rations will be drawn from Bde. Refilling point tomorrow at usual hour. Units will draw camels to deliver them to their lines.

4. TRANSPORT.
All animals and vehicles will be handed in as ordered in Administrative Instructions No. 5 para 5, by 1830 tomorrow. Receipts will be taken.

5. BIVOUAC SHEETS.
(i) Bivouac sheets of 4th Royal Scots and 7th Royal Scots will be dumped in the lines of 4th Royal Scots in bundles of ten, and will be collected by O.C., "D" Section "D" Coy C.T.C. and returned to Div. A.O.D. Receiving Depot, near SURAFEND.

(ii) Bivouac sheets of other units will be returned by them to the same Depot by camel during the morning of 3rd April.

6. LATRINES.
All mobile latrine equipment will be returned to Ord-nance tomorrow night.
　　Trench latrines will be dug. These will be properly filled in before units march out.

7. SICK.
All men likely to fall out on the march will be sent off early under an Officer to the Units' Station Dump.

8. CAMELS/

- 2 -

8. **CAMELS.** Camels will be allotted to units as under on 3rd April:-

    Brigade H.Q............15
    Each Battalion.........45
    M.G. Coy...............15
    T.M. Batty.............15
    1/1st L.F. Amb.........19

The above will be drawn by units from "D" Sect. "D" Coy. C.T.C.
The camels will be taken over by a Divisional Mounted Policeman at the Station and returned to "D" Section lines.

9. **ENTRAINING.** Units will entrain on 3rd April at Siding beside Dumps at LUDD Station as follows:-

Unit.	Time train ready to load.	Time train leaves LUDD.
4th Royal Scots	0700	0851
7th Royal Scots	1000	1151
7th Sco. Rifles	1300	1451
8th Sco. Rifles	1600	1751
(Bde. H.Q............)		
(M.G. Coy............)		
(L.T.M. Battery......)		
(320th Coy A.S.C.....)	1900	2051
(Supply Section......)		
(F.P.O. & Ordnance...)		

A Marching Out State, shewing Officers and Other Ranks entrained, will be handed to a representative of Bde. Staff at the Station.

10. **F.P.O. & Ordnance.** The F.P.O. & Ordnance will move tomorrow at 1800 to Bde. H.Q. Dump at Railway Siding.
Transport arrangements for them are issued separately.
They will return all tents etc to A.O.D. Receiving Depot, YY SURAFEND, before moving out.

11. **SUPPLY SECTION.** The Supply Section will move at 1600 tomorrow to Bde. H.Q. Dump at Railway Siding.
The B.T.O. will send four camels under a mounted orderly to report to the Supply Officer at 1600.

ACKNOWLEDGE.

[signature]

Lieut.
A/Staff Captain, 156th Inf. Brigade.

Issued at_____

Copy No.			Copy No.	
1	to G.O.C.		10	to Supply Officer.
2	4th Royal Scots		11	B.T.O.
3	7th Royal Scots		12	Camel Officer
4	7th Sco. Rifles		13	W.S.O.
5	8th Sco. Rifles		14	D.A/D.O.S.
6	156th M.G. Coy		15	F.P.O.
7	156th L.T.M. Batty		16	Bde. Ordnance.
8	1/1st L.F.Amb.		17	Bde. Sigs.
9	320th Coy A.S.C.		18 & 19	File.
			20	Diary.

War Diary – April 1918.   APPENDIX 3 II

4th. Royal Scots   7th. Sco. Rifles
7th. Royal Scots   8th. Sco. Rifles
156th. L.T.M. Battery.

1. It is probable that the Brigade will remain in its present area until the end of the month, and then be moved into a reserve area behind the line. If, however, any serious situation arises the Brigade may be moved at extremely short notice.

It is essential, therefore, that we should get fit in the shortest possible time and train specially for the conditions we shall find when we next meet our enemy.

2. To effect this, training at the moment should daily consist of:-
   (a) Route marches up to 4 miles
   (b) Short periods of steady drill
   (c) Rapid loading and firing practices (with and without gas masks)
   (d) Gas mask drill – (especially important).
   (e) Rapid deployment and the covering of movement by fire both in attack and retirement.
   (f) Practising movement by signals instead of by word of command.
   This is specially important in view of the difficulty of giving words of command when gas masks are worn.

3. It is of special importance to train all ranks up to the very highest state of efficiency in the use of the gas mask. At all parades masks will be carried and at intervals the alert position should be ordered and afterwards masks will be worn. It is essential that men should be so trained that they will be able to march, manoeuvre and fight in their masks for long periods of time, up to even 6 hours.

The training for this must necessarily be progressive. Short parades must occasionally be held at night to accustom men to donning the mask and working in it in the dark.

4. Lessons to be drawn from recent operations in this country are being summarised, and all information of value to us will be disseminated as early as possible, but on all officers and N.C.Os in particular the following points must be emphatically impressed:-
   (i) That whoever is entrusted with a command no matter how small, must command his men.
   (ii) That in an action, particularly one fought under open warfare conditions, commanders of all formations must display, and will be expected to display great initiative. Situations change so rapidly, and communications are often so interrupted that there will be times without doubt when a Brigade or Battalion Commander cannot be informed of a situation and cannot be appealed to for orders. In such circumstances subordinate commanders must act on their own initiative, and on the action taken by them, success or failure of far reaching dimensions will result. The B.G.C. wants all Officers to remember that in such situations he will take full responsibility if failure does ensue, but in every case where action is taken by an Officer or N.C.O. without reference to superior authority, the Officer or N.C.O. concerned must take immediate steps to inform such superior authority of his action, and, when information of vital importance is transmitted it should be forwarded by more than one runner and by different routes.

5. Training will be limited to 5 hours work per diem (Sundays excluded), and C.Os. will please render as early as possible their training programmes showing hours and places of parade. Special attention will be paid to feet inspection at conclusion of each route march, and the maintenance of the strictest march discipline when on the march.

22nd. April 1918.

Major,
Brigade Major, 156th. Inf Bde

SECRET.   *War Diary. April 1918*   Copy No. 12

156th Infantry Brigade.

APPENDIX III

Administrative Instructions No. 1

Preliminary.

24th April 1918.

1. MOVE.
The 156th Inf. Bde. Group composed as follows will entrain at RUE tomorrow for WIZERNES.
- 156th Bde. H.Q.
- 4th Royal Scots
- 7th Royal Scots
- 7th Sco. Rifles.
- 8th Sco. Rifles.
- 156th L.T.M. Battery.

One Company Divisional Train and Brigade Supply Section.

2. AMMUNITION.
114 Boxes S.A.A. will be drawn by each Battalion before entraining from Bde. S.A.A. Dump at the N. end of RUE Rest Camp Road close to the Station. This S.A.A. will travel in Units' S.A.A. L.G.S. wagons.

3. BILLETING PARTIES.
Billeting Parties as under will travel with the first train and will report at RUE Station to a representative of Bde. H.Q. one hour before the train moves out.

Per Battalion.......... 1 Officer, 1 Senior N.C.O., and a representative of each Company.
Per T.M. Battery....... 1 N.C.O. and 1 Other Rank.

All Billeting Parties will carry tomorrow's rations and will take bicycles.

4. TRANSPORT.
(i) One motor lorry per Battalion and one for L.T.M. Bty. will be available to move Units' baggage to the Station.
These vehicles will later move by road with Units' second blankets. Units will detail 1 O.R. fully armed and equipped, with the day's rations to proceed with each vehicle.

(ii) Units' transport will travel with them by rail loaded according to scale. Water carts will travel full.
NOTE. Each limbered G.S. wagon carries 32,000 rounds of ammunition.

(iii) Train baggage wagons according to scale will report to Units' H.Q. to-day to load Units' baggage.
These wagons will move by rail under train arrangements.
Units will detail one man armed and equipped to move with each wagon. These (men) will carry the day's rations.

5. RATIONS.
(i) The meat ration of the day's ration will be carried in Field Cookers and the remainder on the man.
(ii) One day's ration carried by the train will be issued on arrival.

Issued at _____   A/Staff Captain, 156th Inf. Brigade.
Lieut.

Copy No. 1 to G.O.C.		Copy No. 7 to H.Q. 52nd Division.
2	4th Royal Scots	8	Coy. 52nd Div. Train.
3	7th Royal Scots	9	156th Bde. S.O.
4	7th Sco. Rifles	10	156th Bde. Ordnance
5	8th Sco. Rifles	11	156th Bde. F.P.O.
6	156th L.T.M. Batty.	12 & 13	Diary
		14	File.

SECRET.

War Diary — April 1918   Copy No. 14

156th Infantry Brigade.

Administrative Instructions No. 1a.

APPENDIX IV

24th April 1918.

1. Units will entrain at RUE Station as per attached Time-table.

2. **Entraining Officer.** Lieut. A.S. BILSLAND, attached 156th Inf. Bde. Headquarters.

   Detraining Officer. Capt. G.S. SMITH, attached 156th Inf. Bde. Headquarters.

3. (a) Vehicles and baggage of each train load will be at Station three hours before the train is timed to leave.
   (b) A loading party of 1 Officer and 60 other ranks will be detailed for each train and will arrive at Station at same time as vehicles.
   (c) 4th Royal Scots will provide loading party for Nos 1 and 2 trains and 8th Scottish Rifles for Nos 5 and 6 trains.
   (d) Units concerned will be at Station one hour before their train is due to leave.

4. Baggage wagons detailed in Administrative Instructions No. 1 of to-day's date, para 4 (iii), will be loaded by 10 a.m. tomorrow, and will proceed by No. 6 train under Divisional Train arrangements. 2nd Blankets will be taken by motor lorry to RUE Station and not as stated in Administrative Instructions No. 1.

5. Two motor lorries will be available for each Battalion. Those for the first train will report to Units at 6.30 a.m.

6. A movement order shewing the number of personnel, the vehicles and the animals proceeding by each train will be handed by Units to the R.T.O. on arrival at RUE Station.

7. ACKNOWLEDGE.

Issued at 7 p.m.

H.D. McIntyre
Captain,
Staff Captain, 156th Inf. Bde.

———————oOo———————

Copy No. 1	to G.O.C.		Copy No. 9	to 156th Bde. S.O.
2.	4th Royal Scots		10	156th Bde. Ordnance.
3.	7th Royal Scots.		11	156th Bde. F.P.O.
4.	7th Scottish Rifles		12	Lieut A.S. Bilsland.
5.	8th Scottish Rifles		13	Capt. G.S. Smith.
6.	156th L.T.M. Battery		14 & 15	Diary
7.	H.Q., 52nd Division		16	File.
8.	52nd Divisional Train.			

TIME-TABLE.

No. 1 Train departs 8.44 a.m. 25th instant...... Brigade H.Q.
1 Coy, 1 Cooker and team of 4th Royal Scots
Brigade Signal Section
156th L.T.M. Batty.
Postal Section
Supply Section, and following details of A.S.C. transport, (220th Coy A.S.C.) 1 Officer, 20 other ranks, 10 four wheeled vehicles and teams, 5 cycles,
also cycles of billeting party.

No. 2 train departs 11.34 a.m.   do.   4th Royal Scots, less 1 Coy, 1 Cooker and team

No. 3 train departs 2.24 p.m.   do   7th Royal Scots, less 1 Coy, 1 cooker and team.

No. 4 train departs 5.4 p.m.   do   7th Scottish Rifles, less 1 Coy, 1 Cooker and team.

No. 5 train departs 8.34 p.m.   do   8th Scottish Rifles less 1 Coy, 1 Cooker and team.

No. 6 train departs 12.14 a.m. 26th instant   1 Coy 7th Sco. Rifles
1 Coy 7th Royal Scots
1 Coy 8 th Sco. Rifles
with cookers and teams in each case.
Remainder of A.S.C. Coy and transport.

===============oOo===============

Administrative Instructions No. 1a

ADDENDUM

Reference Administrative Instructions No. 1 and 1a of to-day's date.

The supply wagons of 156th Inf. Bde. Train Coy are proceed:
:ing by first train. After detraining they will wait at the
Station until particular unit whose rations they carry arrives.
Each unit will then pick up its own supply wagons.

SECRET.

War Diary April 1918

156th Inf. Brigade Order No. 33.

Copy No 12

Reference Maps 1/100,000. Sheet 5a.
1/40,000. Sheet 36a.

APPENDIX V

25th April 1918.

1. 156th Infantry Brigade and 220th Coy A.S.C. will move by march route to XI Corps Reserve Area tomorrow, April 26th.

2. The following will not go into Billets on detraining, but will bivouac in the vicinity of WIZERNES Station.
   7th Scottish Rifles.
   8th Scottish Rifles.
   1 Coy 7th Royal Scots.
   Personnel of 220th Coy A.S.C. on No. 6 train.

3. Units will move under their own arrangements via HELFAUT, HEURINGHEN, ECQUES to REBECQ, at which place guides will meet them to lead them to Billeting areas.
   Units will not arrive at REBECQ before noon.

4. Billeting parties will proceed on bicycles and meet a representative of Brigade H.Q. at road junction at East end of REBECQ at 9 a.m.

5. RATIONS. Rations for consumption on 27/4/18 will be drawn tomorrow by first line transport [Train] from a refilling point at road junction a quarter of a mile East of MAMETZ at 3 p.m.

6. TRANSPORT. Two motor lorries will be available for each Battalion at WIZERNES Station at 9.30 a.m. tomorrow. This in addition to the Battalion Train baggage wagons. Half motor lorry will be available for L.T.M. Battery.

7. MEDICAL. Urgent cases of sick requiring evacuation will be sent to 2/2nd East Lancs. Field Ambulance, HALLINES, by 10.30 a.m. tomorrow. If ambulance is required, guide must report to Field Ambulance not later than 9 a.m.

8. Brigade H.Q. will close at WIZERNES at 10 a.m. and will open at MAMETZ at 12 noon.

9. ACKNOWLEDGE.

Issued at _____

Major,
Brigade Major, 156th Inf. Brigade.

========================oOo========================

Copy No.		Copy No	
1	to B.G.C.	8	to O.C., Sigs.
2	4th Royal Scots	9	Bde. S.O.
3	7th Royal Scots	10	Staff Captain
4	7th Sco. Rifles	11	XIth Corps.
5	8th Sco. Rifles	12	Diary
6	156th L.T.M. Battery	13	Diary
7	220th Coy A.S.C.	14	File.

App VI

Effective Strength

156th Infantry Brigade   30th April 1918

	Officers	Other Ranks
Bde HQ	6	25
4 Royal Scots	38	829
7 Royal Scots	39	919
7 Sco Rifles	47	874
8 Sco Rifles	40	859
156 L.T.M.Bty	3	45
	173	3551

Original

VC 2

SECRET.

WAR DIARY
OF
156TH INFANTRY BRIGADE
FOR
MAY - 1918.

VOL - XXXVI

Army Form C. 2118.

156TH INFANTRY BRIGADE

WAR DIARY or INTELLIGENCE SUMMARY.

(Erase heading not required.)

Instructions regarding War Diaries and Intelligence Summaries are contained in F.S. Regs., Part II. and the Staff Manual respectively. Title pages will be prepared in manuscript.

MAY 1918.

Place	Date	Hour	Summary of Events and Information	Remarks and references to Appendices
MAMETZ.	1		2/. Halliwell R.E. was to day attached to Brigade to supervise instruction in Rapid Wiring. Training is being carried out by units in accordance with attached Table.	(Appendix I) J.S. Capt.
—"—	2		B.G.C. visited 1/4th Royal Scots on Range at G.22.d. and later in day visited Corps Trench Mortar School.	J.S. Capt.
—"—	3		B.G.C. and officers of the Brigade attended Lecture by Col. Forbes DSO in TOWN HALL, ALBERT. During this Lecture the Commander in chief addressed the officers and expressed his wishes for the success of 52nd Division in France.	J.S. Capt.
—"—	4		B.G.C. and the whole Brigade attended Gas and Hammenwerfer Demonstrations. MARTHES. Capt. G. Gordon Weir M.C. returned from leave in U.K. and resumed duty as Brigade Transport Officer.	J.S. Capt.
—"—	5		Brigade Order No 34 issued to all concerned. ref. move to XVIII-ii Corps.	(Appendix II) J.S. Capt.
—"—	6		Training continued. Weather fine.	J.S. Capt.
—"—	7		Wet weather interfered with training. Brigade Transport moved by road to DUVION, and will move tomorrow to new area near NEUVILLE ST VAAST.	J.S. Capt.
NEUVILLE ST VAAST	8		Brigade moved by train to ACQ (in two trains) as per Appendix II above, and on arrival was accommodated in hutment area at NEUVILLE ST VAAST, and Mt. ST ELOI.	J.S. Capt.
MONT ST. ELOI	9		Brigade Headquarters moved to WHITEHOUSE MONT ST. ELOI, where units are now all quartered except 7th Royal Scots who remain at NEUVILLE ST VAAST. Leave to U.K. opened today for one O.R. per Brigade per day. B.G.C. visited 155th Bde. in the line, Captain Will M.C. Worcester Regt. attached to Brigade as acting Staff Captain with C.O's.	J.S. Capt.
—"—	10		B.G.C. visited Vimy and area occupied by 155th Bde.	J.S. Capt.

156TH INFANTRY BRIGADE. WAR DIARY   MAY. 1918.   Army Form C. 2118.

INTELLIGENCE SUMMARY.

Place	Date	Hour	Summary of Events and Information	Remarks and references to Appendices
Mont St. Eloi	11		The allotment of leave to U.K. has been increased to 19 per Brigade per day.	A/B Capt.
"	12		It has been ordered that Battalions should adopt a distinguishing mark. The Battalions in 156th Bde will wear coloured bands on the right arm. 1 for 4th Royal Scots. 2 for 7th R.S. 3 for 7th S.R. and 4 for 8th S.R. L.T.M. Bty. will wear one stripe double width.	A/B Capt.
"	12		Units carried out training. Special attention is being paid to Bayonet fighting and Anti-gas training. Battalions are bathing by platoons and fresh underwear will shortly be issued. At present it is not available.	
"	13		Lt. Col. J.M. FINDLAY. D.S.O. 1/8th Scottish Rifles reported back from hospital. B.G.C. and officers of the Brigade visited Right Section of Divisional front, at present occupied by 155th Brigade. B.G.C. went round the line (with B.M. and observed enemy lines.	A/B Capt.
"	14		B.M. 483. Warning Order re relief of 155th Bde by 156th Bde, issued to all concerned. Appendix III Brigade Order No 35. issued to all concerned for Relief to take place tomorrow. Appendix IV Officers of Brigade visited 155th and inspected line to be held. Preliminary arrangements for relief were completed	A/B Capt.
WILLERVAL SECTION.	15		156th Brigade relieved 155th Brigade in the line. The frontage held is about 3000 yards wide, as shown on map attached Appendix VI The 7th Scottish Rifles hold the Right Subsection with 4th Royal Scots in reserve. The 8th ___ ___ ___ ___ Left ___ ___ ___ 7th ___ ___ ___ On the Right of the Brigade is 51st Division; on the left the 157th Brigade. 156th Brigade Head quarters are at THELUS CAVE. Relief reported complete by day and was reported complete by 21/5 , without casualties	A/B Capt.
"	16		The B.G.C. and B.M. visited the line. Certain rearrangements of the dispositions of units set	A/B Capt.

156TH INFANTRY BRIGADE WAR DIARY or INTELLIGENCE SUMMARY.

MAY-1918.

Army Form C. 2118.

Place	Date	Hour	Summary of Events and Information	Remarks and references to Appendices
WILLERVAL 16 SECTION	17		being made.	JSS Cpl
			Water. This was not organised when the Brigade took over. Arrangements are being made to keep Tanks filled in the front line system, the balance of the supply being carried in Petrol tins. There are two pipes running to each Battalion in the line, but these are not sufficient without the use of Petrol tins.	
			Rations. The Light Railway is being utilised as far as possible, and ration stations are opened up which had fallen into disuse.	
			Salvage Dumps are being established and each units' salvage is taken out of the line by the Light Railway. Enemy fired some gas shells into our Right Subsection.	
-"-	18		Enemy has been quiet since we took over line, and our patrols have not encountered any enemy parties, but during this night 18/19/17 a short encounter took place at one of our exposts and we lost 2 men.	JSS Cpl
-"-	19		Patrols by night as usual. No man's land varies in width from 400 to 900 yards, and the enemy appears to hold his front system lightly. Cooking has been a matter of difficulty, but Soyer Stoves 1 per company have been established in the sunken VANCOUVER ROAD, the food being carried to companies in the line in "Thermos" Containers. Weather continues fine.	JSS Cpl
-"-	20		On night of this Brigade quickly adjusted their dispositions and so avoided heavy casualties. The enemy took place on night of 19/17, the men of this	JSS Cpl
-"-	21		By order of the Corps Commander, every man must fire 5 rounds per day and small ranges are being constructed for men not in the front line. Weather very hot. Enemy quiet by day as usual. Our patrols at night saw no enemy.	JSS Cpl

ORDERS 36 issued re Changeover by Battalions APPENDIX V.

WAR DIARY 166TH INFANTRY BRIGADE
or
INTELLIGENCE SUMMARY

Army Form C. 2118

MAY 1918

Place	Date	Hour	Summary of Events and Information	Remarks and references to Appendices
WILLERVAL SECTION	21 22		Hdqrs. of 4th Royal Scots moved into THELUS CAVE, as previous position destroyed by shellfire. Weather continues fine. Quiet day. Patrols out by night. Observation has been good during the past few days, and several points in enemy's line, where M.G. and T.M. emplacements were suspected, have been dealt with by the Artillery.	
	23.		The Brigade having been 8 days in the line, Battalions changed over. During the first half of the tour a great deal has been done to strengthen the line. B.G.C. has been round the line repeatedly, and alterations in the distribution of units have been made in accordance with attached plan. (APPENDIX VI) B.G.C. has directed that each Battalion in the line should send out two Patrols each night. Weather fine. Usual work continued in trenches.	
	24		The Right Subsection is now held by 4th Royal Scots, the Left Subsection by 7th Royal Scots. B.G.C. visited Posts in Left Subsection. Early this morning a large concentration of gas was discharged from the Left Section. Enemy did not retaliate and his guns were much quieter than usual during the day. Patrols by night met no enemy. Weather fine.	
	25		Dull, cloudy day, and high wind. Patrols as usual by night. One patrol, 4th Royal Scots reported 3 men missing on their return, but as no enemy was encountered it is believed these men are in a shell crater, and will return. B.G.C. visited right subsection during afternoon.	
	26		Weather fine. Work in trenches as usual. The post at COUNT'S WOOD is no longer to be held, and it was accordingly evacuated today. Three missing men returned safely.	

Army Form C. 2118

150th Infantry Brigade WAR DIARY or INTELLIGENCE SUMMARY

May, 1918

Instructions regarding War Diaries and Intelligence Summaries are contained in F.S. Regs., Part II. and the Staff Manual respectively. Title Pages will be prepared in manuscript.

(Erase heading not required.)

Place	Date	Hour	Summary of Events and Information	Remarks and references to Appendices
VILLENAL SECTION	27		A more than usually active day on the enemy's part. Much shelling by day and by night. A few Blue Cross gas shells fell in the Right S.C. Section. Patrols by night were troubled by more M.G. fire than usual. Weather good.	WCpt
	28		It has been decided to occupy BORDER POST, and B.G.C. accompanied by O.C. 1/17th Scottish Rifles reconnoitred the site of the old post today and arranged how the new trenches were to be dug. Weather continues fine.	WCpt
	29		Enemy guns quiet. Our own more active. An attempted raid by party of 1/17th S.R. was frustrated owing to enemy vigilance in parts of enemy, and his M.G. activity. B.G.C. visited line and closes at Hdqrs of both forward Battalions.	WCpt
	30		Lt. Genl. Sir Ivor Maxse K.C.B. visiting New Corps visited the Brigade Section and went round the French's. Certain changes in the disposition of the line were decided on, and the main line of resistance will now be the YUKON OTTAWA French line, the system forward of that being held as an outpost line. A test S.O.S. was carried out this evening. The first gun fired six secs. after the first rocket grenade went up in the front line. The Relay Grenade Post system worked well. Patrols by night as usual.	WCpt
	31		A day patrol of 1/17th Royal Scots lay in No Man's Land today and obtained useful information. B.G.C. 159th Brigade and staff visited this section in view of relieving it shortly.	WCpt

156th Infantry Brigade

Army Form C. 2118

WAR DIARY
or
INTELLIGENCE SUMMARY

May, 1918

(Erase heading not required.)

Place	Date	Hour	Summary of Events and Information	Remarks and references to Appendices
WILLERVAL SECTION	31		Brigade Order No 37 issued, re Relief by 157th Brigade. Casualty Return for month of May. Effective Strength at this date. C H Wholfe	(APPENDIX VII) (APPENDIX VIII) (APPENDIX IX)

Brigade Major
156th Infantry Brigade.

SECRET.

PROVISIONAL DEFENCE SCHEME.
WILLERVAL SECTION.

Ref. 1/20,000 Trench Map.

1. The WILLERVAL SECTION is the RIGHT SECTION of the MERICOURT Sector. The 51st Division is on the Right and another Brigade of the 52nd Division on the Left.

Boundaries.

2. The boundaries are as follows:-
Right Boundary. B.10.b.5.8. - B.10.a.7.6. - TIRED ALLEY B.13.b.8.2. - B.13.c.5.8. BORDER POST (inclusive to 52nd Division) - A.12.c.0.0. thence West.
Left Boundary. ACHEVILLE - NEW BRUNSWICK ROAD as far as Railway Embankment at T.26.a.3.9. (exclusive to WILLERVAL SECTION) thence to Cemetery at T.25.d.6.9. (inclusive to WILLERVAL SECTION, thence to BOIS DU GOULOT at T.25.c.0.0. and thence due West along grid line.
Inter-Battalion Boundary.
WESTERN ROAD (inclusive to Right Subsection)

Garrison.

3. The Section is held by one Infantry Brigade Group, consisting of:-
One Infantry Brigade
Field Coy R.E.
Field Ambulance.
It is divided into 2 Subsections, each of which is held by two Battalions, one in the front system and one in reserve.
The latter provides garrisons for the BROWN LINE and Posts along the THELUS RIDGE. The remainder of the two Reserve Battalions are held as mobile reserve in the hands of the Section Commander.

Description of Defences.
(a) First Zone of Defence.

4. The Defences of the Section are organised as follows
The Outpost Line. This consists of a chain of small posts supplied by the front line garrison and thrown forward in front of the Main Line of Resistance. On the right of the line these are situated in shell holes, and on the left in MONTREAL TRENCH.
THE BLUE LINE. This consists of Firing and Support Line of which the Firing Line is the Main Line of Resistance running from the Right Boundary at B.10.b.5.8. along PLUMER TRENCH to Junction with HUDSON TRENCH, thence to T.23.d.9.2. and along NEW BRUNSWICK TRENCH.
Note. It is intended at a later date to withdraw the Main Line of Resistance to B.10.a.7.6. - B.4.a.3.2. - B.4.a.9.6. - T.28.c.7.2. - T.28.a.7.6. - T.23.d.9.2. and thence along NEW BRUNSWICK TRENCH.
The RED LINE. This consists of a series of 7 self contained strong points DURHAM, SUBURB, FOVANT and BARNSLEY in the Right Subsection and WAKEFIELD, SHEFFIELD and CANADA in the Left Subsection. In addition, a firebay :ed length of BEEHIVE TRENCH in the Left Subsection is garrisoned, and a strong point will be constructed.
Each of the above is constructed for a garrison of one platoon, and will be completed for all round defence. These posts are connected by lateral communication trenche

(b) Second Zone of Defence.

The BROWN (FARBUS VIMY) LINE.
This is a continuous line running parallel to and about 300 yards East of the ARRAS-LENS Railway with deep dugouts for the garrison in the Railway Embankment.
The GREEN (THELUS RIDGE) LINE.
This consists of a continuous trench with certain strong points of which the following are occupied and are being put into a state of defence:-
SPUR POST, BORDER POST, FARBUS POST, TAPE POST in Right Subsection, and THELUS POST in Left Subsection.

2.

(c) Flank Defences. For the purpose of local flank defence of the Section, in the event of the enemy penetrating the Section on Right or Left, TIRED ALLEY and CANADA TRENCH are firestepped and wired.

Distribution of Troops

5. The troops holding the line are distributed in depth as follows:- (Appendix A)

(a) The first Zone of Defence in each subsection is garrisoned by one Battalion with three Companies in the BLUE LINE and one Company in the RED LINE (platoon posts).

(b) One Company of each Reserve Battalion is placed at the disposal of the O.C., Forward Battalion, in each subsection, for the purpose of counter-attack and to garrison TIRED ALLEY and CANADA TRENCH respectively.

TIRED ALLEY is permanently garrisoned by a series of 5 combined posts of two sections each. The positions of these are:-
  (a) B.10.a.6.5.
  (b) B.9.b.9.0.
  (c) B.9.d.5.8.
  (d) B.9.c.2.3.
  (e) B.13.b.8.2.

Of these (a), (c) and (e) are commanded by N.C.Os of 51st (Highland) Division, and (b) and (d) by N.C.Os of the Brigade holding the WILLERVAL Section.

(c) The BROWN LINE is garrisoned by one Company of each Reserve Battalion which also supplies garrisons to the GREEN LINE Posts in rear as follows:-

Right Reserve Battalion.
  SPUR POST..........1 Platoon.
  TAPE POST..........1 Platoon
  FARBUS POST........1 Platoon.
  BORDER POST........1 Platoon.

Left Reserve Battalion.
  THELUS POST........1 Platoon.

(d) The remainder of the Reserve Battalions are in mobile reserve, situated as follows:-

Right Reserve Battalion

  Headquarters...THELUS MILL
  1 Coy..........Railway Embankment near FARBUS STATION.

Left Reserve Battalion.
  HILLS CAMP, NEUVILLE ST VAAST.

NOTE. The latter will be moved to THELUS POST as soon as accommodation has been provided.

Action in case of attack.

6. (a). It is the role of the Outpost Line to give warning of an attack and to withdraw fighting to the Main Line (BLUE LINE) when they can no longer serve any useful purpose by holding out.

(b). The role of the Main Line of Resistance (BLUE LINE) is to break up, disorganise and repulse the enemy's attack. The garrison of this line will fight to the last. There will be no retirement.

Local penetrations will be restored by local counter attacks carried out by the platoons in support, and if occasion demands by half Companies in each Subsection retained for that purpose.

(c) The line of Posts will maintain a passive resistance each garrison holding out to the end without reference to what happens on its flanks, thus breaking up the enemy's attack in preparation for the counter attack which will be delivered by the Brigade Reserve.

(d) The Company of the Reserve Battalion in each Subsection which is placed at the disposal of the Battalion Commander of each subsection will be utilised as follows:-

Half Company in Right Subsection will immediately man TIRED ALLEY and defend it against attack from the South. Half Company in the Left Subsection will man CANADA TRENCH and defend it against attack from the North.

(e)

(e) The remaining half Companies will be used by the Os.C. Front Battalions of Right and Left Subsection for the purpose of Counter attack to restore the situation in the BLUE and RED LINES.

(f) The garrisons of the BROWN LINE and the Posts on the top of the ridge will "stand to" ready to man their posts the instant the bombardment lifts.

(g) The remainder of the Reserve Battalions will "Stand to" and send an Officer to the Brigade Headquarters.

ARTILLERY. 7. (a) The Section is covered by the 52nd Army Brigade R.F.A., 9th Brigade R.F.A., and 2 Batteries 56th Brigade R.F.A., amounting in all to,-

    8 Batteries......18 pounders.
    2 Batteries...... 4.5 Hows.

The attached tracing shews the barrage lines (Appendix B)
The barrage is reinforced, as shewn, by Machine Guns.

(b) The Divisional Front is covered by the following Heavy Artillery, all of which is available to cover either Divisional Section:-

    4.............9.2 Hows.
    6.............8" Hows.
    12............6" Hows.
    12............60 pdr. guns.

The S.O.S. points of these are shewn on the attached tracing. (Appendix "C")

MACHINE GUNS.
8. There are 24 Vickers Guns in the Section. Positions and arcs of fire are shewn on the attached tracing (Appendix D)

TRENCH MORTARS.
9. All trench mortars are in purely defensive positions owing to the great width of NO MAN'S LAND. The following are in action, the positions and arcs of fire being shewn on the attached tracing (Appendix E)

X 52 and 4 guns Y 52 Medium Batteries.....10 Newton Mortars
One Light Battery............................ 6 Stokes Mortars

An alternative emplacement has been constructed for one Newton Mortar for offensive fire into ARLEUX.

COMMUNICATIONS.
10. (1). The following means of communication are available:-
  (a) Telephone & telegraph.
  (b) Visual.
  (c) Wireless
  (d) Power Buzzer and amplifier.
  (e) Pigeons.
  (f) Runners.

The above are shewn on the attached diagram. (Appendix F)

(2). In addition to the above means, chains of relay posts are provided for transmitting the S.O.S. signal by rifle grenades. This method is the quickest, but the S.O.S. will be sent simultaneously by all available means.

TRANSPORT. 11. Transport Lines and Quartermaster's Stores are at BERTHONVAL FARM.

SUPPLIES. 12.(a) <u>Rations.</u> are drawn each morning from R.P. at A.2.c.3.9. and are delivered at Quartermasters Stores by Div. Train.

(b) <u>Forwarding of Rations.</u> is carried out as follows:-
Right Subsection Battn. by pack animals to the RED LINE (B.4.c.central)
Left Subsection Battn by pack animals to Battn. Cookhouse (T.28.a.5.2.)
Right Reserve Battn.
  Battn. H.Q. & 1 platoon by limber.
  2 Companies (BROWN LINE) by Light Railway from ZIVY to LONGWOOD (B.15.a.2.8.)
  7 Platoons (3 in WILLERVAL LOCALITY and 1 in each of following FARBUS, TAPE, BORDER, SPUR)
By/

2.

Right Reserve Battn. (Contd)
    By Light Railway from ZIVY to FARBUS Junction
    (B.7.d.5.6.)

Left Reserve Battn.
    Battn. H.Q. & 7 Platoons by limber.
    2 Companies (T.21.d.) BROWN LINE by Light Railway
      from ZIVY to MORRISON (T.36.c.7.4.)
    1 Platoon (THELUS) by Light Railway from ZIVY to
      FARBUS JUNCTION.

Bde. H.Q. By Limber.

L.T.M. Battery. By limber to Battn. H.Q. thence by Carrying
    Parties.
    Rations forwarded by Light Railway are loaded on
    trucks at ZIVY by 7.30 p.m.

(c) Water.

Right Subsection Battn. Water is drawn at LONGWOOD from
    Tanks at pipe lines and conveyed in petrol tins by
    Light Railway to WILLERVAL thence to the line by
    Carrying Parties provided by Right Reserve Battn.

Left Subsection Battn. Water is drawn at MORRISON from 4
    tanks and conveyed in petrol tins by carrying parties
    provided by Left Reserve Battn. Left Coy draws from
    well at NEW BRUNSWICK SUBWAY. (T.16.c.9.4.)

Right Reserve Battn.
    2 Coys (BROWN LINE) from LONGWOOD in petrol tins.
    7 platoons in post from FARBUS in petrol tins.
    Battn. H.Q. from tank A.6.c.8.6.

Left Reserve Battn.
    2 Coys from MORRISON by petrol tins
    1 platoon (THELUS) from FARBUS Junction by petrol tins.
    Battn. H.Q. 7 platoons.. Camp NEUVILLE ST VAAST.

L.T.M. Battery.
    From tanks LONGWOOD & MORRISON (Sect. in Line)
    A.5.b.6.6. Batty. H.Q.

Bde. H.Q. From tank A.6.c.8.6.

Transport. (including animals) at BERTHONVAL.

AMMUNITION. 13. Brigade ammunition dumps are situated as follows:-
    Bde. H.Q. .... A.6.c.6.5.
    LONGWOOD .... B.15.a.2.8.
    FARBUS .... B.2.d.3.1.
    MERSEY .... (B.2.a.7.7.
                    (B.2.a.7.5.
                    (B.2.b.5.0.
    RED BRICK STALK ...... T.26.b.3.2.

The above dumps are refilled from HOOPERS DUMP (AUX RIETZ) by Light Railway to LONGWOOD & MORRISON.

R.E. MATERIAL 14. The main R.E. dump is at ZIVY (A.10.a.4.7.) from which
    material is forwarded by Light Railway to LONGWOOD,
    MORRISON and FARBUS Junction.

RESERVE WATER & RATIONS.
    15. (a) Water. 50 full petrol tins are maintained in each
        subsection. This is being increased.
        (b) Rations. 2 tins (each 25 lbs) biscuits and 56 tins
        preserved meat are held at the following points:-

CANADA	T.22.c.6.3.	SUBURB	B.9.b.9.8.
SHEFFIELD	T.21.d.3.0.	DURHAM	B.9.b.1.4.
BEEHIVE	T.27.b.1.1.	SPUR	B.14.a.5.6.
WAKEFIELD	T.27.d.7.6.	BORDER	B.13.a.4.0.
BARNSLEY	T.27.d.7.1.	TAPE	A.12.d.9.1.
FOVANT	B.3.c.5.8.	FARBUS	B.7.d.7.7.
		THELUS	B.7.a.5.7.

Bde. Reserve FARBUS (B.2.d.3.1.) 146 tins biscuits.
                              63 cases preserved meat
                                (each 48 tins)

STRAGGLERS POSTS. /

5.

STRAGGLERS POSTS. 16. First Line Stragglers Posts are situated at
Commandants House..........B.7.d.5.2.
MERSEY ALLEY................B.1.b.8.4.
VIMY........................T.25.b.5.8.

MEDICAL. 17. (a). Right Subsection Battn.
R.A.P. (B.15.a.0.8.) evacuated through A.D.S. of the neighbouring Division on Right.
(b). Left Subsection Battn.
R.A.P. (T.18.a.4.1.) with relay post at T.26.a.3.9.) evacuated through A.D.S. VIMY. (T.26.a.9.4.)
(c). Supplementary.
R.A.P. (B.2.a.9.8.) with relay post at A.11.b.3.9.
The main Dressing Station for (b) and (c) is at AUX RIETZ (A.8.c.5.5.)

SALVAGE. 18. Salvage is delivered by units to Div. Salvage Dump A.8.c.5.5.

BURIAL. 19. Bodies are conveyed by units to Collecting Stations B.2.b.2.8. (Junction of MERSEY TRENCH and MORRISON VALLEY - BROWN LINE.

Cemeteries .........THELUS.......A.5.c.8.5.
AUX RIETZ......A.8.c.5.9.
They are dealt with by Divisional Burial Officer from collecting station.

C H 2 Metcalfe

Major,
Bde. Major, 156th Inf. Bde.

==

APPENDICES.

"A"........................Distribution of Troops.
"B"........................Barrage Lines, 52nd Army Bde.
R.F.A.
"C"........................S.O.S. points of Heavy Artillery
"D"........................M.G. positions & arcs of fire.
"E"........................Trench Mortar positions & arcs of fire.
"F"........................Communications.

======oOo======

SECRET.   Copy No. 15

156th INFANTRY BRIGADE ORDER No. 3.
==

                                                    2nd
                                                    21st May 1918.

1.   The following reliefs will be carried out on 23rd instant.

   (a) 1/4th Royal Scots will relieve 1/7th Sco. Rifles in the
       Front System Right Subsection.
   (b) 1/7th Royal Scots will relieve 1/8th Sco. Rifles in the
       Front System Left Subsection.

2.   Details of reliefs will be arranged between Battalion
   Commanders concerned. Reliefs to be carried out in daylight.
   Command will pass on completion of each relief.

3.   Communications, Trench Maps, Defence Schemes, Log Books
   and Trench Stores will be taken over and receipts given.
   Lists of Trench stores, together with Sanitation Certificates,
   will be forwarded to Bde. H.Q. 36 hours after completion of
   relief. Lewis Gun Magazines, S.A.A., Tools etc, may be
   exchanged by mutual arrangement.

4.   On relief, the 1/7th Scottish Rifles and the 1/8th Scottish
   Rifles will take over the dispositions of the 1/4th Royal Scots
   and 1/7th Royal Scots respectively.

5.   Existing arrangements regarding supply of rations and
   water will be taken over.

6.   Completion of relief will be reported "Priority" by code
   word "Capt. MACLEAN".

7.   ACKNOWLEDGE.

                                    Major,
Issued at 6 p.m.   Brigade Major, 156th Inf. Brigade.

================================

Copy No. 1 to G.O.C.   Copy No. 9 to Bde. Supply Officer.
         2   4th Royal Scots.   10   B.T.O.
         3   7th Royal Scots   11   157th Inf. Brigade.
         4   7th Sco. Rifles   12   154th Inf. Brigade.
         5   8th Sco. Rifles   13   52nd Division.
         6   156th L.T.M. Bty.   14   412th Field Coy R.E.
         7   Bde. Signals   15 & 16   Diary.
         8   (Staff Captain   17   File.
              (I. Officer   18   Right Group R.F.A.
                                          19   52nd M.G. Battalion.
                                          20   211th M.G. Company.

================================

"E"

Right Section – Defence Scheme
6" Newton Trench Mortar Arcs of Fire & "SOS" Points

Grid North.

RIGHT SECTION – DEFENCE SCHEME.
HEAVY ARTILLERY "SOS" LINES.

"C"

	9.2"	8"	6"	60 Pdr Barrage
General "SOS"	■	▲	●	—
Arleux "SOS"	■	▲	●	—
Méricourt's "SOS"	■	▲	●	—
Oppy "SOS"	▨	▨	●	----

Where two or more occur of the same nature the Black Sign indicates the exact spot.

"1. 156th Inf. Bde
1-6-18."

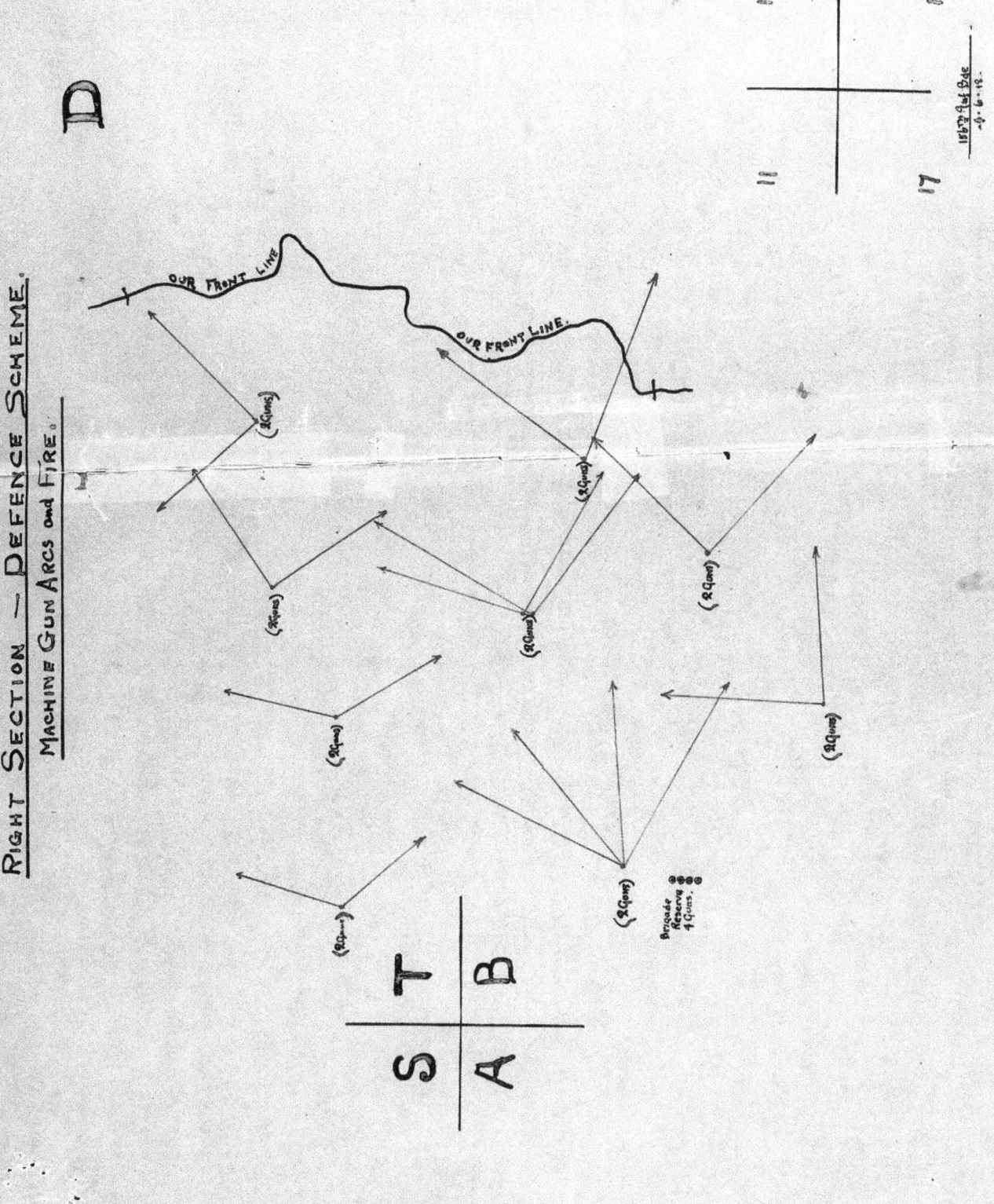

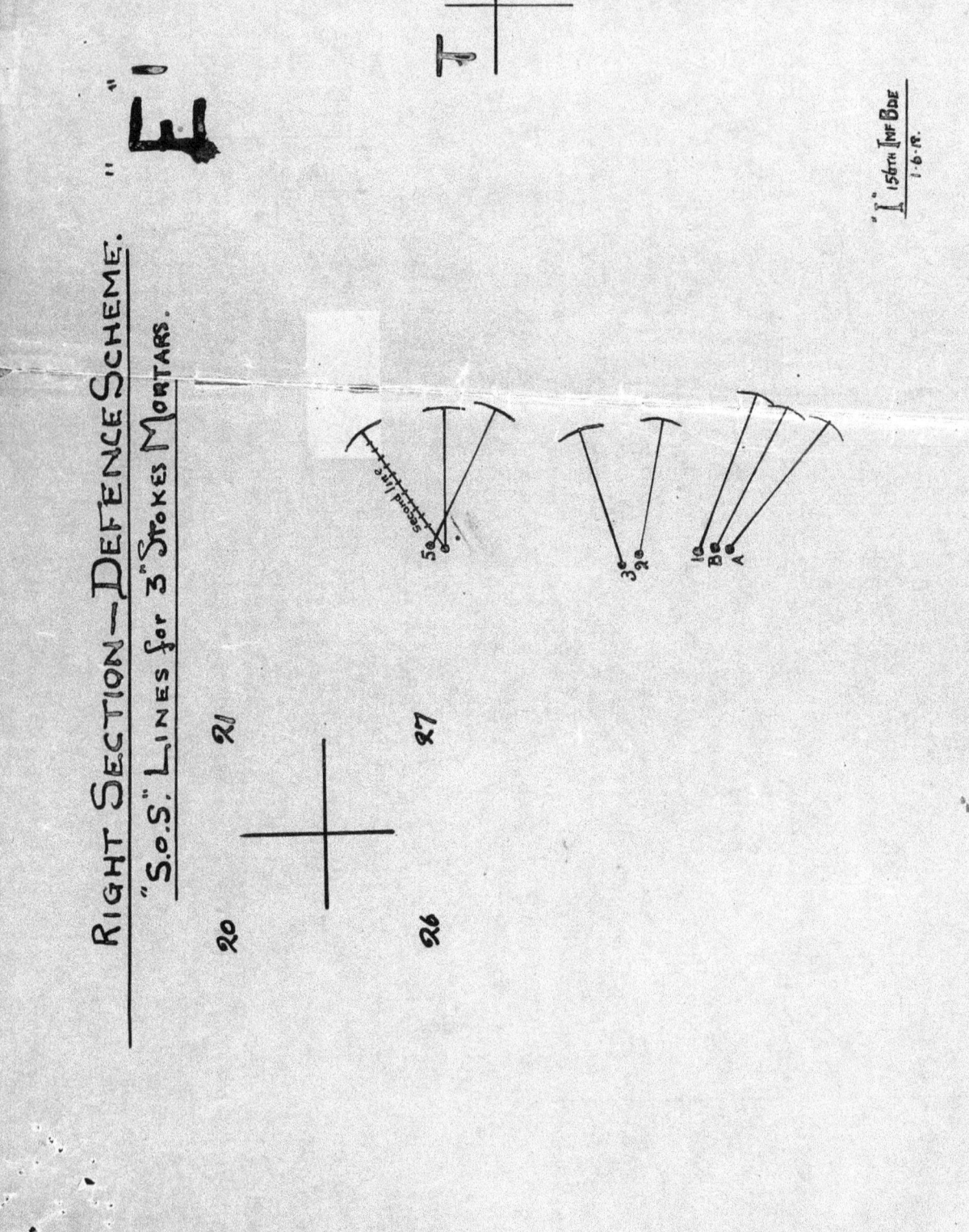

RIGHT SECTION — DEFENCE SCHEME.

18 Pdr. and M.G. "S.O.S" Barrage Lines.

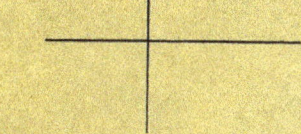

18 Pounder
 FIRST BARRAGE - yellow.
 SECOND — " — - red. THIRD...Blue
Machine Guns _ _ _ _ green.

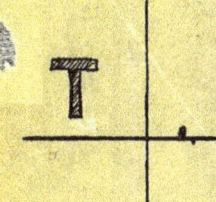

"I" 156TH Inf Bde.
20·5·18.

Right Section – Defence Scheme.
Distribution.

"A"

Blue — Left Subsection
Left Subsection Reserve
Red — Right Subsection
Right Subsection Reserve
Left Res: Battn. HQrs

Canada
Sheffield
Beehive Trench
Wakefield
Left Bn: HQ.
Barnsley
Fovant
Right Bn:Hq. Suburb
Durham

Bde: Hqrs.
Tape
Fargo
Spur
Border

ALLOTMENT OF TRAINING GROUNDS.

```
2d............4th. Royal Scots
2a............7th. Royal Scots (Mondays, Wednesdays & Fridays)
3a............7th. Royal Scots (Tuesdays, Thursdays & Saturdays)
1d)...........7th. Sco. Rifles
2b)
2a............8th. Sco. Rifles (Tuesdays, Thursdays & Saturdays)
3a............8th. Sco. Rifles (Mondays, Wednesdays & Fridays)
3b............156th. L.T.M. Bty.
```

PROVISIONAL ALLOTMENT OF RIFLE RANGES.

Number	Range	Targets
9	50 yards	14
10	120 "	8
11	30 "	5
4..L.G.	30 "	5

One Lewis Gun Range at MARTHES.

	Mondays	Tuesdays	Wednesdays	Thursdays	Fridays	Saturdays
No. 9 & 10	7th S.R.	8th S.R.	7th S.R.	8th S.R.	7th S.R.	8th S.R.
4 (L.G.)	8th S.R.	7th S.R.	8th S.R.	7th S.R.	8th S.R.	7th S.R.
11	7th R.S.	4th R.S.	7th R.S.	4th R.S.	7th R.S.	4th R.S.
X MARTHES(L.G)				4th R.S.		7th R.S.

X From 1 p.m;

Arrangements are being made to secure short and long rifle ranges at CLANQUES and elsewhere, particulars of which will be issued later.

SECRET.

156th Inf. Bde. Order No. 34.   Copy No. 17

Reference Maps 1/100,000 Sheets 5a and 11.   5th May 1918.

1. The 52nd Division is being transferred to XVIII Corps on May 6th, 7th and 8th and will take over the HERICOURT Sector of the line from the 4th Canadian Division on the night May 7th/8th.

2. The 156th Inf. Brigade Group, composed as under, will be in support at NEUVILLE ST VAAST.
   156th Inf. Brigade.
   412th Field Coy R.E.
   219th Coy A.S.C.
   1/1st Low Field Ambulance.

3. Transport and mounted personnel will move by road on May 7th and 8th under orders to be issued by Brigade Transport Officer. They will halt for the night May 7th/8th in the DIVION area. Dismounted personnel will move by tactical trains on May 8th in accordance with attached time table.

4. ENTRAINING. Units will entrain at ARRAS as per attached time-table:-
   Entraining Officer   Captain G.E. SMITH
   Detraining Officer   Lieut. A.D. BILLAND
   (a) The Entraining Officer will report to R.T.O. 2 hours before the start of No. 6 train and will travel in train No. 7.
   (b) Units will arrive at entraining Station as follows:-
      No. 6 Train.
         7th Royal Scots .... 7 A.M.
         8th Scottish Rifles   7.30 a.m.
         1/1st Low. Field Amb. }
         156th Inf. Bde. H.Q.   }   8 a.m.
      No. 7 Train.
         7th Scottish Rifles   4 p.m.
         4th Royal Scots   4.30 p.m.
         156th L.T.M. Batty   }
         412th Field Coy R.E.   }   5 p.m.
   (c) 1/7th Scottish Rifles will detail loading party of 1 Officer and 30 other ranks to report to Entraining Officer 2 hours before the start of the first train. This party will remain on duty until No. 7 train is loaded and will be responsible for loading all baggage etc of the Brigade Group.
   (d) 1/7th Royal Scots will detail a similar party at detraining Station to unload all baggage and stores of the Brigade Group.

5. BAGGAGE ETC. As much kit etc as possible will be sent on the 7th instant by the baggage wagons of the train, only minimum Officers' kits, and blankets, a proportion of cooking utensils, medical equipment, and one or two cycles per unit will be taken on the tactical trains. Instructions for conveying this baggage and one day's rations by lorry to the Station on 8th instant will be issued later also the hour baggage wagons will report on 6th instant. Packs and 1 blanket will be carried on the men.

6. SUPPLIES. Rations will be drawn as follows:-
   From R.P. at 10 a.m. on 6th inst. for consumption 7th inst.. by First Line Transport
   From R.P. at 3 p.m. on 6th instant for consumption on 8th inst.. by First Line Transport.
   From R.P. (time notified later) on 7th inst.. for consumption 8th inst. delivered by M.T.

7. TRANSPORT. The following are numbers of personnel & animals moving by road:-

Unit	Animals	Personnel	
Each Battalion	55	40	(including 4 cyclists)
Bde. H.Q.	26	25	
412th Fd. Coy R.E.	72	72	3 "
1/1st Low. Fd. Am.	45	47	

7. TRANSPORT. (Continued)

The transport will carry unconsumed portion of rations for 7th instant and 1 days rations for 8th and will refill for 9th instant at DIVISION on arrival of special M.T. Convoy.

8. TRAINS.

A Movement Order showing the number of personnel proceeding by each train will be handed by units to R.T.O. on arrival at entraining Station, a copy of which will be given to the entraining Officer.

10. Brigade H.Q. will close at MAMETZ at 7 a.m. on May 8th, and will open at NEUVILLE ST VAAST on arrival.

11. ACKNOWLEDGE.

CH? Metcalfe

Major,
Brigade Major, 156th Inf. Bde.

Issued at _____

Copy No. 1 to B.G.C.
    2   4th Royal Scots
    3   7th Royal Scots,
    4   7th Sco. Rifles
    5   8th Sco. Rifles,
    6   156th L.T.M. Battery,
    7   156th Bde. Signals
    8   R.T.O.
    9   B.S.O.
    10   S.C.
    11   412th Field Coy R.E.
    12   1/1st Low. Field Amb.
    13   219th Coy A.S.C.
    14   52nd Division.
    15   Captain SMITH.
    16   Lieut. RICHLAND.
   17 & 18   War Diary.
    19   FILE.

TIME TABLES FOR ENTRAINMENT

Date	Unit	Entrain No. of Train	Time of Departure	Time of Arrival	Detrain at	Remarks
May 4th	15th Bn Bde H.Q. 16th Signals 7th Royal Scots 8th Res. Rifles 1/1st Lr. Field Amb)	Alma	6	9.8 a.m.	1.12 p.m.	Ath
	4th Royal Scots 7th Sc. Rifles 16th L.N.L. Bdy 41st 16th Div Cy R.)	Alma	7	6.8 p.m.	10.12 p.m.	Ath

SECRET.

4th. Royal Scots
7th. Royal Scots
7th. Sco. Rifles
8th. Sco. Rifles
156th. L.T.M. Bty.

WARNING ORDER.

1. 156th. Inf. Brigade will relieve 155th. Inf. Brigade in the RIGHT SECTION of the Divisional Line in daylight on the 15th. inst.

2. Battalions will be disposed as follows:-

    7th. Sco. Rifles......RIGHT SUBSECTION, Front Line System

    8th. Sco. Rifles......LEFT SUBSECTION, Front Line System

    4th. Royal Scots......RIGHT RESERVE

    7th. Royal Scots......LEFT RESERVE

3. Advance parties, consisting of 1 Officer per Coy., 1 N.C.O. per platoon, Nos. 1 of all Lewis Guns in action, and proportion of signallers and runners will go into the line tomorrow afternoon.
They will be rationed up to and including the 15th. inst.

4. Relief of Trench Mortar Battery will take place on 16th. inst.

5. Detailed orders will be issued later.

                                              Major,
                             Brigade Major, 156th. Inf. Bde.

Copy to 155th. Inf. Brigade
Staff Captain.

SECRET.

156th Inf. Brigade Order No. 35.  Copy No. 19

Reference Maps 1/100,000 Sheet 11.
1/20,000 Trench Map.   14th May 1918.

1.   156th Inf. Brigade will relieve 155th Brigade in the RIGHT (WILLER-
:VAL) SECTION of the Divisional Sector on May 15th.

2.   Battalions will relieve as follows:-

1/7th Sco Rifles relieve 1/5th K.O.S.B. in RIGHT SUBSECTION (Front System)
1/8th Sco Rifles   "   1/4th K.O.S.B.   LEFT SUBSECTION (Front System)
1/4th Royal Scots   "   1/5th R.S.F.   RIGHT RESERVE
1/7th Royal Scots   "   1/4th R.S.F.   LEFT RESERVE.
     The method of holding the Line is now being changed and the final
dispositions are shown on attached Schedule. In the event of this change
not being completed at the time of relief, the line will be taken over as
it is held and the readjustment completed the following day.

3.   The Battalion boundaries will be as follows:-
   <u>Right Boundary</u>+ TIRED ALLEY - SPUR POST (B.14.a. central) - LONE TREE
                POST (B.13.a.) all inclusive.
   <u>Inter-Battalion Boundary.</u> WESTERN ROAD (inclusive to Right Battalion)
   <u>Left Boundary.</u>   ACHEVILLE - NEW BRUNSWICK ROAD, as far as Railway
                embankment in T.26.a.3.9. (exclusive to Right Section)
                - GRAND TRUNK TRENCH T.25.a.9.3. (inclusive to Right
                Section) - T.25.c.0.0. and thence West along grid line.

4.   All movement East of LA TARGETTE Cross Roads will be by platoons
at 200 yards distance.
     Troops for Right Subsection will move by TIRED ALLEY and Troops
for Left Subsection by HERSEY ALLEY.

5.   The leading platoons of Battalions will pass the Road Junction
A.9.b.2.8. (East end of NEUVILLE ST VAAST) at the following times:-
          1/7th Sco. Rifles................11 a.m.
          1/8th Sco. Rifles................12 noon
          1/4th Royal Scots................ 1 p.m.
          1/7th Royal Scots................ 2 p.m.
     While waiting at NEUVILLE ST VAAST, Companies will be sufficiently
separated as to avoid appearance of a concentration.

6.   Advance Parties will be sent into the line on May 14th in
accordance with instructions already issued.

7.   156th L.T.M. Battery. will relieve 155th L.T.M. Battery on 16th
May. During the period between the completion of the Infantry and Trench
Mortar reliefs 156th L.T.M. Battery will be under the orders of B.G.C.,
155th Inf. Brigade.

8.   Details of reliefs and meeting places for guides will be arranged
between O.Cs concerned.

9.   Communications, Trench Maps, Defence Schemes, Log Books, and
Trench Stores will be taken over and receipts given. Lewis Gun Magaz-
:ines and Stokes Mortars may be exchanged by mutual arrangement.

10. Completion of Relief will be reported "Priority" by code word "VIMY"
     The command of the Section will pass to B.G.C., 156th Inf. Bde.
on completion of the Infantry relief.

11. Battalions will go into the line with 22 Officers per Battalion
and 1 N.C.O. and 6 men per section. All personnel in excess of these
will proceed to RISPIN CAMP (X.19.c.9.8.) on May 16th. An Officer from
each unit will report to the Commandant by 10 a.m. for instructions as to
accommodation.

2.

12. Administrative Instructions will be issued separately by the Staff Captain.

13. Brigade H.Q. will close at MONT ST ELOY at 2 p.m. May 15th and open at A.6.c.5.5. at the same hour.

14. ACKNOWLEDGE.

C.H.J. Metcalfe

Major,
Brigade Major, 156th Inf. Brigade.

Issued at....................

No. 1 Copy to G.O.C.
    2   4th Royal Scots.
    3   7th Royal Scots.
    4   7th Sco. Rifles
    5   8th Sco. Rifles
    6   156th L.T.M. Batty.
    7   156th Bde. Signals
    8   Staff Captain
    9   Intelligence Officer
   10   Bde. Supply Officer
   11   B.T.O.
   12   219th Coy A.S.C.
   13   155th Inf. Brigade
   14   157th Inf. Brigade.
   15   154th Inf. Brigade
   16   52nd Division.
   17   1/1st Low/ Fd. Amb.
   18   412th Fd. Coy R.E.
 19 & 20   Diary.
   21   File.

DISPOSITION OF TROOPS IN RIGHT (WILLERVAL) SECTION.

Issued with Brigade Order No. 35, dated 14-5-18.

DISPOSITIONS.

UNIT	EX SUBSECTION	BATTALION H.Q.	DISPOSITIONS.
1/7th Sco. Rifles	Right	WILLERVAL	3 Companies in Blue Line, each with 2 Platoons in the Front Line and 2 platoons in support. 1 Company in Red Line and one Platoon in each of the following works:— BARNSLEY, FOVAN, SUBURB and DURHAM. (1 Coy 1/4th Royal Scots placed at disposal of O.C., 1/7th Sco. Rifles for purposes shewn below.
1/8th Sco. Rifles	Left	MERSEY ALLEY (T.26.d.3.2)	3 Companies in Blue Line, each with 2 platoons in the Front Line and 2 platoons in support. 1 Company in Red Line with one Platoon in each of the following works:— CANADA, SHEFFIELD, BEEHIVE and WAKEFIELD. (1 Coy 1/7th Royal Scots placed at disposal of O.C., 1/8th Sco. Rifles for purposes shewn below)
1/4th Royal Scots	Right Reserve	HILL CAMP NEUVILLE ST VAAST	1 Coy garrison of Brown line. 1 Coy living in Brown line but at the disposal of O.C., 1/7th Sco. Rifles for following purposes (a) half Coy to garrison TIRED ALLEY in the event of an attack on the Right Flank (b) half Coy for counter attack as required. 1 Platoon in Garrison SPUR POST; 1 Platoon garrison FARBUS POST 2 Coys (less 2 Platoons) HILL CAMP, NEUVILLE ST VAAST.
1/7th Royal Scots.	Left Reserve	HILL CAMP NEUVILLE ST VAAST.	1 Coy garrison of Brown Line. 1 Company T.21.9.9.4. at disposal of O.C., 1/8th Scottish Rifles for following purposes. (a) half Coy garrison of CANADA TRENCH in the event of an attack on the left flank (b) half Coy for counter attack as required. 1 Platoon garrison THELUS POST. 2 Coys (less 1 Platoon) HILL CAMP, NEUVILLE ST VAAST.

NOTE. The Front or "Blue" Line is at present marked by Notice Boards as "Red" Line. This will be changed after relief.

Right Section — Defence Scheme.
Communications.

Legend.

- ⊙ Signal Office.
- △ Linesman's Post.
- ⊕ Power Buzzer Stn:
- A Power Buzzer Amplifier Stn:
- T△ Wireless Trench Set Stn:
- ······ Visual Route.
- ∿∿ Runner's Course.
- R Relay Post.
- ✸ Visual Station.
- 🕊 Pigeon Station.
- ✱ Rocket Station.
- ——— Buried Cable
- ------ Route Between Power Buzzer Amplifier Stns:
- ∿∿∿ Route Between Wireless Stns:

Left Coy: Hqrs.
Right Coy: Hqrs.
To Right Sub-Section of Left Section.
Left Sub-Section Hqrs.
R.T.U.
Right Sub-Section Hqrs.
R.L.U.
Brigade Message & Rocket Station
To Left Sub-Section of Right Section
To Left Section Hqrs.
To Right Section Hqrs.
To Div:
To Div:
Section Hqrs.

deNeeds Lt. Re...
1502 Inf Bosched.
1.6.18.

Vol 3

SECRET.

WAR DIARY
OF
156th INFANTRY BRIGADE
FOR
JUNE 1918.

VOLUME XXXVII

156th INF. BRIGADE

WAR DIARY or INTELLIGENCE SUMMARY

Army Form C. 2118.

JUNE, 1918.

Place	Date	Hour	Summary of Events and Information	Remarks and references to Appendices
WILLERVAL SECTION	1		FOOTHILL – 1/110,000 – VIMY – MHA S.W.3 – 1/10,000 – ROUVROY – MHA S.W.4 1/10,000	
			A daylight Observation Post of 17th Royal Scots in NO MAN'S LAND furnished useful information.	(APPENDIX I)
			Advanced Parties of 157th Brigade came into the line prior to relief to be carried out tomorrow. Bde. Major and Staff Capt. 157th Brigade visited these Hdqrs. and afterwards went round part of the line.	SSg Capt
Mont St. Eloi	2		Brigade relieved by 157th Brigade. (Br. General Allan Commdg.) On relief this Bde. proceeded to quarters in huts at MONT ST ELOI, with 1st Scottish Rifles at NEUVILLE ST VAAST. Relief took place in daylight without casualties. Brig. General A.H. LEGGETT. D.S.O. proceeded on leave to U.K. Lt. Col. J.C.P. ROMANES D.S.O. Commdg. 17th Scottish Rifles took over command of the Brigade.	SSg Capt SSg Capt
—	3		Resting and cleaning up. Bathing commenced. Divisional Band played in Camp.	SSg Capt
—	4		Training commenced (platoons.) Major J. Hurst, Yank Corps lectured to Officers of 156th Bde. on Cooperation of Infantry and Yanks in the attack.	SSg Capt
—	5		Brigade Commander visited units during training. 4th and 7th Royal Scots took part in attack practice in cooperation with Yanks.	SSg Capt
—	6		7th and 8th Scottish Rifles took part in attack practice in cooperation with Yanks. Brig. Genl. A.H. LEGGETT. D.S.O. returned from leave in U.K. and resumed command.	SSg Capt

156TH INF. BRIGADE WAR DIARY or INTELLIGENCE SUMMARY

Army Form C. 2118

JUNE. 1918

Place	Date	Hour	Summary of Events and Information	Remarks and references to Appendices
Mont St Eloi	7		Brigade Order No 38 issued to all concerned, re Relief by this Brigade of the Left Section of Divisional front, at present occupied by 155th Infantry Brigade. Administrative Instructions No 4. issued to all concerned.	APPENDIX II APPENDIX III
"	8		Training carried on by Companies. Weather continues good. B.G.C. visited training grounds and Ranges. Reserve Defence Scheme issued. O.C. 1/7th Royal Scots and 1Bn Scottish Rifles visited XVIII Corps School. FRESSIN.	APPEND IV
"	9		Supplement to LONDON GAZETTE announces that Brig. Genl A.H. LEGGETT. D.S.O has been awarded the C.M.G. Church Parades by Battalions.	
"	10		Major C.H. METCALFE, D.S.O. Brigade Major proceeded to U.K. on leave. Captain W.R.KERMACK. 1/7th Royal Scots took over duties of Brigade Major. Advance Parties from this Brigade proceeded to Left Sub-section of Divisional front where 156th Bde will tomorrow relieve 157th Brigade.	
"	11		Brigade moved up the line again to relieve 157th Brigade. Men were carried by Motor Lorries beyond NEUVILLE ST VAAST. Relief was carried out by day, and a heat haze afforded good cover from possible aerial observation by enemy.	

WAR DIARY or INTELLIGENCE SUMMARY

Army Form C. 2118

156th INFANTRY BRIGADE

JUNE. 1918.

Place	Date	Hour	Summary of Events and Information	Remarks and references to Appendices
S 27 b.0.5. CHAUDIERE SECTION.	12	9am	Bde. Took over CHAUDIERE SECTION. Two Battalions in front, (1/7th S.R. on the right and 1/6th S.R. on the left) Two Battalions in support (1/4th R.S. on right, 1/7 R.S. on left). ~~despatition of Battalions~~ [strikethrough] Orders have been issued that certain parties in the front line are to fire their 5 rounds (daily practice) from TOLEDO TRENCH (see Appendix VII) to lead enemy to believe that this trench is held in strength by us. B.G.C. visited Headqrs of 4th and 7th Royal Scots. Weather fine.	MCyh MBCyh MBCyh
— " —	13		B.G.C. visited all Battalion Headqrs and conferred with Battalion Commanders regarding work to be done to improve the line. The day was dull and as visibility was not good, it was exceptionally quiet on the front.	MBCyh
— " —	14		Work is now under way, and in addition to usual French improvements, which are badly needed, there is an enormous quantity of material of all kinds lying in disused trenches, all of which will require to be salved. B.G.C. visited Vimy village area during afternoon. Captain J.J. McCombie, M.C. 8th Scottish Rifles attached to Brigade Hdqrs as understudy to Acting Brigade Major. Patrols are going out nightly from both Battalions in the line, but so far no enemy parties have been encountered. Enemy is heavily wired in, and shows no sign at present of any intention to take the offensive.	MBCyh

156th INFANTRY BRIGADE WAR DIARY or INTELLIGENCE SUMMARY

JUNE. 1918

Army Form C. 2118

Place	Date	Hour	Summary of Events and Information	Remarks and references to Appendices
CHAUDIERE SECTION	15		Work on trenches includes blocks which are being constructed in all the communication trenches, with a loophole and a stronger section of trench ahead of it. These are now under construction.	Hy Capt
" "	16		B.G.C. visited Left Subsection and Left Subsection Reserve Bn. Hdqrs. Five Non Commissioned Officers of the United States Army were today attached to the Brigade for instruction. They are to live with the four Battalions special attention being paid to scouting. Bde Order No 39 (Battn. Reliefs) issued (APPENDIX V) Bde Intelligence Officer attached to Hdqrs of Left Subsection in the line.	Hy Capt
" "	17		Brigadier General Commdg. visited Right Subsection and inspected work done on BROWN LINE. Maj. General J. Hill, CMG, DSO, Commdg 52nd Division, inspected 156th Brigade Transport at Daycamp Fl.u.b.2.0. Patrol of 8th Scottish Rifles obtained identification (23rd Reserve Infantry Regiment) which is normal.	Hy Capt
" "	18		Bde I.O. returned from Hdqrs. Left Subsection. Weather cooler and dull. 59th Brigade relieved 60th Brigade on Left flank of this Brigade.	Hy Capt
" "	19		B.G.C. held conference of Battalion Commanders at Hdqrs 1/4th Royal Scots. Reference new defence scheme proposed by XVIII Corps. Weather wet during day, but in the evening became fine.	Hy Capt
" "	20		Battalions in line relieved by Battalions in Reserve (see Appendix V) 157th Infantry Brigade, on Right Flank, relieved by 155th Inf. Brigade.	Hy Capt

WAR DIARY or INTELLIGENCE SUMMARY

Army Form C. 2118

156TH INFANTRY BRIGADE

JUNE 1918

Place	Date	Hour	Summary of Events and Information	Remarks and references to Appendices
CHAUDIERE SECTION	21		Five Non-commissioned officers of U.S. Army left to rejoin their units. Weather cold and wet. B.G.C. visited Left subsection.	
	22		During the present week work has been actively carried out on wire and on trenches. Patrols have been active but no enemy patrol has yet been engaged in action.	
	23		Patrol of 1/7th Royal Scots, under Lt. S.J. Spence, had an encounter in No Man's Land with enemy patrol and took 2 prisoners. We suffered no casualties.	
	24		Lt. Genl. Sir Aylmer Hunter-Weston KCB.DSO. assumed command of VIII Corps vice Lt. General Sir Ivor Maxse, KCB. CVO. DSO.	
	25		During the night of 24/25th our guns shelled MERICOURT area with gas. Brigade Order No 40 issued to all concerned, reference redistribution of Battalions in the Line consequent on the withdrawal of the 1/8th Scot Rifles, to come in to force on 27th instant. (APPENDIX VI)	
	26		B.G.C. visited Headqrs 1/8th Scottish Rifles in the forenoon. In the afternoon Capt. J.J. McCombie A/OSS. Bde Major left to rejoin 8th Sco. Rifles.	
	27		1/8th Scottish Rifles. Lt. Col. J.M. Findlay, D.S.O. Commdg. withdrawn from 156th Brigade. At 6 pm. the Battalion was inspected by the Corps Commander, and prior to the inspection the B.G.C. saw the Battalion, and expressed his regret that they were going and his good wishes for the	

WAR DIARY
or
INTELLIGENCE SUMMARY

Army Form C. 2118.

156TH Infantry Bde.

JUNE 1918.

Hour, Date, Place		Summary of Events and Information	Remarks and references to Appendices
CHAUDIERE SECTION	27	Future Brigade frontage now distributed as per plan attached. Brigade Order No 41 ref. Relief by 157th Bde. issued to all concerned.	APPENDIX VIII APPENDIX VIII G.
—	28	B.G.C. saw departure of 1/8th Sco. Rifles at Mt. St. Eloi.	
—	29	Brigade Commander 157th Bde. visited Hdqrs. and discussed arrangements and disposition of line with B.C.C. Section Defence Scheme issued. Brigade relieved by 157th Inf. Bde. (Lt. Col. Anderson, Commdg.)	APPENDIX VII Lt Col A/Capt
Mont St. Eloi	30	Relief reported complete by 5.30 p.m. Battns. distributed as per appendix. Battalions resting and cleaning up. Casualty Return for the month Effective Strength of Bde. on this date	APPENDIX IX A/Capt APPENDIX X A/Capt

W.P. Kermack   Capt.
Acting Brigade Major.
156th Infantry Brigade.

30th June 1918.

REPORT of DAY PATROL, 1/7th Royal Scots, at T.29.b.0.8
31st May 1918.

No. 302909. Cpl. P. CRANE.
301116 Pte. R. STENSON,
12555 Pte. B. JOHNSTON.

1. Approaches to our line.
   (a) From the East the approach to HUDSON BLOCK would seem to be impossible without a considerable wirecutting bombardment. Even were the wire cut successfully, the enemy would have to cross a space of 300 yards in view of our post at the block and also from portions of our front line.
   (b) MONTREAL TRENCH is well protected by wire, but from NO MAN'S LAND the gaps are very obvious by day.

0230 – The post established itself in a shell hole on the forward slope of the crest which runs E. & W. across NO MAN'S LAND. The covering party then withdrew towards HUDSON BLOCK. About three minutes after their departure, the O.P. spotted two Hun patrols, one of 20 men and the other of 6. The smaller patrol was S. of the O.P. and they moved over the crest making towards ARLEUX.
   The large patrol followed our covering party towards our wire. 20 minutes later they appeared again moving N.E. towards WINNIPEG TRENCH. They passed very close to our O.P. and when about 100 yards beyond it they were challenged and halted by a sentry who appeared to be on duty near HUDSON TRENCH at T.29.b.4.8.

0300 – ~~Considerable movement~~ M.G. flash bearing 110° T estimated 600 yards from the O.P. Sound bearing to another M.G. 160° T estimated 1000 yards distant.

0330 – Considerable movement seen in front line especially in ARLEUX LOOP SOUTH, loud laughing and talking heard, and heads shewing above parapet as if men standing to.

0400 – Party of 20 men came out of HUDSON TRENCH at T.23.b.8.5. and started to repair the wire in front of this trench. This party worked for an hour and then disappeared into a trench again. New pickets were driven in, and new wire put up. A trip wire was run out about 10 to 20 yards in front of the fence wire.

0430 – Large amount of wheel traffic moved S.W. along road in T.24.a.E.& c. also T.30.a. & c.

0500) – One E.A. hovering overhead prevented observation and
0600)   movement in O.P.

0650 – Numerous clouds of smoke seen in HUDSON POST from T.24.a.27 TO T.24.c.59.65 also at ARLEUX LOOP SOUTH in U.29.d.

0730) – No movement at all. No day posts seen in front line.
1700)   Observers exposed themselves to try to attract attention but no notice was taken of this. The front line appears to be entirely evacuated by day.

1720 – FRESNOY TRENCH was being repaired by a party of not less than 20. White dust seen to rise. Men also seen pulling sandbags off the parapet.

1800 – A line of men at one yard interval moved down TICKLER & HUDSON TRENCHES (T.24.a. & c.) This continued for 15 minutes.

1820 – Loud talking and laughing in WINNIPEG TRENCH.

1950 – Wiring party of 20 reappeared and continued work at T.23.B.8.5.

2020 – Wiring party relieved by other 20 men.

2050 – One E.A. over our line, flying under 2000 feet.

ENEMY/

ENEMY LINE.

The front line is protected by two apron fences 15 feet wide 3 feet high. O.P. looked into the wire, not over it, and the distance between fences was not easily judged, but they are thought to be very close to one another. No gaps could be seen although a very careful search was made for them. The large enemy patrol seemed to enter about T.23.d.7.5. (see Patrol Reports of Lt. McDONALD, 27-5-18, and of Lt. WEIR, 25-5-18. A night Post was situated about 150 yards North of enemy block in HUDSON TRENCH This Post challenged enemy's returning patrol of 30 and possibly it was only there to protect the rear of the patrol or to mark the gap in the wire in case of a hasty return on the part of the patrol.

This Post communicated with patrol by whistling frequently.

1-6-18.

(Sgd) Wm. M. COWAN, Lt.
I.O., for O.C., 1/7th Royal Scots.

SECRET.   156th Inf. Brigade Order No. 38.   Copy No. 19   II

Ref. Map MARQEUIL, 1/20,000.   7 June 1918.

1. 156th Inf. Brigade will relieve 155th Inf. Brigade in the LEFT SECTION on June 11th and 12th.

2. Reliefs will take place as follows:-

June 11th. 7th Sco. Rifles relieve 5th K.O.S.B. in Front Line
                                        RIGHT SUBSECTION.
            8th Sco. Rifles relieve 4th K.O.S.B. in Front Line
                                        LEFT SUBSECTION.
            4th Royal Scots relieve 5th R.S.F. in RIGHT RESERVE.
            7th Royal Scots relieve 4th R.S.F. in LEFT RESERVE.
June 12th. 156th L.T.M. Battery relieve 155th L.T.M. Battery.

3. Units in camp at MONT ST ELOY will move by Motor Lorry as follows:-
   7th Sco. Rifles.....To Barrier on LA FOLIE FARM Road at S.28.d.8.8
                       starting at 9 a.m.
   4th Royal Scots.....To Barrier on LA FOLIE FARM Road at S.28.d.8.8
                       starting about 12.15 p.m.
   7th Royal Scots.....Via ARRAS-SOUCHEZ Road, CAMPBELL Road to
                       S.28.a.3.8., starting about 12.15 p.m.
   8th Sco. Rifles will march from HILLS CAMP, the leading platoon arriving at S.23.a.3.8. at 9.30. a.m.

4. Guides will meet Units as follows:-
   7th Sco. Rifles.....At Barrier S.28.d.8.8. at 9.30. a.m.
   4th Royal Scots.....At Barrier S.28.d.8.8. at 12.30. p.m.
   8th Sco. Rifles.)
   7th Royal Scots.)...Chain of picquets from debussing point to
                       BLIGHTY TRENCH where guides from Battns
                       will be assembled at 9.45. a.m. and 12.45
                       p.m. respectively.
   In addition, guides will be at LA TARGETTE Cross Roads at 9.15 a.m. for RIGHT SUBSECTION and 12.15 p.m. for LEFT SUBSECTION to guide first relay of Lorries to Debussing points. All the above are being arranged for by 155th Inf. Brigade.
   Battalions going into RIGHT SUBSECTION will move by HUMBER, PEGGIE and TOAST TRENCHES. Those going into LEFT SUBSECTION will move by BLIGHTY, GLACE and HYTER TRENCHES.

5. Movement will be by platoons at 200 yards distance.

6. 7th Sco. Rifles and 7th Royal Scots will each detail an Officer from the nucleus to be left behind to act as Debussing Officers at S.28.d.8.8. and S.28.a.3.8. respectively.

7. Advance Parties consisting of 1 Officer per Company, one N.C.O. per platoon, Nos 1 of all Lewis Guns in action, Gas N.C.Os, and a proportion of Signallers and Runners, will go into the line on June 10th. Guides to take them to Battalion H.Q. will meet them as follows:-
   7th Sco. Rifles)
   4th Royal Scots)....At Barrier S.28.d.8.8. at 3 p.m.
   7th Royal Scots)...
   8th Sco. Rifles)...At 155th Inf. Brigade H.Q. at 3 p.m.

8. Details of relief will be arranged between C.Os. concerned.

9. Communications, Trench Maps, Maps of NO MAN'S LAND, Defence Schemes, Log Books and Trench Stores will be taken over.

10./

10. Personnel of Units to be left out of the line will proceed to VILLERS CAMP, arriving there by 3 p.m. June 11th.

11. Between the completion of the Infantry and L.T.M. Battery Reliefs, 156th L.T.M. Battery will be under orders of B.G.C., 155th Inf. Brigade.

12. Completion of relief will be reported by the code word "JUSTICE".

13. B.G.C., 156th Inf. Brigade, will assume command of the SECTION at 9 a.m. June 12th, at which hour Brigade H.Q. will close at ST ELOY and reopen at S.27.central.

14. ACKNOWLEDGE.

Major,
Brigade Major, 156th Inf. Brigade.

Issued at 1/pm

=======oOo=======

```
Copy No.  1 to G.O.C.              Copy No. 11 to B.T.O.
          2    4th Royal Scots              12    119th Coy A.S.C.
          3    7th Royal Scots              13    155th Inf. Bde.
          4    7th Sco. Rifles              14    157th Inf. Brigade
          5    8th Sco. Rifles.             15          Brigade.
          6    156th L.T.M. Bty.            16    52nd Division.
          7    156th Inf. Bde. Sigs.        17    1/1st Low. Fd. Amb.
          8    Staff Captain                18    412th Fd. Coy R.E.
          9    Intelligence Officer    19 & 20    Diary.
         10    Bde. Supply Officer          21    File.
```

SECRET.　　　　　156th Infantry Brigade.　　　　　　　　　No. 18

7th JUNE, 1918.

ADMINISTRATIVE ORDERS, No. 4.

Ref. Map : MAROEUIL, 1/20,000.

Ref. 156th Inf. Bde. Order No. 38 -

1. **BILLETS.**
(a) All Billets and Camps must be left scrupulously clean, and a certificate signed by an Officer of the incoming unit stating that the Camps have been taken over in a clean and sanitary condition will be forwarded to Bde. Hdqrs. by 9 a.m. on 12/6/18.
(b) A list of Area Stores as per schedule to be handed over to incoming unit, will be forwarded to Brigade Hdqrs. by 12 noon on 10/6/18.
(c) Certificates will be obtained from the Area Commandant that there are no outstanding claims for damage to Government property.

2. **TRANSPORT.**
(a) The lines at present occupied will be vacated by 2 p.m. on 11/6/18 and certificates obtained that the lines were taken over in a clean and sanitary condition.
(b) Transport will be brigaded at DALY CAMP (F.11.b.20.). Separate orders will be issued by the Bde. Transport Officer.
(c) Completion of relief will be wired Bde. Hdqrs. by the Brigade Transport Officer by the code word "ROSS".

3. **MOBILE STORES.**
Mobile stores, blankets and spare kits will be taken to DALY CAMP.

4. **TRENCH STORES.**
List of Trench Stores taken over will be furnished, as per schedule, to reach Bde. Hdqrs. not later than 36 hours after relief.

5. **SUPPLIES.**
(a) Commencing 11th inst. supplies will be drawn from Refilling Point at LEADLEY SIDING (A.2.c.6.8.) and delivered to Transport Camp by the Supply Section of the Train.
(b) Rations will be taken to ZIVY STATION and loaded on trains by 8-15 p.m. daily for the following points:

Right line Battn.	-	CANADA DUMP. (T.20.b.6.3.)
Left line Battn.	-	VICTORIA DUMP. (T.13.b.3.3.)
Right Reserve Battn.	-	2 Companies and Batt. Hdqrs., BRUNSWICK DUMP. (T.26.a.8.9.)
		2 Companies, CANADA DUMP. (T.20.b.6.3.)
Left Reserve Battn.	-	2 Companies and Batt. Hdqrs., CAYUGA DUMP. (S.24.7.6.8.)
		2 Companies, VICTORIA DUMP. (T.13.b.3.3.)
L.T.M.Battery.	-	VICTORIA DUMP. (T.13.b.3.3.)

(Note.) Forward of VICTORIA and CANADA DUMPS, the two front line Battalions push up their rations on Trollies as far as the front system.
(c) Company Quartermaster Sergeants will proceed each night with the rations from ZIVY and are responsible that the rations are delivered to their Companies.

(d) The Quartermaster or Transport Officer of each Battalion will travel nightly with the Ration Train and report to their Battalion Hdqrs. for orders. Quartermasters will visit their Battalions in the line at least every two days.

(2).

3. **COOKING.**
Cooking for the Battalions in the line will be as follows:-
1. (a). Right Line Battn. By means of Soyer Stoves and Camp Kettles in a Quarry near Battn. Hdqrs. and conveyed to Companies in Food Containers.
   (b). Left Line Battn. By means of Soyer Stoves which are well dug in, and conveyed to Companies in Food Containers.
2. (a) A proportion of Soyer Stoves and Food Containers will be handed over to all Battalions.
   (b) Fresh meat will be cooked at Transport Camp, forwarded by Light Railway, and heated up by the Soyer Stoves.

7. **RESERVE RATIONS.** Distributed as follows:-
(a). Brigade Reserve.

	Map Reference.	Biscuits.	Meat.
Right Line Battn.	(T.16.c.9.5.)	775	744
Left Line Battn.	(T.8.d.3.7.)	750	768
Right Reserve Battn.	(S.24.d.1.2.)	750	756
Left Reserve Battn.	(T.7.d.9.5.)	750	760
		3025	3028

(b). Localities.

Right Reserve Bn. NOVA SCOTIA.		
(T.21.a.3.3.)	600	576
Left Reserve Batt. BOIS DE LA CHAUDIERE.		
(T.7.d.9.5.)	600	576

8. **WATER SUPPLY.**

MONT FOREST SYSTEM.
(T.15.b.7.6.)	3,	400 gallon tanks.
(T.13.c.3.8.)	3,	Do. Do.
(T.13.c.9.2.)	1,	Do. Do.
(T.16.d.2.7.)	3,	Do. Do.
(T.19.b.9.1.)	3,	Do. Do.

GIVENCHY MAIN.
(S.12.b.9.6.)	1,	W.B.F. (12 taps.)
(S.12.b.8.5.)	2,	400 gallon tanks.
(T.8.a.0.0.)	1,	Do. Do.
(T.8.a.7.8.)	4,	Do. Do.
(T.8.d.5.3.)	4	Do. Do.

VIMY.
(S.18.c.9.3.)	2	S.P.
(S.24.b.2.9.)	2	200 gallon tanks.
(T.20.c.3.1.)	2	Do. Do.

9. **WATER PICQUETS.**
The following picquets will relieve those found by 155th Infantry Brigade by 2 p.m. on 11/5/18.

Right line Battn.	1 N.C.O., 5 men for MONT FORET SYSTEM.
Left line Battn.	1 N.C.O., 2 men for GIVENCHY MAIN. (T.8.a.0.0.). (T.8.a.7.8.).(T.8.d.5.3.)
Right Reserve Bn.	1 N.C.O., 4 men for GOODMAN MAIN and VIMY. (T.20.c.3.1.)
Left Reserve Bn.	1 N.C.O., 3 men for GIVENCHY (S.12.b.9.6.). (S.12.b.8.5.) and VIMY. (S.18.c.9.3.). (S.24.b.2.9.)

Picquets will be in possession of their duties in writing per 52nd Dvn. Administrative Memo No. 7 para 5 (i) (ii), and will be rationed by the unit concerned.

(3).

10. **AMMUNITION SUPPLY.**
   1. The ammunition is distributed as follows:-
      (a) With Companies.
      (b) Battalion Dumps.
      (c) Forward Brigade Dumps.
      (d) Main Brigade Dump.
   2. Battalions restock from a convenient forward Brigade Dump on application to Brigade Headquarters.
   3. Location of Brigade Dumps:-
      MAIN DUMP.   CAYUGA.   (S.24.c.8.5.)
      FORWARD DUMPS. CULVERT.   (T.20.d.5.1.)
                      PEGGIE.   (T.19.b.7.8.)
                      NANAIMO.   (T.13.a.2.7.)

11. **STRAGGLERS POSTS.**
    Stragglers posts are as follows:-
    S.11.d.4.2,   S.18.c.9.2,   S.24.b.4.6,   T.19.c.2.5.
    manned by personnel found by A.P.M.

12. **PRISONERS of WAR.**
    Prisoners of War Cage. AUX REITZ. (A.8.c.3.7.)

13. **SALVAGE.**
    Salvage dumps are situated as follows:-
    Right line Battn.   -   CANADA DUMP.
    Left line Battn.   -   VICTORIA DUMP.
    Right Reserve Battn. -   BRUNTSWICK DUMP.
    Left Reserve Battn. -   CAYUGA DUMP.

14. **MEDICAL.**
    MAIN DRESSING STN.   AUX REITZ.(A.8.c.5.5.)   ] 3rd L.Fd.
    ADVANCED DRESSING STN.   LA CHAUDIERE.(S.18.c.9.5.)] Amb.
    (a). Regimental Aid Posts.
         Right line Battn.   T.13.c.6.0.
         Left line   " .   T.8.c.2.6.
         Right Reserve " .   Battn. Hdqrs.
         Left Reserve " .   Battn. Hdqrs.
    (b) Relay Posts.
         Right Battalion.   T.20.b.2.7.
         Left Battalion.   T.13.7.8.

15. **BURIAL.**
    The following cemetries will be used:-
    THELUS. A.5.c.8.5.   AUX RIETZ. A.8.c.5.0.
    An advanced collecting post is established at T.19.b.8.4. and units are responsible for taking bodies to the station. Units will wire Divisional Burial Officer, AUX RIETZ, when any bodies have to be collected, and arrangements will be made to remove these from the Collecting Station by the Dvnl. Burial Party.

13. ACKNOWLEDGE.

                                              Captain,
                                           Staff Captain,
                                    156th Infantry Brigade.

P.T.O.

(4).

Issued at 9.40 p.m.

Copy to :-

No. 1. B.G.C.
2. 4th Royal Scots.
3. 7th Royal Scots.
4. 7th Sco. Rifles.
5. 8th Sco. Rifles.
6. 156 L.T.M.Bty.
7. Bde. Major.
8. Bde. Sigs.
9. Bde. Supply Officer.
10. Bde. Transport Officer.
11. O.C., Light Railways, ZIVY.
12. 1/3rd. L.F.A.
13. 219 Coy. A.S.C.
14. 155th Inf. Bde.
15. 52nd (L) Division.
16. File.
17. Diary.
18. "

ACTION of RESERVE BRIGADE.

Reference Map MAROEUIL, 1/20,000/

1. The Divisional Reserve consists of:-
   156th Inf. Brigade;
   1 Coy 52nd M.G. Battalion (less 10 guns).

2. The action of the Divisional Reserve is dependent on the extent and direction of the enemy's penetration into our line, but roughly may be considered under three headings:-
   (a) Forming a Defensive Flank to the South;
   (b) Forming a Defensive Flank to the North;
   (c) Counter-attack to restore a broken centre.

3. The following general instructions are laid down to meet the three contingencies mentioned above:-
   (a). In the event of the enemy breaking through South of WILLERVAL, the Battalion in the NEUVILLE ST VAAST Area will move at once to occupy the ECURIE SWITCH from THELUS POST (exclusive) to the THELUS TRENCH in A.17.b., Battalion H.Q. being established at A.J. Test Box, A.6.a.5.0. (RIGHT SECTION HEADQUARTERS).
   The remainder of the Brigade will move to NEUVILLE ST VAAST area and will assemble as follows:- (see attached tracing)
   4th Royal Scots....PADDOCK SWITCH TRENCHES, South of LICH-
   :FIELD POST No. 1.
   7th Royal Scots....PADDOCK SWITCH TRENCHES, North of LICH-
   :FIELD POST No. 1.
   7th Sco. Rifles....In Old Trenches about 300 yards West of LICHFIELD POST No. 1.
   O.C., 156th L.T.M. Battery will detail a half Battery to come under the orders of O.C., 8th Scottish Rifles for the defence of ECURIE SWITCH.
   156th L.T.M. Battery, less half Battery, will assemble at LICHFIELD POST No. 1.
   Brigade H.Q. and H.Q. 4th and 7th Royal Scots will be at A.E. Test Box, LICHFIELD POST NO. 1.   H.Q., 7th Scottish Rifles, will be at old Canadian Battalion H.Q. about A.3.d.central.
   (b). In the event of the enemy breaking through from the North, the Brigade will concentrate in the neighbourhood of Hill 130, proceeding there by the routes already reconnoitred.   The position of units will be as follows:-
   4th Royal Scots   ... ... S.20.d.5.6.
   7th Royal Scots   ... ... S.20.a.9.5.
   7th Sco. Rifles   ... ... S.20.a.2.5.
   8th Sco. Rifles.)
   156th L.T.M. Bty.) ... ... S.20.c.5.2.
   Bde. H.Q. at S.J. Test Box, S.20.a.4.0.
   (c). In the event of a penetration into our front line the Battn. at NEUVILLE ST VAAST will move at once to occupy that portion of the GREEN LINE between S.22.d.6.1. and A.5.b.7.3., pushing forward Posts well down the Eastern slopes of VIMY to cover the BONVAL RE-ENTRANT and the LENS-ARRAS ROAD. Battalion H.Q. will be at S.Q. Test Box at S.28.c.5.5.
   The remainder of the Brigade will move as detailed in para 2 (a).
   (d). Units will complete reconnaissances for the above dispositions and will arrange for Notice Boards to be erected shewing the assembly position of each Company.

3. The probable future action of the Brigade after arriving at the position of assembly will be as follows; and the necessary reconnaissances will be carried out.

In 2 (a).
   The 7th Sco. Rifles & half Battery 156th L.T.M. Bty will be pre-
   :pared to man the ECURIE SWITCH from THELUS TRENCH to LILLE Redoubt (inclusive)
   Bde. H.Q. will remain at H.E. Test Box.

2.

In 2 (b).
The Brigade will be prepared to support the 2nd C.I.W. Battalion (Col. McKINERY, D.S.O.) who will be manning the GREEN LINE from its junction with the PADDOCK SWITCH in S.29. to junction with Bully Switch in M.20.d.
In this case Battalions will be disposed as follows:-
8th Sco. Rifles...from Junction GREEN LINE and PADDOCK SWITCH in S.29. to Junction GREEN LINE and BLIGHTY in S.22.a.
4th Royal Scots...thence to Road at S.15.6.0.6.
7th Royal Scots...thence to BOIS EN HACKE (S.2.c.) inclusive.
7th Sco. Rifles...in reserve at position of assembly.
156th L.T.M. Battery will detail a Section to come under the orders of each Battalion in the GREEN LINE,- the Battery, less 3 Sections, remaining in reserve at Brigade H.Q.
Brigade H.Q. will remain at S.J. Test Box, S.20.a.4.0.

In 2 (c).
(i). 4th Royal Scots will be prepared to man the GREEN LINE from A.5.b.7.3. to THELUS POST (exclusive)
Brigade H.Q. will remain at A.E. Test Box.
(ii). The Brigade, less 8th Sco. Rifles, will be prepared to move by night across the VIMY RIDGE and concentrate under cover of VIMY about the following positions:-
    4th Royal Scots, ... S.18.d.8.0.
    7th Royal Scots, ... S.24.c.6.4.
    7th Sco. Rifles, ... S.24.c.0.2.
    156th L.T.M. Bty, ... to positions covering the GREEN LINE.
Brigade H.Q. will move to S.23.c.2.2.

4.   The actions of the Company, 52nd M.G. Battalion, will be:-
In 2 (a).
Send 2 guns to each of the following positions:-
    JERUSALEM M.G. POST ... A.17.c.30.60.
    RAILWAY POST ... ... A.11.d.40.40.
    JORDAN POST ... ... A.12.c.45.40.
    TAPE POST B.7.c.15.45
    THELUS POST ... ... B.7.a.85.00.
The Company, less 10 guns, will move into reserve at LICHFIELD POST No. 1.

In 2 (b).
Send guns to the following positions:-
    1 gun ... ... S.22.d.62.82.
    1 gun ... ... S.22.d.70.75.
    2 guns ... MAPLE ... S.22.a.62.40.
    2 guns ... BEECH ... S.22.a.42.94.
    2 guns ... ELM ... S.16.c.35.25.
The Company, less 8 guns will move to join Bde. H.Q. at S.J. Test Box, S.20.a.4.0.

In 2 (c).
Send 2 guns to each of the following positions:-
    HOW M.G. POST ... S.30.d.48.70.
    THISTLE M.G. POST. S.30.a.63.34.
The Company, less 4 guns, will Stand by in CUBITT CAMP, send-:ing an Officer to report to Bde. H.Q. at A.E. Test Box.

5.   Battalions will be ready to move in one hour from the order to "Stand to", and will move immediately on the order "SITUATION (a), (b) or (c)" being communicated to them.

6.   The necessary reconnaissances will be completed as early as possible and a statement forwarded shewing position of ammunition reserves in the GREEN LINE and ECURIE SWITCH, and the quantities of extra ammunition required and points at which it should be dumped. The whole of Units ammunition reserve should be considered available.

7.   The attached Map shews the above dispositions, positions of units being marked as follows:-
    Situation (a) ... ... YELLOW.
    Situation (b) ... ... BLUE
    SITuation (c) ... ... GREEN.

Major,
for Bde. Major, 156th Inf. Brigade

SECRET.   Copy No. 18

156th INFANTRY BRIGADE ORDER No.39.

16th June 1918.

1. The following reliefs will take place on 20th inst:-

    (a) 1/4th Royal Scots will relieve 1/7th Scottish Rifles in First Zone Right Sub-Section.
    (b) 1/7th Royal Scots will relieve 1/8th Scottish Rifles in First Zone Left Sub-Section.
    (c) Battalions relieved will take over dispositions of battalions which relieve them.

2. Reliefs will be completed by 7 p.m. and reported by Code Word "IMSHI".

3. Details of relief will be arranged between C.O's concerned.

4. On relief, platoon of 1/7th Scottish Rifles which is to proceed shortly to Musketry Camp, will be allotted quarters near Brigade H.Q. by Staff Captain. From 21/6/18 it will come on ration strength of Bde.H.Q.

5. Trench Stores will be taken over and receipts given, one copy to be forwarded to Bde.H.Q. 36 hours after the relief.

6. Existing arrangements regarding supply of rations and water will be taken over.

7. Acknowledge.

                                    W R Kermack Captain,
                                    A/Brig.Major, 156th Inf.Brigade.

Issued by runner at 12 noon

Copy No.1 to	G.O.C.	Copy No.12 to	157th Inf.Brigade
2	4th Royal Scots.	13	80th Inf.Brigade
3	7th Royal Scots.	14	52nd Division.
4	7th Sco.Rifles.	15	413th Coy. R.E.
5	8th Sco.Rifles.	16	Left Group R.F.A.
6	156th T.M.Batt.	17	Left Group 52nd M.G.Bn.
7	Bde.Signals.		
8	Staff Captain.	18 & 19	Diary
9	I.Officer.	20	File.
10	Bde.Supply Officer.		
11	B.T.O.		

SECRET.   Copy No. 15

156th. INFANTRY BRIGADE ORDER No. 40.

Ref. Map - TARGETTE 1/20,000   25th. June 1918.

1.   The Brigade will be redistributed in the Left Section of the 52nd. Divisional Sector in three instead of four Battalion areas from 3 p.m. 27th. June, the 1/8th. Scottish Rifles being withdrawn from the Brigade.

2.   Names and boundaries of these areas will be as follows:-
   (a) TOAST AREA, the Right Sub-section of the front zone of defence, bounded by VESTA TILLEY (exclusive) to its junction with TEDDIE GERRARD, thence South-west to T.15.a.0.0, thence South-south-west to junction of JULIA JAMES with GERTIE (exclusive), thence to junction of the two railway embankments (exclusive) in square T.13.d, thence South-east, parallel to and 300 yards west of the embankment to junction of the embankment and PEGGIE (inclusive), thence to T.20.a.8.6, thence to Section boundary at T.21.c.7.6.
   (b) BETTY AREA, the Left Sub-section of the front zone of defence, bounded by TOAST AREA on the South, to junction of embankments (inclusive) in square T.13.d, thence North-west to Brigade section boundary at its junction with ARRAS-LENS Road (inclusive).
   (c) VIMY-CHAUDIERE AREA, the second zone of defence comprises the remainder of the Brigade Area.

3.   BLUE Line will be the first Battle Line. BLACK Line (CANADA-GERTIE-JAMES-HAYTER-GLADYS-DARTMOUTH) will be the second Battle Line, and BROWN Line (including VIMY and CHAUDIERE localities) will be the third Battle Line.

4.   Distribution will be as follows:-

   (i) 4th Royal Scots will hold TOAST AREA with their four Companies in line disposed in depth, each company having one-and-a-half platoons in First Battle Line, and two platoons holding CANADA-GERTIE Trenches.
   Each Company will have one half platoon day and night in the line of observation (MONTREAL-QUEBEC-LILY ELSIE).

   (ii) 7th. Royal Scots will hold BETTY AREA with their four Companies in line disposed in depth, each Company having two platoons in First Battle Line. In Second Battle Line the two centre Companies will have two platoons each holding respectively HAYTER and GLADYS Trenches, the Right flank Company having one platoon holding JAMES and one holding HALIFAX Trench, and the Left flank Company having one holding DARTMOUTH and one holding PICTOU Trench. The platoons in HALIFAX and PICTOU will give special attention respectively to the trench junctions with RED and AMHURST Trenches.
   The platoons at the junctions of KEANE with BETTY and TEDDIE GERRARD with VESTA TILLEY will each have one section in the observation line at the junctions of TOLEDO with BETTY and VESTA TILLEY and another half way along BETTY and VESTA TILLEY.

   (iii) The liaison Section with 20th. Division which is posted at the junction of RED Trench with the LENS-ARRAS Road will be supplied by Left front zone battalion (1/7th. Royal Scots).

   (iv) 1/7th. Scottish Rifles will hold VIMY-CHAUDIERE AREA. They will have two Companies in VIMY locality from GRAND TRUNK to LENS-ARRAS Road (inclusive) as at present; one Company in BROWN Line, relieving one company 1/8th. Scottish Rifles; and one Company in CHAUDIERE-GLACE of which two platoons will be in GLACE, and one platoon in CHAUDIERE in support. The fourth platoon will hold BROWN LINE from LENS-ARRAS Road (exclusive) to S.23.b.7.10. This Company also relieves one Company 1/8th. Scottish Rifles.

   (v) /

2.

(v) The A.A. Lewis Gun and team of 3 other ranks of 1/8th. Scottish Rifles at present on duty at Brigade Transport Camp will be relieved by 1/7th. Scottish Rifles.

(vi) Headquarters, 1/4th. Royal Scots will be established at T.26.a.3.8. Headquarters of 1/7th. Royal Scots and 1/7th. Scottish Rifles remain as at present.

4 (a) 1/7th. Scottish Rifles will take over anti-aircraft Lewis Gun posts at S.17.b.2.4.
1/4th. Royal Scots will take over Anti-aircraft Lewis gun post at T.15.a.6.8.

5. Relief will be completed by 3 p.m. and notified to Brigade H.Q. by code word "WELLINGTON RIDGE".

6. Details of relief will be arranged between C.Os concerned.

7. Communications, trench maps, Defence Schemes, Log Books, and Trench Stores will be taken over by relieving units.
1/7th. Scottish Rifles will take over 1/8th. Scottish Rifles Headquarters, and all relay posts and other dispositions of 1/8th. Scottish Rifles not taken over by 1/7th. Royal Scots. Battalion H.Q. 1/7th. Scottish Rifles will not move from present position.

8. As relieved, 1/8th. Scottish Rifles will move in parties not stronger than one platoon by CENTRE, GLACE and BLIGHTY Trenches to embussing point at S.26.a.3.8 (CAMPBELL ROAD). Buses will be at embussing point from 11.30 a.m. onwards and will convey 1/8th. Scottish Rifles to MONT St. ELOI. O.C., 1/8th. Scottish Rifles will detail an embussing Officer.

9. Details of 1/8th. Scottish Rifles at 52nd. Division Reception Camp will rejoin their unit at MONT St. ELOI by 12 noon under arrangements to be made by O.C. 156th. Brigade Details Reception Camp.

10. Camps to which 1/8th. Scottish Rifles will proceed will be notified later.

11. ACKNOWLEDGE.

WRKermack Captain,
A/Brigade Major, 156th. Inf. Bde.

Issued by runner at _____

Copy No.		Copy No.	
1	to G.O.C.	9	to O.C. 156th. Bde. Details 52nd. Div. Reception Camp.
2	4th. Royal Scots		
3	7th. Royal Scots		
4	7th. Sco. Rifles	10	Bde. S.O.
5	8th. Sco. Rifles	11	H.Q. 52nd. Divn.
6	156th. T.M. Batt.	12	155th. Inf. Bde.
7	Staff Captain	13	59th. Inf. Bde.
8	S.T.O.	14 & 15	War Diary
		16	File

SECRET.   BM 1/71/1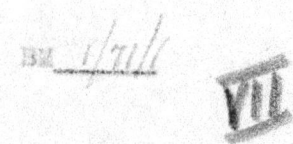

1. Herewith one copy of 156th Inf.Bde. Defence Scheme for LEFT SECTION, 52nd Division Sector.

2. Please ACKNOWLEDGE.

28th June 1918.

W R Kermack Captain,
A/Bde.Major,156th Inf.Brigade.

Distribution of Copies.

1. G.O.C.
2. Right Front Zone Bn.   (4th Royal Scots)
3. Left Front Zone Bn.   (7th Royal Scots)
4. Reserve Battalion.   (7th Sco.Rifles)
5. T.M.Batt.
6. Staff Captain.
7. Right Section 52nd Division.
8. Right Section 20th Division.
9. Left Group F.A.
10. Left Group 52nd Division M.G.Bn.
11. I.O.
12. B.M.
13 &14. War Diary.
15. File.
16. Darwin

CONTENTS.

1. Tactical description of the Section.
    A. Boundaries. B. Topography.
2. Organisation of the Area for Defence.
    A. Defensive Framework. B. Distribution of Defence Infantry.
3. Plan for the Conduct of the Defence.
    A. Troops available. B. Action against Frontal Attack.
    C. Action against Flank Attacks.
Appendix 1.   Probable Enemy Action.
Appendix 11. Organisation of Anti-Aircraft Defences.
Appendix 111. Action of Artillery and Trench Mortars.
Map 1. Distribution of Battalions.
Map 2. Communications.
Map 3. Machine Guns and Stokes Mortars.

SECRET.

1. Tactical Description of the Section.

(A) BOUNDARIES.

On the North. Junction of BILLIE BURKE and BETTY Trenches (inclusive) westward along Grid Line to T.2.c.3.0 - T.1.d.7.3 - junction of RED Trench with the LENS - ARRAS Road (inclusive) - along RED Trench and CYRIL Trench (both exclusive) - S.11.c.0.4 - S.15.central - thence to LA TARGETTE - SOUCHEZ Road at S.19.a.5.0.

On the South. The ACHEVILLE Road (exclusive) - NEW BRUNSWICK Road (exclusive) up to its junction with BROWN LINE at T.20.c.5.0. Thence down to junction of BROWN LINE with GRAND TRUNK Trench (inclusive) - through CEMETERY (exclusive) in square T.25.d - BOYS DE GOULOT at T.25.c.0.0 - thence due west along GRID Line.

(B) TOPOGRAPHY.

1. The VIMY RIDGE from the SCARPE Valley to that of the SOUCHEZ River runs approximately N.N.W. and S.S.E. Its length from Point du Jour on the St.LAURENT-BLANGY- GAVRELLE road is 6 1/2 miles, its height throughout more than 100 metres above sea level and more than 40 above the level of the plain to eastward. The highest point of the Ridge, Hill 145 (S.16.c.) falls just within the northern boundary of the Brigade Section, but the crest rises to over 140 metres at two other places also, the Ecole Commune (S.22.d.) and Thelus Mill (A.6.central). These two latter are partially separated on the East by the BOIS DE BONVAL re-entrant (S.30;C.) which comes just within the Southern boundary of the Section. The North-Eastern slope of the Ridge is much steeper than the Western; there is, for example, from BOIS DU CHAMP POURRI (S.23.b.) to the ECOLE COMMUNE a rise of 65 metres in about 900, that is, a slope of approximately 1 in 14. The crest and Eastern slopes of the Ridge are wooded, from FARBUS to about 800 yards S.E. of GIVENCHY. The trees have been considerably thinned by shell fire, but there is in spring and summer much young undergrowth which gives cover. The Ridge commands a very distant view both over the plain between and beyond LENS and ARRAS to the East, and over the more undulating and higher ground to the West.

2. East of the Ridge a gently rolling plain stretches between LENS and ARRAS. Across this plain spurs run from the Ridge in a general N.E. direction. In the area under consideration such spurs are:-
    (a) The HUDSON SPUR, on which stands FARBUS, ACHEVILLE, BOIS-BERNARD. Its general height is over 60 metres. Where it is crossed by the VANCOUVER ROAD between MONT FORET QUARRIES and WILLERVAL it is over 75 metres (OTTAWA TRENCH).
    (b) The VIMY SPUR, over 60 metres in height, on which stands PETIT VIMY and VIMY villages, runs first almost due East for 2500 yards and then (at CANADA and KURTON TRENCHES) turns N.E. pointing to between MERICOURT and AVION. The knoll on which the ruins of VIMY Village stands covers the BOIS DE BONVAL re-entrant.

    (c)/

(c) The CHANDIERE SPUR, which has its highest ground at Hill 165, immediately West of the BOIS DE LACHANDIERE and the LENS/ARRAS RAILWAY EMBANKMENT.
(d) The ARTHUR'S SEAT - BOIS DE L'HIRONDELLE SPUR (in the Divisional Sector on our left) runs, southward of the SOUCHEZ RIVER, from GIVENCHY at the northern end of the VIMY RIDGE to the N.W. corner of AVION, rises to a height of 95 metres, and flanks and to a large extent commands on the North the plain which lies between the VIMY RIDGE on the S.W. and the line AVION-ACHEVILLE on the N.E.

3. Two other important features must be noticed, because they furnish, along with, in a less degree, other similar features in this area, such marked lines as the enemy's customary tactics make it likely he will follow in an advance. They are:-
(a) The main LENS/ARRAS ROAD, which crosses the VIMY RIDGE immediately North of the BONVAL re-entrant, making an angle of about 70° with the main line of ridge.
(b) Approximately parallel with this Road, and about 1000 yards East of it, runs the steep-sided embankment of the LENS-ARRAS RAILWAY. Opposite LA CHANDIERE (at S.13.d.) a branch of the embankment curves westwards towards the ARRAS ROAD at the LA CHANDIERE, and at the same point the main course of the embankment begins to swing S.S.E., to round the south end of the VIMY RIDGE at BAILLEUL.

2. ORGANISATION OF THE AREA FOR DEFENCE.

(A) THE DEFENSIVE FRAMEWORK.

1. The Section is divided into three areas. Their boundaries are as follows:-
   (i) TOAST AREA, the Right Sub-section of the front zone of Defence, is bounded:-
   By VESTA TILLEY (exclusive) to its junction with TEDDIE GERRARD, thence S.W. to T.15.a.o.o., thence S.S.W. to junction of JULIA JAMES with GERTIE (exclusive), to junction of two Railway Embankments (exclusive) in square T.13.d., thence S.E. parallel to, and 200 yards West of the Embankment to junction of Embankment and PEGGIE (inclusive), thence to T.20.a.8.6., thence to Section boundary at T.21.c.7.6.
   (ii) BETTY AREA, the Left Sub-section of the front zone of Defence is bounded:-
   On the South by TOAST AREA, to junction of Embankments (inclusive) in square T.13.d., thence N.W. to Brigade boundary at its junction with ARRAS-LENS ROAD (inclusive).
   (iii) VIMY-CHAUDIERE AREA, the second zone of defence, comprises the remainder of the Section.
   Each Area is held by a battalion of Infantry, organised in depth.

2. In the first zone of defence are comprised:-
   (i) An Observation and S.O.S. line- MONTREAL-QUEBEC- LILY ELSIE- VESTA TILLEY-TOLEDO- BETTY TRENCHES.
   (ii) The FIRST BATTLE LINE (Outpost line-BLUE LINE)- the NEW BRUNSWICK-TEDDIE GERRARD- KEANE-ACTRESS TRENCHES.
   (iii) The SECOND BATTLE LINE (BLACK LINE)- the CANADA-GERTIE-JAMES-HAYTER-GLADYS-DARTMOUTH TRENCHES.
   In the second zone of defence is:-
   (iv) The THIRD BATTLE LINE (BROWN LINE) - VIMY locality and BROWN LINE TRENCHES, with the CHAUDIERE locality in advance of BROWN LINE.

(B) DISTRIBUTION AND ALLOCATION TO DUTIES OF DEFENCE INFANTRY.

1. The two battalions holding the front zone are distributed as follows:-
   (i) Each battalion has its four companies side by side distributed in depth.
   (ii) Each company has two platoons in the BLACK LINE (Second Battle Line), two platoons each less one half platoon in the First Battle Line (Outpost Line) and one half platoon in the Line of Observation, except in the case of the two centre companies of the left battalion, which have no men in the Line of Observation, but two full platoons in the First Battle Line.
   (iii) The Sections in the Line of Observation are in this Line by day and by night, each Section posting a double sentry with S.O.S. Signal Rocket. All withdraw to the First Battle Line after the S.O.S. is sent up and responded to by barrage fire in the event of attack.
   In the event of a raid or surprise attack the "Red Barrage" comes down for three minutes in front of the Observation Line and then lifts back to the front of the First Battle Line (Outpost Line).

(iv)/

(iv) Every effort will be made to persuade the enemy that the Observation Line is a Battle Line. To this end at least one patrol of section strength will be sent daily in early forenoon and late afternoon to TOT Trench, to repair any damage done to the trench and to fire their five rounds S.A.A. from its vicinity in order to give the impression to the enemy that this trench is still occupied. As many sections of the garrison of the First Battle Line as possible will fire their daily five rounds from the line of observation.

2. The battalion holding the second zone of defence is distributed differently from those in the front zone being on a wider front. Two companies are in VIMY Locality and BROWN LINE as far as its junction with the ARRAS-LENS ROAD (inclusive). Each Company has three platoons in line, and one platoon in support. One company less one platoon is in LA CHAUDIERE Locality (GLACE Trench) with one of its platoons in support, and one company is in BROWN LINE, similarly disposed. The fourth platoon of the CHAUDIERE company is in BROWN LINE immediately West of the ARRAS Road.
No troops in the second zone of defence are available to reinforce the second or first Battle Lines, or to counter-attack to restore the situation in the front zone of defence.

3. In order to secure maintenance of touch with the Right Brigade of the 20th Division on the Left of the Section front, combined posts, of one section from each Division, under a Sergeant, are established at the following points:-
(a) T.2.d.5.4. Trench junction ACTRESS TRENCH.
(b) T.2.c.2.4. Trench junction in PARTRIDGE TRENCH.
(c) S.12.b.9.4. crossing of RED TRENCH and LENS-ARRAS ROAD.
B.G.C. Left Brigade, 52nd Division, is responsible for post (a) and provides a Sergeant who is in charge.
Posts (b) and (c) are under B.G.C. Right Brigade, 20th Division, and commanded by a Sergeant of that Division.
All three Sections are furnished by Left front zone battalion.

4. Battalion Headquarters of the two front line battalions are behind the Railway Embankment, at T.26.a.3.8. and T.13.b.5.o.
Headquarters of the second zone battalion are at S.24.a.2.o.
Brigade headquarters are at S.27.central.

T.25.b.80.95

5.

3. PLAN FOR THE CONDUCT OF THE DEFENCE.

(A) Troops available.

The troops available for the defence of the Section are:-
- 1 Infantry Brigade Headquarters, 3 battalions and
- 1 Light Trench Mortar Battery.
- 2 Sections Field Company R.E.

In addition, but not under the immediate orders of the Brigade Commander, there are-
- 4 6" Newton Mortars.
- 24 Machine Guns under Divl. M.G. Officer (who lives at Bde. H.Q).
- 1 Section of these held in Reserve at S.23.b.7.5.
- 1 Composite Brigade R.F.A. of 4 18 prs. batteries and 2 4.5" How. batteries (H.Q. Left Group F.A. are situated at Inf.Bde.H.Q.)
- + 3 Heavy Batteries (60 prs.)
- + 4 Siege Batteries.

Anti-Tank defence is provided by 3 15pr. guns situated at:-
- T.19.b.77.75.
- T.19.c.75.95.
- T.26.a.58.15.

In addition all the Machine Guns in the Section are provided with at least one belt of armour-piercing bullets.

+ These are not available exclusively for defence of Left Brigade Section front, but for whole Divisional Sector.

There is a F.A. Liaison Officer with Bn.H.Q. of each of the two front line battalions, and a Liaison Officer for the Heavy and Siege Batteries is attached to Bde.H.Q.

The frontage of the Brigade Section measured along The First Battle Line is approximately 2800 yards long. Taking each battalion's strength at 600 rifles, this gives one rifle for every 1½ yds. of front. There are available 1 Vickers or Lewis Gun for every 27 yds. of front, and one field gun or howitzer for every 88 yds.

(B) ACTION AGAINST FRONTAL ATTACK.

The front of the Section is too great to allow of the retention of an infantry reserve by the Brigade Commander or by the C.Os. of ~~the two~~ battalions. ~~in the first zone of defence.~~ It is, in any case, more important, that companies should have platoons available for immediate counter-attack. ~~In the second zone of defence each battalion Commander has one company in local reserve for counter-attack or reinforcement; and~~ In the second zone each company Commander in the line has one platoon in support.

The Divisional reserve (one Brigade of infantry and one M.G. Coy.) in the event of a break through by the enemy, is available for use by the G.O.C. Division, either for deliberate counter-attack or to occupy the GREEN LINE (THELUS-RIDGE LINE) - ECURIE or PADDOCK SWITCHES (vide:- Action of Reserve Brigade Divisional Defence Scheme).

The principle of defence of the Brigade Section is that for the troops allotted to the defence of the three Battle Lines (BLUE, BLACK, & BROWN)," there is only one degree of/

"of resistance, and that is to the last round and to the last man". Troops allotted to rear localities must not reinforce forward to a front locality; otherwise rear lines will be left without their garrisons, and a further penetration by the enemy may take place. Each of the Second and Third Battle Lines are therefore in course of organisation into defended localities capable of all-round defence. These are at present:-

(a) CANADA and KURTON Trenches from their junction with TOAST on the right to junction with PEGGY on the left.
(b) CHAUDIERE (1 Company) less 1 platoon)
(c) VIMY Locality- Garrison ~~1 battalion~~ 2 companies.

If such localities are held, penetration between them by bodies of the enemy will not be able to make progress.

(C) ACTION AGAINST FLANK ATTACKS.

(i) To arrest a break-through by the enemy on the north or an advance between the HIRONDELLE and CHAUDIERE Spurs, or down the line of the LENS Railway Embankment, the line PICTOU- CENTRE- GLACE and BLIGHTY Trenches should be held.

(ii) In the event of penetration south of our area, the defended localities of CANADA- KURTON; VIMY, and part of GRAND TRUNK Trench in the second zone, and TOAST Trench in the front zone will form a defensive flank.

2. PLAN FOR THE CONDUCT OF THE DEFENCE (continued)

D. ACTION AGAINST RAIDS.

(1) To deal with a small raid of 50 men or less, Company Commanders of the two front zone battalions will each detail one of their platoons in BLACK LINE which will be available for them as a counter-attack platoon to restore the situation.

(2) To deal with a larger raid or minor attack, the company of the reserve battalion which holds the northern flank of VIMY locality and part of BROWN LINE (to the ARRAS Road inclusive), together with the support platoon of the second company in VIMY locality, will be available for counter-attack to restore the situation in BLACK LINE and the outpost zone forward of BLACK LINE. It will only be so used by the Reserve battalion commander on an order from the G.O.C. Brigade. When this company is withdrawn from VIMY locality its place will be taken by the support platoon of the company in CHAUDIERE locality.

APPENDIX 1.

PROBABLE ENEMY ACTION.

1. The dominating strategical and tactical feature is the VIMY RIDGE. Its position relative to ARRAS means that its loss by us would entail the loss of ARRAS, and afford the enemy direct observation to westward as far as NOTRE DAME DE LORETTE and MONT ST.ELOY, and much further yet S.W. of MONT ST.ELOY. The loss of the ARRAS SALIENT would make much more difficult the retention of GIVENCHY (lez-la Bassée) and BETHUNE.

2. An attack may take any of the following forms:-
   (a) A small raid by a company or less.
   (b) A large raid by approximately a battalion or more.
   (c) A general attack, probably upon the normal lines of this year's (1918) tactics, i.e. an intense but short (3/4 hours) bombardment of the front 1500 yards in depth with gas shell and trench mortars, and of the trench lines in rear by heavy artillery, wire being cut partly by Trench Mortars and partly by Tanks advancing in co-operation with the infantry.
   (d) A surprise general attack, without any preliminary bombardment, Tanks being used against the wire and infantry co-operating with them, on the CAMBRAI model (September 1917).
   (a) and (b) can probably be efficiently dealt with by the S.O.S. barrage and the reserves in the hands of Company Commanders.
   (d) could only be of limited application owing to the unsuitability of the ground for Tanks, the Railway Embankment forming a serious obstacle.
   (c) may be considered as coming (1) frontally, (2) from the north, (3) from the south.

3. Our Observation Line is 5000 yards as the crow flies in advance of the THELUS-RIDGE line (GREEN line) which is a trench line sited=slightly on the reverse slope of the Ridge. The Third Battle Line (BROWN line) is approximately 2500 yards in advance of GREEN line. Further, on this Section front "No Man's Land" is 1000-1500 yards across..
   An advance by the enemy therefore which stopped short of the actual possession of VIMY RIDGE would not be of great tactical advantage to him, as it would give us better observation, and bring him more closely under the fire of our guns. In such a position it would also be difficult for him to bring forward artillery and trench mortars to support a further advance against the RIDGE itself. The steep eastern slope of the RIDGE and the steep Railway Embankment across our front considerably restricts the possibilities of an advance made in co-operation with Tanks. This advantage is however less marked by the case further to our right. The loss of the minor spurs which run northeastward from the RIDGE would give the enemy valuable observation of its eastern slopes at close range, but would only slightly affect our artillery positions, and would not deprive us of our much superior advantages in observation.

4. On our northern flank, on the front of the Brigade on our left, a frontal attack on a grand scale would meet considerable physical difficulties in debouching from the ruins of LENS and AVION. As against this, the district is suitable for a concealed concentration of troops.
   The flooded condition of the SOUCHEZ River South west of LENS would divide an attack in its initial stages. "No Man's Land" is about 800 yards across.

5. On our southern flank conditions are rather less favourable to us. The German line is nearer here to the VIMY RIDGE, and this too where the slope of the RIDGE is more gradual than on our own Section front. It is therefore likely that any enemy attempt to get a direct footing on the RIDGE would be made south of WILLERVAL and west of BAILLEUL rather than against our immediate front. Such an attempt successfully carried out would/

Would
- (i) give the enemy observation over much of the ground we hold W. of the VIMY RIDGE.
- (ii) compell the withdrawal from their present positions of a large number of our guns.
- (iii) seriously threaten our remaining positions east of and on the RIDGE itself.

While it is thus thought that the most favourable line of attack for the enemy is probably against the S.E. end of the VIMY RIDGE, it must be kept in mind that such an attack, or a similar one on the north, might be extended to include our own Section front. In such circumstances the loss of HIRONDELLE Spur (in the 20th Division Sector) or of VIMY Spur would make it very difficult to hold the ground between them. Forward of the VIMY RIDGE itself, therefore, these two localities seem to be the most vital for our defence.

APPENDIX II.

ORGANISATION OF ANTI-AIRCRAFT DEFENCE.

Lewis Guns for defence primarily against low-flying enemy aircraft are organised in three lines, each of four guns, approximately at the three Battle Lines:-

LINE.	CO-ORDINATE.	UNIT.
OUTPOST	T.16.c.85.25	Right Bn.
"	T.15.b.60.55	"
"	T.15.a.8.8.	~~Left A Bn.~~ Left B Bn.
"	T.8.a.8.5.	
BLACK	T.20.b.3.5. (c.7.9.)	Right Bn.
"	T.13.b.4.2.	Left Bn.
"	T.13.b.8.7.	"
"	T.7.b.1.1.	"
BROWN	T.~~26.a.5.9.~~ 20.c.20.15.	~~Right~~ Reserve Bn.
"	S.24.b.7.0.	"
"	S.24.c.2.o.	"
"	S.17.b.2.4.	~~Left~~ Reserve Bn.

APPENDIX III.
ACTION OF ARTILLERY AND TRENCH MORTARS.

A. FIELD ARTILLERY.

1. The following is the "normal" procedure for "S.O.S." Barrage.
   On the S.O.S. signal or message, the Barrage comes down in front of the Observation line for 15 minutes at following rates:-

   5 minutes intense.
   5 minutes rapid.
   5 minutes normal.

   After this fire will depend on the situation.

2. Lanes are left in the Artillery Barrage, which is by this means thickened to one gun to 45 yards and is 200 yds. in depth. It is thus a serious obstacle and it is hoped that the enemy will be deflected into the lanes, which are covered by machine guns and trench mortars.

3. In the event of a cloud gas attack, all 18 pr. batteries fire 3 rds. gun fire on S.O.S. lines and continue with short bursts of fire. 4.5" Howitzers place "blocks" on enemy's communication trenches.

4. During an intense hostile bombardment, which is evidently the prelude to an attack, counter preparation will be undertaken. It will consist mainly of frequent rolling barrages by 18 prs. fired at irregular intervals backwards and forwards over the zones allotted to them, while 4.5" Hows. fire on selected targets. The object is to prevent the enemy sending forward patrols and M.G. parties to establish themselves in NO MAN'S LAND.

B. HEAVY AND SIEGE ARTILLERY.

1. The fire of 12 60-pr. guns and 22 Siege howitzers can be directed on to either of the two section fronts. In the event of a General S.O.S. 6 60-prs. and 10 Siege Howitzers would be available for the left section front.

2. Available guns are left laid on either Counter Battery, General, or Brigade S.O.S. lines as circumstances indicate; the Counter Battery S.O.S. being designed to deal with such hostile bombardment as may precede an infantry attack.

3. The rate of fire is:-
   5 minutes INTENSE.
   5 minutes RAPID (for 8" and 9.2" Howitzers-this amounts to 1 rd. per gun per minute.)
   5 minutes NORMAL (half rate of RAPID).

   In the case of 8" and 9.2" howitzers a hostile gas neutralization would probably reduce this rate by at least one third.

C. MEDIUM TRENCH MORTARS.

Six 6" Newton Mortars are available for the defence of the Section front. They are distributed as follows:-

Bty.	GUNS.	LOCATION.	S.O.S.point.	REMARKS.
Y/52	Y 1	T.22.a.71.60	T.17.a.85.15)	Forward Mortars
	Y 2	T.22.a.73.60	T.17.a.40.60)	silent for S.O.S.
	(2 guns)	T.19.d.central	to cover BLACK & BROWN LINES	
				New positions.
	Y 7	T.13.b.50.35		
	Y 8	T.13.b.60.70		
	Y 10	T.17.c.60.10		Forward offensive position when required. Gun taken from Y 1.

"S.O.S." Fire is 3 rds. per gun per min. for first 5 minutes on S.O.S. points. Then 1 rd. per gun per min. till further orders.

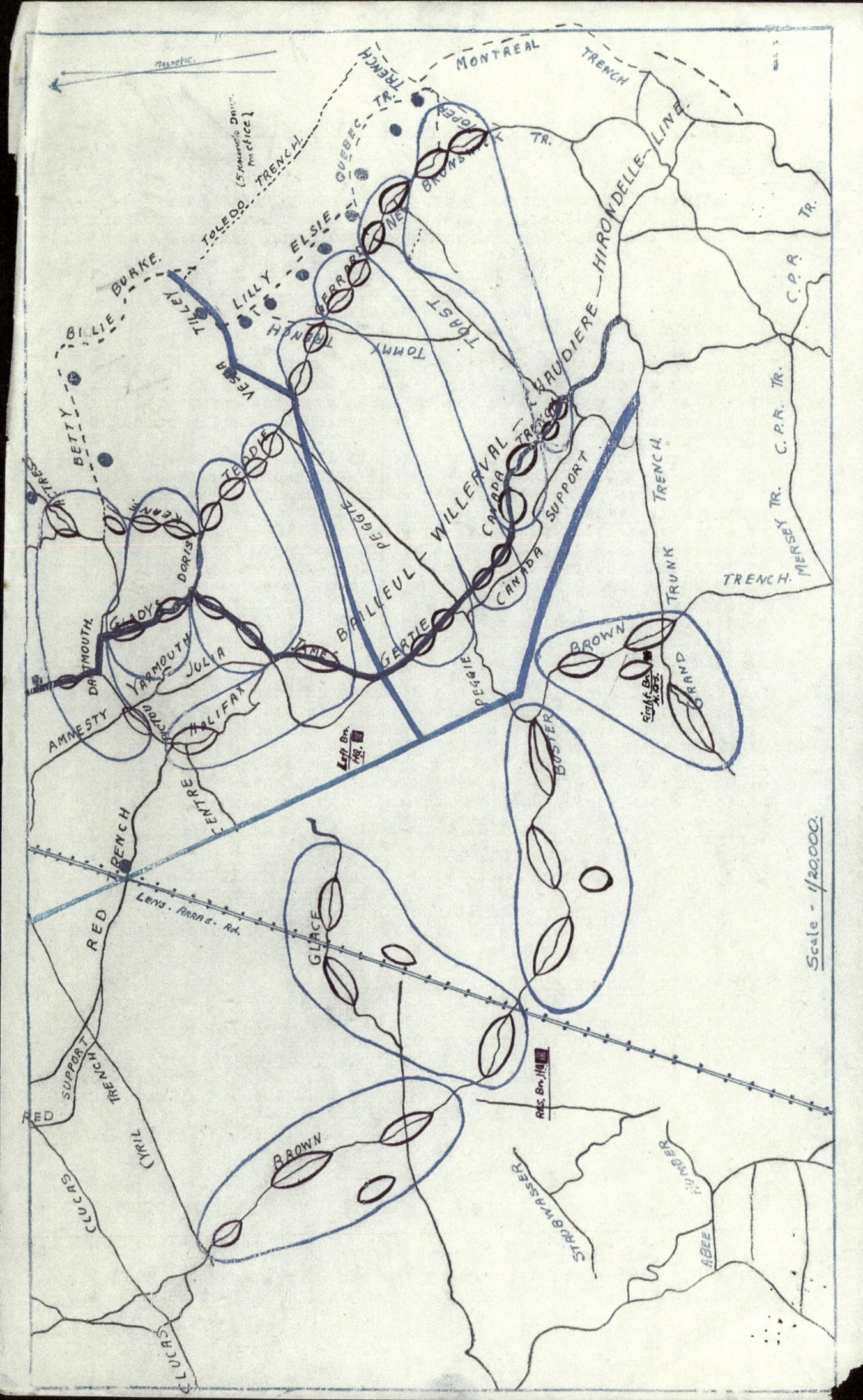

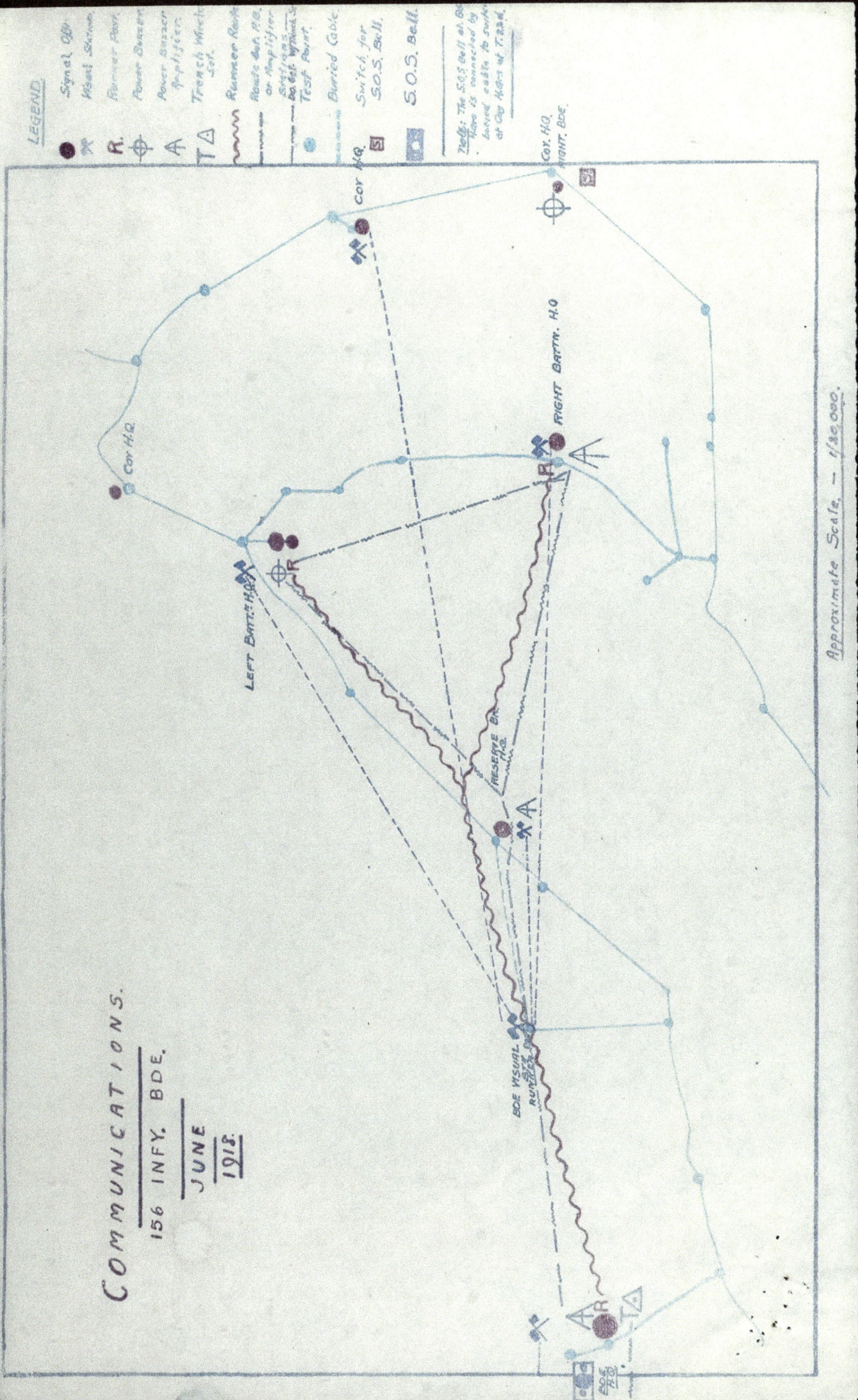

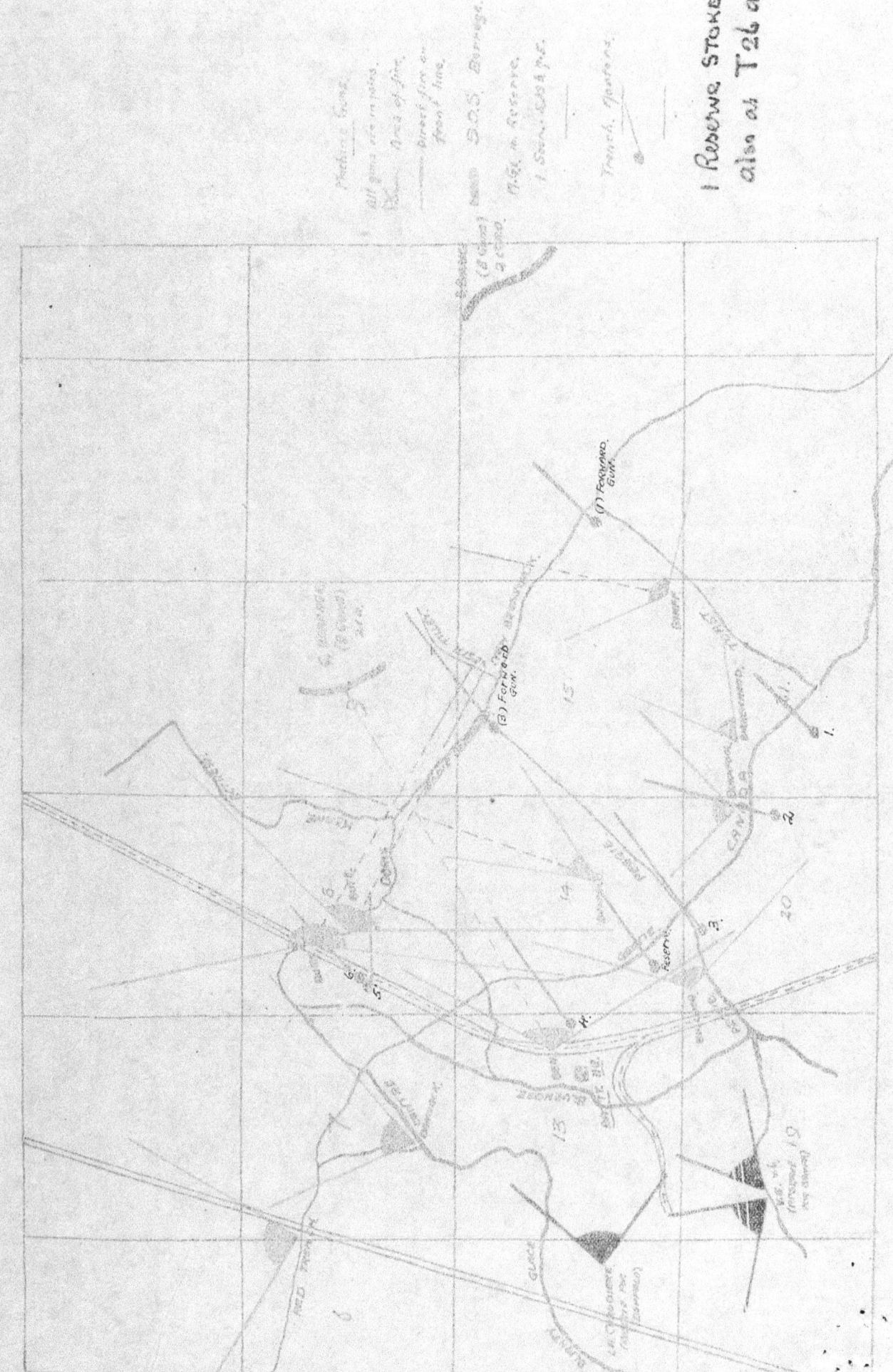

SECRET. (For the information of Unit Commanders only)   BM.1/70/1

O.C.
4th. Royal Scots   7th. Sco. Rifles
7th. Royal Scots   156th. T.M. Batt.

The following instructions for action are additional to those given in Left Section Defence Scheme of this date. They will be handed over with that Scheme personnally to the C.O. of the unit which relieves you.

28th. June 1918.   W R Kermack Captain,
                                      A/Brigade Major, 156th. Inf. Bde.

Copies to:- G.O.C.
             52nd' Division
             Right Section, 52nd. Division
             Right Section 20th. Division
             Left Group R.A.
             Left Group 52nd. Division M.G. Bn.
             War Diary.

1. On receiving certain warning of a hostile attack in force, the order "Prepare for Action" is to be issued by G.O.C. 52nd. Division.

2. On receipt of this order, the following action will be taken by platoons in and forward of the First Battle Line (BLUE LINE):-
   (a) One platoon per Company will be withdrawn to a position in support to BLACK LINE, where it will be available either for reinforcement or counter-attack.
   (b) In three Companies of each front line battalion one platoon per company will be withdrawn to strengthen the garrison of BLACK LINE.
   (c) In the remaining Company one platoon will remain in BLUE LINE. It will furnish 2 observation Posts which will push forward about 150 yards into "NO MAN'S LAND", in front of our own wire. Here they will be safe from our own and the enemy's barrage.
       Their duty is to send the "S.O.S" alarm by all means available, and to engage the enemy scouts. They will not withdraw.
       The "S.O.S" signal will be repeated from BLUE LINE and BLACK LINE.
       This platoon in observation will be relieved every 6 hours.
   (d) In the Right Battalion Sub-section the Company supplying this platoon will be the left centre Company. When in the observation line as described above this platoon will find personnel to man the "S.O.S" electric alarm gong in the Test dug-out TN at T.32.d.9.4 which communicates with Bde H.Q. Left Section.

3. On an "S.O.S" message <u>by telephone</u> from BLACK LINE an "S.O.S" barrage will be brought down in front of BLACK LINE instead of the normal barrage.

TO all recipients of
155th Inf.Bde. LEFT SECTION DEFENCE SCHEME.

BM 1/71/2

Please note that the following alterations should be made in above Scheme, if not already made:-

1. "Defensive framework" para.4. For "T.35.a.3.8." read "T.35.b.5½.9½"
2. "Conduct of the Defence" para. (A). For "4 Battalions" read "3 Battalions".
   Read "One rifle for every one and a half yards of front" and "One Vickers or Lewis Gun for every 21 yards".
3. (B) "Action against Frontal Attack" - Delete lines six and seven, and in line eight delete "-ment and".
4. Next page, line 10, - Garrison of CHAUDIERE is "One company less one platoon".
   Line 11, Garrison of VIMY Locality is "two companies".
5. Appendix II. Gun at T.15.a.5.5. is supplied by the Right Battalion. (Line 5).
   Line 8, Read "T.20.a.5.9."
   Line 12. Read "T.20.c.20.15".
   All four guns in BROWN LINE are supplied by the reserve Battalion.

W R Kermack   Captain,
A/Bde.Major,155th Inf. Brigade.

SECRET.   Copy No. 16

156th. INFANTRY BRIGADE ORDER No. 41.

Ref. Map HASEBROUK - 1/20,000   27th. June 1918.

1.   The 156th. Inf. Bde. is to be relieved by the 157th. Inf. Bde. in the Left Section on June 29th. and 30th., and will take over on relief the billets and dispositions of the 157th. Inf. Bde.

2.   Reliefs take place as follows:-
        June 29th. - 4th. Royal Scots relieved by 7th. H.L.I.
                     7th. Royal Scots   do.   6th. H.L.I.
                     7th. Sco. Rifles   do.   5th. H.L.I.
        June 30th. - 156th. T.M. Batt.   do.   157th. T.M. Batt.

3.   Advanced parties of units of the 157th. Inf. Bde. are going into the line on 29th. June. They will be met by guides as follows:-
(a) Advanced parties of 7th. H.L.I. and 5th. H.L.I. at Barrier, LA FOLIE FARM Road (S.28.d.8.8) at 3 p.m. by one officer per battalion and one other rank per company, 1/7th. Sco. Rifles. One officer and 4 other ranks (1 per Coy) 1/4th. Royal Scots will meet this party at foot of HUMBER Trench at 3.30 p.m. and from there act as guides to advanced party of 7th. H.L.I.
(b) Advanced party of 6th. H.L.I. will be met at S.29.a.3.8 (top of CAMPBELL ROAD) at 3 p.m. by one Officer and 4 other ranks (1 per Coy) of 7th. Royal Scots.

4.   On 29th. June one officer and one other rank per battalion H.Q., one officer per company and one other rank per platoon from each battalion will meet relieving units at debussing points as follows:-
    4th. Royal Scots at Barrier - S.28.d.8.8..............9.15 a.m.
    7th. Royal Scots at CAMPBELL ROAD - S.29.a.3.8........9.15 a.m.
    7th. Sco. Rifles at Barrier, Bn. H.Q. & 2 Coys) 12.15 p.m.
                     at CAMPBELL Road,   2 Coys)
These guides will be acquainted with routes to be followed.

5.   From debussing points routes to be followed are:-
        (a) For Right Sub-section Battalions -
            HUMBER-RED TRAIL-BROWN LINE- PEGGIE and TOAST Trenches.
        (b) For Left Sub-section Battalions -
            BLIGHTY-GLACE-HAYTER or CENTRE Trenches.

6.   Details of relief will be arranged between C.Os.

7.   Motor lorries bringing relieving units will be available to take troops to MONT ST. ELOI and will continue to run till all troops are evacuated.

8.   After relief troops will move to debussing points, 200 yards distance to be kept between platoons. If necessary platoons will move by sections on the enemy side of the RIDGE. Routes same as used by relieving units.

9.   1/7th. Sco. Rifles and 1/7th. Royal Scots will each detail one embussing officer for the Bde. at Barrier and CAMPBELL Road respectively. Names of Officers detailed will reach this Office by 6 p.m. 28th. inst.
        These Officers will make any necessary alterations in embussing arrangements in the event of enemy shelling and will report action taken by runner to Bde. H.Q.

10.   Units will supply their own debussing officers at MONT ST. ELOI.

11./

2.

11. Commands of areas will pass on completion of battalion reliefs.

12. Completion of relief will be reported by code word "MOULTING" and completion of arrival in camp by code word "PARROT".

13. Following will be distribution of units while in Divisional reserve:-

  4th Royal Scots - HILL'S CAMP - (6th H.L.I.)
  7th Royal Scots - FRASER & LANCASTER CAMPS (6th H.L.I.)
  7th Sco.Rifles - OTTAWA CAMP (7th H.L.I.)
  156th T.M.Batt. - KANSOM CAMP.

14. Between passing of commands of Section from G.O.C./Inf. Bde. to G.O.C. 157th Inf.Bde. and relief of 156th T.M.Batt. by 157th T.M.Batt., the former will be under orders of O.C. 157th Inf.Bde.

15. Details of units at Divisional Reception Camp will rejoin units in respective billets on 29th June by 12 noon.

16. Brigade H.Q. will close at present position, X.27.central, and open at WHITE HOUSE, MONT ST.ELOI, on 29th June on completion of Infantry reliefs when command of the Section will pass.
  Messages for Brigade H.Q. may be sent to WHITE HOUSE from 5 p.m. onwards.

17. ACKNOWLEDGE.

Issued by Runner at _____   W.R.Kermack Captain,
           A/Bde.Major,156th Inf.Brigade.

  COPY No. 1 to G.O.C.
     2   4th Royal Scots.
     3   7th Royal Scots.
     4   7th Sco.Rifles.
     5   156th T.M.Batt.
     6   Staff Captain.
     7   I.O. & Gas Officer.
     8   Bde.Sigs.Officer.
     9   Left Group Comdr. 52nd M.G. Bn.
     10   R.T.O.
     11   52nd Division.
     12   155th Inf.Bde.
     13   157th Inf.Bde.
     14   60th Inf.Bde.
     15   Bde.R.O.
     16 & 17 War Diary.
     18   File.

War Diary Appendix

Effective Strength — ~~two~~ June 1918.

Unit	Week ending 8th		Week ending 15th		Week ending 22nd		Week ending 29th	
	O.	OR.	O.	OR.	O.	OR.	O.	OR.
4 Royal Scots	42	839	42	843	41	836	46	858
7 Royal Scots	40	912	40	891	40	865	44	868
7 Sco. Rifles	47	867	47	850	46	853	46	917
8 Sco. Rifles	40	854	40	852	40	828	—	—
	169	3472	169	3436	167	3382	136	2643

War Diary Appendix

Casualties – June 1918

Unit	Killed O.	Killed O.R.	Wounded O.	Wounded O.R.	Killed Gas O.	Killed Gas O.R.	Wounded Gas O.	Wounded Gas O.R.	Missing O.	Missing O.R.
Bde. H.Q.	-	-	-	-	-	-	-	-	-	-
4 Royal Scots	-	1	-	11	-	-	-	1	-	-
7 Royal Scots	-	1	-	7	-	-	-	-	-	-
7 Sco. Rifles	-	3	1	5	-	-	-	-	-	-
8 Sco. Rifles	-	-	-	3	-	-	-	-	-	-
156 T.M. Batt.	-	-	-	1	-	-	-	-	-	-
	-	5	1	27	-	-	-	1	-	-

Original

Vol 4

War Diary

of

156th Infantry Brigade

1st to 31st July 1918.

Volume XXXVIII

Confidential

WAR DIARY or INTELLIGENCE SUMMARY

Army Form C. 2118.

155th Infantry Brigade

July 1918.

Volume XXXVII

Ref Map. **MARŒUIL 20000**

Hour, Date, Place	Summary of Events and Information	Remarks and references to Appendices
Mont St. ELOI 1st / 10.00 am.	Lieut Col. G.P. Romans D.S.O. 7/8 The Cameronians resumed command of the Brigade, owing to the absence of Brig. Gen. A.H. Leggett, C.M.G., D.S.O. on leave to U.K. The Brigade was inspected by H.R.H. The Duke of Connaught, on the open ground west of MONT ST. ELOI. After inspection, the March Past was carried out by 4/5th The Royal Scots. The General Officers and Divisional Commanders were present (Lt. Gen. Sir H.S. Horne, K.C.B, K.C.M.G., Lt. Gen. Sir A. Hunter Weston K.C.B, D.S.O. and Maj. Gen. J. Hill, C.B, D.S.O. G.O.C.). 6/7 Scottish Rifles, 7th Scottish Rifles, supplied to H.Q. guard & H.Q. piece Capt. G.S. Smith, G.T.O., on leave to U.K. The Brigade Commander and A/Brigade Major carried out recce.	Appendix I.
2nd	VIMY area in accordance with Recent Brigade Recce Scheme. Divisional Commander's conference. Brigade Commander visit ambulances training.	
3rd		
4th	The Brigade Commander visited 155th Brigade H.Q. in the Right Subsection of the Divisional Sector.	

WAR DIARY or INTELLIGENCE SUMMARY

155 INFANTRY BRIGADE

Army Form C. 2118.

JULY 1918   Vol. XXXVII

REFM A P MAREUIL 1:20,000.

Hour, Date, Place	Summary of Events and Information	Remarks and references to Appendices
MONT ST ELOY 5th 6th	Brigade Order No. 42 issued. (Runlop 155th Inf. Bde.) The Corps Commander, General Sir A. Hunter-Weston, K.C.B., D.S.O., visited the Brigade and inspected the training. Capt. H. Sayer, M.C. rejoined the Brigade as Adjutant. 2nd Lt. G.N. Haugh, 7th Scottish Rifles, Brigade I.O., rejoined from U.K.	Appendix II (Appendix I 155th Inf Bde) Appendix III 155th Inf Bde
7th	Administrator General H.Q. 6 issued. Lieut. Col. G.A. Mitchell, D.S.O., 1/5th Bn The Royal Scots, assumed command of the Brigade. The Brigade Major visited the Right Section of Divisional Sector. (155th Inf Bde)	155th Inf Bde
8th	The Brigade relieved the 153rd Bde in the Right Section. Battalions moved up from MONT ST ELOY by bus. Dispositions: two battalions in the line distributed in depth, from left to right, 7/5 Royal Scots, 1/4 Royal Scots, and 1/5 Scottish Rifles.	155th Inf Bde
RIGHT SECTION (H.S.T.6.c.6.6.) 9th	The Brigadier Commander and Brigade Major visited the Right Sub-Sector. Considerable aerial and artillery activity. Enemy aircraft dropping 12 down in Brigade Sector. Sound mirror.	155th Inf Bde

WAR DIARY
or
INTELLIGENCE SUMMARY

Army Form C. 2118

15th Infantry Brigade, Part II.

REF. MAP. MAROEUIL 1/20,000. Vol XXVIII. JULY 1918.

Place	Date July	Hour	Summary of Events and Information	Remarks and references to Appendices
RIGHT SECTION (Hd 7.6.c.6.5)	10th		The Brigade Commander visited the Centre Sub-Sector. Little artillery or aerial activity during the day, visibility being poor owing to rain.	QRSgt
"	11th		The Brigade Commander visited the Left Sub-Sector. Wet night with bright intervals. Quiet day.	QRSgt
"	12th		Our artillery active during the afternoon. Maj Gen J Hill, CB, DSO visited Brigade HQ. "Gleras Beam" attack carried out by the Division on the Left Section front.	QRSgt Appendix IV
"	14th		Order No 43 issued re-eligibility by 4th Canadian Divn to Leave. A.E. BIRD, A/IO, proceeded on leave to U.K. Administrative Order No 7 issued.	July 14 Appendix V
"	15th		Brig. General A H LEGGETT, CMG, DSO returned from leave to U.K. and resumed command of the Brigade. Capt G. STANLEY SMITH A/IO returned from leave to U.K. and took over duties of A/Bde Major. Returns as per Order No 43 carried out.	July 15
"	16th		Lt-Colonel A MACLAINE MITCHELL, A/Bde Commander reported 1/4th Royal Scots. G.O.C. visited VIMY AREA and settled the dispositions of the 4th S.R. with the OC of the unit	July 16

Army Form C. 2118.

WAR DIARY
INTELLIGENCE SUMMARY

157th Infantry Brigade   July 1918   Vol XXVII

R/Map LENS 1/100,000, Page 4

Place	Date 1918 July	Hour	Summary of Events and Information	Remarks and references to Appendices
RIGHT SECTION	17th		G.O.C. and B.M. visited the line	full lt / full lt
	18th		G.O.C. and B.M. visited the line	full lt
	19th		G.O.C. and B.M. visited the line	full lt
	20th		Order No 44 issued	Appendix VI
	21st		Relief for Order No 44 carried out. Order No 45 issued. During the tour in the line the enemy opposite the Brigade front have been inactive. Patrols have been out every night but on only one occasion was an enemy patrol met with and shots were exchanged. Enemy artillery activity has been slight. Our artillery has carried out many destructive shoots and harassed the enemy generally. Brigade inspected by Lieut General A. Hunter Weston, Comdg VIII Corps.	Appendix VII / full lt / full lt
ST ELOY	22nd		Move carried out as per Order No 45.	full lt
BARLIN	23rd		B.O.C., B.M. and S.C. reconnoitred fork for Embussing and visited the training station. B.M. No 24/8 issued. — Bde to be ready to move at 4 hrs notice.	full lt / Appendix VIII / full lt
	24th		G.O.C. and B.M. visited thennits at BOIS D'OHLAIN.	full lt
	25th		G.O.C. and B.M. visited thennits at training.	full lt
	26th		G.O.C. and B.M. visited thennits at training. Instruction in Embussing issued. One Company per Bn to carry out a Route March each day.	full lt

Army Form C. 2118.

WAR DIARY
or
INTELLIGENCE SUMMARY.

152nd Infantry Brigade

Ref Map LENS 1/10000 July 1918 Map XXXVII

Place	Date	Hour	Summary of Events and Information	Remarks and references to Appendices
BARLIN	26th		Two Lewis Gun Instructors from the Brigade reported for duty to the 1/12th Field Coy. R.E. B.G.C. accompanied by the Brigade Major inspected the transport of the Brigade in the transport lines. 1/6 B.G.C. and B.M. visited the units.	Appx.
	27th		Weather unsettled. Showers with lightning and very heavy rain. B.G.C. and B.M. visited Bounds at training. B.M. 301 issued (Loaded of 1st L.N. Transport Limbers)	Appendix IX
	28th		G.306/6/for Army. During week ending Augt 3rd every unit during hours of training will wear their S.B.R.s for 10 minutes at every clock hour. All ranks throughout the Bde not actually training will wear their S.B.R.s for 10 to 10.15 a.m. daily.	Appx It
	29th		Today has been counted a Sunday owing to Sunday being a training day on account of men having been allotted on Sunday. Bde Order No 6 issued.	Appx X
	30th		Move carried out as per Order No 6 with the exception that the Bde was billeted at E COIVRES instead of at MAROEUIL. Bde Order No 4 issued - Relby of 11th Canadian Brigade B.G.C. B.M., S.C., I.O., Sign Off and C.O.s and Adjts. visited	Appendix XI

WAR DIARY

INTELLIGENCE SUMMARY

156th Infantry Brigade

Army Form C. 2118.

July 1918 Vol XXVIII

Ref Map LENS 1/100,000 Page 6

Place	Date	Hour	Summary of Events and Information	Remarks and references to Appendices
ECOIVRES	July 1		11th Canadian Infantry Brigade and arranged details of the relief.	
CHATEAU MEURICE	3rd		11th Canadian Infantry Brigade relieved in GAVRELLE SECTION. We trained without incident to get buses for 4th Royal Scots. Brigade Order No 48 issued.	Appendix XII.
			During the period the Brigade was in G.H.Q. reserve. Its units were camped under canvas in BOIS D'OHLAIN. As the weather was wet and there were no floor boards, the men had a rather uncomfortable time of it.	Appendix XIII / Appendix XIV / Appendix XV
			— Casualties —	
			— Strength —	
		✗ Insert	4th Royal Scots carried out the march in good order. Casualties to our side during relief 5 O.R. wounded (Enemy shell fire)	

A. Taylor, Capt.
Brigade Major 156th Infantry Brigade.

War Diary July

BM 83

Appendix I

```
G.O.C.              4th Royal Scots.
Lt.Col.ROMANES,D.S.O.  7th Royal Scots.
B.T.O.              7th Sco.Rifles.
B.M.                156th T.M.Batt.
Staff Captain.
```

In view of an inspection by the DUKE OF CONNAUGHT on Monday next, it is essential that we should smarten up as much as possible during tomorrow.

It is not yet known what form the inspection will take, except that the March Past at its close will be in fours only.

Battalion Commanders will tomorrow see that:-
(1) Mens hair is cut.
(2) Special attention given to cleanliness of finger nails. (this is a point always looked to by the Duke.)
(3) Replacement of unserviceable boots and clothing with new or serviceable clothing and boots.
(4) Cleaning up of equipment.
(5) Practice the March Past in fours.
(6) Practice all Officers in saluting.
(7) Practice in handling of arms.
(8) Tam O' Shanters will be worn.

2. The massed Pipers of the Brigade will play during the Inspection, and play each unit past to its own Regimental March.

3. During the March Past all Officers will salute with the right hand on arriving at the saluting point, at the same time turning head and eyes to the right.

Each platoon on reaching the saluting point will be given the command "Eyes Right" by its own Commander. The Company Commander will **not** give the order "Eyes Right" to his company.

All ranks will be warned that the head and eyes must be turned smartly to the right or left as the case may be on receiving such an order from their respective platoon Commanders, and that the free arm must swing very freely throughout the March Past.

There is an idea in some units that on reaching the saluting point, the free arm is to remain rigid by the side. This is wrong and must not be.

4. There is not much time for preparation, but the fullest use must be made of what time there is.

29th June 1918.

W R Kermack
Captain,
A/Bde.Major, 156th Inf.Brigade.

SECRET.   BM 96

1.   H.R.H. THE DUKE OF CONNAUGHT is to inspect the 156th Inf.
Brigade at 10 a.m. on 1st July on the ground in front of WINNIPEG
CAMP.

2.   The Brigade will be formed in hollow square at 8.30 a.m.,
each Battalion having two Companies in line with two Companies in
rear of them at a distance of six paces from rear rank to rear rank.

3.   Companies will be equalised and sized, and each platoon will,
as far as possible, be commanded by an Officer, but seconds-in-command
of Companies will not command platoons. C.Q.M.S's will not parade.
C.S.M's will act as right guides.

4. (a). Dress – Walking out order, with rifles.
   (b). Tam o' Shanters will be worn.
   (c). S.B.Rs will not be carried on parade.
        4th Royal Scots will dump S.B.Rs clear of the parade ground
        under a small guard.
   (d). Officers will not carry gloves or canes.
   (e). Mounted Officers may wear leggings or field boots. All other
        Officers will wear puttees.

5.   All Officers will be dismounted on the parade. For the March
Past C.Os, Seconds-in-Command and Adjutants, will be mounted.

6.   "Arm-Badges" of runners, scouts, and signallers will be removed.
The red distinguishing Battalion bands will not be removed.

7.   No Lewis Guns will be carried on parade.

8. (a) Handling of arms will be done in the same time as the beat of
       the left foot in marching in quick time.
   (b) All Officers will salute on the third motion of the present
       and cut the hand away on the second motion of the
       slope (or order).

9. (a) Transport will parade in line at 80 yards distance behind
       7th Royal Scots, with pack animals in the front line in front
       of limbers.
   (b) Drivers will stand to their horses.
   (c) Wagons will be as for G.O.C's inspection recently.

10.   R.S.M. RHIND, M.C., will act as Brigade Sergt. Major. Markers
will report to him at 8.15 a.m.   7th Royal Scots will supply 8 markers
(two per Company) to include markers for 4th Royal Scots. 7th Sco.
Rifles will supply 4 markers (one per Company).

11. (a) After the inspection H.R.H. is to present medals to ten W.Os,
        N.C.Os or men of the Brigade.
    (b) These men will fall in two paces behind the supernumerary rank
        of the 7th Royal Scots during the inspection. Just before H.R.H.
        has finished inspection of the last Battalion, they will be
        marched by an Officer to the saluting base by the Brigade Sergt.
        Major.
    (c) They will wear clean fatigue dress with belt and bayonet only.
        Their medal ribbons will not be worn.

12.   After the presentation, Battalions will unfix bayonets, and
march off the ground by the most Westerly exit, each followed by
their own transport; then left wheel down the main road to ST ELOY,
and march past H.R.H. in column of route. H.R.H. is to be at a
selected point on the bank on the North side of the main road.

13.   On the March Past:-
    (a) Six paces will be kept between platoons, ten between Companies,
        100 between Battalions.
    (b)/

2.

 (b). Two signal flags will mark the points for giving the commands "Eyes Left" and "Eyes Front".
 (c). Seconds-in-Command will follow the Infantry of their Battalion and precede the Transport.
 (d). Transport Drivers and Brakesmen will be specially warned to keep their <u>eyes</u> turned to the left between these two flags.
   Rifles will be slung on the left shoulder by Brakesmen.

14. The Divisional Band will play on the inspection parade. Battalion Pipe Bands will play the Brigade past on the March Past. They will be massed 50 yards on the right of H.R.H.

15. 7th Royal Scots and 7th Scottish Rifles will each supply two A.A. Lewis Guns and teams (2 other ranks) for the vicinity of the parade ground. They will be in position at 8.30 a.m. on 1st July. Lewis Gun Officer of 7th Royal Scots will point the positions out to one N.C.O. of each Battalion at a time to be arranged by him. Lewis Guns will also be in position for parade tomorrow afternoon (see para 16).

16. (a). A practice parade for 7th Royal Scots and 7th Sco. Rifles will be held tomorrow afternoon at 6 p.m. on the parade ground.
 (b). Dress - As for the parade.
 (c). Transport will not be present.
 (d). Lieut. Col. J.G.P. ROMANES, D.S.O., will be in command.
 (e). Bands of all three units will parade massed.

17. 4th Royal Scots Band will be billited by 7th Sco. Rifles from tomorrow till after the parade. They will report as soon as convenient to O.C., 7th Sco. Rifles. O.C., 4th Royal Scots, will please make any necessary arrangements with Lieut. Col. ROMANES.

18. Motor Lorries will be available to bring 4th Royal Scots from HILLS CAMP at 7.30 a.m. on 1st July, and to take them back.

29th June 1918.   *W R Kermack* Captain,
             A/Brigade Major, 156th Inf. Brigade.

 Copies to:-

  G.O.C.
  4th Royal Scots.
  7th Royal Scots.
  7th Sco. Rifles.
  156th T.M. Battery.
  Lieut. Col. ROMANES, D.S.O.
  Brigade Major.
  Staff Captain
  Brigade Transport Officer.
  52nd Division (for information).

War Diary
July
Appendix VI

SECRET.

TO all recipients of

186th INFANTRY BRIGADE ORDER No. 42.
○○

Reference Brigade Order No.42, para. 14, for "BERTHONVAL" read "LATTA".

This will be permanent camp for 186th Bde. Transport. A/Staff Capt. will allot units areas today at an hour to be notified later.

6th July 1918.

W R Kermack Captain,
A/Bde. Major, 186th Inf. Brigade.

SECRET.   Copy No. 15

155TH INFANTRY BRIGADE ORDER NO.49.

Ref.No.M150.999 (Baddeley).   **5th July 1918.**

1. The 155th Infantry Brigade will relieve the 157th Infantry Brigade in the Right Section of the 52nd Division Sector on the 8th and 9th July.

2. Reliefs will take place as follows:-

July 8th. 1/7th Sco.Rifles will relieve 1/5th H.L.I. in the Right Sub-Section.
           1/4th Royal Scots will relieve 1/6th H.L.I. in the Centre Sub-section.
           1/7th Royal Scots will relieve 1/7th H.L.I. in the Left Sub-Section.

July 9th. 155th T.M.Batt. will relieve 157th T.M.Batt.

3. On 7th July advanced parties consisting of Battalion Intelligence Officers, one officer per company, one N.C.O. per platoon, two battalion runners, two runners per company, two battalion signallers, Battalion scout N.C.O., Lewis Gun N.C.O. per company, Battalion and company Gas N.C.Os., will go into the line. They will be met at 9:15 a.m. by guides from the Battalion Headquarters and companies they are relieving as follows:-

   1/7th Sco.Rifles at Junction of Plank Road with NEUVILLE ST.VAAST-MOUNT ROAD (A.11.a.4.7.)
   1/4th Royal Scots and 1/7th Royal Scots at Right Brigade Headquarters (A.5.d.7.5.) at 9:30 a.m.
   Three motor lorries will convey advanced parties of 1/7th Royal Scots and 1/7th Sco.Rifles to A.11.a.4.7., leaving FRASER CAMP at 8:45 a.m.

4. On 8th July Units will be met by guides from Battalion Headquarters, Company Headquarters, and platoons of the units they are relieving as follows:-

   4th Royal Scots at A.11.a.4.7. from 9:15 a.m. till 10 a.m.
   7th Sco.Rifles at A.11.a.4.7. at 10 a.m.
   7th Royal Scots at A.11.a.4.7. at 12:15 p.m.
   Lorries will be at OTTAWA CAMP from 7:30 a.m. onwards to convey 1/7th Sco.Rifles, and at FRASER CAMP from 11:45 a.m. for 1/7th Royal Scots.

5. 4th Royal Scots and 155th T.M.Batt. will march from NEUVILLE ST.VAAST.

6. Units will appoint their own entraining and detraining Officers. These Officers will make any necessary alterations in event of enemy shelling, and report by wire or cyclist to Brigade.

7. Left and Centre Battalions will use TOMMY ALLEN Communication Trench. Right Battalion will use TIGER ALLEY.

8. Details of relief and exchange of Lewis Gun Magazines, etc. will be arranged between O.Cs. concerned.

9. Till reaching the communication trenches, platoons will move at 200 yds. distance. On the enemy side of the Ridge movement will be by Sections.

10/

2.

10. Commands of sub-sections will pass on completion of Battalion relief.

11. Completion of relief will be reported by code word "UNIFORM".

12. Between passing of Command of Section from G.O.C. 155th Infantry Brigade to G.O.C. 156th Infantry Brigade and relief of 155th L.M.Batt. by 156th L.M.Batt., 155th L.M.Batt. will be under orders of G.O.C. 156th Infantry Brigade.

13. In the event of an enemy attack while relief is in progress companies will assemble in the nearest defences and report to the nearest Battalion Commander or Brigade Headquarters.

13. Details of Units not proceeding into the line will move to Divisional Reception Camp by 2 p.m., 9th July.

14. Transport will be brigaded at BERTHENVAL by 2 p.m., 9th July.

15. Command of the Section passes on completion of the Infantry relief at which hour Brigade Headquarters will close at WHITE HOUSE, ST. ELOI, and open at Right Section Headquarters.

16. ACKNOWLEDGE.

W R Kermack Captain,
A/Bde. Major, 156th Inf.Brigade.

8th July 1915.

Issued by Runner at _____

Copy No. 1   G.O.C.
        2   4th Royal Scots.
        3   7th Royal Scots.
        4   7th Cam. Riflers.
        5   155th L.M.Batt.
        6   Staff Captain.
        7   I.O. & Bde. Sigs.
        8   D.H.Q.
        9   52nd Division.
        10   155th Inf. Bde.
        11   157th Inf. Bde.
        12   Bde.Supply Officer.
        13   2nd Lowland Field Ambulance.
    14 & 15 War Diary.
        16   File.

SECRET.   156th Infantry Brigade.   Copy No. 14

ADMINISTRATIVE ORDERS NO. 6.

Appendix III

Ref. 156th Infantry Brigade Order No. 48.

1. **BILLETS AND CAMPS.**
   (i). All billets and camps will be left absolutely clean before Units march out.
   (ii). Certificates from O.C., Advance Party, of incoming units that billets, camps and horse standings were taken over in a clean and sanitary condition, and a Certificate from the area Commandant that there are no outstanding claims for damage to Government property, will be sent to Brigade H.Q. by noon on 9th July.

2. **TRANSPORT AND QUARTERMASTERS STORES.**
   (i). Units will take over the horse standings and camps allotted to them by the A/Staff Captain at LATTA CAMP and the Camp West of it. They will be vacant by 2 p.m. on 8th July.
   (ii). The B.T.O. will issue any further instructions necessary. He will report completion of move by wire to Bde. H.Q. by code word "PARIS".
   (iii) The B.T.O. will forward to Bde. H.Q. within 48 hours of arrival in camp a return of stores taken over, made out on Div. Trench Stores Pro Forma.
   (iv) Baggage Wagons of the Divisional Train will report to Units' H.Q. at 8 a.m. on 8th July.

3. **BLANKETS AND OFFICERS' KITS.**
   Blankets and Officers' kits will be conveyed to units' Q.M. Stores LATTA CAMP under their own arrangements.

4. **RATIONS.**
   (i). Refilling Point, commencing 8th July:-
       LEADLEY Siding - A.2.c.5.9.
   (ii). Rations will be drawn at 3 p.m. and delivered by the Supply Section of the Train at Units' Q.M. Stores, LATTA CAMP.
   (iii). DISTRIBUTION.
       (a). Right Battalion.
           3 Companies by limber to B.3.c.8.7.
           1 Coy and Battalion H.Q. by limber to Battn. H.Q.
       (b). Centre Battalion.
           3 Coys by limber to Cookhouses, VANCOUVER, T.28.a.4.3.
           1 Coy and Battn. H.Q. by train from ZIVY to MORRISON.
       (c). Left Battalion.
           3 Coys by limber to Cookhouses, VANCOUVER, T.28.a.4.2.
       (d). T.M. Battery.
           By rail from ZIVY to MORRISON.
       (e). Brigade H.Q. ... by Limber.
   (iv). Rations forwarded by light railway will be loaded on trucks at ZIVY by 7.30 p.m. nightly.
   (v). The B.T.O. will inform Transport Officers the hour at which Transport may proceed over VIMY Ridge.
   (vi). An Officer of each Battalion Administrative H.Q. will proceed with rations each night, and report at their Battalion H.Q.
   (vii). C.Q.M.Ss. will proceed to their Coy H.Q. each night with rations which they will hand over at their Coy Cookhouses.

5. **WATER.**/

2.

5. **WATER.**
   (i). *Right Battalion.*
      (a). Drinking water is conveyed by Light Railway each night to four 200 gall. tanks at DURHAM POST - B.9.b.2.3. - filled under Water Supply Officer's arrangements.
         Battalion H.Q. and 1 Coy draw from LONGWOOD, at which there are four 200 gall. tanks, filled each night by the Division on the Right.
      (b). Washing water is drawn from WILLERVAL WELLS.
   (ii). *Centre Battalion.*
      (a). Drinking water is drawn from MERSEY - B.2.a.9.7. - and FARBUS - B.2.d.1.9. - both filled by pipe line. Water for 3 forward Coys is filled from MERSEY into petrol tins by Battalion Water Picquet by day and dumped at B.2.a.7.8. where it is collected by limber at night and conveyed to VANCOUVER.
      (b). If this supply fails, petrol tanks will be filled at MORRISON.
      (c). Washing water may be drawn from FARBUS WOOD WELLS.
   (iii). *Left Battalion.*
      (a). Drinking water is drawn from four 200 gall. tanks at MORRISON - T.26.c.6.5. - filled nightly by Light Railway under Water Supply Officer's arrangements.
        It is filled in petrol tanks and conveyed as follows:-
          For 3 Coys by push lines to B.3.a.7.8. thence by limber to Cookhouses, VANCOUVER.
          For 1 Coy and Battn. H.Q. by push lines to Battn. H.Q.
      (b). If this supply fails water may be drawn from VIMY Brewery - T.26.a.5.0. - from pipe-filled tanks.
      (c). Washing water may be drawn from FARBUS WELLS.
   (iv). *T.M. Battery H.Q.* Drinking water is drawn from MERSEY.
   (v). *Brigade H.Q.* Drinking water is drawn from 400 gall. tank, filled daily by pipe.
   (vi). Petrol tins, dixies, or food containers will not be used for drawing water from wells.
   (vii). C.Os will ensure that each man has at least one gall. of water per day.

6. **Water Picquets.**
   (i). Water Picquets will be found by units, as per attached list which is issued to all concerned. They will report at H.Q. of the unit to be relieved at 10 a.m. on 8th July.
   (ii). Only units of the Brigade and Amb. personnel attached will be allowed to draw water from water sources in the area.
   (iii). Standing Orders for water picquets will be issued separately.

7. **AMMUNITION.**
   (i). Brigade Dumps:-
         LONGWOOD ... ... B.15.a.2.8.
         FARBUS ... ... B.2.d.3.1.
         MERSEY ... ... B.2.a.7.7.
         BRICKSTACK ... ... T.26.d.3.3.
     Ammunition Guards as follows will report to Sergt. MORRIS, Brigade Ammunition N.C.O. at Brigade H.Q. THELUS CAVE, at 9 a.m. on 8th instant:-
         4th Royal Scots ... 3 Ptes. for LONGWOOD.
         7th Royal Scots ... 2 Ptes for Farbus.
         7th Sco. Rifles ... 2 " for MERSEY.
         7th Sco. Rifles ... 2 " for BRICKSTACK.
     Transport arrangements for Ammunition Guards and Water Picquets will be issued later.
   (ii). *Brigade Reserve Dump.* THELUS CAVES - A.6.c.6.5.
   (iii). Except in emergency, application for Ammunition from these Dumps will be made to Brigade H.Q.

8. **R.E. MATERIAL.** /

3.

8. R.E. MATERIAL.
(i). R.E. Officers keep in touch with C.Os. and R.E. material required is sent up by Light Railway from ZIVY to the nearest junction (LONGWOOD, MORRISON or FARBUS).
(ii). Material for wiring should be conveyed by limber to VANCOUVER.

9. MEDICAL.
(i). Right Battalion. R.A.P. – B.9.a.9.8.
  Routes of evacuation:-
   (a). Via TIRED ALLEY. Relay post at B.14.a.0.8.
   (b). Via Relay Post – B.2.d.3.4.
(ii). Centre Battalion.)
   Left Battalion.   ) Combined R.A.P. at T.27.d.4.4.
    Evacuation to Relay Post – T.26.a.4.9.
(iii). A.D.S. – B.2.a.9.5.
    Evacuation by push trucks to motor ambulance post – T.25.a.9.5., or by returning ration trucks.

10. FIRST LINE STRAGGLERS POSTS.
  Commandant's House ... B.7.d.5.2.
  MERSEY ALLEY ... ... B.1.d.9.9.
  VIMY ... ... T.25.b.5.8.

11. SALVAGE.
  Evacuation.
(i). By returning ration limbers.
(ii). By rail from VANCOUVER, MORRISON or FARBUS.
    Units sending salvage by (ii) will notify Brigade H.Q. 24 hours previously.

12. BURIAL.
Units will convey bodies to collecting station at B.2.b.2.8. and notify Brigade H.Q.

13. ACKNOWLEDGE.

6th July 1918.
                              Lieut.
              A/Staff Captain, 156th Inf. Brigade.

Issued at..........

═══════════════════════════════════════

Copy No. 1 to Brigade Commander   Copy No. 10 to 219th Coy A&S.C.
         2   4th Royal Scots.   11   W.S.O.
         3   7th Royal Scots.   12   155th Inf. Bde.
         4.   7th Sco. Rifles.   13   A.D.M.S.
         5.   156th T.M. Battery   14 & 15   Diary.
         6.   52nd Division.   16   File.
         7.   Bde/ Major.
         8   B.T.O.
         9.   Bde. Sig. Officer.

War Diary
July

SECRET.

Copy No. 16

156th Infantry Brigade Order No. 42.   Appendix IV

Reference MARŒUIL Sheet 1/20,000.   14th July 1918.

1.   The 4th Canadian Division is relieving the portion of the 52nd Division South of WATLING ROAD (inclusive to 4th Canadian Division) as far as R.S.O.O.S., thence due West to junction of HERSEY ALLEY and Railway Embankment, thence to A.13.a.8.5.

2. (a). On 14th July the 50th Canadian Infantry Battalion will relieve all troops of the 7th Scottish Rifles and the 4th Royal Scots East of, and including, the BLACK LINE.
    (b). The 47th Canadian Infantry Battalion will relieve all troops of 7th Scottish Rifles and 4th Royal Scots at present situated in the BROWN LINE.
    (c). Relief will commence at approximately 8.30 p.m. in both cases.
    (d). All details of the reliefs will be arranged between O.C. Battalions concerned.

3.   On relief, as above, the 4th Royal Scots will relieve the 6th H.L.I. in the Right Sub-Section of the Left Section of the Divisional Sector, and the 7th Scottish Rifles will relieve the troops of 7th H.L.I. in VERY and in the BROWN LINE between NEW BRUNSWICK ROAD and S.24.central. They will also relieve One Company 4th Royal Scots, in the BROWN LINE between HERSEY ALLEY and NEW BRUNSWICK ROAD.

     Details of relief to be arranged between Battalion Commanders concerned.

4.   10th Canadian T.M. Battery will relieve that portion of the 156th T.M. Battery in the present Brigade area South of WATLING ROAD.

     On relief, O.C. 156th T.M. Battery will relieve all guns of the 157th T.M. Battery situated in the Right Sub-Section of the Left Brigade Section.

     Details of reliefs will be arranged between O.C. concerned.

5.   O.C. 7th Scottish Rifles and 4th Royal Scots will arrange to supply such guides as may be required by relieving Battalions. Details as to numbers, times, rendezvous and routes will be arranged by O.C. concerned.

6.   Advance parties, on relief, of incoming units will report at Headquarters of the unit which they are to relieve at 8 a.m. on 15th July:-
     Battalion Works Officer.
     1 Officer & 1 N.C.O. per Battalion Headquarters.
     1 Officer per Company.
     1 N.C.O. per platoon.
     Battalion Gas N.C.Os.
Guides are not required for these parties.

7./

2.

7.   No party larger than the equivalent of a platoon will move off together, and intervals of 200 yards will be maintained between platoons.

8.   In the event of an enemy attack during relief O.C. 4th Royal Scots and 7th Scottish Rifles will send an Officer to report to Brigade Headquarters.

9.   All maps, Defence Schemes and Log Books will be handed over.

10. All reliefs will be completed by 5 a.m. on 16th July.

11. Completion of reliefs will be reported to Brigade Headqrs by the following code:-
     Completion of Relief of 7th Bon. Rifles in BLACK LINE
                              and BROWN LINE ....NAKED.
        do.   do.   4th R. Scots in BLACK LINE and
                              BROWN LINE ....ETHDEN
        do.   do.   8th H.L.I. by 4th R. Scots...........TALATA.
        do.   do.   7th R.Sct. by 7th R. Scots...........ARDAA.
        do.   do.   156th T.M. Batty by 10th
                              Canadian T.M. Battery..........RANGA
        do.   do.   157th T.M. Batty by 155th T.M. Bty...SETTA

12. Command of area to be taken over by 47th and 50th Canadian Infantry Battalions will pass to G.O.C. 10th Canadian Brigade on completion of relief of 4th Royal Scots and 7th Scottish Rifles in the BLACK and BROWN LINES, and of the Right SUB-SECTION of the Left Section to G.O.C. 156th Infantry Brigade, on completion of reliefs mentioned in para 5.

13. Brigade Headquarters will remain in present position.

14. ACKNOWLEDGE.

                                            H. Sayer
                                            Captain,
                                   Brigade Major, 156th Inf. Brigade.

Issued at 10.20 p.m.

Copy No. 1 to 4th Royal Scots.
        2   7th Royal Scots.
        3   7th Scot. Rifles.
        4   156th T.M. Battery.
        5   Sthd. Division.
        6   10th Canadian Infantry Brigade.
        7   157th Inf. Brigade.
        8   412th Field Coy R.E.
        9   Brigade Commander.
       10   Brigade Major.
       11   Staff Captain.
       12   Signals.
       13   Right Group R.A. Commander.
       14   Right Group M.G. Commander.
       15   R.T.O.
    16 & 17 War Diary.
       18   File.

SECRET.   Copy No. 14

155th INFANTRY BRIGADE.
ADMINISTRATIVE ORDER No. V.

Reference 155th Inf.Brigade Order No. 81.

1. RATIONS.

Rations will be distributed as follows:-

1/4th Royal Scots.
    Battn.H.Qrs., by train from NIVY to NEW BRUNSWICK.
    4 Coys.   Do.   do. CANADA.

1/7th Sco.Rifles.
    Battn.H. & 1 Coy. by Limbers.
    1 Coy.   by train from NIVY to MORRISON.
    1 "   Do.   do. NEW BRUNSWICK.
    1 "   Do.   do. BORDEN.

2. TRENCH STORES.

All ammunition and trench stores will be handed over and receipts taken, except the following which will be retained:-

    Yukon Packs.
    Soyers Stoves.
    Food Containers.

Receipts will reach Bde.H.Qrs. 24 hours after relief. The usual procedure will be carried out in taking over the Trench Stores of 157th Inf.Bde.

3. AMMUNITION.

After reliefs, Bde. Dumps will be located as follows:-

    THELUS CAVES   A.C.C.S.F.
    HELMET   B.2S.Y.7.
    BRICKSTACK   L.23.A.4.5.
    CANUCA   S.24.C.3.5.
    CULVERT   T.23.C.5.1.

The Guards at LONGWOOD and PARRUS Dumps will be relieved by 10th Canadian Inf.Bde. at 3 a.m. on 15th inst. 1/7th Scottish Rifles will relieve Guards of 157th Inf. Bde. by 12 noon on 14th inst. at following Dumps:-

    1 N.C.O. & 2 men   CANUCA.
    1 N.C.O. & 2 men   CULVERT.

4. WATER PICQUETS.

Water picquets will be handed over by the Battalions concerned.

5. MEDICAL.

Separate orders will be issued.

6. ACKNOWLEDGE.

                                      Captain,
14th July 1918.   Staff Captain, 155th Inf.Brigade.

Issued at 2 p.m.

Copy No.1 to Brigade Commander.   Copy No.8 to B.M.O.
    2. 4th Royal Scots.   9. Bde.Signal Officer.
    3. 7th Royal Scots.   10. Bde.Supply Officer.
    4. 7th Sco.Rifles.   11. 157th Inf.Bde.
    5. 155th T.M.Batt.   12. 10th Canadian Inf.Bde.
    6. 52nd Division.   13. Diary.
    7. Bde.Major.   14. File.

2.

Copy No. 1 to 4th Royal Scots.
2. 7th Royal Scots.
3. 7th Cameronians (Sco. Rifles)
4. 156th T.M. Battery.
5. 52nd Division.
6. 155th Inf. Brigade.
7. 23rd Inf. Brigade.
8. 10th Canadian Inf. Brigade.
9. 412th Field Coy R.E.
10. 1/1st Lowland Field Amb.
11. B.G.C.
12. Brigade Major.
13. Staff Captain
14. Intelligence Officer.
15. Signals.
16. Brigade Transport Officer.
17. Brigade Supply Officer.
18 & 19 War Diary.
20 File.

SECRET. *War Diary* Copy No. 18

156th INFANTRY BRIGADE ORDER No: 44.

Ref. Map MAROEUIL. 1/20,000.   *July*   20th July 1918.
Appendix

1. The 52nd (Lowland) Division is being relieved by the 8th Division in the RIGHT SECTION of the VIII Corps Front on the 20th JULY 1918, and subsequent dates, and, on relief, is coming into G.H.Q. Reserve.

2. (a). The 156th Inf. Brigade will be relieved by the 23rd Inf. Brigade in the ACHEVILLE SECTION on the 21st July in accordance with Table attached.
   (b). Details of reliefs will be arranged between Commanders concerned.

3. (a). Guides for relieving units as far as the entrances to MERSEY ALLEY and PEGGIE TRENCH will be arranged for as follows:-
   (i). 1/7th Cameronians will provide a chain of picquets from the Debussing Point (S.28.d.central) along HUMBER TRENCH, thence along the RED TRAIL to entrance of PEGGIE TRENCH.
   (ii). 1/7th Royal Scots will provide a chain of picquets from the Debussing Point at A.11.a.4.7. to entrance of MERSEY ALLEY.
   The above chains to be in position by 1 p.m.
   (b). Guides forward of the above mentioned points will be arranged for by C.Os concerned.

4. Communications, Trench Maps, Maps of NO MAN'S LAND, Aeroplane Photographs, Log Books and Trench Stores will be handed over. Copies of receipts for all of the above will be sent to Bde. H.Q. 48 hours after relief.

5. Command of Subsection will pass to O.C. Relieving Units on completion of each relief.

6. Outgoing Troops, on leaving the Communication Trenches, will move at not less than 200 yards distance between platoons.

7. (a). Busses will be available for the transport of units to MONT ST ELOY. Embussing Points will be as shown in column "E" of the attached Table.
   (b). An Officer from each Battalion will be detailed to supervise the embussing and debussing of their respective units.

8. In the event of an alarm during the relief, troops will man the nearest defences and send an Officer to the nearest Battalion H.Q.

9. Completion of relief and arrival in camp will be reported "Priority" by Code word "CHEERIO" and "GOOD BYE".

10. Brigade H.Q. will close at present position and open at WHITE HOUSE, MONT ST ELOI, on completion of reliefs, when command of the Section will pass to G.O.C., 23rd Inf. Brigade.

11. ACKNOWLEDGE.

H. Sayer
Captain,
Brigade Major, 156th Inf. Brigade.

Issued at 9 p.m.

SECRET.

MARCH TABLE

HEAD QRS. 16th 1/BRIGADE.
(Issued with 16th Inf. Brigade Order No. 44.)

"A" Serial No.	"B" Units in order of march	"C" Place	"C" Starting Point.	"C" Time.	"D" Route.	"E" Destination	"E"	"F" Remarks
1.	(a) 7th Cameronians } (b) Bde. Hqrs. }	Road Junction F.1.s.7.9.		11 a.m.	GAMBLAIN L'ABBE - LES 4 VENTS GD SERVINS - Cross Roads Q.22.d.5.9. - VERDREL	(a) BOIS D'OLHAIN (b) BERLIN		Bde. H.Q. to fall in in rear of Batn.
2.	7th Royal Scots	do.		11.45 a.m.	As Serial No. 1.	BOIS D'OLHAIN		
3.	4th Royal Scots } 16th T.M. Bnty.}	do.		12.45 p.m.	As Serial No. 1	do.		T.M. Bty to fall in in rear of Batn.
4.	413th Field Coy R.E.	do.		1.30 p.m.	As Serial No. 1	do.		
5.	"B" Coy 22nd M.G. Batn.	Road Junction W.18.d.25.60		3.45 p.m.	GD SERVINS - Cross Roads at Q.22.d.5.9. - VERDREL.	do.		
6.	1st Lon. Field Ambulance.	do.		4.30 p.m.	As Serial No. 5.	do.		

SECRET.

ISSUED WITH 156TH INFANTRY BRIGADE ORDER No. 44.

"A" Serial No.	"B" Unit to be Relieved	"C" Relieving Unit.	"D" Route for Incoming Unit.	"E" Route for Outgoing Unit.	"F" Destination.	Remarks.
1.	4th Royal Scots.	2nd Batn. Middlesex Regiment.	Debussing Point (S.28.d.Central) HUBBER TRENCH - PEGGIE TRENCH.	PEGGIE TRENCH - RED TRAIL - HUBBER TRENCH Debussing Point (S.28.d.Central)	LANCASTER CAMP, MONT ST ELOI.	Relief of 4th Royal Scots will probably commence at 1.30 p.m.; of 7th Royal Scots at 3 p.m.; and 7th Cameronians at 4.30.
2.	7th Cameronians.	2nd Batn. West Yorks Regiment.	Debussing Point (S.28.d.Central) HUBBER TRENCH - RED TRAIL.	RED TRAIL - HUBBER TRENCH. Debussing Point (S.28.d.Central)	OTTAWA CAMP, MONT ST ELOI.	
3.	7th Royal Scots.	2nd Batn. Devonshire Regiment.	Debussing Point (A.11.a.4.7.) MERSEY ALLEY - C.P.R. TRENCH.	C.P.R. TRENCH - MERSEY ALLEY. Debussing Point (A.11.a.4.7.)	FRASER CAMP, MONT ST ELOI.	
4.	156th T.M. Battery.		Debussing Point (A.11.a.4.7.) MERSEY ALLEY -	MERSEY ALLEY - Debussing Point (A.11.a.4.7.)	DURHAM CAMP, MONT ST ELOI.	

War Diary July 1918
Appendix VIII

Ref.Map:- Sheet 44 B. 1/40,000.

4th Royal Scots.	"B" Coy. 52nd M.G.Bn.
7th Royal Scots.	415th Field Coy. R.E.
7th Cameronians (S.R.)	1/1st Lowland Field Amb.
155th T.M.Batt.	219th Coy. A.S.C.

BM 248

1. In continuation of this Office BM 242 of today, the 52nd Division is in G.H.Q. Reserve, and the 155th Brigade Group will be ready to move by Bus or Tactical Train at nine hour's notice.

2. MOVE BY TACTICAL TRAIN.

(a) Entraining Station will be GALMAIND- HIGOUART. Brigade starting point for march to entraining Station will be CROSS ROADS at P.10.b.0.8.

(b) Route from Starting Point will be as follows:-
HOUDAIN - DIVION - FOSSE de la CLARENCE - Railway Bridge at I.19.a.6.8.

(c) Order of March to entraining Station will probably be as follows:-

   4th Royal Scots.
   7th Royal Scots.
   7th Cameronians (S.R.)
   155th T.M.Batt.
      (to march with 7th Sco.Rifles).
   "B" Coy. 52nd M.G.Bn.
   415th Field Coy.R.E.
   1/1st Lowland Field Amb.

(d) The above order of march is provisional only and may have to be altered on receipt of a definite order to move, but it will, if possible, be adhered to.

(e) All Unit Commanders will, as soon as possible, reconnoitre the shortest and best roads to the Starting Point. A report will be sent to these H.Qrs. giving the route selected, and the time which it is estimated it will take to get to the Starting Point from present camps or billets.

(f) As there will probably only be limited accommodation for Transport on the trains, a portion of the 1st Line Transport only will be taken. The remainder will proceed by Road.
Further orders will be issued on this point.

(g) All Lewis, Vickers and Stokes Guns will be taken on the train together with all possible ammunition which can be carried in the portion of the Transport taken by train.

3. MOVE BY BUS.

(a) Embussing Point will be on the MAISNIL-RANCHICOURT Road, with its head at P.8.c.00.80.
Head and Tail of Embussing Point will be marked by boards.

(b) The Brigade Starting point will be the Road Junction at J.30.c.1.1.

(c) Order of march will probably be as in para.2 (c) above.

(d) Reconnaissances will be carried out as laid down in para.2 (e) above, and a similar report sent to these H.Qrs.

(e) All Lewis, Vickers and Stokes Guns will be taken in the busses together with at least 24 drums per Lewis Gun and 10 filled belts per Vickers Gun. Full complement of Stokes shells will be carried.

(f) One complete day's ration will be carried on the men and the unconsumed portion.

(g) Embussing Strengths will be sent to Bde.H.Qrs. immediately on receipt of an order to move.

(h) The attention of all concerned is drawn to 52nd Divisional Administrative/

Administrative Circular Memorandum No.8, dated 27th May 1918.

4. ACKNOWLEDGE.

H. Sayer

                                              Captain,

23rd July 1918.   Bde.Major, 156th Inf.Brigade.

COPIES TO:-

        Staff Captain.
        B.T.O.
        Signal Officer.
        Bde.Supply Officer.
        War Diary (2)
        File.

****

4th. Royal Scots   7th. Sco. Rifles   BM 301
7th. Royal Scots

First Line Transport limbers will be loaded as undernoted
pending the complete supply of golf bags carriers and racks.
These loads must not be exceeded except for a minimum of
signallers and pioneers equipment.
28th. July 1918.   (Sgd) H. SAYER, Captain,
                     Brigade Major, 156th. Inf. Bde.

4 wagons each loaded with
    Front portion.
                                      4 Lewis Guns   )
                                      18 Magazine Cases   )

    Rear Portion.   5 Lewis Guns   )
                                      12 Mag. Cases   ) $18\tfrac{1}{2}$ cwts
                                      2   "   A.A.   )
                                      8 Spare parts   )
3 Wagons, each loaded with   Range Finder   )

                                    22 Boxes S.A.A.   ) $17\tfrac{1}{2}$ cwts
2 wagons each loaded with   8 boxes grenades   )

                                    Picks and Shovels   )
                                    Axes etc.   )
                                    Armourers Tools   )
                                    Vet Chest   )
                                    Farrier's kit   ) $7\tfrac{1}{2}$ cwts.
                                    Saddler's kit   )
                                    6 boxes grenades   )
1 Wagon, loaded with 400 drums (50 magazines)   21 cwt.
10 Wagons

Copies to Brigade Major   Transport Officer:-
           Staff Captain   4th. Royal Scots
           Bde. Transport Officer   7th. Royal Scots
                                          7th. Sco. Rifles.

SECRET. *War Diary* Copy No. 20

150th INFANTRY BRIGADE ORDER No. 45.

July Appendix VII

Ref Map Sheet 51c.
Sheet 44b. (late 36b.)　　　　　　　　　　21st July 1918.

INFORMATION. 1. The 52nd (Lowland) Division is moving into the XVII Corps area on the 21st July and subsequent dates.

MOVE. 2. 150th Inf. Brigade will march to Billets and Camps in BOIS D'OLHAIN and BARLIN on 22nd instant in accordance with attached March Table. Units will march independently.

TRANSPORT. 3. Transport of Units, including Train wagons, will march in rear of Units.
Water Carts will be full, and all mobile stores will be carried.

DISTANCES ON THE MARCH. 4. The following distances will be maintained on the march:-

　　　Between Battalions　...　500 yards.
　　　Between Coys　...　100 yards.
　　　Between Unit and its
　　　　Transport　...　100 yards.

PROTECTION FROM ENEMY AIRCRAFT. 5. One Lewis Gun Section, ready for action, will accompany each Battalion Transport in order to deal with low-flying E.A.

GUIDES. 6. Guides from Advance Parties will meet units at the Road Junction in VERDREL (Q.21.a.4.6.) to conduct them to areas allotted for Camps or Billets.

PACKS. 7. Mens packs will be carried in lorries in accordance with para 8 below.

LORRIES. 8. (a). Motor lorries will report at 8.30 a.m. on 22-7-18 to carry packs and baggage as follows:-
　　9 lorries to Bde. Transport Officer, LATTA CAMP, 3 for each Battalion.
　　1 lorry to 412th Field Coy R.E. at position to be notified later.
　　1 lorry at 1/1st Low. Field Amb. at VILLERS AU BOIS.
　　1 lorry to "B" Coy 52nd Division M.G. Coy at RISPIN CAMP, VILLERS AU BOIS.
　　2 lorries Bde. H.Q. at WHITE HOUSE, MONT ST ELOI. for Bde. H.Q. and 150th T.M. Batty.
(b). The lorry to accompany Bde. Group will report at Bde. H.Q. at the same hour.
(c). Units will detail unloading party of 1 N.C.O. and 2 men to accompany each lorry.
(d). All lorries after loading will rendezvous on Main Road at Y.M.C.A., OTTAWA CAMP, at 10 a.m. and will move independently to Road Junction VERDREL at Q.21.a.4.6., where they will be met by representatives of Billeting parties.

SUPPLIES. 9. Rations for 22nd instant will be drawn by 1st Line Transport from present refilling point on 21st instant, and for 22rd instant will be carried in the Supply Wagons of the Train. Refilling point for 24th instant, CITE DU No. 9 (Q.2.d.6.5.)

TRAIN/

SECRET.   156th INFANTRY BRIGADE ORDER No. 37.   Copy No. 21
==

Ref. Map MAROEUIL 1/20,000.   31st May 1918.

1.   156th Inf. Brigade will be relieved by 157th Inf. Brigade in the WILLERVAL SECTION on the 2nd and 3rd June.

2.   Reliefs will be carried out in daylight and will be as follows:-
June 2nd. 4th Royal Scots will be relieved by 5th H.L.I.
                          in the Front System, RIGHT SUBSECTION.
           7th Royal Scots will be relieved by 6th H.L.I.
                          in the FRONT SYSTEM, LEFT SUBSECTION.
           7th Sco. Rifles will be relieved by 7th H.L.I.
                          in RESERVE RIGHT SUBSECTION.
           8th Sco. Rifles will be relieved by 5th A. & S.H.
                          in RESERVE, LEFT SUBSECTION.

June 3rd. 156th L.T.M. Bty. will be relieved by 157th L.T.M. Bty.

3.   Details of reliefs will be arranged between C.Os concerned.
4.   Communications, Trench Maps, Maps of NO MAN'S LAND, Defence Schemes, Log Books and Trench Stores will be handed over.
        Lewis Gun Magazines may be exchanged by mutual arrangement.

5.   Advance Parties from 157th Inf. Brigade are going into the line tomorrow, 1st June.   Guides will be arranged as follows:-
        7th Sco. Rifles....Guides for all Posts and Coys at 2 p.m. at Bde. H.Q.
        4th Royal Scots....1 Guide to take party to Battn. H.Q. at 2.15 p.m.
                                       at Brigade H.Q.
        7th Royal Scots....1 Guide to take party to Battn. H.Q. at 2.30 p.m.
                                       at Brigade H.Q.
        8th Sco. Rifles....Under arrangements to be made direct with 5th A &S.H.

6.   Relieving troops for the BROWN LINE and EAST thereof will be guid-:ed to the point at which the Railway crosses TIRED ALLEY and MERSEY ALLEY respectively under Brigade arrangements as shewn below.   Beyond these two points and for the posts West of the BROWN LINE, arrangements will be made between C.Os.
        1/7th Sco. Rifles will provide a chain of picquets along the tracks from the NEUVILLE ST VAAST - LES TILLEULS ROAD to the Junction TIRED ALLEY - THELUS RIDGE LINE and to the end of MERSEY ALLEY, thus avoiding CANADIAN MONUMENT.   These chains will be in position by 10 a.m.   Units of 157th Inf. Brigade will be directed as follows:-
        5th H.L.I..By TIRED ALLEY.
        6th H.L.I..By MERSEY ALLEY.
        Forward Coy 7th H.L.I. and Coy for THELUS RIDGE
             POSTS...By TIRED ALLEY.
        2 Companies for BROWN LINE.........................By MERSEY ALLEY.
        5th A. & S.H.......................................By MERSEY ALLEY.

7.   Outgoing troops, on leaving the Communication Trenches, will move at not less than 400 yards distance between Platoons.

8.   On relief, Units will move into Camps as follows:-
        4th Royal Scots........LANCASTER CAMP (Vacated by 1/5th H.L.I.)
        7th Royal Scots........FRASER CAMP (Vacated by 1/7th H.L.I.)
        7th Sco. Rifles........OTTAWA CAMP (Vacated by 1/6th H.L.I.)
        8th Sco. Rifles........remain in HILLS CAMP.
        156th L.T.M. Bty.......CUBITT CAMP.

9.   Details at RISPIN CAMP will rejoin their Units at the Camps shewn above at 3 p.m. on June 2nd.

10.   Completion of relief and arrival in Camp will be reported by the Code Words "NEBY" and "SAMWIL" respectively.

11.   Administrative Instructions will be issued by the Staff Captain.

12./

2.

12. Brigade H.Q. will close at THELUS MILL at 0900 on 3rd June and reopen at MONT ST ELOY at the same hour.

13. ACKNOWLEDGE.

                                        Major,
                  Brigade Major, 156th Inf. Brigade.

Issued at 7 p.m.

Copy No.		Copy No.	
1	to G.O.C.	12 to	211th M.G. Coy.
2	4th Royal Scots.	13	52nd M.G. Battalion
3	7th Royal Scots.	14	Staff Captain
4	7th Sco. Rifles	15	Bde. Signals
5	8th Sco. Rifles	16	Intelligence Officer
6	156th L.T.M. Bty.	17	Bde. Transport Off.
7.	155th Inf. Bde.	18	Bde. Supply Officer
8.	157th Inf. Bde.	19	52nd Division.
9	152nd Inf. Bde.	20	1/1st Low. Fd. Amb.
10	Right Group R.F.A.	21 & 22	Diary.
11	412th Field Coy R.E.	23	File.

AMENDMENT
to
156th Inf. Brigade Order No. 37

1st June 1918.

Delete para 12, and substitute:-

"Command of Right Section will pass to B.G.C., 157th Inf. Brigade, at 12 noon on 2nd June, at which hour 156th Inf. Brigade Headquarters will open at MONT ST ELOY."

Issued at 7 p.m.

Major,
Brigade Major, 156th Inf. Brigade.

To all recipients of 156th Inf. Brigade Order No. 37.

War Diary - Appendix   (VIII)

Casualties - May, 1918

Unit	Killed		Wounded		Wounded (Ga.)		Missing	
	O	OR	O	OR	O	OR	O	OR
Bde HQ	-	-	-	-	-	-	-	-
4 Royal Scots	1	2	3	3	-	3	-	-
7 Royal Scots	-	3	1	2	-	-	-	-
7 Leo Rifles	-	2	-	6	1	21	-	2
8 Leo Rifles	-	1	-	2	-	-	-	-
	1	8	4	13	1	24	-	2

War Diary Appendix

Effective Strength - May 1918

IX

Unit	Week ending 3rd		Week ending 10th		Week ending 17th		Week ending 24th	
	O	OR	O	OR	O	OR	O	OR
4 Royal Scots	40	822	40	819	41	789	39	823
7 Royal Scots	40	916	40	914	41	902	41	940
7 Sco Rifles	48	856	48	846	48	828	47	877
8 Sco Rifles	40	855	40	852	41	837	41	868
	168	3449	168	3431	171	3356	168	3508

War Diary July. Appendix X

SECRET. Copy No. 17

156th Infantry Brigade Order No. 46

Ref Maps. 1/40,000. Sheets 36b and 51c.

29th July 1918.

1. **RELIEF.** The 52nd (Lowland) Division is relieving the 4th Canadian Division in the Left Subsector of the ARRAS SECTOR on the night 31st July/1st August and subsequent days.

2. **MOVE.** The 156th Inf. Brigade Group will march to Billets and Camps at MAROEUIL in accordance with the attached March Table.

3. **TRANSPORT.** Transport will march with units.

4. **DISTANCES ON MARCH.** The usual distances will be maintained on the line of march.

5. **ADVANCE PARTIES.** Advance Parties will meet Units at Cross Roads at F.22.d.80.00 and guide them to their Billets or Camps.
   Arrival of units in billets will be reported to Brigade H.Q. by the code word "Blast".

6. **SUPPLIES.** Rations for 31st instant will be drawn at 4 p.m. to-day and carried in the Supply Wagons of the Train.

7. **TRAIN WAGONS.** Baggage and Supply Wagons will report at Units Headquarters by 7 p.m. today, 29th instant.

8. **LORRIES.** Motor Lorries will report at 7.15 a.m. tomorrow, 30th instant to carry men's packs as follows:-
   - 2 .... Headquarters, 1/4th Royal Scots.
   - 2 .... do. 1/7th Royal Scots.
   - 2 .... do. 1/7th Scot. Rifles.

   A second run will be made as follows:-
   One man from each of the following units will report to Battalions as detailed below at 7.30 a.m. to proceed with the Lorries and guide one back to their respective Billets or Camps:-
   - 156th T.M. Battery ... to ... 1/4th Royal Scots.
   - 412th Field Coy R.E. ... to ... 1/7th Royal Scots.
   - "B" Coy 52nd M.G. Battn. to ... 1/7th Sco. Rifles.
   - 1/1st Low. Field Amb. to ... Bde. Headquarters.

   Each Battalion may make a second run with their remaining lorry if necessary.
   One Lorry will proceed in rear of column. This Lorry will deal with breakdowns, stragglers etc. No man will, however, be allowed to ride on the lorry without written permission from an Officer.

9. **MEDICAL.** One ambulance wagon will call at Battalion H.Q. by 7.30 a.m. tomorrow to collect any sick for evacuation.
   One ambulance wagon will proceed with each Battalion in the rear of their transport.

10. **BILLETS.** Billets and Camps must be left scrupulously clean, and a certificate of cleanliness obtained from the Town Major or Area Commandant; also that there are no outstanding claims for damage to Government property.

11. **BRIGADE H.Q.** Brigade H.Q. will close at BARLIN at 12.15 on the 30th July and re-open at the same hour at MAROEUIL.

12. **ACKNOWLEDGE.**

H. Sayer
Captain,
Brigade Major, 156th Inf. Brigade.

Issued at _____

2.

TRAIN WAGONS. 10. Supply and Baggage Wagons of the Train will report at Units' Transport Lines at 6 p.m. on 21st instant and will remain there during the night of 21/22nd.

STORES. 11. The following trench stores will be carried by units, and will not be handed over:-
(a) Yukon packs.
(b) Anti-Gas Combination clothing.

MEDICAL ARRANGEMENTS. 12. Two ambulance wagons will call at Battalion Camps by 6 a.m. on 22-7-18 for hospital cases.
One ambulance wagon will report to each Battalion Camp 30 minutes before Battalion moves on 22-7-18 to accompany Units on march.

REPORTING ARRIVAL 13. Units will report arrival to Bde. H.Q. immediately after they reach new area.

Brigade H.Q. 14. Bde. H.Q. will close at WHITE HOUSE, MONT ST ELOI, at 2.30 p.m. on the 22nd instant and open at the same hour at BARLIN.

15. ACKNOWLEDGE.

H. Sayer
Captain,
Brigade Major, 155th Inf. Bde.

Issued at _____

```
Copy No.  1 to 4th Royal Scots.
          2    7th Royal Scots.
          3    7th Camercnians (Sco. Rifles)
          4    155th T.M. Batty.
          5    52nd Division "G".
          6    52nd Division "Q".
          7    412th Field Coy R.E.
          8    "B" Coy 52nd M.G. Battn.
          9    1st Low., Field Ambulance.
         10    52nd M.G. Battalion.
         11    52nd E.P. Coy.
         12    52nd Divisional Train.
         13    S.O.C.
         14    Brigade Major
         15    Staff Captain
         16    Intelligence Officer.
         17    Signals
         18    R.T.O.
         19    Bde. S.O.
      20 & 21  War Diary.
         22    File.
```

a.

```
Copy No.  1 to  4th Royal Scots.
          2      7th Royal Scots.
          3      7th Sco. Rifles.
          4      155th T.M. Battery.
          5      412th Field Coy R.E.
          6      1/1st Low. Field Amb.
          7      "B" Coy 52nd M.G. Battn.
          8      219th Coy A.S.C.
          9      52nd Division.
         10      B.G.C.
         11      Brigade Major.
         12      Staff Captain
         13      Intelligence Officer.
         14      Signals
         15      B.T.O.
         16      Bde. Supply Officer.
      17 & 18    War Diary.
         19      File.
```

War Diary July Appendix XI

SECRET.

156th. Infantry Brigade Order No. 47   Copy No. 20

Ref. Map MARŒUIL - 1/20,000   30th. July 1918.

1. **Relief by 52nd. Division.** In continuation of 156th. Infantry Brigade Order No. 46 of yesterday, 52nd. Division is relieving a portion of the 4th. Canadian Division from TOWEY ALLEY inclusive to WESTERN ROAD on 31st. July and succeeding days.

2. **156th. Infantry Brigade Relief.** 156th. Infantry Brigade will relieve 11th. Canadian Infantry Brigade on July 31st. in accordance with attached table marked "A". Units will as far as possible take over present dispositions of the various units they relieve.

3. **Advance parties** as under will assemble at Brigade Headquarters at 8.45 a.m. on the 31st. inst. and proceed by motor lorry to the units which they are relieving. They will be met by guides on the scale of two per battalion at ROCLINCOURT Cross Roads.
   Composition of advance parties per battalion:-
   One officer per Coy.
   One N.C.O. per platoon
   Intelligence officer and four scouts
   Signalling officer
   Gas N.C.O.

4. **Guides.** Guides as set out below will meet relieving units at ROCLINCOURT at following times:-
   4th. Royal Scots ... 1.30 p.m.
   156th. L.T.M.Batty.)
   7th. Sco. Rifles   ) 2.45 p.m.
   7th. Royal Scots ... 4.30 p.m.

   2 per Battalion H.Q.
   1 per Coy. H.Q.
   1 per platoon
   2 for L.T.M. Battery

5. **Safety precautions.** During the whole of the relief distances of 500 yards between platoons or corresponding units will be maintained.
   All movement East of the BROWN LINE will be by trenches.

6. **Action in case of attack.** In the event of an attack taking place during the relief units will man the nearest defences and report to the H.Q. of the unit they are relieving, giving their location. They will also send an officer with the above information to Brigade H.Q.

7. **Details of Relief.** All other details of relief will be arranged between unit Commanders concerned.

8. **Handing over.** All maps, aeroplane photographs, schemes, log books, tables of work, trench stores etc will be taken over.

9. Command of Battalion Sections will pass to O.C. relieving Battalion on completion of each relief and of the Bde. Sector to G.O.C. 156th. Infantry Brigade on completion of all infantry reliefs.

10. **Reporting completion of relief.** Completion of reliefs will be reported to Bde. H.Q. by the following code word "FORTNUM"

11. Brigade /

- 2 -

11. <u>Brigade H.Q.</u> will close at the Chateau, ECOIVRES, at 7 p.m. on the 31st. and re-open at the same hour at B.20.b.2.6

12. ACKNOWLEDGE.

J. Sayer
Captain,
Brigade Major, 156th. Inf. Bde.

Issued at 11.30 p.m.

```
Copy No  1 to 4th. Royal Scots
         2    7th. Royal Scots
         3    7th. Sco. Rifles
         4    156th. L.T.M.Batty.
         5    11th. Canadian Inf. Bde.
         6    187th. Inf. Bde.
         7    412 Field Co. R.E.
         8    1/1st. Low. Field Amb.
         9    "B" Coy. 22nd. M.G. Bn.
        10    52nd. Division
        11    4th. Canadian Division
        12    219th. Coy. A.S.C.
        13    B.G.C.
        14    Brigade Major
        15    Staff Captain
        16    Intelligence Officer
        17    Signals
        18    Bde. Transport Officer
        19    Bde. Supply Officer
    20 & 21   War Diary
        22    File
```

MARCH TABLE

(Issued with 155th Inf. Brigade Order No. 46 of 29/7/18.)

Serial No.	"A" Units in order of March.	"B" STARTING POINT. PLACE	"C" TIME.	"D" ROUTE	"E" DESTINATION	"F" REMARKS.
1.	4th Royal Scots } Brigade H.Q.(a) }	Road Junction at Q.14.b.2.6.	8 a.m.	VEDREL - FRESNICOURT - Road Junction P.30.4.8.4. - LES 4 VENTS GAMBLAIN LABBE - MONT ST ELOY	HAROEUIL.	(a) To march in rear of 4th Royal Scots. (b) To march in rear of 7th Cameronians
2.	7th Royal Scots	As for Serial 1	8.30 a.m.			
3.	7th Cameronians } 155th T.M. Bty.(b)	As for Serial 1	9 a.m.			
4.	"B" Coy 52nd M.G. Battalion	Railway Bridge in Q.8.4.0.	9.5 a.m.	Road Junction at Q.14.b.3.6. and thence as for Serials 1, 2 & 3.		
5.	412th Fd. Coy R.E.	As for Serial 4	9.35 a.m.			
6.	1/1st Lon. Field Ambulance	As for Serial 4	10.5 a.m.			
7.	219th Coy A.S.C.	To be arranged by O.C. 219th Coy A.S.C.				

TABLE "A"

(Issued with 156th. Infantry Brigade Order No. 47 of 30/7/18)

(A) Serial No.	(B) UNIT	(C) Unit to be relieved.	Starting Point Place (D)	Time (E)	(F) Route.	(G) Remarks.
1.	7th. Cameronians	54th. Canadian Inf. Battalion (Right front line)	Head of embussing Point. 500 yards West of Cross Roads, F.15.a.0.6	2.15 p.m.	Cross Roads at A.8.a.5.7 - LHWS- ARRAS Road as far as MAGASCAR CORNER (A.25.d.3.3) - BOURIN.	By Bus to ROCLINCOURT. Debussing point Cross Roads ROCLINCOURT.
2	156th. L.T.M.Batt	11th. Canadian L.T.M. Batt. No. 1	as for serial No. 1	2.15 p.m.		By bus to ROCLINCOURT. Will use last 3 buses of the column. Debussing point as for serial No. 1
3	7th. Royal Scots	102nd. Canadian Inf. Bn. No. 1 (Left front line)	as for serial No. 1	4 p.m.		By bus to ROCLINCOURT. Debussing point as for serial No. 1.
4.	4th. Royal Scots	87th. Canadian Inf. Bn. (Support line)	Canadian Cross Roads - F.15.a.0.3	10 a.m.		By march route. Usual intervals will be maintained Rine of march until ROCLINCOURT after which 500 yards distance will be maintained between platoons. If a halt is made for a mid-day meal the Battalion must be concentrated in G.2 or G.3.a and C.

All Battalions will use DUSE ALLEY when approaching the BROWN LINE or trenches beyond.

Appendix XII

SECRET.

155th. Infantry Brigade Order No. 48   Copy No. 17

Ref. Map MAROUIL. - 1/20,000.   31st. July 1918.

1. On 1st. August 1918 the Northern Brigade Boundary will be altered to the following line:- B.29.a.0.7 - B.23.a.0.8 - B.21.b.0.0 - B.22.d.0.8 - B.22.c.9.8 - B.21.central - along North side of Sunken Road to B.20.d.0.8 - along North side of GULL LANE (inclusive to 155th. Infantry Brigade).

2. The troops between the above mentioned line and the Northern Brigade Boundary as constituted on the night 31st.July/ 1st. August will be relieved as follows:-
    (a) 7th. Royal Scots by 6th. H.L.I. in the front line and POST LINE.
    (b) 4th. Royal Scots by 8th. H.L.I. in the BROWN LINE.
All details of the relief will be arranged between the Battalion Commanders concerned.

3. The Stokes Gun situated at B.10.c.5.8 will be relieved by the 157th. L.T.M. Battery but the Gun situated at B.22.a.7.2 will continue to be manned by 155th. L.T.M.Battery and will maintain its present arc of fire.
Details of relief to be settled between Commanders concerned.

4. 7th. Royal Scots will hand over their present H.Q. to 6th. H.L.I. and will establish new H.Q. at those now occupied by L.T.M. Battery at B.29.d.0.8. O.C. 155th. L.T.M.Battery will reconnoitre a new H.Q. and will report its position to Bde. H.Q. as soon as possible.

5. At 6 p.m. on the 1st. August the Inter-Battalion Boundary as at present constituted will be altered to the following line:- B.29.a.0.5 - B.23.b.4.8 - Junction of FERN ALLEY and POST SUPPORT TRENCH (B.23.c.1.8) - along Southern side of FERN ALLEY to its junction with BROWN LINE (B.17.d.4.9).
O.C. 7th. Scot. Rifles and 7th. Royal Scots will arrange to make the necessary adjustments by the above mentioned hour.

6. Completion of reliefs will be wired to Bde. H.Q. by the following code words:-
    (a) Relief of 7th. R.S. by 6th. H.L.I. "BATTLE"
    (b) Relief of 4th. R.S. by 8th. H.L.I. "GO"
    (c) Relief of 7th. C.R. by 7th. R.S. "PUSH"

7. ACKNOWLEDGE.

H. Sayer
Captain,
Brigade Major, 155th. Inf. Bde.

Issued at _____

Copy No. 1 to 4th. Royal Scots   Copy No. 10 to R.S.O.
        2   7th. Royal Scots   11   D.M.
        3   7th. Sco. Rifles   12   S.O.
        4   155th. L.T.M.Batt.   13   M.O.
        5   157th. Inf. Bde.   14   Signals
        6   52nd. Division   15   S.T.O.
        7   4th. Canadian Division   16   Bde. H.Q.
        8   "B" Coy. 52nd. M.G. Bn.   17 & 18   War Diary
        9   412 Field Coy. R.E.   19   File.

War Diary Appendix XIII
156th Infantry Brigade

Casualties - July, 1918

Unit	Killed		Wounded		Missing	
	O.	OR	O.	OR	O.	OR
156 Inf Bde HQ	-	-	-	-	-	-
4 Royal Scots	-	-	-	8	-	-
7 Royal Scots	-	-	1	7	-	-
7 Sco Rifles	-	-	-	4	-	-
156 L.T.M. Bty	-	-	-	-	-	-
	-	-	1	19	-	-

War Diary Appendix XIV   156th Infantry Brigade

Strength - July 1918

Unit	Week Ending 6th		Week Ending 13th		Week Ending 20th		Week Ending 27th	
	O	OR	O	OR	O	OR	O	OR
4 Royal Scots	47	883	48	934	46	971	46	984
7 Royal Scots	44	900	44	944	44	927	45	940
7 Sco. Rifles	45	895	45	905	44	924	44	979
	136	2678	137	2783	134	2822	135	2903

On His Majesty's Service.

No. 42.

CONFIDENTIAL.

Officer i/c
A.G's Office,
At the Base.

War Diary,
A.D.P.S., Canadian Forces,
August 1st - 31st 1918.

POST OFFICE.

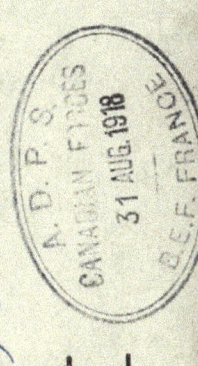
A.D.P.S.
CANADIAN FORCES
31 AUG. 1918
B.E.F. FRANCE

HQ 156 Supply Btn
VA
Apl '18

Original

Confidential

War Diary
of
156th Infantry Brigade
1st to 31st August 1918

Volume XXXIX

156th Infantry Brigade

WAR DIARY or INTELLIGENCE SUMMARY

Army Form C. 2118.

August 1918. Vol XXIX

Place	Date 1918 Augt	Hour	Summary of Events and Information	Remarks and references to Appendices
B.20.6.2.6. MARŒUIL	1st	12ⁿ	Reliefs carried out as ordered in Brigade Order No 48 (See July War Diary). B.G.C. visited the Battalion H.Q.s and the BLACK LINE and arranged the dispositions with the Commanding Officers.	
	2nd		Dry and very warm day. Visibility improved in afternoon. Major General J.Stelle. G.O.C. 52nd Div. visited Bde H.Q.	
			Misty and rainy day. Visibility poor. RFA will phone Bde learn order received that 56th Bde and 9th Bde both the Bde. 56th Bde will be – Battn. learn with 157Bde. 9 with Bde with Right Battalion.	
			It is important that enemy should not obtain identifications at this junction. Patrols will therefore be of a purely defensive nature. Use of phone in advance of Battn H.Q. is forbidden except in case of emergency.	
	3rd		B.G.C. & S.B.M. visited the line. Reconn. still held around a portion of the line. Capt Kinnoch reported from leave to U.K. Visibility good. Warm sunny day. Orders issued that every opportunity should be taken to study No man's LAND for day O.P.s established in front of our lines. Very necessary owing to patrols being purely defensive when around a part of the line	
	4th		B.G.C. and Capt Kinnoch	

War Diary / Intelligence Summary

157th Infantry Brigade

August 1918 — Vol XXIX — Page 2

Army Form C. 2118.

Place	Date	Hour	Summary of Events and Information	Remarks and references to Appendices
MARŒUIL 1/20 000-a R/Map				
B.20.6.26.	3rd Aug	4².⁴⁵	T/Captain J. R. Sadler, 1/7th Northumberland Fusiliers attached to this Bde for instruction in Staff Duties. Visibility quite good today. B/Aps + pleasant day. Recommended to Div that have Shag tobacco be continued. Upon his no further Orders issued to examine that all five bays are so built up that bottoms of wire front trench cannon can but fire to bear by direction of Dummy Boundary stakes. Laying down the direction of Dummy & added scare questions suggests that following questions be added:- "Are Tanks being used in this attack? If so, are they to follow the Platoon Commander? Should we ask humbly before an attack to take over objectives captured by them, or are they to join the infantry & help in the capture of Strong Points to the final consolidation 2) Army N.C.O's + men thoroughly understand the method of working with Tanks that is to be employed in this attack? 3) Do I and my men know the method of communication between Infantry and Tanks? Lt 1/H detailed operation of the line Lt TM By to prove daily from front line 30 men per Co to 2 hrs at Baths & ROCLINCOURT BATHS.	Visibility varied all day light ./. fully ./.

Army Form C. 2118.

156 Infantry Brigade

WAR DIARY
or
INTELLIGENCE SUMMARY.
(Erase heading not required.)

August 1918   Vol XXIX

Instructions regarding War Diaries and Intelligence Summaries are contained in F.S. Regs., Part II. and the Staff Manual respectively. Title pages will be prepared in manuscript.

Page 3

Place	Date 1918	Hour	Summary of Events and Information	Remarks and references to Appendices
B20.b.9.6	5th		MAROEUIL 1/20,000. Teams for Army Rifle Meeting given use of range for practice from today onwards.	
	6th		Bde Order No. 49 issued. Boundary alterations. B.G.C. & B.M. met O.C. 1/7 S.R. & 412 R.E. at STIRLING POST and arranged for POST to be turned into a Strong Point. Capt Kynoch proceeded to Division to understudy the Staff.	Appendix I
	7th		Dull day but visibility very good. Great deal of movement and a large number of trains observed. B.G.C. feels that additional harassing arrangements. Army Rifle meeting 9/8 Bde v 54 Bde. Bde Rifle teams (7th) moves as far Bde Order No. 49 completed. B.G.C. and B.M. visited 172nd Bde of the 57th Div. (Boisrionnay(?))	July
	8th		Dry day but visibility was low. Enemy registered a number of points in our front line suggesting raid. B.G.C. and B.M. went round the left subsection. Information received that qualifying period for officers leave had been reduced to 5 months. Dull day and visibility poor. B.G.C. spoke to units, Second-in-commands re their duties not left in the line. B.M. memo No. issued on same subject.	Appendix II

WAR DIARY
or
INTELLIGENCE SUMMARY.

Army Form C. 2118.

156th Infantry Brigade

August 1918

Vol XXIX

Ref Map MAROEUIL 1/20,000.

Page 4

Place	Date 1918 Augt	Hour	Summary of Events and Information	Remarks and references to Appendices
B.20.b.2.6	9th		B.G.C. and B.M. went round the right subsection. Lieut A. E. BIRD, M.C. 1/7th Cameronians (Sco Rif) reported for duty as A/Intelligence Officer. Bright day day of good visibility. Restrictions re patrols speaking on phone removed	JWH/6
	10th		B.G.C. and B.M. went round the Support Area Sections — turn line to be kept up to strength i.e. 1 N.C.O. + 6 men per Instruction and 2 N.C.O.s + 9 men per L.G. Section. If possible & country will be replaced by a man who really belongs to the Section but otherwise by temporarily attaching a man from another Section. B.M. 672 "Co. to attacks" issued. Appendix II Bright day day of good visibility. Capt S. Ballard Staff Captain proceeded on leave to U.K. Bde. Order No 50 issued "1st 4th R.S. to relieve 7th R.S."	JWH/7 Appendix III
	11th		Bright day day of good visibility B.M. attended a demonstration by a platoon of the 4th A.C. B.C. visited the Support Br. W.D. Doherty in course of construction with C.R.E.	JWH/8
	12th		Bright day very warm day of low visibility	

Army Form C. 2118.

151st Infantry Brigade

WAR DIARY or INTELLIGENCE SUMMARY.

August 1918   Vol XXIX

Ref Map   Page 5.

Place	Date	Hour	Summary of Events and Information	Remarks and references to Appendices
MAROEUIL B.20.c.26.15	13 Aug		B2C and B13 M visited a portion of the Line, handed over. Relief carried out by 151st Division received. Relief completed & Bde Op.Ord. No. 50 carried out. Bright day warm day. Inability to be issued Recommend that Dr Hall Gum Boots, thigh, for winter wear with the ankle boot, with wooden soles. B.S.C and A/B.M attended a demonstration by a platoon of the #A.C.	
	14		Last night purely defensive patrols were out and today instructions were sent out that no more active patrols would take place while the Bde remained in the Line. Orders were received this morning that the Bde would be relieved on 16/17th but these were cancelled about 4 p.m this evening & Bde will be relieved tomorrow 15th and night 15/16th Bde O/day No. 51 issued re relief. Lieut. Col Co dg 154=Of Bde (relieving Bde) his B.M a d his S.C visited these Head qrs this afternoon and arranged details of the relief	Appendix IV

Army Form C. 2118.

WAR DIARY or INTELLIGENCE SUMMARY.

(Erase heading not required.)

151st Infy Bde

August 1918 Vol XXIX

Place	Date 1918 Augt	Hour	Summary of Events and Information	Remarks and references to Appendices
B.20.b.6.	14th		MARDEUIL 1/20,000. R/Map. Page 6. Was reviewed & award of Legion of Honour + Croix de Guerre to Lieut Colonel D.M. Bradley D.S.O. Comdg 1/5th Bn The Cameronians (Scot Rif) the 8th the 13th left in at 2.5pm Guide from 34th Divn. Appendix V	KWH/k
	15th		Bright warm day of fair visibility. Brigade Order No. 52 issued re move to new area. Great difficulty was experienced in making any arrangements owing the lack of orders from higher authority to the fact that train programmes had to be frequently changed = Order 20pm. but the priority the return was completed at 9pm. Information did not reach there till 12 midnight. Brightest warm day of low visibility.	
	16th		The move was completed about 4 a.m. Times delayed considerably owing to shelling and gas shelling. Still the shell in the line was a very quiet one. The shelling and unsatisfactory over the forenoon turning however and to the ensuing of patrolling. changes in how clears and to the restrictions of patrolling. No enemy patrols were even seen. His attitude was a purely defensive one and it would appear that he was awaiting a British attack. No identifications were	KWH/k

WAR DIARY or **INTELLIGENCE SUMMARY**

Army Form C. 2118.

156th A/Bde

August 1918 Vol XXXV

Ref map 1/40,000 Page 7

Place	Date	Hour	Summary of Events and Information	Remarks and references to Appendices
CHATEAU BERLES D.14.b.5.7	1918 Aug 16th		44 B and 51st C obtained or lost. He had a nasty habit of putting down barrages with gas with HE on our lines and our batteries and carrying out little area shoots but a deamon was made by us to wave all feeling between infantry and artillery by immediate retaliation to his strong barrages and by crooks on his W.Q. He known with the Canadian Weavers was apla did on & they carried out quite a number of shoots for us & landing over the 154th Def Bde they were advanced to have OPPY WOOD burned up with H.S. incendiary shells sent to the Bocher habit of using Batteries as observation posts. Owing to a raid one night on the front of the Bde on our right a barrage (S.O.S.) costing £33,000 was put down in front of our lines & on the enemy's lines and communications Lessons learnt (1) Vital necessity of good signal and runner communications (2) The value of negative reports. Intelligence Summaries attached B.G.C & O.B.M. visited the units "blld5". Appendix VI. The day was spent by the units in cleaning washing up and resting	Hwlf Lt Hwlf

Army Form C. 2118.

WAR DIARY
or
INTELLIGENCE SUMMARY.
(Erase heading not required.)

156th Inf Bde

Ref Maps 1/40,000   1/44 B and 51.C

August 1918.   Vol XXXIX   Page 8.

Place	Date 1918	Hour	Summary of Events and Information	Remarks and references to Appendices
CHATEAU BERLES D.14.6.5.7.	16th		Bright warm day. B.G.C. attended a conference at Divisional Headquarters and afterwards proceeded to reconnoitre and B.M. reconnoitred the training areas.	
	17th		Dull day. The 52nd Division is now under XVII Corps but is in G.H.Q. reserve at 24 hours notice to move. More will probably be by strategical train. Div will very likely have to go into action immediately on its arrival at its destination. Plans to be cut & dried & preparation made to reduce kits to a minimum. (A Divisional store for surplus kit will shortly be formed (Stores from B.M. 717) B.G.C. B.M. & A/M/S.C made a reconnaissance accompanied by the three battalion commanders.	
	18th		Fine bright day. Mules started to arrive. St. John Skills sent to dump.	
	19th		A/S/C attended a conference of Staff Captains at Div HQ and B.M. visited D.H.Q. B.G.C. B.M. and A/S.C made a reconnaissance once. Dull dry day with bright intervals.	
	20th		Dull day but very warm day. About 11am the Bde was warned that it would probably have to move a few miles South during the night.	

A7023. Wt. W12859/M1297 750,000. 1/17. D. D & L., Ltd. Forms/C2118/14.

Army Form C. 2118.

WAR DIARY
or
INTELLIGENCE SUMMARY.

(Erase heading not required.)

156th Inf. Bde.

R. Myles 1/40,000   August 1918   Vol XXXIX

                                                  Page 9

Place	Date	Hour	Summary of Events and Information	Remarks and references to Appendices
CHATEAU BERLES AU BOIS	20th Aug		4th Bn. & 51st C. Bde moved off about 11.30 p.m. and marched to BERNEVILLE. As the men had already done a full day's training they found the march a very stiff one. The night was also an exceptionally close one.	
BERNEVILLE	21st		Passed 4th R.S. and 1/7th Bty BERNEVILLE & 4th R.S. WAN QUETIN Y & S R WARLUS	Jul 4/9
	22nd		Exceptionally warm day. Brigade rested. Exceptionally warm day. At 9 A.M. B.& C. and A.S.C. proceeded by motor bus and attended a Divisional Conference at BLAIRVILLE QUARRIES at same time all C.O.'s and Coy Cdrs and 1 other officer per Coy together with A/B.M. and (Bde I.O.) proceeded by motor bus and attended a Bde Conference at BLAIRVILLE QUARRIES. 7/B.G.C. and three other officers after the meet of the day undertook a reconnaissance. Meanwhile the remainder of the Bde was proceeding by road up to and under Bus and BRETENCOURT and BLAIRVILLE to take up its place in M.33.d (51B S.W.) Strunk with the greatest difficulty owing to congestion on roads and lack of bivouacs that the 11th Bde managed to get up for up to the bye before the barrage came down at 4.55. a.m. Bde attached arrived and Fd Arty SPINNEY AVENUE T.1.b.4.d HENIN TRENCH T.1.a & N.31.c and road M.3.6.a & d	Jul 4/9
BLAIRVILLE QUARRIES	23rd			

Army Form C2118.

Army Form C. 2118.

WAR DIARY
or
INTELLIGENCE SUMMARY.

(Erase heading not required.)

155th Lf Bde

Army 1918 Page 10.

Place	Date 1918 Augt	Hour	Summary of Events and Information	Remarks and references to Appendices
BLAIRVILLE QUARRIES	23rd		Advanced Bde HQ S.4.A.3.4. Very warm day.	
	24th	7am	Bde attacked captured and held the road N.26 a b c d	
			west part N.33 c	
			Advanced at Boisleux S.5.b.6.8. Bright dry day	
	25th		Consolidating and patrolling. Bright dry day	
T.1 & 1.5.	26th		Bde concentrated in the afternoon and eventually moved	
			to N.21 a & N.27. Rain morning but bright + dry afterwards	
N.34a. & 6. 27th		10a	Bde attacked captured and held line — U.2 d and U.3 a	
N.36.d.6.8. 28th			Bde relieved by Canadians + early morning and moved	
S.5 6 6 8			back to open ground in N.35 and 36 and S.5 a & 6. dry day	
			very open weather. Bright dry day. Capt Allen returned from leave.	
	29th		Bde resting + re-organising. Bright dry day. Capt Sadler proceeded on leave.	
	30th		Bde resting + re-organising. Bright dry day.	
			B.B.C. attacked entrance at D.H.Q.	
	31st		Bde relieved 167th Lf Bde in support of the Battle Line	
			running through BULLECOURT — See Order No 53 issued	App. VII
			Dry cold day	

WAR DIARY or INTELLIGENCE SUMMARY

Army Form C. 2118.

Vol XXXIX

156th Inf Bde — August 1918 — Page 11

Place	Date	Hour	Summary of Events and Information	Remarks and references to Appendices
			Report on Operations 20/28th August 1918.	Appendix VIII
			Effective Strength	Appendix IX
			"Casualties"	Appendix X

A. Hope, Captain,
Brigade Major, 156th Inf Bde.

SECRET

OPERATION ORDER No 1.   Copy No _____
****
156th Infantry Brigade.
****

22nd August 1918.

1.   The 156th Inf. Bde. in conjunction with the 56th Division on its right will tomorrow, 23rd instant, attack the enemy's trench line (S. to N.)

   (a) BOIRY TRENCH up to and inclusive of Pt. T.1.d.5.0. on COJEUL RIVER.
       All to 56th Division.

   (b) BOIRY TRENCH at T.1.d.5.0. - SPINNEY AVENUE - HENIN TRENCH as far as N.31.c.4.3. - DOG SAP - Pt. M.36.b.5.8. in MYRTLE TRENCH.
       All to 156th Inf. Bde.

2.   Zero hour for attack, 4.55 a.m.

3.   The 156th Inf. Bde. will be deployed for attack not later than 4.30 a.m. on a taped line running (S. to N.) S.6.c.3.0. - S.6.a.3.3. - M.36.c.5.4. - M.36.a.5.7.

4.   The deployment on the above line will be covered by existing posts held by 49th Division E. of that line, but at Zero minus 15 min. these posts will be withdrawn slightly nearer our line of deployment, resuming their original positions after our attack has developed.

5.   The 156th Inf. Bde. will be deployed for attack as follows:-
   (a). Right Attack. 4th Royal Scots.
           From S.6.c.3.0. - S.6.a.3.3. (road exclusive)
       Final objective 4th Royal Scots
           From T.1.d.5.0. along SPINNEY AVENUE to junction of that avenue with MARTIN TRENCH exclusive.

   (b) Centre Attack. 7th Royal Scots.
           From S.6.a.3.3. (road inclusive) to M.36.c.5.4.
       Final Objective 7th Royal Scots.
           From junction of SPINNEY AVENUE and MARTIN TRENCH (inclusive) along HENIN TRENCH up to and inclusive of N.31.c.3.3.

   (c). Left Attack. 7th S. Rifles.
           From M.36.c.5.4. up M.36.a.5.7.
       Final objective 7th Sco. Rifles
           From N.31.c.3.3. (exclusive) along sunken road to DOG SAP - M.36.b.5.8. in MYRTLE TRENCH, from whence their left will be refused along sunken road for 200 yards.

6.   Tanks.
   (a). A group of three tanks will operate with each Battalion and by 1 a.m. 23rd instant will be formed up just E. of the Sunken Road running through M.35.c. and S.5.a. and c.
       At Zero hour (4.55 a.m., 23rd) all tanks will make forward towards and through the infantry line of deployment, which they must have reached by Zero plus 12 minutes at latest, and follow the artillery barrage as closely as possible.
       Certain enemy posts which tanks will give special attention to and destroy have been pointed out to Tank Coy Commander.

   (b). After reaching the line of final infantry objectives as mentioned in para 5 (a), (b) and (c), Tanks will push on beyond that line supported by one Company of each Battalion to exploit the area East of final objective, for a distance of roughly 400 yards, but they will withdraw from the exploitation area after 30 mins. from time final objectives were reached, and return home

7/

7. The attack of the 156th Inf. Bde will be supported by the fire of 6 artillery Brigades R.F.A. and heavy guns.

The artillery barrage will come down at 4.55 a.m. precisely on a line approximately 300 yards E. of the infantry line of deployment; the barrage will remain on its opening barrage line for 12 mins and then lift forward by bounds of 200 yards to and beyond final objectives.

Smoke shells in proportion of one smoke to 6 shrapnel will be used in this creeping barrage.

8. The rate of advance of Battalions of 156th Inf. Bde. will vary.
RIGHT ATTACK 100 yards every 4 mins. to conform to rate of advance of left Battalion of 56th Div. (London Scottish Battn)
CENTRE ATTACK. 100 yards every three minutes.
LEFT ATTACK. 100 yards every two minutes.

9. The 412th Field Coy will detail two Sections of 1 N.C.O. and 6 men each to accompany the centre attack and assist O.C. 7th Royal Scots in establishing two blocks in HENIN TRENCH, N.31.c.3.4. and MARTIN TRENCH, T.1.b.1.5.

10. Each Battalion will, on attaining its final objective, exploit its own front in conjunction with tanks for a distance of approximately 500 yards. This will be done in each case by the second Company waves of each Battalion. They will closely support the Tanks and clear all pockets and dug-outs of the Bosche before withdrawing.

If severe opposition is encountered, exploiting Companies and tanks will not persist, and in any case will withdraw behind the line of final objectives after 30 mins from the time of first occupation of the same.

11. Machine Gun Companies. 16 guns, 177th Inf. Brigade will employ barrage and harassing fire from fixed points from ZERO to Zero plus 15 min Targets have already been indicated which it is specially desirable to deal with. 16 guns 52nd Div. M.G. Bn. have separate orders already issued, by which 12 guns go forward and take up positions 450 yards west of final objectives and 4 guns remain in reserve about M.36.c.9.3.

12. Os.C. Battalions will detail one Battn. Scout to each tank to act as infantry observer.

13. Aeroplane flares will be lit by our most advanced line at Zero plus 1 hour, and again at Zero plus 3 hours when they will be called for by contact aeroplanes.

Flares must be lit at these times.

14. Consolidation must be taken in hand as soon as final objectives are attained. 52nd Div. Pioneer Battn. are detailing one Coy to improve old trench connecting SUMP and HENIN TRENCHES, and 1 Coy to bury cable forward.

Picks and shovels in proportion of 2 shovels to 1 pick will be drawn from tool dump established at M.33.c.7.4. by Battns. prior to moving forward to line of deployment. Every man to have one heavy entrenching tool.

15. Battalion Commanders will take steps to ensure that there is no overcrowding in any captured trenches, and particularly on the final objective line, which should be thinly held.

Battalions must be distributed in great depth.

All ranks will be warned to expect the Germans to retaliate largely with gas, and to be prepared for it, and to take special precautions to meet it after the sun rises.

16. Each man will carry two grenades (No 23) 220 rounds of S.A.A. and one aeroplane flare. Each Section Commander will carry one S.O.S. rocket.

17./

17. Administrative arrangements are being notified in a separate order to units.

18. Each man will clearly understand that he will go straight through without a halt to the objective assigned to his platoon or company. That all ground won is to be held at all costs, and that all Bosche encountered are to be killed without any hesitation. Prisoners are a nuisance, and are not wanted.

19. Advanced 156th Inf. Bde. H.Q. and report centre will from 3 a.m. 23rd instant, be established at present H.Q. 2/6th Durham L.I. at S.M.a.1.5.
 Main Brigade H.Q. will be at present H.Q. of 177th Inf. Bde. at R.34.d.central (quarry). All reports by telephone and runner to be to advanced 156th Inf. Bde H.Q.

20. ACKNOWLEDGE.

        (Sgd) A.LEGGETT,
         Brigadier General,
       Commanding 156th Inf. Brigade.

****

Issued by Special D.R. at 12.45 a.m. 23.8.18.

```
Copy No 1 to 52nd Div.
        2    168 Inf. Bde.
        3.   177 Inf Bde.
        4.   176 Inf. Bde.
        5    O.C. 1/7th Royal Scots.
        6         1/4th Royal Scots.
        7         1/7th Sco. Rifles.
        8    412th Field Coy R.E.
        9    O.C. Tank Coy
       10    P.C. Coy, 52nd Div. M.G. Bnz
       11    Right Group R.F.A.
       12    Left Group R.F.A.
       13    Staff Captain.
```

****

Casualties First Phase - 22nd to 28th August 1918.

Unit	Killed		Wounded.		Wounded (Gas)		Wounded at duty		Missing		Total	
	O.	O.R.	O.	O.R.	O.	O.R.	O.	O.R.	O.	O.R.	O.	O.R.
4th Royal Scots	-	27	2	110	3	98	1	4	-	10	6	249
7th Royal Scots	1	16	5	80	2	251	-	-	-	1	8	348
7th Sco. Rifles	-	10	2	86	-	42	1	3	-	-	3	141
TOTAL	1	53	9	276	5	391	2	7	-	11	17	738

NAMES OF OFFICER CASUALTIES.

4th Royal Scots.

Wounded.
    Lieut. G. GARDNER, ... 4th Royal Scots
    Lieut. J. HALLEY, ... 8th Royal Scots.

Wounded (Gas)
    Capt. W.M. CARMICHAEL,. 4th Royal Scots.
    2/Lt. A.W. BANNERMAN... 4th Royal Scots.
    2/Lt. J.S. MARSLAND ... 4th Royal Scots.

Wounded (at duty).
    2/Lt. A.E. ABBOTT, ... 4th Royal Scots.

7th Royal Scots.

Killed.
    Captain K. MACKENZIE,.. 9th Royal Scots.

Wounded.
    Lieut. T. McLAUCHLAN, M.C. 7th Royal Scots.
    Lieut. S.J. SPENCE. M.C., 9th Royal Scots.
    Lieut. J. McNAB, ... 6th Royal Scots.
    Lieut J.C. McCULLOCH... 9th Royal Scots.
    2/Lt. J.S. WEIR, ... H.L.I.

Wounded (Gas)
    Lieut. C.A. COLE, ... 4th Yorks.
    2/Lt. D. McLENNAN. ... 4th Royal Scots.

7th Scottish Rifles.

Wounded.
    2/Lieut. F.J. DEACON... 7th Sco. Rifles.
    2/Lt. R. GLASS, ... 7th Sco. Rifles.

Wounded (at duty).
    Lieut. W.M.D. ANDERSON. 7th Sco. Rifles.

PRISONERS CAPTURED 1st PHASE 22/28th August 1918.

UNIT.	OFFICERS	OTHER RANKS.
4th Royal Scots	4	440
7th Royal Scots	3	250
7th Sco. Rifles	3	41
TOTAL	10	731

WAR MATERIAL CAPTURED FIRST PHASE 22/28th August 1918.

4th Royal Scots.

```
Machine Guns      ...    ...   40
Guns.
      5.9         ...    ...    1
      77 mm       ...    ...    2
      Field       ...    ...    2
      Anti-tank   ...    ...    3
      Minenwerfer ...    ...    4
      Trench Mortars     ...    2
Quantity M.G. & 77 mm Ammunition.
```

7th Royal Scots.

```
Machine Guns      ...    ...   23
Guns.
      Field       ...    ...    2
      Minenwerfers       ...    3
Anti-tank Rifles         ...    2
   -do-   Ammunition, rds,      6
Telephones        ...    ...    1
Signalling Lamp, Electric       1
Range Finders     ...    ...    1
Large quantity Rifles, S.A.A.
```

7th Sco. Rifles.

```
Machine Guns      ...    ...   16
Guns.
      Anti-tank   ...    ...    1
      Trench Mortars     ...   10
M.G. Ammunition...    boxes    11
M.G. Ammunition...    Belts    70
Aerial torpedoes...   Boxes    15
Rifles      ...   ...   ...   400
Bombs, 2000 approx.   ...   2000 approx.
Shells      ...   ...   ...   168
Stock Grenades ...    Boxes    16
Ball Grenades  ...    Boxes    13
Bombs       ...   ...   Boxes  40
Pineapple Minenwerfers         52
```

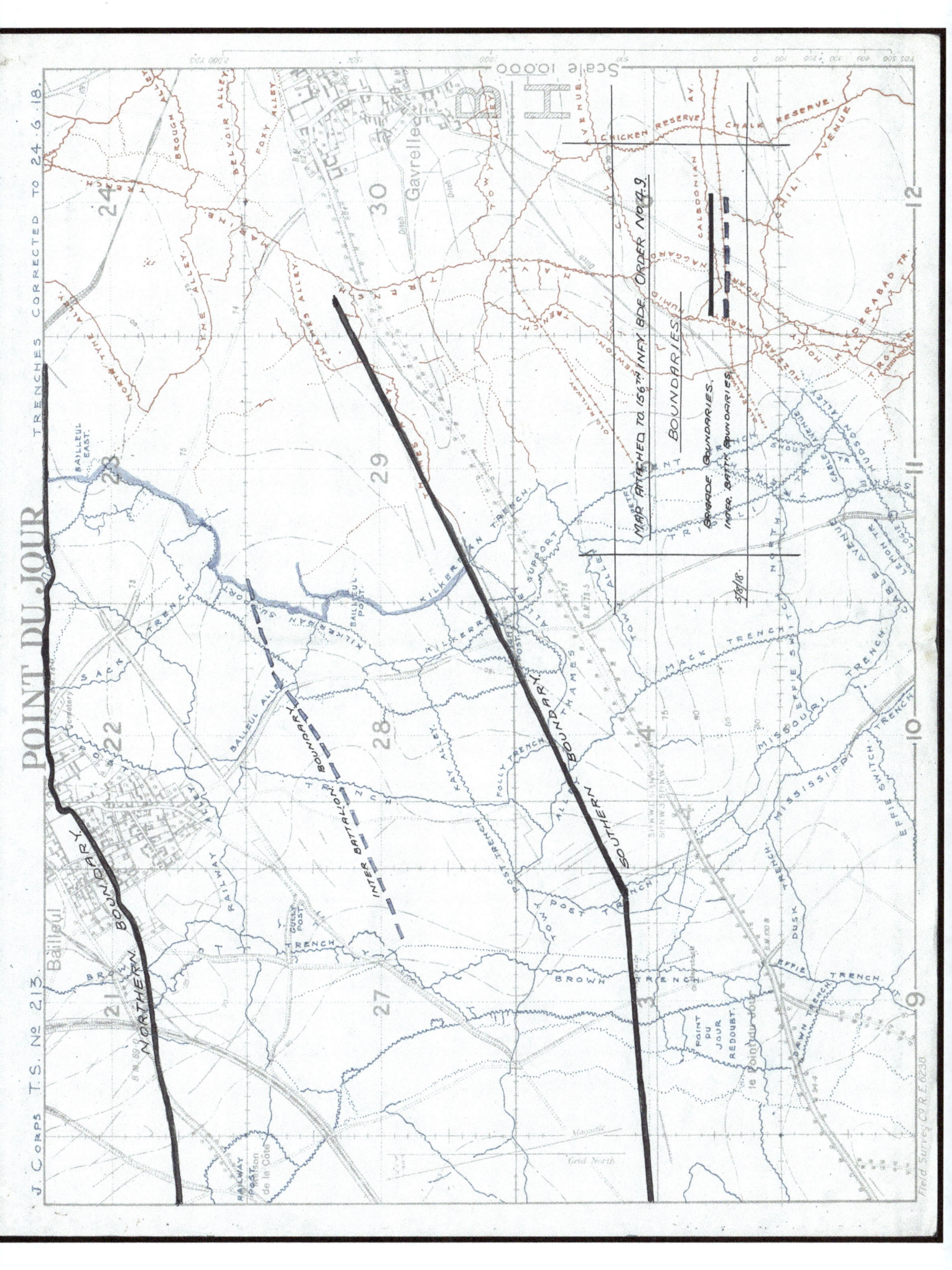

War Diary
August 1918
Appendix I

War Diary Appendix

GAVRELLE SECTION
INTELLIGENCE SUMMARY No 6
(From 6am 5/8/18 To 6am 6/8/18)

REF MAP Foothill 1/20,000 3rd Ed.   6th August 1918

I OUR ACTIVITY
  (a) OPERATIONS
        Usual forward night positions established
by Right Sub-section.
        Left sub-section defensive patrols to B.23.b
15.05, and B.29.a. 70.80. From 10.30 pm to
2.45 am
        Nothing to report. —

  (b) ARTILLERY
        During the day, various calibres were very
active on ENEMY front & support systems rah
B.24.b, B.30.a central, C.19.a & C.31.a.
        4.5 Hows. shelled Sunken Road at C.7
central, C.15.a & FRESNES.
        Distant back areas were also shelled.
        Field Guns put over some shrapnel on
C.31.d, B.24.b, C.14.c & C.31.a.H.8
        U.27.c. OPPY, B.24.a, I.1.c, I.2.c & GAVRELLE
also received a good deal of attention.
        Harassing fire was actively kept up on
GAVRELLE/

2.   6th August 1918

I. OUR ACTIVITY (contd.)
  (b) ARTILLERY (contd.)
    GAVRELLE & trenches in front till 1.30 AM, salvoes at
    10 minute intervals on same points from 1.30 am to
    3.30 AM. Back areas were also shelled
    during the night.

  (c) AERIAL
          Apart from 1 plane at 4.15 pm flying
    low & machine gunning ENEMY trenches, there
    has been no activity today.

II. HOSTILE ACTIVITY
  (a) OPERATIONS

                  NIL

  (b) ARTILLERY

Time	Rounds	Calibre	Target
9. AM	7 rds	H.2	B.27.c, and
	5.9; registered front line at B.29.c		
9.15	20 rds	H.2	KAY ALLEY B.28.c.9.5.
	10 rds	5.9	B.22.d.
9.35	70 rds	77 mm	B.19, B.31.a & B.32.a.
11.15	10 rds	77 mm	H.11.b.5.5.
	40 rds	77 mm	H.6.d, H.7.d, & H.9.b.
11.15 to 12 noon	42 rds	H.2	H.7.d, H.8.b & H.9.b.

3.   6th August 1918

II. HOSTILE ACTIVITY (contd)
    (b) ARTILLERY (contd)

Time	Rounds	Type	Location
12.10 PM	1 rd.	77 mm	B.21a.77.
12.30 "	15 rds.	do	BAILLEUL
	50 rds.	5.9	Distributed fire on B.21a.68 & B.15a. OUSE TUNNEL & OUSE Comm. Trench W. of Tunnel
2.35 "	26 rds.	H.2.	B.21a. H.9
2.35 to 4.30 "	40 rds.	5.9 (sens fuze)	B.26b (Rly cutting) & area at H.2.
3.15 "	25 rds.	H.2.	BROWN LINE (B.21d.4.7) 2 bays damaged
	4 rds.	Blue Cross Gas	on B.20d.
4.10 "	4 rds.	77 mm	RAILWAY POST area
4.15 "	12 rds.	H.2.	OUSE ALLEY B.16d.
5.45 "	15 rds.	77 mm	B.23d.
	2 rds.	5.9	H.2.c
6.15 "	5 rds.	H.2.	B.17c.4.5
	6 rds.	Heavy Shrapnel	ROAD B.20.
6.30	25 rds.	H.2.	EMBANKMENT B.21a.10
9.40-10.20 "	26 rds.	H.2	TONY ALLEY H.4a.
10.50-11.15	15 rds.	H.2	close behind KILKERRAN SUPPORT
1.20 AM	40 rds.	H.2 & 5.9	H.3.c.
3.0 AM	21 rds.	H.2	H.5a.

Gas shells were put over the vicinity of H.3, H.12.d, B.26, & H.5.c during the night.

(c) TRENCH MORTARS

| 9. AM | Registered front line - B.29c. - 5 rounds. |

4   6th August 1918

II. HOSTILE ACTIVITY (contd)

  (d). MACHINE GUNS

      Usual bursts along front line at intervals during the night, and, at "Stand to".

  (e) WORK

9.40 to 10.5 AM — 6 men working on wire in front of trench from Road at C.36a.28 to C.36a.35

11.20 to 12 noon — Small working party (5) on FRESNES-ROUVROY LINE, C.27c central.

  (f) MOVEMENT

      There was much individual movement on FRESNES GAVRELLE ROAD, & in & around GAVRELLE generally. Much movement also centred around C.19 central, & a few ENEMY moved S. from NEUVIREUIL on Road in C.15 a & c. Slight movement on Road in C.13d.9.5 in N.W. direction, at intervals at C.31a.28; I.2.a.8.2 & C.15a.H.7

    TRENCHES — 2 men - B.31b.31 - 4 men C.31a.28 - 1 man C.31b - 2 men C.25a.8.4 - 2 men C.26d.5.3.

      Carrying party of 5 from MAUVILLE FARM C.16d to Trench C.23b.5.4. It would appear that carrying parties leave FARM for various trenches in the locality. At 6 am this morning party /

5.   6th August 1918

II. HOSTILE ACTIVITY (contd)
  (f) MOVEMENT (contd)
            party of 16 men (carrying picks & shovels)
            walking S. at C.19.c. disappeared behind ridge.
5.40-6 pm   A great deal of movement round Trenches from C.19.d.
            to C.25.b, and at C.21.a.2.8
6 AM   Horse limber on track at C.17.a, being loaded by 3
(6th)   men. moved towards FRESNES.
            3 parties of 6, carrying boxes from C.21.c.4.9 to C.20.a.3.0
            (box was carried by 2 men, suggesting S.A.A. or T.M. shells)
            10 men left C.19.d. carried boxes as above.
  (g) AERIAL
7.30 AM   One low E.A. (2000 ft) flying W over TRENT
            TRENCH.

III. GENERAL
            Trains on VITRY BEAUMONT RLY as follows:-
              4 going N. at 1.10 PM, 2.30 pm, 3.12 pm
                & 3.25 pm. (at D.8.2.)
              2 going S. at 2.30 pm, & 3.25 pm (D.8.2.)
            At 8.40 pm, 1 train moved N.
5.45 AM   Motor bogey moved along Light Railway from
            C.27.b. to C.32.c.
            Visibility varied, and was low at times
            owing to mists.

                                    Brig. General,
                        Commanding, 155th Infantry Brigade.

GAVRELLE SECTION
INTELLIGENCE SUMMARY N° 7.
(From 6 a.m. 6/8/18. To 6 a.m. 7/8/18).

REF. MAP. FOOTHILL 1/20,000. 3rd Ed.   7th August 1918.

I OUR ACTIVITY.
   (a) OPERATIONS

   Left Sub-Section Defensive Patrols to B.23.c.90.40.
   and B.23.b.15.15. — nothing to report.
   Left Sub-Section Day O.P. Report from B.29.a.22 Report A.
   Right Sub-Section Reconnaissance Report. Report B.

   (b) ARTILLERY.

   H.V. slows were active on GLOSTER WOOD,
   (C.27.a.b.); FRESNES-ROUVROY LINE, (C.21.b.), &
   FRONT LINE SYSTEM - (B.18 & B.24).

   Field Guns were very active on GAVRELLE
   areas (B.30.a); B.29.a; C.19.c; C.25.a; HOLLOW
   COPSE (C.27.c.); and at I.1.c, & I.2.c; area
   in immediate rear of OPPY WOOD was also
   shelled.
   60/rs engaged guns active at C.6.c.5.8. —
   (True bearing 74° from B.30.b.2.4.)
   Harassing /

2.   7th August 1918.

I OUR ACTIVITY (contd)

(b) ARTILLERY (contd)

Harassing fire was kept up by night chiefly on targets in vicinity of VITRY, GLOSTER WOOD, & back areas. Heavy fire on GAVRELLE & C.19.c.

(c) AERIAL.

Slight activity today. Formations of 4 & 5 over ENEMY lines at times were fired on by A.A. Guns & M.Gs., without result.

Some activity by night. A few bombs were dropped on ENEMY Back areas. ENEMY used searchlights from about C.29.a & b.

II HOSTILE ACTIVITY.

(a) OPERATIONS

NIL.

(b) ARTILLERY.

Activity was below normal.

Time	Rounds	Calibre	Location
11 AM	30 rds.	5.9	B.26.a.
11.35 "	2 rds.	5.9	H.3.b.
	20 rds.	5.9	H.3.a.&c
11.50 "	12 rds.	77mm	KO

3.   7th August 1918.

II HOSTILE ACTIVITY (contd)
(b) ARTILLERY. (contd)

3. P.M.	6 rds.	5.9	— KAY ALLEY · B.28.c.
	2 rds.	4.2	— C.21.a.8.8.
3.35 "	8 rds.	4.2	— H.3.6.5.6.
	30 rds.	5.9	— KAY ALLEY · B.28.c.
4.30 "	6 rds.	5.9	— H.4.c.
5.30 "	30 rds.	5.9 & 77 mm — TONY ALLEY · H.4.c.
5.45 "	16 rds.	5.9	— KAY ALLEY · B.28.c.
9.30 "	20 rds.	5.9	— H.3.a.1.c.
10.15	15 rds.	4.2 & a few gas shells on B.30.b.
12 mid.} 12.30 am}	12 rds. Gas (4.2) on H.1 central.
4.40 AM.	28 rds. 77mm — Right sub section front & support lines.

(c) TRENCH MORTARS.
Inactive, NIL.

(d) MACHINE GUNS.
Normal. Usual bursts by night, at regular intervals.

(e) WORK.

4.   7th August 1918.

II HOSTILE ACTIVITY (cont'd).

(e) WORK.
No new work reported.

(f) MOVEMENT.

6 - 6.35 A.M.   There was considerable movement in C.25.a. central & C.19 central. 36 men, in parties, left trench, C.19.c.5.3 & walked to SQUARE WOOD.

9. A.M.   Horseman left GAVRELLE & disappeared W. of FRESNES, 40 minutes later.

During the day there was individual movement at the following points viz:- B.30.a.6.5; B.30.d.8.3. ~~B.24.c.2.0.~~, C.19.b; C.19.c.1.4; C.30.b.; C.31.b.& d; C.25.a. & C.16.a. 3.2; Slight movement at I.1.d. & I.2.C. & B.18.c.8.4. 2 men (with food containers?) at C.19.c.1.4.

7 - 8 P.M.   Small parties of 5 & under, moving on Roads & tracks at:-

C.10.a.4.; C.25.C.; C.9.d. & near MAUVILLE FARM. at C.23.a.1.8.

4 parties, of 6 men each, moved NW from IZEL-LES-EQUERCHIN & disappeared at U.30.d. 3.2. They moved very slowly & appeared to be heavily laden. Visibility was low at this time & it could not be seen whether they carried rifles & equipment.

5.   11th August 1918.

II HOSTILE ACTIVITY (contd.)
    (g) AERIAL
            NIL.

III GENERAL
     Trains on VITRY BEAUMONT RLY as follows:-
     12 going S.- at 8.25 a.m.; 10.40 a.m.; 1.5 p.m.
        1.50 p.m., 3 at 2 p.m. (following each other)
        3.35 p.m.; 4.35 p.m.; 7 p.m.; 7.30 p.m. &
        7.40 p.m.
     3 going N. - 10.40 a.m. - 2 p.m. & 3.10 p.m.
     Flash bearing of Heavy Gun - 79° T. from
        B.21.a.1.3.
     -Do- A.A. Guns 92° & 93° T. from B.20b.2.4.
     Motor Van moved S.W. towards FRESNES
     Visibility was generally good.

                            Brig: General,
                        Commanding 156th Infy. Bde.

GAVRELLE SECTION.
INTELLIGENCE SUMMARY NO. 8.
(From 6 a.m. 7/8/18 to 6 a.m. 8/8/18.)

REF. MAP. Foothill. 1/20000 3rd Ed.   8th August 1918

I. OUR ACTIVITY.
   (a) OPERATIONS.
   Usual night positions taken up by Right Sub-Section. Left Sub-section defensive posts at B.23.b.7.05 & B.23.c.85.29 from 10.15 p.m. to 2.15 a.m.
   Nothing to report.

   (b) ARTILLERY.
   Heavies shelled FRESNES-ROUVROY line in C.15 a. & C.21; FRESNES-GAVRELLE ROAD at C.21.c.d.; RAILWAY COPSE C.27.d.; GLOSTER WOOD (C.29.b.7.9). & FRESNES (C.28.a.) were also shelled at intervals during the day by various calibres.
   18 prs directed fire on OPPY & GAVRELLE areas, chiefly at C.13.b.9.5, C.19.a, C.26.c, B.24.b.7.5 & B.30 a &c.
   Usual harassing fire by night on ENEMY back areas, chiefly in vicinity of FRESNES

2.   8th August 1918

I OUR ACTIVITY (cont'd).
   (b) ARTILLERY (cont'd)
       areas at C.19., C.20., NEUVIREUIL, C.25,
       IZEL-LES-EQUERCHIN. Between 5 & 6 A.M., 3rd Cdn
       Guns actively shelled OPPY areas.

   (c) TRENCH MORTARS.
       12 rounds on GAVRELLE areas.

   (d) AERIAL.
       A good deal of patrol activity today.
       Formations of 5 and under, frequently flew
       along ENEMY lines & were fired on by
       AA. & M.Gs.
       At 3.30 P.M. 3 planes dropped bombs in
       vicinity of C.21.b.16., & were very heavily
       engaged by A.A. & M.G.
       Battle planes were active towards evening.
       Some patrol activity between 5 & 6 a.m.

II HOSTILE ACTIVITY.
   (a) OPERATIONS.
              — NIL. —
   (b.)

3.   7th August 1918.

II. HOSTILE ACTIVITY (contd.)
(b) ARTILLERY

6 AM.	3 rds. H.2	B.28.d.7.9.
	15 " H.2	B.29.c.6.1.
9.30 "	2 " H.2	TOWY ALLEY. H.H.L.
10.45 "	10 " H.2	Do Do
11.0 "	5 " 5.9	DITCH POST.
12 noon.	12 " H.2	H.4.b.
1. P.M.	77 mm registered NOMANS LAND (B.17a.1.d) & BAILLEUL.	
	118 rds. 77mm	B.23 cent.
1.5 "	6 rds. H.2	KAY ALLEY. B.28.d.
5.0 PM.	1 round each (5.9).	B.29.b.98. & B.29.b.5.9. (probably registering from their own lines)
5.5 "	18 rds. 77mm	B.22. central.
6.50 " (6.5?)	48 rds. H.2	H.2. B.25 & B.26.
10 PM	15 rds. H.2	B.29.a.
1.30 AM.	8 rds. 77mm	BROWN LINE & BAILLEUL.

Enemy appeared to register B.17.C. 20.85.
B.17.C. 60.05, B.23.a. 25.55, B.23 central & B.23.c. 45.25

GAS SHELLING

6.30 PM	311 rounds Green Cross	B.27.C.5.0.
7.10 "	250 " in vicinity of TONGUE POST. H.2.c
8.50 "	50 Green Cross B.26.d. & B.27.C.5.1.
10.45 to 12.15 PM	~~mixture of~~ ~~gas shells~~ B.28.a.7.7.

(c) TRENCH

8th August 1918

4.

II HOSTILE ACTIVITY (cont'd)

(c) TRENCH MORTARS.
NIL.

(d) MACHINE GUNS.
Usual night fire.

(e) WORK.
NIL

(f) MOVEMENT.
Observation on ENEMY lines was rendered difficult by ground mists, but the following is reported:-

10.50 AM 5 thinking men were seen at GAVRELLE
b.   HOLLOW COPSE. (C.26.c.40.95.) + BIACHE
4. P.M.   ST.VAAST; 3 men walking in N. direction at C.H.C. & movement in Tr. etc. at B.18.6.9.2.
7.15.PM   Enemy moving a park bridge? at C.30.b.

(g) AERIAL
More activity today. At 9.30.AM.
5.EA. flying at about 8000 ft. dropped 30-40 small hand grenades on BAILLEUL + B.22 etc.

10.40 AM 2 EA flying high over sector area, were driven off in S.E. direction by AA. Gun fire.

5.   8th August 1918.

II HOSTILE ACTIVITY. (Cont'd)
(g) AERIAL. (cont'd).

11.15.AM 3. E.A. flying at 10,000 ft. flew W. over Section.
7.50 P.M 1 Low flying E.A. over High Hub. Section area
(at about 1500 ft) was engaged by L.G. fire
& rifle fire without effect. At same time 2
other E.A. at about 5000 ft. hovered overhead.
One of our patrolling planes engaged the low
flying plane & ENEMY Planes retired over
their own lines. I fired starlight. Nothing
followed.

III GENERAL.

A.A. Guns active on true bearing of 95° from
B.20.b.2.4. (Vide O.P).
Flash bearings from same point - 80°? 88°,
88°, 100°, & 113°. (all True) - Field Guns.
84°. & 96° (H.V. Guns) - Bearing of H.V.
Gun I from B.27.c.7.1
93°. & 82°. (Heavies) from B.20.b.2.1
Motor cars travelling N. at high speed
along Road at C.17.a.6.2.
True bearing taken from Blind Gas Shell -
107°. from B.27.c.5.1.
At 11.pm. a shell explosion was heard
behind GAVRELLE.
Flash bearing of H.V. Gun from B.27.S.7.1. - 96°.T.
                (Sgd) Jno. Haugh.
                   for Brig General
                       Comdg. 15th Bde.

BM Please see return

GAVRELLE SECTION INTELLIGENCE SUMMARY NO. 9
(For 24 hours ending 6 a.m. 9th August 1918)

REF. MAP. FOOTHILL. 1/20,000. 31.8.Ed.   7th August 1918.

I. OUR ACTIVITY

(a) OPERATIONS

Usual night operations were carried out
by Right Sub Section.

Defensive Patrols from Right Sub Section
to B.29.6. 30.00, & B.29.a. 80.90.
Nothing unusual to report.

(b) ARTILLERY

Activity was normal during the period.
FRESNES, GAVRELLE, NEUVIREUIL, ROUVROY
FRESNES System (C.21.b.d. & C.27 cent) Areas
in C.13.C. C.19.C. C.21.d. & C.25. were shelled by
Heavies during the day.
Field Guns were active on systems
in B.18.c. B.24 cent. OPPY & B.30 a & b.
Harassing fire by night.
4.5 & 6" Hows were active on
GAVRELLE areas, on C.19. & C.25 between 5 & 6 a.m.
this morning.

(c) AERIAL.

2.   9th August 1916

I. OUR ACTIVITY (contd)

   (c) AERIAL.

        Considerable patrol activity during the day. Places on rear & prominently over ENEMY front line were fired on by A.A. Guns & M.G., without result. Large formations of 10 H.S. were active between 7 & 8 p.m.

        There was some slight activity.

II. HOSTILE ACTIVITY

   (a) OPERATIONS

        NIL.

   (b) ARTILLERY.

9.A.M.	13 rds. 77 m/m	B.27.a.
	4 rds. H.2.	TOWY ALLEY. H.11.B.
9.55.	4 rds. 77 m/m	B.26.a.& b.
10.to 2.30 P.M.	50 rds. H.2.	Forward Gun Position. B.7a
11.15.	4 rds. 5.9	H.5.b.
11.20.	5 rds. H.2.	B.28.c.
11.45.	2 rds. H.2.	B.22.a. 9.0.
11.30 to 1.P.M.	82 rds. H.2.	TOWY ALLEY. H.11.b.
12.30 P.M.	4 rds. 5.9	B.22.a. 90.10.
3 P.M.	16 rds. H.2.	H.11.b.
4.30	12 rds. H.2.	H.3.c. & H.11.b.
7.40	A few gas shells.	B.26.b.
11.0	63 rds. H.2. & 77 m/m	B.368.
1.115 to 3.40	250 rds. 77 m/m, H.2 & 5.9	H.3.C.7.2. to B.27.b. 88.

3.   9th August 1918.

I. HOSTILE ACTIVITY. (contd.)

(b) ARTILLERY   B.??6.
4.30 a.m. Shelled left sub. sector areas at B.29.a, b.
           put down a left barrage in front of his own line

(c) TRENCH MORTARS.
        NIL.

(d) MACHINE GUNS.
    Short bursts of fire at 6.30 a.m. Considering
    59° T. from B.29.c.33. Probably from the M.G. Emplacement
    suspected at B.29.c.90.65.
    Very little fire during the night.

(e) WORK.
    Working party of 6 men at C.21.c.9.5.

(f) MOVEMENT.
    Much individual movement on FRESNES-
    GAVRELLE ROAD during the day. Between
    GAVRELLE & ridge at C.19.c. between 6 & 8 P.M.
    There was also some movement in & around
    SQUARE WOOD (C.27.c.05.10.); C.15.b,
    C.21.b, & B.18.d.30.
         Movement at C.16 was rather pronounced.
         Small parties of ENEMY were seen in French
    ary

II HOSTILE ACTIVITY (contd)

(f) MOVEMENT (contd)

at C.9a.1.0 - C.9a.7.6. Driven off & dispersed.

7.5. 3 men at C.16a.28. 40.36 & 5.6.

Slight movement on Roads. Tracks at C.16a.5.1. & C.15c.4d.

Men observing from Trench. B.30.b.67.

Motor Van on Road at C.16.b. 6.5.

3 men on Road, C.16.a. were forced to take cover from our shell fire.

Party of 10 men at I.11a. S.W. were engaged by a pounder gun & scattered.

8 men at C.9a.5.1.7. (This is a suspected permanent post of some kind).

Troops moving behind OPPY WOOD. Artillery fired a few rounds. 3 men seen in the WOOD.

(g) AERIAL

(a) Ordinary

8 am. 1 E.A. over battery area (4000 ft) was engaged & driven off by A.A. guns.
9.05 2 E.A. Do. (7000 ft) Do. Do.
5.15 2 E.A. Do. (6000 ft) Do. Do.

(b) Low Flying

1. Flying under 1000 ft. over Bde. areas was engaged by M.G. fire & driven off.

III GENERAL

GENERAL

Operation orders to take MAIVILLE
CMDAKA

Smoke used throughout the day
Obb.113

[illegible struck-through line]

Tank [illegible] C.19. d. tail.
Heavy MG + [illegible] artillery on Truck bearing ofa
630 M. - 13 tank y. 11 - 18 rounds between
[illegible] report. Approximate location C.9d.02
2. AA guns acted on bearing of 85° T.
and C.204 y.11.
Gun flashes on bearing of 710°, & 869 [illegible]
0.30 a.m.

Enemy [illegible] relieved in [illegible] downwind
[illegible] by our [illegible] MG on a bearing
of 55° [illegible] M. 9 a. 400. [illegible]
no [illegible]

Abt 10 PM, 2 km Inland S. of VITRY.
BEAUMONT Rly. relieved N. at 7 PM
Visibility good during the day.

Brig: General.
Commanding 66th Infy. Bde.

GAVRELLE SECTION INTELLIGENCE SUMMARY. No 10.
(for 24 hours ending 6 p.m. 10th August 1918)

REF:MAP. FOOTHILL 1/10,000 (Edn.)   10th August 1918.

I OUR ACTIVITY
   (a) OPERATIONS

       Defensive Patrols from Left Sub-Section to
       B.28.b.15.15 & B.23.c.90.10.

       Nothing unusual to report.

   (b) ARTILLERY
       At intervals during the day, Heavies fired
       chiefly on targets in C.13.b.; GAVRELLE;
       ROUVROY-FRESNES trench system at C.14.b. &
       C.21.b.&d.; NEUVIREUIL (C.9.c.) and on C.10.a.
       & C.16.d.
           Field Guns engaged movement at C.8.b.1.9,
       C.8.b.11.2. & C.17.a. Individual movement
       on C.19.c. was engaged by 60 pdr.
           At "Stand to", 18 pdrs. put over 30 rnds on GAVRELLE.
           Harassing fire was normal by night
       except between 2 a.m. & 3 a.m., when fire was
       rather heavy. 3 explosions were heard behind
   (c) AERIAL   enemy at 8.45 p.m.
       Much

2.   10th August 1918.

I OUR ACTIVITY (contd)
  (c) AERIAL. (contd).

Much patrol activity in the early morning. Planes crossed ENEMY front areas. Observation Balloon forced to descend by our planes at 7.5 am. Activity was maintained during the day was slightly above normal in the evening. Planes were fired on heavily by M.Gs. & by A.A. Guns from about C.31.d.5.3, C.32.d.4.4. & (C.30.d. cent?)

Propaganda pamphlets were dropped in NO MAN'S LAND from our planes.

II HOSTILE ACTIVITY.
  (a) OPERATIONS

                    NIL

  (b) ARTILLERY.

Time	Rounds	Calibre		Target
8.40 AM	4 rds.	H.2	–	H.3.a.
	9 rds.	77 m/m	–	BAILLEUL.
9.30 "	5 rds.	5.9	–	B.26.C.
9.35 to 10.15 "	10 rds.	77 m/m	–	B.26.C. (every 2 minutes)
9.30 "	10 rds.	H.2	–	H.1.
10.20 "	2 rds.	Shrapnel	–	DO.
1.30 PM	3 rds.	5.9	–	B.17.C.
3.0 "	10 rds.	H.2	–	H.3.b.
3.15 "	6 rds.	H.2	–	H.3.b.8.8.
3.35 "	12 rds.	H.2	–	H.3.a.4.6.
4.15 "	6 rds.	H.2	–	H.10.b.
5.30 "	10 rds.	H.2	–	H.5.a.
6.0 "	30 rds.	H.2	–	POST TRENCH. H.3.b.

3.   10th August 1918.

II. HOSTILE ACTIVITY. (cont'd)
   (b) ARTILLERY.
   10. P.M.   19 rds. 77 mm.   -   B.23.a. (Frontline).
   10.30 "   A few rds.(Yellow Cross) - B.27.a & c & d.
   1.0. A.M   20 rds. H.2.   -   H.3.a.
   2.0 A.M   12 rds. H.2.   -   H.H.a.
   2.30 A.M   10 rds. 77 mm.   -   KAY. EXT?. B.28.d.

   (c) TRENCH MORTARS.
            NIL.

   (d) MACHINE GUNS.
         Usual bursts of fire during the night, along
   front line.

   (e) WORK.
         No new work reported.

   (f) MOVEMENT.
         2 men tracked from C.13.c.9.H. to C.19.b.18.
         A good deal of individual movement on FRESNES-
         GAVRELLE ROAD - (engaged by Artillery.)
         5 men moving about behind camouflage screen
         C.21.a.2.H.

10th August 1918.

II. HOSTILE ACTIVITY. (contd)

(f) MOVEMENT. (contd).

1 man left trench at C.13.d.9.4. followed by 2 others. - all proceeded to OPPY.

6 men moving about in trenches at C.16.b.4.c.

6 men moving N.E. at C.31.b.3.7. disappeared from view behind scrub at about C.23.a.9.9.

20 men in 3 parties, on Road from C.17.a. central to C.16.d. cent. were sniped at by artillery.

Much individual movement from C.19.c. to C.20.b. Also at cross roads in C.15.c.7.3.

2 men left MAUVILLE FARM, proceeded N.W. disappearing at C.21.b. 10.30.

Individual movement was normal at C.21; C.27.d. to FRESNES; C.19.c.4.5. to C.19.a.4.5; C.26.a. central to C.22.c.8.1. & at C.8.d.1.9. & C.8.b.11.2.

(g) AERIAL

9.5 A.M.	5 E.A. flying high over our front line areas (Left Sub Section) was engaged by A.A. Guns & driven off.
11.35 A.M.	1 E.A. dropped white signal light at about M.9. 8.10. Many were fired over their circuit immediately thereafter.
5.30 A.M.	1 Low flying E.A. (1500 ft) over section area was engaged by A.A. & L.G.s

III GENERAL.

5.   10th August 1918.

III. GENERAL.

11.15 pm	1 train going N. from VITRY.
	Flash bearings as follows:-
	5.9. — 74° True from B.31a.1.3.
	77mm. — 68° True from B.30b.8.1.
2. am	1 red light followed by a double red, put up from about B.30a. — nothing resulted.

Visibility was good at times during the day.

                    Brig: General,
        Commanding, 156th Infantry Brigade.

GAVRELLE SECTION · INTELLIGENCE SUMMARY. NO. 11.
(For 24 hours ending 6 a.m. 11-8-18.)

REF. MAP· FOOTHILL· 1/20,000. 3rd Ed.   11th August 1918

OUR ACTIVITY.

(a) OPERATIONS — PATROLS &c.

Lt. L.R. BINNIE & 2 sections (left subsection) — No enemy posts were located. Wiring party of 50 or 60 were seen were at B.23.d.85. was in good condition & double apron fences, 4ft high, with gap of a foot belt.

Report of DAY O.P. established by Left Sub Section. — attached.

(b) ARTILLERY.

Heavies have been very active today. Two destructive shoots were carried out. viz:—
9·2's. 25 rounds, on MAUVILLE FARM. C.16d.
6" Hows. 50 rounds on suspected H.Q. at C.21a. 75·80.

H.V. Gun active behind IZEL·LES·EQUERCHIN was engaged — also some counter battery work. (C.9c.50. & C.37.).

B.11a; ROUVROY· FRESNES·LINE at C.15d. & C.21b; OPPY, NEUVIREUIL, & FRESNE were/

2.   11th August 1918.

I. OUR ACTIVITY. (contd)
   (b) ARTILLERY (contd)
       were shelled at various times during the day.
           Field Guns harassed areas behind OPPY,
       ENEMY FRONT LINE at B.18., B.24.a, & B.30.1
       engaged movement in C.36.
           Harassing fire was normal till 3 A.M. At 3AM
       S.O.S. was put out by Right Flank Brigade & taken
       up by flanks supports. Barrage was put down
       in 7 minutes & continued till 3.50 a.m. At 4.30
       A.M. Section front was quiet.

   (c) MACHINE GUNS.
           Responded to S.O.S. very quickly.

   (d) AERIAL.
           Patrol activity was above normal during
       the day. Large formations of from 4 to 10., over
       Section areas frequently crossed Enemy front
       line & were engaged by his A.A. & M.Gs.
           Activity was maintained till 7.15 p.m.

II HOSTILE

3.   11th Augt. 1918.

II HOSTILE ACTIVITY
  (a) OPERATIONS

                    NIL

  (b) ARTILLERY

Time	Rds	Type	Location
8.30 AM	15 rds.	5.9	H.2c & d.
9.30 "	18 "	H.2 & 77mm	B.27b. H.1.H.d.
9.45 "	21 "	H.2	B.28 b. cent.
10.0 "	8 "	H.2	H.H.a. 3.6
10.30 "	3 "	5.9	B.19 b. 3.8.
11.30 "	37 "	5.9 & 77mm	B.21 a. 3.3 & H.2c & d.
12.30 PM	5 "	77mm	OUSE ALLEY. B.17d. H.2.
1.0 "	35 "	H.2	H.H.a. & H.10a.
1.45 "	5 "	(Heavy. H.V.)	areas in A.7. back areas
2.0 "	55 "	77mm	H.1b. & H.H. areas.
2.10 "	30 "	77mm	THAMES ALLEY.
4.0 "	12 "	H.2	TONY ALLEY. H.H.a. H.2
4.15 "	10 "	H.2	H.9. central.
5.0 "	20 "	5.9	H.1.b.
9.15 "	30 "	H.2	H.10.b.
9.30 – 10 PM	30 "	H.E. & Gas.	H.36.b.4.5. to H.36.b.4.5.60. (In front of Brown line)
12.15 AM	107 "	77mm	H.H.b.
3 AM	Bombardment of GAVRELLE front System with minnenwerfer, 5.9, H.2. 77mm for 15 minutes. Renewed again/		

H   11th August 1918.

II. HOSTILE ACTIVITY. (contd)

   (b) ARTILLERY (contd)

      again at 3.40 am. til 4.10 AM. At 5.35am
      3 minutes bombardment on sector Iron System.

   (c) TRENCH MORTARS

12.15 A.M. & at   Barrage on front & support lines from
2.15 A.M.   right of RIGHT Sub-Sector, to the right.

   (d) MACHINE GUNS

      Normal.

   (e) WORK.

      Suspected new work at C.30.a.6.7.

   (f) MOVEMENT.

      4 men on track at point C.2b.3.2.
were fired on by Sniping Guns from over
ridge at C.2b.6.4.

      Some movement to & from MAUVILLE FARM
3 men left FRESNES & disappeared at C.19.c.4.4.
2 men left House I.6.c. & went to I.5.a.
Motor car & 2 Horsemen going E. on
Road, D.26.6.1.

      3 men running out Telephone cable on
Road at point C.15.a.7.7. to suspected H.Q. C.21.a.2.8.

5.   11th August 1918.

II HOSTILE ACTIVITY. (contd).

(f) MOVEMENT. (contd).

Movement in Trenches at C.20a, C.20a.4.7.
C.21a.9.3, & C.10d.7.0. - C.27d.7.0. - C.27d.9.1.
on tracks at C.21b.5.9, C.15.c.9.0, C.20b.0.5.
C.17a. & FRESNES GAVRELLE ROAD.

Convoy of 15 limbers, 12 drawn by team of 4, remainder
by 2, 2 drivers on each limber. Escort of 8 men with 1st
4 limbers, remainder 1 mounted man each, & about 11
men on foot. Convoy was proceeding N. (Artillery notified).

(g) AERIAL

(1) Ordinary

8.35 A.M.	2 E.A. flying low over ENEMY front lines & were engaged by Lewis Guns.
9.15 "	1 E.A. over section area (at 7000 ft.) was engaged by A.A. Guns & driven off.

(2) Low Flying.
NIL.

III GENERAL

A number of explosions were seen behind
ridge which forms skyline S.E. of Right Sub. Sector
front line. (behind VITRY.)

1 Train went S. through IZEL-LES-EQUERCHIN.

Smoke from H.V. Guns. Grid 730 from B.27d.7.4.
No flash was visible, but interval between smoke &
report. 28½ seconds.

A.A. Gun active at C.23d.1.2.

6   11th August 1918.

III GENERAL. (cont'd)

    Gun flashes seen at C.6.c. & C.16.c.
    Do. Do. on bearing of 87°.T. from B.21a.1.3.

7.15 P.M. & Smoke rising from Trench, B.16.b.3.2. A
8.30 -   thick blue smoke appeared to come out of a funnel or pipe & rise to a height of about 2 feet, before drifting with the wind.

                              Brig: General,
              Commanding 156th Infantry Brigade.

GAVRELLE SECTION. INTELLIGENCE SUMMARY. No. 12.
(For 24 hours ended 6 a.m. 12.8.18.)

REF MAP. BETHUNE - 1/20,000.   12th August 1918

1. OUR ACTIVITY.
    (a) OPERATIONS.
        Lt. A. W. McLaurin (Scout Officer) & Sec.Lt. R. Glass, 2
        Rifle Sections & 1 Scout. - Patrol to B.30.a.1.8.
        (Right Sub section.)   Report A.

        Lt. J.C. McCulloch, 2 Rifle Sections & 1 Lewis Gun - Patrol to
        B.24.c.30.30. (Left Sub section).   Report B.

    (b) ARTILLERY.
            Heavies shelled ROUVROY - FRESNES LINE at
        C.14.d, C.15.c, C.15.d, & C.21.b.d., NEUVIREUIL,
        GAVRELLE, IZEL-HOF FARM. (C.10 central) & FRESNES
            C.19.c., C.25.d., C.27.b.7.9. Front line
        in B.24 & 29 also received attention.
            Heavies & Field Guns shelled OPPY areas, & a
        few rounds fired at a suspected Sniper in OPPY
        WOOD - (Observer referred to in Day O.P. Report of 11/8/18)
                Harassing fire by night on pre-arranged
        targets was normal.

    (c) AERIAL.
            None.

2.   12th Augt. 1918.

OUR ACTIVITY (contd.)
(c) AERIAL.

There was some patrol activity in the early morning. Flights crossed ENEMY lines & were slightly engaged by MGs. There was very little AA. gunfire. During the day activity was below normal, only one formation of 6 being active at 3.20 p.m.

There was some night flying & H.E. explosions were heard in direction of VITRY.

II HOSTILE ACTIVITY.
(a) OPERATIONS.
                    NIL

(b) ARTILLERY.

Time	Rounds	Calibre	Location
6.55 - 9.15 AM	34 rds.	5.9	H.10.a.
9.0 "	16 rds.	5.9	B.36 cent. Ne.
10.15 "	30 rds.	H.2	H.15.b.
2.55 "	38 rds.	H.2	B.36.d.2.8.
3 - 4.15 "	10 rds.	5.9	B.36 cent.
3.10 - 5.30 "	475 rds. 5.9. H.2 & 77mm.		Vicinity of Railway Cutting - B.36.C.3.3.
3.30 "	10 rds.	H.2	POST TRENCH
4.0 "	40 rds.	5.9	POST SUPPORT & THAMES ALLEY
4.10 "	Harassing fire on BAILLEUL - (about 70 rds. H.2. & 5.9).		
6.0 "	1 rd.	5.9	B.28.c.5.3.
7.15 "	10 rds.	5.9	H.4.c.
9.0 "	50 rds.	Heavies	Back areas.

3.   13th August 1918.

II. HOSTILE ACTIVITY. (contd)

(b) ARTILLERY. (contd)

11. P.M.   10 rds. H.2 - H.3 a.

A few gas shells - (Blue cross) on right
sub-section, heavy gas shelling on B.26 & H.H. cent.

10 P.M. to
midnight.   About 300 77 m.m. Gas shells - B.27.C.2.2. to Rly. cutting.

(c) TRENCH MORTARS.
                    NIL

(d) MACHINE GUNS.
        More active than usual, particularly from
        direction of GAVRELLE ROAD.

(e) WORK.
        Small wiring party of the enemy behind trench
        C.15. c. to a.6.

4/ MOVEMENT.
10.45. A.M.   5 men in trench C.19.d. H.5.
11.0. A.M.   A man walked from C.35.b. 7.7. to C.36.c. 5.8.
              men walking in trenches at B.30.a. 5.4.   at
B.30.a.H.3   they were almost fully exposed. Trench appears to be
              blown in at that point.
              12 men working about at C.19.C.
11.15. P.M.   men running along road at C.21.C. 8.3.
              entered FRESNES.
              2 men with NAUVILLE FARM in trench at
              C.21.b. 1.9.

4.   13th August 1918.

1. HOSTILE ACTIVITY (cont'd)
   (f) MOVEMENT (cont'd)

4.15 PM	1 man looking over parapet at B.30.a.5.5.
	0 dividual movements observed NEUVIREUIL (12 men)
6.45 "	3 men observed from I.H.b.5.3 to I.11.a.1.8 — 1 detained later.
8.10 "	2 men from Trench at C.30.b.50 to C.30.c.8.2. stood there, apparently at mouth of dugout or emplacement. They were joined by a third man, who came up from dugout. Latter left party at 8.30 pm. This appears to be a ? position of some kind.

   (g) AERIAL.

8.45 – 10.15 AM	Planes flying low over our lines registering for artillery, were fired on by our L.Gs.
9.55 AM	1 E.A. crossed our lines at high altitude flying SN.
9 to 10 am	1 Low flying E.A. (2000 ft) over KILKERRAN Trench
10.30 AM	1 E.A. over our lines driven off by F.A. Guns & L.G.
8.30 PM	1 Low flying E.A. over Action area, was driven off in a S direction by Scary A.A. Gun fire.
	There was considerable activity during the night.

5.   13th August 1918

III. GENERAL.
   Smoke rising from following points:-
C.14d., C.31a.2.8. From Trench at C.19c.
A.A.Gun active – 106° T from B.27d.7.H.
Large cloud of smoke at C.24c.2.H.
Appeared to be a dump burning.
Smoke seen on Railway at D.20b.
Gun flashes on T.bearings of 69°, 98° & 107°
from B.20b. 2H.

                              Brig: General,
              Commanding 156th Infantry Brigade.

GAVRELLE SECTION. INTELLIGENCE SUMMARY. NO. 13.
(For period 6a.m. 12/8/18 to 6a.m. 13/8/18.)

REF: MAP: FOOTHILL 1/20,000 3rd Ed.   13th August 1918

I. OUR ACTIVITY.
  (a) OPERATIONS.
      2n/Lt. F.J. DEACON, 2 Rifle Sections, Scout Corpl &
      1 Scout - Patrol to B.29.c.60.35 (Right
      Sub-section.) ———————————————— Report "A".
      Lt. T.A. HERDMAN, Cpl. J.C. McCULLOCH, 2 Rifle
      Sections & Lewis Gun — Patrol to B.24.c.20.15
      (Left Sub-Section). ———————————— Report "B".

  (b) ARTILLERY.
          Heavies shelled C.19.c. areas; Trench System
      C.19 b & d; - NEUVIREUIL; GAVRELLE; & FRESNES
      C.28.c. & d.
          Field-guns more active during the day
      on ENEMY SUPPORT LINE from C.7. central
      to C.35; and in vicinity of B.24; MARINE
      TRENCH, at B.30.a; & in near vicinity of
      OPPY WOOD.
          At 1.30 P.M. retaliation was called for &
      responded to. - Guns of various calibres putting
      over some 300 rounds on B.30d; C.19; and
      OPPY WOOD.
          Heavies/

2.   13th August 1918.

I. OUR ACTIVITY (contd.)
   (b) ARTILLERY (contd.)

        Heavies & field guns fired about 300 rounds
   at 6 P.M. on B.24d, & B.30a. on call for
   retaliation.

        Harassing fire by night chiefly in vicinity
   of OPPY. & C.31.d.

   (c) AERIAL

        Patrol activity was normal during the
   day. — Formations approaching ENEMY lines
   being engaged by A.A. guns & M.G.s.
        There was a little activity during the
   night, & in the early morning.

II. HOSTILE ACTIVITY.
   (a) OPERATIONS
                      — NIL —

   (b) ARTILLERY.

   1. A.M. | 55 rds. | H.2. & 77mm — B.27.c.7.1. & close vicinity
            | 64 rds. | H.2 & 77mm   — RAILWAY CUTTING.
   1.10 " | 109 rds.| 77mm Gas Shells—(not identified) on
            | | H.1.a, B.26.d, B.27.c.
   5.30 " | 36 rds. | H.2.   — B.26.a.
   6.20 " | 37 rds. | H.2 (H.E. & gas) — B.26.c.

3.   13th August 1918.

II HOSTILE ACTIVITY. (contd.)

(b) ARTILLERY. (contd.)

6.50 P.M.	17 rds. H.2.	- B.26 c & d.
9.10 "	12 rds. H.2.	- H.9 b.
10.30 "	113 rds. 77 m/m	- B.28.
11.5 "	83 rds. 77 m/m	- areas in H.5
11.30 "	10 rds. (H.V. Gun)	- Back areas.
11.35 "	15 rds. 77 m/m	- _Do._ (about H.11.)
2 A.M. to 4 A.M.	65 rds. H.2. & 77 m/m at intervals on B.28 d. to H.5 a &c.	

(c) TRENCH MORTARS.
NIL.

(d) MACHINE GUNS.
Normal.

(e) WORK.
Listening posts of Right Company (Right Subsection) heard ENEMY working party 7/800 yds away in an Easterly direction.

(f) MOVEMENT.

10.15 A.M.	2 men walked from C.20.c.H.8 to C.20.c.3.1.
10.30 "	2 men standing on parapet - C.15.C.1.5.
10.40 "	2 men at C.19 b. 3.1. & 4 men on ridge C.19 c.

H. 13th August 1918.

II. HOSTILE ACTIVITY (contd)
    (f) MOVEMENT (contd)

11:30 A.M.   3 men, from C.20.b. to C.20.b.7.6.

12 noon.   3 men, from C.21.a.5.9 to C.20.b.5.4.

12:35 P.M.   2 men moving S. along POUVROY. FRESNES LINE at C.15.c. central. entered Trench at C.21.a.9.9. 2 men at C.22.b. 4.6 walked into FRESNES.

3:30 "   3 men walked from GAVRELLE to B.30.c. 6.9. At same time 2 men entered GAVRELLE.

5:30 "   Considerable individual movement at C.19.c.

5:45 "   3 men moving S. on Road. C.15.c., entered H.Qrs. at C.21.a.2.8.

6:15 "   Light Limber at MAUVILLE FARM, followed tracks through C.16.a. disappeared at C.10.c.
        Individual movement in C.15, C.21.d.

7:35 "   5 men from direction of FRESNES, disappeared at C.22.a.2.3.
        Enemy transport heard from direction of GAVRELLE ROAD at 3.30 a.m.

    (g) AERIAL

9:15 a.m.   2 E.A. flying very high crossed our lines going S.W.

4:45 P.M.   2 E.A. flying E. over our lines (at about 3000 ft.) were engaged by A.A. Guns & M.G.'s & driven off.

5.   13d August 1918.

II HOSTILE ACTIVITY (cont'd)
(9) AERIAL (cont'd)

10.5 p.m.   1 E.A. flying over our back areas.
11.0 P.M.   1 E.A. dropped parachute lights, West
             of Brigade H.Qrs. Lights burned for
             20 minutes.

III GENERAL

8.25 P.M.   Signal Lamp flashing in C.31.b.
             Ground mists & haze rendered observation
             on ENEMY lines difficult.
             Helio in operation in Wood C.27.d.6.9.

                        AM   Brig: General,
             Commanding, 156th Infantry Brigade.

GAVRELLE SECTION INTELLIGENCE SUMMARY No 14
(Period from 6 a.m. 13/8/18 to 6 a.m. 14/8/18)

14th August 1918.

REF MAPS FOOTHILL 1/20000 3rd Edn
51 B N.W. Ed. 10a (Local) 1/20000

I OUR ACTIVITY

(a) OPERATIONS

Defensive night posts were established in front of our line. Nothing to report.

(b) ARTILLERY

Shelled ROUVROY FRESNES LINE at C.14, C.21, HOLLOW COPSE (C.27), OPPY areas (C.13), C.10b, and at I.15a. A few rounds on FRESNES & C.25 b. rd. MAUVILLE FARM also received attention.

C.19.C, and trench trench systems at B.18.b. rd. B.24, & B.29.b. rd. were shelled by Field Guns.

Heavies carried out some concentrated fire on hostile batteries & long range guns fired 5 rounds on RAILWAY EMBANKMENT. D.16a.

Harassing fire by night.

2.   14th August 1918

I. OUR ACTIVITY (contd.)

(c) AERIAL

Apart from some patrol work, there was very little activity during the day.

By night, bombs were dropped on ENEMY back areas.

II. HOSTILE ACTIVITY

(a) OPERATIONS

— NIL —

(b) ARTILLERY

Time	Rounds	Type	Location
12.30 PM	10 rds	H.2	KAY ALLEY B.28 d.
3 pm - 3.15 pm	40 "	H.2	B.28 b. 9.5, & B.28 d.
3.30 PM	50 "	H.2 77mm	B.26 c & d.
4. PM	25 "	H.2	TONY ALLEY. H.4 a.
	15 "	77mm	H.3 b.
5.10 PM	35 "	H.2	H.5 a & H.4 b.
10.30 PM	12 "	77mm	H.5 a & H.4 b.
	20 "	H.E & Gas (Blue Cross)	B.26 d. H.3 a.
11 PM	6 Gas shells		B.23 a 5.3 B.28 c
3.30 AM	17 Gas shells		B.15 c central. & B.16
3.50 AM	31 rds	H.2	B.22 c central & B.28 c

(c) TRENCH

3.   14th August 1918.

II HOSTILE ACTIVITY (contd)

(c) TRENCH MORTARS

        NIL

(d) MACHINE GUNS

    Normal activity. Usual short bursts of fire.

(e) WORK

        NIL

(f) MOVEMENT.

    Much individual movement in vicinity of Trenches C.31.b.5.2, on track at C.27.b. & trenches in I.10.d. during the day.

10.20 AM	3 men on top of trenches I.6.c. moved to I.4.d.9.2
10.45	1 man entered trench C.31.b.
2.30 PM	6 men carried material from C.16.d.9.2 to Trench C.32.b.5.5.
2.40 "	2 men behind Trench at C.14.C.0.3.
3.0 "	5 men moved from C.36.d.11. to SQUARE WOOD C.36.d.9.3.
3.40 "	2 men from HOLLOW CORSE to trench C.26.d.1.0
4.0 "	1 man walked from Ridge C.19.c. to FRESNES
4.30 "	3 men walking along Trench line at C.26.7.4
5.0 "	Sentry in trench at C.27.d.3.8.
5.30 "	4 men left FRESNES went to C.19.c.
5.55 to 6 pm.	8 men moving about in C.32.b.5.8

4.   14th August 1918.

II HOSTILE ACTIVITY (contd.)

(f) MOVEMENT (contd.)

6 PM. — 2 men from MAUVILLE FARM walked to FRESNES

6.5 — 7 men seen for a few seconds at C.21.b.25.35
(trench)

7.10 — Considerable individual movement at C.33.a.30.
was engaged by artillery.

7.20 — 5 men (1 carrying a large white paper) from
C.15.c.8.5. to C.15.a.5.5.

7.15 – 8 pm } movement at C.31.d. & C.16.d.5.1.

(g) AERIAL

(a) Ordinary.

9.10 AM — 1 EA flying W. over section area about 6000 ft
was engaged by AA Guns & driven off in a
northerly direction.

10.50 " — 5 EA flying E over our lines were engaged
by AA Guns.

6.45 PM — 3 EA flying high over section were driven off
by AA Guns.

There was some activity by night, & H.E.
bombs were dropped at ~~TUNNEL DUMP~~
B.15.c.5.4. close vicinity of TUNNEL DUMP.

(b) Low flying

9.10 AM to 9.20 AM } 1 EA over section area was twice driven off
by Lewis gun fire.

5.   10th August 1918.

III. GENERAL

Several explosions were heard behind ENEMY lines, during the day.
Dump exploded approximately at D.9. Appeared to be an oil dump. Huge clouds of smoke were seen rising.
Motor train at C.22.C.4.4. approx.

7.45PM Train moved S. to VITRY.
Signal lamps in operation at BEACH ST. VAAST.

1AM-2AM Flash of Heavy gun (shelling back areas) was distinctly seen 3 times on a T bearing of 79° from B.30.b.2.4.

Visibility varied during the day.

                                    Brig. General
                        Commanding 156th Infantry Brigade

GAVRELLE INTELLIGENCE SUMMARY. NO. 15.
(For period from 6 a.m. 14/8/18 to 6 a.m. 15/8/18).

REF. MAPS :- 51 B N.W. Ed. 11A. 1/20,000.   15th August 1918.
FOOTHILL. 1/20000 3rd Ed.

I OUR ACTIVITY.

(a) OPERATIONS.

Defensive night posts were established in front of our line. — No Enemy were seen. Day Observation Report (Right Subsector). "A"

(b) ARTILLERY.

GAVRELLE, NEUVIREUIL, OPPY, FRESNES-ROUVROY LINE, (C.14.c. C.15.c. & C.21.); & front Trench system, in B.18 & B.24., were shelled by Heavies during the day. There was also intermittent fire on ridge at C.19.c.

Long Range Guns shelled back areas.

Field Guns harassed trenches in B.12.b, B.18.d, & B.30.c., and a few rounds at intervals were put over on FRESNES-GAVRELLE ROAD.

Harassing fire by night, chiefly in vicinity of OPPY, & C.19.a. cent. & C.26.c.6.5.

(c) AERIAL.

2. 15th August 1918.

I. OUR ACTIVITY (cont'd)

(c) AERIAL.

Patrol activity was normal, & formations frequently flew along ENEMY LINES, & were engaged by A.A. guns & M.Gs.

There was some activity from 10PM - 2AM. Bombs were dropped on ENEMY Back areas.

II. HOSTILE ACTIVITY.

(a) OPERATIONS.
    NIL.

(b) ARTILLERY

Time	Rounds	Calibre		Location
7.45 AM	20 rds	H.2	—	B.27.c
9.0 "	20 rds	77m	—	TONY COMM. TRENCH.
	6 rds	H.2	—	B.28.d
9.50 "	3 rds	77m	—	B.23.d. (registered on NO MANS LAND)
	5 rds	77m	—	B.27.d. & 7.H.
	2 rds	H.2	—	B.23.b. 2.1
9.55 "	12 rds	H.2	—	B.28.d.
10.10 "	4 rds	H.2	—	B.29.c. 3.H.
10.35 "	5 rds	5.9	—	B.26.a. & B.27.d. (Brown Line)
	20 rds	H.2	—	H.5.a.
11.15 "	60 rds	77m	—	H.5.a.
	16 rds	5.9	—	B.14.b. & B.8.b.d.
12 noon	20 rds	Blue Cross(?)	—	H.3.a.H.
	10 rds	H.2	—	H.11.d. & H.5.a.

3.   15th August 1918

"7. HOSTILE ACTIVITY. (contd.)
    (b) ARTILLERY. (contd.)

2.30 p.m.	30 rds.	77 m.v.	–	BROWN LINE, H.3, & B.27.
2.35 "	10 rds.	do	–	B.21.d.
2.50 "	30 rds.	do	–	B.23.d.5.2 & B.28.b.
3.0 "	10 rds.	5.9	–	KILKERRAN TRENCH, B.29.c.59
3.25 "	6 rds.	H.2	–	B.29.d.5.8.
3.30 "	4 rds.	5.9	–	B.29.c.8.2
4.0 "	30 rds.	H.2	–	H.6.c.3.5 & B.21.d.
7.0 "	6 rds.	H.2	–	H.3.a.
10.15 "	30 rds.	H.2	–	H.4.b.
11.45 "	30 rds.	77 m.v.	–	B.29.a. H.3.
12.15 "	24 rds.	H.2	–	B.15.b. H.3 & H.6.
1.10 a.m.	60 gas shells on B.23.a. (suspected yellow cross)
	& 200 gas shells (type not known) on approx.
	B.21.a & b.
3.a.m.	60 rds. 77 m.v. – B.22.d. B.28.d. & H.21.a.
5 a.m.				

        (c) TRENCH MORTARS.

                 NIL.

        (d) MACHINE GUNS
            Swept trench frequently throughout the
        night. – particularly active at morning & evening
        "stand to".

        (e) WORK.
                 NIL.

4.   15th August 1918

II. HOSTILE ACTIVITY. (contd)
   (f) MOVEMENT.

8.30 A.M.	4 men from C.31.d.1.2 to C.31.d.7.8 followed 5 min. later by 2 other men.
9.20-9.30 A.M.	Individual movement in C.23.b. apparently on tracks about 9 men in all moved from C.23b.3.0. to C.17.c.2.3.
10 A.M.	3 men moved N. at B.30.b.3.5.
12.15 P.M.	1 man signalling with white flag, I.2.c.4.5
1.30 P.M.	1 man entered Trench, C.19.b.6.6.
	4 men moved from HOLLOW COPSE, C.87c.4.8 to C.36.c.4.9.
	men from C.31.b.3.4. entered FRESNES
3.30 "	1 man looking over parapet at B.30.a.3.1.
3.40 "	1 man entered Trench, C.31.d.5.6.
	Movement in trenches, C.19.d.2.4. to C.19.d.2.9.
4.30 "	Individual movement on Road in I.10.a.4.
	3 men moved N. from B.30.b.3.5. to GAVRELLE.
5.45 "	1 man walking N. from Trench C.25.b.7.1, entered Trench C.25.a.3.9.
6.10 "	2 men appeared to disappear suddenly in C.19.d.
7.5 "	1 man on tracks at C.25.a.3.9.
7.40 "	2 men walking S. on Road at C.15.a.7.2.

(g) AERIAL

8.a.m.	1 E.A. over station areas was driven off by A.A. guns.
10.30	1 E.A. flying high in S. direction, fired on by A.A. guns. 4 E.A.'s over our sector at night activity

5.   15th August 1918.

II. HOSTILE ACTIVITY

III. GENERAL

Sentries in KILKERRAN TRENCH at about B.28.d.9.7 were occasionally sniped at.

11.30 p.m. Smoke power barrage moving NE. at D.26 + D.27.
Flash Lamp signalling in WOOD - 920 T. from B.27.d.7.4.

Visibility low during the greater part of the day.

Brig: General,
Commanding 156th Infantry Brigade.

156 Infy Bde Order No 53   Appx VII

Copy No 10

Ref. map sheet 1/20,000 51.B.S.W.

31st Aug. 1918.

1. (a) The 52nd Division is relieving the 56th Division in the Battle Line about HENDECOURT and BULLECOURT.
   (b) 155th Infy Bde is relieving 169th Infy Bde in the actual Battle Line on the 31st inst.

2. 156 Infy Bde will relieve 167th Inf. Bde in the Support Line on the night 31st August / 1st September.

3. Battalions will march off from Bivouac Areas at following times:—

7th Cameronians & Bde HQ	4.30 pm
4th R. Scots & T.M. Bty.	4.50 pm
7th R. Scots.	5.10 pm

and will concentrate in the neighbourhood of the road junction at T.4.c.4.4. by 6.45 pm whence they will proceed to take over from the Battalions of the 167th Inf. Bde.

4. B Coy 52nd M.G. Bn is attached to 156th Infy Bde and will concentrate

with other units at T.4.c.4.4 whence it will relieve the M.G Coy attached to the 167th Inf Bde. under arrangements to be made by Commanders concerned.

5. Battalions will not pass the line T.4.d - T.10.b and d before 8 pm

6. Completion of relief of the Battalions of the 167th Inf Bde will be wired "PRIORITY" to Bde. HQ

7. Bde HQ will close at present location at 6.30 pm and re-open at U.7.c.9.8 at same hour.

8. ACKNOWLEDGE.

Captain
Bde. Major 156 Inf Bde.

Issued at

<u>War Diary Append.</u> X   156th Inf. Bde.

Casualties – August 1918

Unit	Killed		Wounded		Wounded (Gas)		Wounded (at duty)		Missing		Total	
	O.	OR	O	OR	O	OR	O	OR	O	OR	O	OR
4 Royal Scots	–	27	4	124	3	98	1	4	–	10	8	263
7 Royal Scots	1	17	6	85	2	251	–	–	–	1	9	354
7 Sco Rifles	–	10	3	94	–	42	1	3	–	–	4	149
	1	54	13	303	5	391	2	7	–	11	21	766

Copies to:-
No 1 to 4th Royal Scots
   2 " 7th   Do
   3 " 15th Sco. Rifles
   4 " 156 L.T.M. Bty.
   5 " SC
   6 " Bde. Sigs
   7 " 412th Fld Co R.E.
   8 " B.T.O.
   9 " B Coy M.G. Bn
  10 & 11 " Diary
  12 " File

War Diary App. IX   156th Inf. Bde.

Effective Strength – August, 1918

	Week ending 10th		Week ending 17th		Week ending 24th		Week ending 31st	
	O	OR	O	OR	O	OR	O	OR
4th Royal Scots	43	962	41	981	43	956	42	795
7th Royal Scots	47	936	47	937	45	918	41	759
7th Sco. Rifles	43	972	44	968	44	939	43	824
	133	2870	132	2886	132	2813	126	2378

App VIII

REPORT
on
OPERATIONS
of
156th INFANTRY BRIGADE.
****

20th - 28th August 1918.
(both days inclusive)
*****

Ref. Map.
1/20,000, Sheet 51b. S.W. (attached).

20th August.

The Brigade was concentrated in the area
BERNEVILLE - WARLUS - WANQUENTIN - LATTRE ST QUENTIN - with
H.Q. in BERNEVILLE.

21st August.   No change.

22nd August.

At 7.45 a.m., a Divisional Warning Order was
received to the effect that the Brigade would move during
the day to the neighbourhood of MERCATEL, with a view to
attacking next morning the enemy's defences covering
HENIN and the HINDENBURG LINE, N.E. of that Village.

The B.G.C., accompanied by Battalion Commanders
and three Officers per Company, went forward to reconnoitre
and make necessary arrangements for the forthcoming oper-
:ations, leaving Seconds-in-Command to bring on the
Battalions.

Time was short and the heat excessive, but by
8.30 p.m. all necessary arrangements had been made and
verbal orders and instructions issued.

The Battalions, however, had not arrived, due to
the fact that only half the number of busses promised
were forthcoming at the embussing points, and unexampled
congestion of traffic of all kinds on the roads.

These difficulties were only overcome by deter-
:mined/

:mined action and energy displayed by Major CURTIS, G.S., 52nd Division, and Captain H. SAYER, Brigade Major, 156th Infantry Brigade, to whose efforts can be attributed the fact that the Brigade concentrated in time to attack at the hour laid down, viz. 4.55 a.m. on 23rd August.

23rd August.

Each Battalion, on arrival, concentrated in open ground in M.33., space marked ⊠, where extra S.A.A., bombs, flares and entrenching tools were issued to the men prior to moving off to their lines of deployment for attack. 1/7th The Royal Scots arrived first at about 11.30 p.m., follow:ed by 1/7th Cameronians at about 1.30 a.m. on the 23rd, and the 1/4th The Royal Scots at 3 a.m.

By arrangement with the C.R.E. of the 59th Division, a white deployment tape was laid by him on the Brigade frontage between S.6.c.3.0. and M.36.a.5.7., as shewn in blue on Map. The Brigade frontage being approximately 1820 yards.

Gaps in our wire were also cut by him, and trench bridges thrown across our front line trenches at points opposite the gaps.

Guides for each Battalion were furnished by the existing garrison of the Line, viz. 1/6th Bn. The Durham Light Infantry. Considerable annoyance was occasioned, and casualties caused by hostile bombing, harassing fire and gas shelling of forward areas while Battalions were moving from the position of assembly to the line of deployment. It had the desirable effect of seriously annoying the men, particularly those of the 1/7th The Royal Scots who suffered most from gas, and at the appointed hour of attack all were intensely eager to come to close grips with the enemy.

The Scheme of Attack, composition of the attacking force, objectives and frontages assigned to each unit and general instructions and orders issued, were as laid down in 156th Inf. Brigade Operation Order No 1, dated 22nd August (attached)/

(attached) and it is only necessary to add that all orders were carried out to the letter, except in so far as the Tanks were concerned. At Zero, plus 12 minutes, they had not reached the Infantry Line of deployment. The Infantry did not wait for them, and reached and took their objectives before the Tanks caught them up.

Here the Tanks passed through them, and, assisted by one Company per Battalion, all ground for a distance of some 500 yards East of the final objective line (marked Red) was exploited and cleared of the enemy. This took about 30 minutes, at the expiration of which, Tanks and exploiting parties returned.

At 7.35 a.m. it was reported that all objectives had been gained, and that consolidation was proceeding satisfactorily. Prisoners were being brought back in fair numbers, many Machine Guns and Minenwerfers were reported captured, and our casualties were said to be light.

At the same hour, it was reported that the 168th Brigade of the 56th Division had advanced Eastward as far as the BOIRY RESERVE TRENCH S. of the COJEUL RIVER. To conform to their movements, the 1/4th Royal Scots were directed to advance their right and occupy the part of that trench which lies N. of the River. This was successfully accomplished.

In order to advance our line as far as possible, patrols from 1/7th Royal Scots were directed to push forward and ascertain whether the road running into HENIN VILLAGE from the West through N.31.c. and d. would constitute a good defensive line. It proved to be of no value, and as it was apparent that the enemy were still strongly posted to the N. and N.E. at FRITZ's STRUCTURE and N.31.b.9.9., the idea of a further advance was abandoned, and the 1/4th Royal Scots were directed to swing back their left from T.2.a.4.1. by means of Section Posts, to ling up with the right of the 1/7th Royal Scots at T.1.b.1.5. This was done, and our line on the right and centre on the evening of the 23rd ran as shewn on map, "B.B.B."

In/

In the meantime, patrols were pushed forward from the Left Battalion, 1/7th Scottish Rifles, up HENIN TRENCH towards FRITZ's STRUCTURE and towards THE MAZE in N.25.a.

By 6.30 p.m. these patrols reported FRITZ's STRUCTURE, HENIN TRENCH at N.25.d.9.9., and N.26.c.0.0. strongly held by Minenwerfer and Machine Guns, but that THE MAZE was occupied by Canadians, with the trench running to it from the South clear of the enemy.

A Section of Machine Guns and 1 Company 1/7th Scottish Rifles were at once directed to occupy that portion of the trench which lies in N.25.c., while Canadians, ex:
:tending their old line S.E. from M.30.central, linked up with the left of the 1/7th Scottish Rifles in the neighbour-
:hood of MYRTLE SAP. The left of the 156th Inf. Brigade line therefore at midnight 23/24th was as shewn by letters "C.C.C." on map.

The contributory causes to the entire success of the day's operations, which resulted in the capture of over 200 prisoners, numerous Machine Guns, Anti-Tank rifles and Minenwerfer, can be classified under four heads:-

(1). Artillery Barrage - very thick, (roughly one gun to 12 yards of front), and extremely even and accurate in 'Lift' and direction.

(2). The manner in which the leading wave of the attack followed close up to the artillery barrage.

(3). The Section 'blob' formations used by each Company in the attack, and the fact that each Battalion advanced on a one Company front or its equivalent.

(4). No halt until final objectives were reached.

24th August.   The Brigade was directed to advance at 7 a.m. in conjunction with an advance of the 157th Inf. Brigade on/

on its right. The latter's objective was HENIN HILL and that part of the HINDENBURG LINE which runs through it.

The objective of the 156th Inf. Brigade was the line of the sunken road connecting MARTIN and HENIN TRENCHES in N.26. Two Battalions, the 1/7th The Royal Scots, on the right, and the 1/7th Scottish Rifles, on the left, were each allotted half the objective mentioned, the 1/4th Royal Scots being ordered to concentrate and remain in Brigade Reserve about T.1.b.2.5. as soon as the 157th Inf. Brigade had passed through them and cleared their front.

The attack commenced at 7 a.m. and all objectives made good by 8 a.m. without any serious opposition being encountered. The Canadians, on our left, having taken the SUGAR FACTORY, touch was obtained with them during the afternoon and the line linked up, but at 9.30 p.m. orders were received to withdraw that part of our line running N.W. through N.26 central and refuse it back from that point to N.25.a.8.9. in view of next day's operations.

On our right, a considerable gap existed between the right of the 1/7th Royal Scots at N.32.b.7.8. and the left of the 157th Inf. Brigade, about T.3.central. In consequence, one Company 1/4th Royal Scots and one Section Machine Gun Company were ordered to fill the gap and establish a strong point at Cross Roads in N.33.c.7.5., and keep touch by means of Section Posts with units to right and left. This was done, and by 4 p.m. our line is as shewn in Green on map. A feature of the day's operat-:ions was the good patrol work carried out by 1/7th Royal Scots and 1/7th Scottish Rifles. Frequent patrols pushed forward up MARTIN and HENIN TRENCHES, and established the fact that the enemy were holding the HINDENBURG LINE strongly with Machine Guns.

The/

The shelling of our forward lines was severe at times and Minenwerfer troublesome.

The strong point garrison were heavily gassed with Yellow Cross throughout the night, and at dawn of the 25th, were withdrawn until the gas cleared, when the post was again reoccupied.

25th August.   The Brigade maintained its positions of the previous day.

26th August.   Orders were received during the night 25th/26th that the 155th Inf. Brigade would move forward, pass through our line and attack the HINDENBURG LINE in N.20.d. and N.27.a. - Zero hour 3 a.m.

The attack was successful.

At about 10 a.m., a Divisional Order was received directing one Battalion of 156th Inf. Brigade to follow up 155th Inf. Brigade, and take over that part of the HINDENBURG LINE captured by it. This was done, and at the same time a strong patrol of the 1/4th Royal Scots was thrown forward to ascertain whether the HINDEN:BURG LINE in N.34. was held by the enemy. This patrol reconnoitred the line from S. of the COJEUL RIVER down to T.5.a.central, up to which point it found 'all clear', but immediately S.E. of the last mentioned point it came under heavy Machine Gun fire and was forced to withdraw.

The 155th Inf. Brigade immediately occupied the cleared portion of the HINDENBURG LINE mentioned, and the 156th Inf. Brigade concentrated at night as follows-

    1/7th Scottish Rifles   at   N.28.c.7.5.
    1/4th Royal Scots   at   N.34.a.5.7.
    1/7th Royal Scots   along CROW TRENCH in N.29.d.
                                               in touch with Canadians to the North.

27th August. /

7.

27th August.   At 5.a.m. orders were received from Division for the Brigade to attack, in conjunction with the 157th Inf. Brigade on its right and the Canadians on its left.

The Brigade was assigned two objectives:-

First Objective.   the line U.2.central - O.32.cent.
Second Objective.   the line U.11.cent. - U.17.cent.

Zero hour, 10 a.m.

Preceeded by an extremely effective creeping barrage which came down at 10.3 a.m. on the line N.36.c.5.7. - N.30.d.5.2., the 1/7th Royal Scots on the left and 1/4th Royal Scots on the right swept forward through a maze of trenches and wire towards their first objective; the 1/7th Scottish Rifles remaining in Brigade Reserve at N.34.a.7.6. with two Sections, "B" Coy, 52nd M.G. Battalion.

By 1.30 p.m., the two leading battalions of the Brigade had reached their first objectives, had sent back over 500 prisoners of war, and reported the capture of over 80 Machine Guns.

Moreover, owing to the 157th Inf. Brigade on the right having somewhat edged off to the right of their first objective, which included the village of FONTAINE CROISILLES, the 1/4th Royal Scots extended their right to include that Village, and had it in their possession by 2. p.m.

At this juncture, Brigade H.Q. and the Brigade Reserve moved forward to N.36.b.5.0. in anticipation of a further advance towards HENDECOURT. The latter did not materialize owing to the Canadians on our left being held up by severe M.G. fire immediately E. of CHERISY, and the 157th Inf. Brigade being delayed for a similar reason about U.17.central.

The 1/7th Royal Scots established touch with/

with the Canadians on their left by nightfall, and the 1/4th Royal Scots by 1 a.m. on the 28th had gained touch with the 157th Inf. Brigade on their right. The line held by the 156th Inf. Brigade at 1 a.m. on the 28th, when it was relieved by the 2nd Canadian Division, is as shewn in purple on the Map.

28th August.   c   The Brigade withdrew for three days' rest to S.5.b. Attached are appended:-

    A. Casualties in the Brigade by units.
    B. Prisoners of War captured by units.
    C. War Material captured by units.

12th September 1918.

          A Leggett
          Brig. General,
      Commanding 156th Inf. Brigade.

180th. Infantry Brigade Order No. 49   SECRET
                                                    Copy No. 18

                                              5th. August 1918.

1. The Southern Boundary of the 52nd. Divisional Front is being
    altered on the 6th. August to the following line -
    H.30.a.2.3 - H.3.d.8.7 - H.5.a.0.0 - H.2.c.5.2.

2. On the 6th. August the Northern and Southern Boundaries of
    the 180th. Infantry Brigade will be altered in accordance with
    the attached map as follows:-
    (a) Troops of the 7th. Cameronians South of the new Southern
        Boundary will be relieved by troops from 1st. Royal
        Munster Fusiliers and 2/4th. Battalion South Lancashire
        Regiment.

    (b) Troops of the 4th. Royal Scots North of the present
        Northern Boundary will be relieved by troops of the
        6th. H.L.I.

    (c) 7th. Royal Scots will relieve the troops of 6th. H.L.I.
        in that portion of the POST LINE North of the present
        Northern Boundary Line.

    (d) Troops of 7th. Royal Scots in the Outpost Zone North
        of the new Brigade Boundary Line will be relieved by
        troops from 6th. H.L.I.

    (e) The gun at present manned by 180th. L.T.M. Battery at
        H.3.d.1.7 will be relieved by the 172nd. L.T.M. Battery.

    All arrangements for the above reliefs will be made by
    Commanders concerned.

3. The Inter-Battalion Boundary will be altered on the 6th.
    August in accordance with the attached map.
        The necessary adjustments will be carried out under arrange-
    ments to be made by Os.C. 7th. Royal Scots and 7th. Cameronians.

4. All reliefs will be carried out by day and will be completed
    by 6 P.M.
        Completion of reliefs will be reported "Priority" to these
    H.Q. by code word "CHANGE".

5. H.Qs of 4th. Royal Scots, 7th. Royal Scots and 7th. Cameronians
    will remain as at present.

6. ACKNOWLEDGE.

                                        Stanley Smith Captain.
Issued at 1.15 p.m.   for Brigade Major, 180th. Inf. Bde.

Copy No. 1 to 4th. Royal Scots   Copy No. 10 to D.A.C.
       2   7th. Royal Scots   11   Staff Captain
       3   7th. Cameronians   12   Intelligence Off. *
       4   180th. L.T.M. Battery   13   Bde. Sig. Off.
       5   119th. Inf. Bde. *   14   Gas Officer   *
       6   172nd. Inf. Bde. *   15   Bde. S.O.   *
       7   52nd. Division   16   Bde. T.O.
       8   412th. Field Co. R.E.   17   R.F.A. Liaison Off.
       9   "D" Coy. 52nd. M.G. Bn. * 18 & 19 War Diary
                                          20   File

            * No map attached

4th. Royal Scots
7th. Royal Scots
156th. L.T.M. Battery.

War Diary August   BM 549   *Appendix II*

1. With reference to attached 52nd. Divisional letter G 20/9/37, the number of Officers at the nucleus Camp will for the present be reduced to 1 Coy. Commander per Battalion. All other Officers, including 2nds-in-command will join their units in the line forthwith. Battalions will issue the necessary instructions.

2. The **duties** laid down for the 2nd-in-command whilst up in the line under these circumstances are as under:-

    (a) To instruct Platoon Commanders in their duties as regards trench routine and administration.
    (b) To instruct Platoon Commanders in the tactical handling of a platoon in trench warfare. Small tactical schemes should be set to each platoon commander in order to make him think out his course of action under the varying circumstances that may arise.
    (c) To see that Trench discipline is rigidly enforced throughout the Battalion area.
    (d) To ensure that the provisions of 52nd. Division Trench Standing Orders are in all cases adhered to.
    (e) The following points should receive special attention:-
      (1) Cleanliness of trenches
      (2) Sanitation of Trenches
      (3) Cleanliness of men
      (4) Equipment properly hung up on pegs when not in use.
      (5) Rifles placed in proper rifle racks.
      (6) The proper proportion of men wearing equipment, and all men wearing gas masks and steel helmets.
      (7) The boots of each man to be off for at least half an hour during each 24 hours.
      (8) Cleanliness and care of arms and equipment.

3. The above duties will occupy the whole time of the 2nd-in-command and he will, therefore, be employed on no other duty. The normal duties of the 2nd-in-command will be performed by the next senior Officer.

9th. August 1918.

(Sgd) H. Sayer, Captain,
Brigade Major, 156th. Inf. Bde.

War Diary Append II A

O.C.
4th. Royal Scots

SECRET

BM 572

(Cancelled)

1. With reference to para 4 of this Office BM 467 of the 5th. August, the Division have now laid down that "in normal circumstances (i.e. until the order " Man Battle Stations" has been issued) the Battalion in support in the BROWN LINE is at disposal of G.Os.C. Brigades for a counter attack to restore a local situation either in the main line of resistance or the outpost zone".

2. For this purpose, the Coy. from your Battalion, located in GULLY POST, should at all times hold itself in readiness to deliver an immediate counter attack either on the POST LINE or on the OUTPOST LINE in the event of necessity arising and the necessary reconnaissances should be carried out.

The B.G.C. does not consider it likely that the whole of your Battalion will be used to deliver an immediate counter attack on either the POST LINE or the OUTPOST ZONE, but all Coy. Commanders and other officers should carry out reconnaissances of possible lines of counter attack, so that any Coy. of your Battalion, in addition to the one in GULLY POST, could be made available for such a counter attack in the event of the necessity arising.

3. With above exception, the provisions of BM 467 of the 5th. inst. remain unaltered.

10th. August 1918.

(Sgd) H. SAYER, Captain,
Brigade Major, 156th. Inf. Bde.

Copies to 7th. Royal Scots
7th. Cameronians (Sco. Rifles)

War Diary
August Appendix III

SECRET.
Copy No. **16**

156th. Infantry Brigade Order No. 80

Ref. Map POINT DU JOUR - 1/10,000   13th. August 1915.

1. On 13th. August 1915, 4th. Royal Scots will relieve 7th. Royal Scots in the Left-Sub-section, and on relief 7th. Royal Scots will take over portion of BROWN LINE at present held by 4th. Royal Scots.

2. All details of relief will be arranged between Battalion Commanders concerned.

3. Lists of maps and lists of trench stores etc. taken over will be forwarded to Brigade Headquarters.

4. After relief, Headquarters of Battalions will be as follows:-

    4th. Royal Scots B.21.a.9.2
    7th. Royal Scots B.27.a.2.5
    7th. Cameronians (S.R.) B.27.c.7.5

    Battalion Headquarters at POINT DU JOUR (B.5.c.4.7) will be vacated by 7th. Cameronians (S.R.) by 2 p.m. on 13th. inst.

5. Reliefs will be carried out by day and will be completed by 6 p.m. Completion to be reported to these Headquarters by the code word "BIEN".

6. ACKNOWLEDGE.

Issued at 7 am

Stanley Smith Captain,
for Brigade Major, 156th. Inf. Bde.

    Copy No. 1 to 4th. Royal Scots
            2   7th. Royal Scots
            3   7th. Cameronians (S.R.)
            4   156th. L.T.M. Battery
            5   272nd. Inf. Bde.
            6   157th. Inf. Bde.
            7   Staff Captain
            8   Intelligence Officer
            9   Bde. Sig. Officer
           10   Bde. T.O.
           11   78th. Bde. R.F.A.
           12   412th. Field Co. R.E.
           13   1/1st. Lowland Fld. Amb.
           14   "B" Coy. 52nd. M.G. Bn.
           15   Bde. S.O.
        16 & 17   War Diary ✓
           18   File

War Diary August Appendix IV

SECRET.

COPY No. 17

189th INF. BRIGADE ORDER No. 61.

Ref. Map HARDINVAL, 1/20,000.
& POINT DU JOUR.

14th August 1918.

1. The 52nd (Lowland) Division is being relieved by the 51st (Highland) Division on the nights 14th/15th, 15th/16th, and 16th/17th August, and on relief will probably be located in the BAVY – AUBIGNY Area.

2. The 155th Infantry Brigade will be relieved on August 15th, and night 15th/16th in accordance with attached Relief Table. Relief to be completed by 4 a.m. on the 17th August.

3. Advance parties from relieving units will report during the afternoon of 16th August.

4. Guides for relieving troops will be supplied in accordance with attached table.

5. Distances of 200 yards will be maintained during the relief between platoons or equivalent formations.

6. All 1/10,000 and 1/20,000 Maps, Log Books, Aeroplane Photographs, Plans of Projected Operations, Trench Stores, Communications etc will be handed over and receipts obtained.
   Special care is to be taken to hand over all details of pending gas operations.

7. All other details will be arranged between Commanders concerned.

8. Command of Battalion Subsections will pass on completion of respective reliefs.

9. Completion of relief will be reported by "Priority" wire to these H.Q. by the code word "OLD".

10. Orders for moves after relief will be issued later.

11. Command of Brigade Section will pass to O.C., 154th Inf. Brigade on completion of relief, at which time Brigade H.Q. will close at its present location. Further orders will be issued as to opening of a new Brigade H.Q.

12. ACKNOWLEDGE.

Issued at 10-30 pm

H. Taylor
Captain,
Brigade Major, 155th Inf. Brigade.

Copy No 1 to 4th Royal Scots.
   2   7th Royal Scots.
   3   7th Cameronians. (S.R.)
   4   155th L.T.M. Battery.
   5   52nd Division.
   6   154th Inf. Brigade
   7   Right Group, 51st Div. Arty.
   8   410th Field Coy. R.E.
   9   1/1st Low. Field Amb.

Copy No 10 to "C" Coy, 51st M.G. Bn.
   11   S.S.O.
   12   Staff Captain.
   13   Intell. Officer.
   14   Bde. Sig. Officer.
   15   Bde. Transpt. Officer.
   16   Bde. Supply Officer.
   17 & 18. War Diary
   19   File.

War Diary August 1918
Appendix V

SECRET.

Copy No. 16

156th. Infantry Brigade Order No. 52.

Ref Maps HAREUIL - 1/20,000 &
Sheets 56B and 51C - 1/40,000   15th August 1918.

1. **MOVE.**   On relief by the 154th Inf. Brigade, the 156th Inf. Brigade will proceed by Light Railway to Billets and Camps in the SAVY Area.

2. **ENTRAINING.**
   (i). Units will entrain at ECOURIE Light Railway Station in the following order:-

   (Brigade H.Q.
   (156th L.T.M. Battery.
   4th Royal Scots.
   7th Cameronians. (S.R.)
   7th Royal Scots.
   "B" Coy, 52nd M.G. Battalion.

   (ii). Battalions will entrain as complete units, and no mixing of Battalions will be allowed.
   (iii). Forming up places in the vicinity of the Railway Station will be selected by Battalions.
   (iv). Entraining Officer will be Lieut. A.S. BILSLAND.
   Each Battalion will appoint an entraining Officer who will report to the Brigade entraining Officer at ECURIE Station at 10.30 p.m.

3. **LEWIS GUNS.**
   (i). Battalions will take all Lewis Guns and 16 drums per gun on the train from ECURIE.
   (ii). It is hoped to get a train for the balance of Lewis Gun drums and Yukon Packs and anti-gas combination suits. This train will start at midnight from B.27.a.1.4.
   One Sergeant and 12 men per Battalion will travel with this train, under an Officer to be detailed by 7th Royal Scots. All drums etc to be loaded on this train must be at the loading place by 11.30 p.m., at which hour battalion parties will report to the Officer mentioned above.
   7th Royal Scots will wire Brigade H.Q. the name of the Officer selected.
   (iii). In the event of above train not being available, the alternative is that limbers will lift surplus drums etc. This transport will be arranged for by Bde. H.Q.

4. **DETRAINING.**
   (i). Detraining Station will be at SAVY; length of journey 5 hours.
   (ii). Brigade Detraining Officer - Captain G.S. SMITH.
   Units will detail a Detraining Officer who will proceed with the first train to leave ECURIE. They will report to Bde. Detraining Officer at ECURIE Station at 10.30 p.m.

5. **BILLETING.**
   (i). On arrival, units will be billeted as follows:-

Brigade Headquarters,	CHATEAU BERLES.
4th Royal Scots	(VILLERS BRULIN. (BETHONSART.
7th Royal Scots	(BERLES. (VANDELICOURT.
7th Cameronians	(SAVY. (BERLETTE.
156th L.T.M. Battery	BERLES.

   Billeting parties, which were sent forward this morning, will meet units at detraining Station and guide them to Billets.
   (ii)./

5. BILLETS, Continued.
    (ii). Units will report arrival in Billets by code word "DEAR"

6. TRANSPORT. Battalions Transport is proceeding to new area to-day under the orders of Bde. Transport Officer, and will be billeted with units on arrival in the new area.

7. RATIONS. Rations for the 16th instant are proceeding with Battalion Transport by road to-day. Rations for 17th inst. will be delivered at Q.M. Stores in the new area.

8. NUCLEUS. "Nucleus" of Battalions will proceed by road tomorrow under orders to be issued by Bde. H.Q.

9. ORDERLIES. Two cyclists per Battalion and one from 156th L.T.M. Battery will report to Brigade H.Q. on arrival in the new area. They will be retained and rationed at Bde. H.Q.

10. BRIGADE H.Q. Brigade Headquarters will open at CHATEAU BERLES at 5 a.m. on the 16th instant.

11. ACKNOWLEDGE.

Issued at _____
                              Captain,
                      Brigade Major, 156th Inf. Brigade.

Copy No 1 to 4th Royal Scots.
       2   7th Royal Scots.
       3   7th Cameronians. (S.R.)
       4   156th L.T.M. Battery.
       5   52nd Division.
       6   154th Inf. Brigade.
       7   412th Field Coy R.E.
       8   "B" Coy, 52nd M.G. Battalion.
       9   B.G.C.
      10   Staff Captain.
      11   Intelligence Officer.
      12   Bde. Sigs. Officer.
      13   Bde. Transport Officer.
      14   Bde. Supply Officer.
  15 & 16   War Diary.
      17   File.

RELIEF TABLE.

Issued with 154th Inf. Brigade Order No. 51.

"A" SERIAL No	"B" UNIT.	"C" To be relieved by	"D" Meeting point for Guides	"E" Time for Guides to be at Meeting Point.	"F" Route to be followed by relieving unit	"G" REMARKS.
1	7th Camerons (S.R.)	4th Seaforth Highlanders	Junction of KOM TRAK and ROUCH at B.Sn.G.3.d.	6.45 p.m.	KOM TRAK - KOM ALEH	(a). Guides for Battalions will be provided at the following rates:- 1 Per Platoon 1 Per Coy H.Q. 2 Per Battn. H.Q. and for L.T.M. Battery at the rate of 1 per Section.
2.	4th Royal Scots	7th Argyle & Sutherland Highlanders	Western end of OUSE ALLEY	6.15 p.m.	OUSE ALLEY	
3.	7th Royal Scots	4th Gordon Highlanders	(a Right hand Coys as for Serial No 1......7.45 p.m. (b Main H.Q. & Left hand Coys, as for Serial No 2 ....7.15 p.m.		KOM TRAK - KOM ALEH OUSE ALLEY	(b). Units will ensure that all guides using the route laid down for Serial No 1 are thoroughly acquainted with it.
4	154th L.T.M. Battery.	154th L.T.M. Battery.	As for Serial No 2	6 p.m.	OUSE ALLEY.	

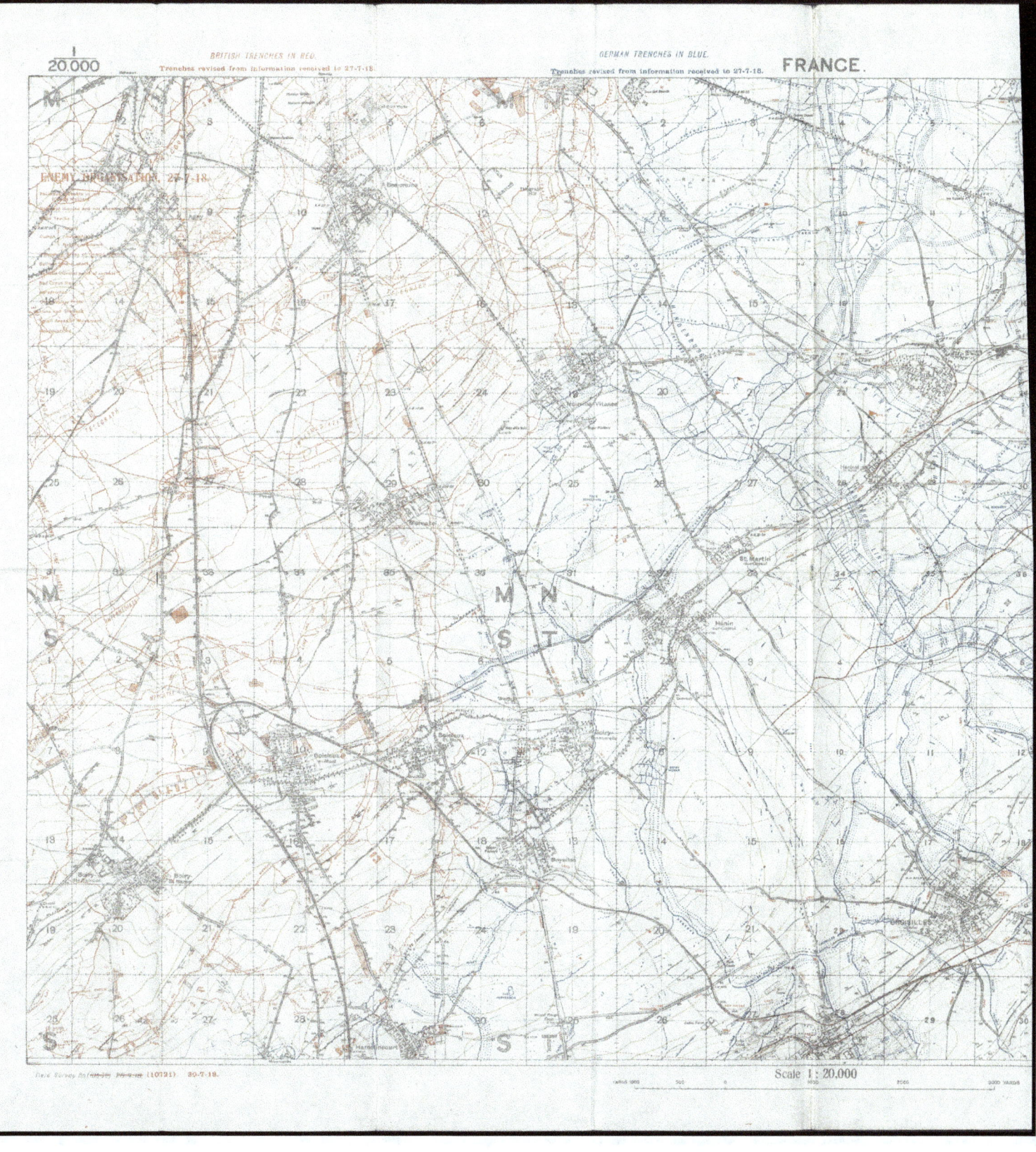

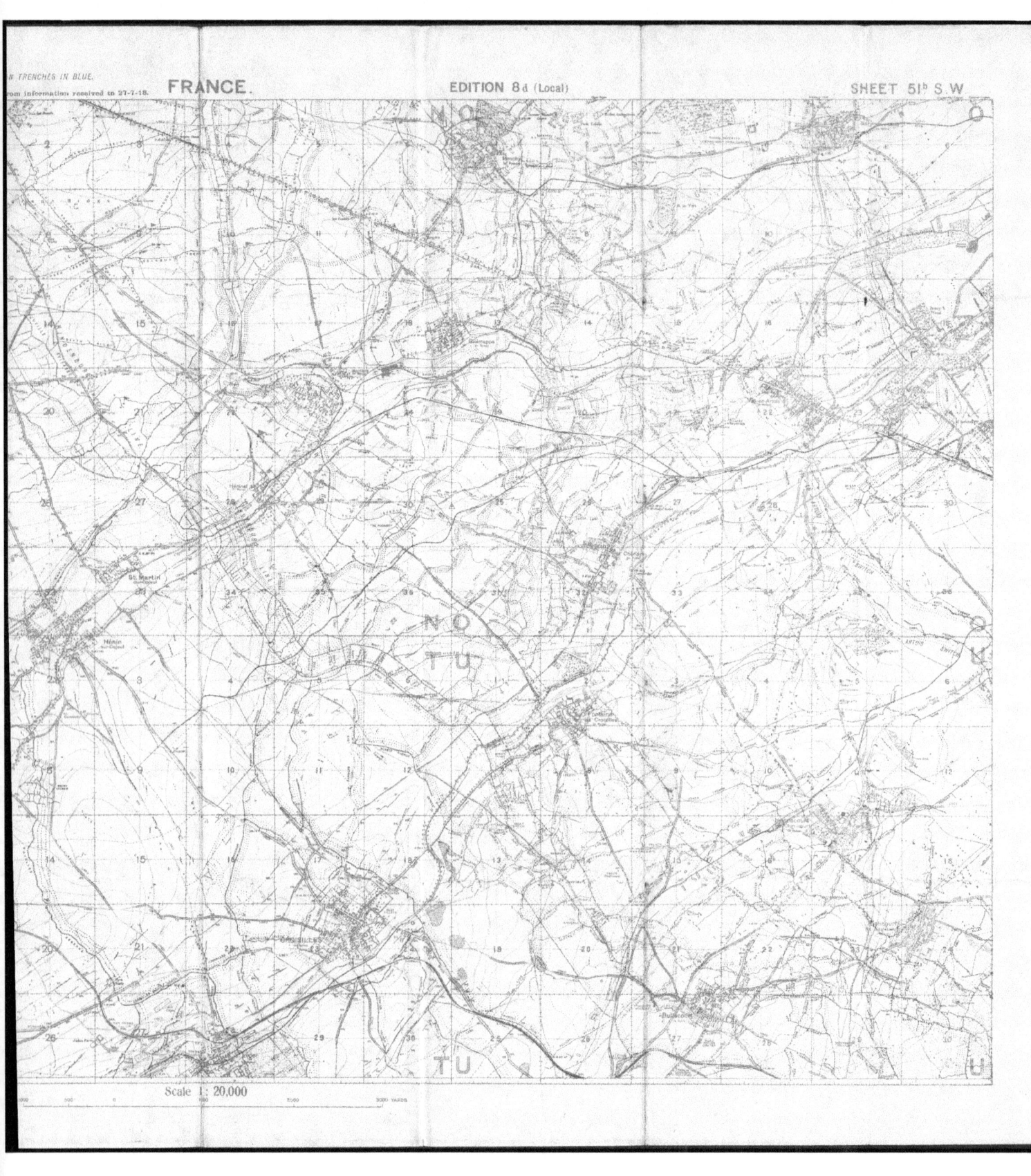

FRANCE. EDITION 8d (Local) SHEET 51b S.W

Scale 1: 20,000

On His Majesty's Service.

156th Bde INF
Sept 18

Confidential.   10-10.

H.Qrs.,
   52nd Division.

        Herewith Bde. War Diary,
(Volume XL) and relative
appendices, for the month of
September, 1918.

                        Archd. E. Bird Lieut.
                        A.T.O. for Brig. General,
                        Commanding 156th Inf. Bde.

16th Octr., 1918.

Original

Confidential No 6

War Diary
of
156th Infantry Brigade

1st to 30th September 1916

Vol XL

WAR DIARY
INTELLIGENCE SUMMARY

155th Infantry Brigade

September 1918

Ref Maps 57BSW 57BSE
57cNW 57cNE /20000

Army Form C. 2118.

Page 1.

Place	Date 1918 Sept	Hour	Summary of Events and Information	Remarks and references to Appendices
U.4.c.9.5.	1st		Brigade in Support to the Battle line running through BULLECOURT. B.C. visited 155th Inf Bde and reconnoitred position for a new Bde HQ. A conference of C.Os was held in the morning and verbal orders were given for operations which were subsequently confirmed. In the evening the Bde was moved up in support of the 155th Inf Bde whose attack east of BULLECOURT.	
U.20.a.9.6	2nd		Early morning Bde moved up to TANK AVENUE and TANK SUPPORT TRENCHES & GORDON RESERVE TRENCH. Bde HQ moved forward & established a joint HQ with 155th Inf Bde at THE KNUCKLE U.20.a.9.6. At 8.45 a.m. Bde attacked HINDENBURG LINE from C.6.2.90. to MOULIN SANS SOUCI.	
V.30.d.5.3.	3rd		Bde concentrated in V.30.d. Bde HQ V.30.d.5.3. Harry Lauder visited the Bde and sang songs and addresses to the troops. His visit was very much appreciated by all ranks.	

WAR DIARY
INTELLIGENCE SUMMARY

151st Infantry Brigade

September 1918

Page 2.

Place	Date	Hour	Summary of Events and Information	Remarks and references to Appendices
D 1 a 3.5	4th		Bde renewed concentrated Bde H.Q. moved to D 1 a 3.5. Information received this Division would be relieved by 56th Divn on 5th inst	
	5th		Our advance fastura proceeded from at - and 52nd Divn advance to their anticipated position was cancelled about 11 a.m.	
	6th		Information received that Divn would [illegible] entire with Corps Support in ST LEGER area on 7th inst Bde Order No BM.101. issued	Appendix I
B 3 c 3 6	7th		Bde moved back to B 2 3 c d 8. Bde H.Q. B 3 c 3 6 Report ref. 31/8/18 – 7/9/18 Lessons learnt during Operations 28/8/18 – 7/9/18	Appendix II & III July/r Jul/r
	8th		Bde rested and cleaned up.	
	9th		Bde rested and re-equipped was commenced preceded by G.S. wagon to the baths.	
	10th		Training commenced Range practice begun Platoon demonstration in No 1 & 2. Training 3rd Army	Jul/r
	11th		Training continued Information received that Div would probably relieve 52nd Div in the	Jul/r

Army Form C. 2118.

WAR DIARY
or
INTELLIGENCE SUMMARY

157th L.T.M. Bde.

September 1918

Page 3

Place	Date	Hour	Summary of Events and Information	Remarks and references to Appendices
B3.c.3.6.	12th		Training continued. Battery of Bde. completed.	
	13th		Show carried on. B.G.L. & C.O. remounted positions in the line. The Bde. to be in Bde Reserve.	
	14th		Bde. addressed by 174th Inf Bde Commander - Scouts examined & awards, and an Officer per Coy attended a tank demonstration. C.O. and Coy Cmdrs visited the line.	
			[struck through] Capt. I. Jones, Ag. Adjt. proceeded on 14 days leave to U.K.	
			Lieut. J. Austin A/Staff Capt proceeded on 14 days leave to U.K.	
			Bomb. Lay. Sgt. A. S. Johnson of the London Regt. who had rendered great service as Bde. Sig. Sgt. on Aug 31st returned to 52nd Divn. went sick thru much run down, was admitted to Hosp. about Sep. 12th	
			Lieut D. L. Grant & Sergt. Scott the Reg. Sig. Officer is now in charge of the Section.	
		5.30 p.m.	Bde Order No. 5 issued re relief of 174th L.T. Bde. 57th Divn. Administration. No 11 issue Appendix I	

Army Form C. 2118.

WAR DIARY
or
INTELLIGENCE SUMMARY.
(Erase heading not required.)

151st Df/Bde

September 1918

Page 4

Place	Date 1918 Sept.	Hour	Summary of Events and Information	Remarks and references to Appendices
B.3.c.3.6.	15th		Church Parades. Major-General J. HILL, Comdg. 52nd Divs. presented ribbons of M.M. won recently by men of the Bde. Administrative Instructions No. 11 issued. Capt. J. R. Sadler A/Staff Capt returned from leave to U.K.	Appendix V Full 4
C.6.6.4.8.	16th		Moves as per Bde Order No. 55. Violent thunderstorm during the night.	
			During the period 7/15th Sept. what Bde was in Corps Support the weather was wretched making life under a bivouac sheet somewhat uncomfortable. The weather also interfered very considerably with training of the Bde. B.G.C. and B.M. visited the units & also 151st Inf Bde and attached the enemy's positions Reserve Brigade Defence Scheme issued considerable amount of rain during the night.	Full 4 VI Full 4
	17th		Bright dry day. B.G.C. attended Conference at Div. H.Q.	
	18th		Dry day with very dull intervals.	

Army Form C. 2118.

WAR DIARY
or
INTELLIGENCE SUMMARY

156 Infantry Bde.

September 1916 Page 5

Place	Date	Hour	Summary of Events and Information	Remarks and references to Appendices
C.6.6.4.5.	19		The Brigade relieved by the 3rd Canadian Bde, and moved to Huesne area in D.14. 15. and 16. B.M. 2 issued	Appendix VII
	20.		Orders received that the Brigade would relieve the 153rd Infantry Brigade on the night of 20/21st Sept. Conference of Battalion Commanders at Bde HQ. after which representatives from units visited the lines in the MOEUVRES Sector. Bde Order No. 52 issued.	Appendix VIII
			The relief was carried out according to instructions. A great deal of gas (Yellow Cross) was experienced during the relief.	
D.15.6.67. MOEUVRES H.Q. Sector.	21		Our line in front of MOEUVRES was subjected to a considerable amount of shelling during the morning. At 3.30pm a very heavy barrage was brought down on MOEUVRES and our line E. of the J. villages, held by the 4th & 7th Royal Scots. At 3.45pm a strong attack was delivered against our defences in E.14. b.o.d. on the left of the 4th Royal Scots were actively engaged, but the enemy obtained a footing in our defences on the right flank. He was ejected by our immediate counter attack, and the situation was completely restored by 7.30pm. During the night the 4th Royal Scots attacked, and captured the enemy post at E.14 central. The day's operations yielded us 5 machine guns, and a few prisoners. (See history of operations.)	Appendix IX

Lieut. (illegible) Bde. I.O. wounded during operations. Lieut (illegible) for duty as A.T.I.O.

Army Form C. 2118.

M of Reference.
57 NE.

WAR DIARY
152 Infantry Brigade
or
INTELLIGENCE SUMMARY.

September 1918

Instructions regarding War Diaries and Intelligence
Summaries are contained in F.S. Regs., Part II.
and the Staff Manual respectively. Title pages
will be prepared in manuscript.

Page 6.

Place	Date Sept.	Hour	Summary of Events and Information	Remarks and references to Appendices
D.15.b.6.7. HQ MOEUVRES Sector	22.		The Brigade Sector heavily shelled at intervals throughout the day. During the night, a determined counter attack was carried out against our new post in E.14 central. This was preceded by heavy artillery and trench mortar fire, this attack was completely repulsed with heavy casualties to the enemy. Brig. Genl. G/8 Gynge's official report exhibited prisoners from Gasher Ordres received that the Brigade would be relieved by the 155 Inf. Bde. on the night of 23/24 Sept. Bn. O 64 issued. Relief carried out without incident.	A/Br/8/6
	23.			Appendix X A/B/8/12
Bde H.Q. D.7.a.c.3	24		Battalions resting.	
	25		Instructions received for attack on CANAL DU NORD. Brigade's Instructions No 12/15 sued. No 1, and Administrative Instructions No 12/15 sued.	Appendices XI and XII
	26.		Instructions received that the attack would take place on 27 Sept. Bde. Order No 57 issued. Brigade moved out to assembly area after dusk. HQ opened at E.19.a.2.9 at 6pm.	Appendix XII
E.19.a.2.9	27.	5.20am	– Our barrage opened. Stiff opposition was met with W. of the CANAL, and in LEOPARD TRENCH	
		10.45	L.10H TR. in our hands.	
		11am	All ground N. of CAMBRAI Road secure. KANGAROO and BOW trenches gave considerable trouble, and required help by Tanks at 4pm.	(Sgd) History of Operations
		4.30am	All objectives secured. Prisoners 470 – machine guns 50	Appendix XIV A/B/8/6

A/0921. Wt. W12839/M1297 750,000. 1/17. D. D & L., Ltd. Forms/C2118/14.

Army Form C. 2118.

Map Reference 57cNE

152 Infantry Brigade. WAR DIARY or INTELLIGENCE SUMMARY.

September 1918 (Erase heading not required.)

Page. 7.

Place	Date Sept.	Hour	Summary of Events and Information	Remarks and references to Appendices
H.Q. E.19.a.2.9.	28		The Brigade remained in captured area. Brig. Gen. G.H. Leggett C.M.G. D.S.O. proceeded on special leave to U.K. Lt Col J.G.P. Romanes D.S.O. assumed command of the Brigade.	O.B./3/5/r O.B.3./r app XV
	29			
	30		Brigade rested, and carried out salvage work. Reorganisation was commenced. Strength on 30th Sept.	

J Stanley Smith
Capt.
a/Brigade Major
152 Infantry Brigade.

APPENDIX I Secret

156th Infantry Brigade Order No 54

Copy No. 3

Ref. Maps 51B.S.W. & 51B.S.E.   1st September 1918
57C.N.W. 57C.N.E.

1. (a) The Canadian Corps of 1st Army on our left will attack the DROCOURT-QUEANT Line, tomorrow, 2nd September

   (b) The 3rd Division of VI Corps on our Right will capture LAGNICOURT and push on towards BEAUMETZ-LES-CAMBRAI

   (c) The XVII Corps will co-operate with the attack of the Canadians and, by pushing its left forward endeavour to gain position to attack QUEANT from the north

   (d) The 57rd Divn. on the left of the XVII Corps will not make a frontal attack on the DROCOURT-QUEANT line, but will pass through a gap made by the Canadian Corps in V.13 and then turn South-east.

2. The 52nd Division will conform to the

2.

the movements of the 57th Divn. and move forward to assault when it is know that 57th Divn. is advancing

3. (a) The 156th Inf.Bde. will pass through the 155th Inf.Bde. and attack under a barrage and clear the area MOULIN-SANS-SOUCI - The Road in U.30.b as far as cross roads in V.25.c.b.2 D.Ka.5.1 - C.6.b.9.0

(b) The barrage will go down on the line Road U.30.c.5.0 - U.30.b.5.7 at ZERO hour, remain there for 10 minutes and then creep forward at rate of 100 yards per four minutes to final objective line in front of which a protective barrage will remain for 15 minutes

(c) ZERO hour will be notified by Bde. H.Q and will depend on the success of the assault further north.

4. The 155th Inf.Bde will move up, their right to keep touch with 3rd Divn. on extreme right and the Right of the 156th Inf.Bde attack, and after the 156th Inf.Bde has obtained its

3.

objectives, will attack the QUEANT-LAGNICOURT ROAD, passing partly through the right of the 156th Inf. Bde.

5. The 156th Inf. Bde. will be ready to move East of the TANK AVENUE-TANK SUPPORT Line (V.22.d - V.28.b & d.) and attack when ordered any time after 0530 tomorrow, 2nd September. The order to units to move from present positions to the TANK AVENUE Line will be issued from 156th Bde. H.Q.

6. The 156th Inf. Bde. will attack as follows:-
Right attack. 1/7th Cameronians
  Final objective C.6.b.9.0 -
  D.1.a.5.1 - V.25.c.6.2 (Cross Roads inclusive)
Left attack. 1/4th Royal Scots
  Final objective V.25.c.6.2 (Cross Roads exclusive) along Road in U.30.b to MOULIN SANS-SOUCI inclusive.
The line of deployment for attack will be the most advanced

4.

line held by the 155th Inf Bde.
after its attack tonight, and it
is hoped that it will be the
line of that Brigade's final
objective which has already been
notified (see BM 16).
   The 1/7th Royal Scots will be
in reserve to the attack and on
receipt of orders from Bde. H.Q.
will move into GORDON RESERVE
with H.Q. at approx. U.22.C.3.2.

7. One section M.G. Coy. will accompany each
of the Battalions of the Bde. The remaining
section will move into Bde. Reserve at
GORDON RESERVE when ordered by Bde.
H-Q. and there await further orders.

8. On receipt of orders from Bde. H-Q.
156th L.T.M. Battery will move up to
GORDON RESERVE. Four T.Ms will
be ready to move forward to assist the
attacking Bns. any time after 0530.

9. When ordered to move forward to
TANK AVENUE and TANK SUPPORT
LINE O's C. 1/7 Cameronians and
1/4th Royal Scots will establish
their HQ at approx. the undermentioned

5.

points:-
 1/7 Cameronians at U.28.d.5.8
 1/4 Royal Scots at U.22.d.6.3

10. Contact aeroplanes will call for flares at 0600, 0700, 0800 and 1000 tomorrow.

11. Bde. H.Q. will open at U.20.a.9.6 at 0500 at which hour its present office will close.

12. ACKNOWLEDGE BY WIRE.

Issued at 8.15 p.m.

H Jaffe
Captain
Brigade Major

Copy to 1 to 4th R.S.   7 to 15 7 S/Bde
       2   7th R.S   8   52 Divn
       3   7 Cameronians   9+10 War Diary
       4   156 L.T.M.Bty   11   File.
       5   B.Bty. 52 M.G.Bn.
       6   155 Inf Bde

Diary of Operations
September 1st - 3rd

APPENDIX II

At 6pm 1st September the Battalion concentrated in trenches just in rear of BULLECOURT. 154th Infantry Brigade Order No. 531 was received about 9 pm. Briefly, this laid down the front of attack for the Brigade as follows:-

4th Royal Scots — from MIN.SANS SOUCI to V.25.c.6.2.

7th Cameronians — from V.25.c.6.2. to D.1.a.8.1. to C.6.& 9.0.

Jumping off place for both these Battalions the old British front line trenches running north and south through U.29.d and C and 5.b. and d. Position of assembly for attacking Battalions TANK SUPPORT Trench just in front of BULLECOURT. Accordingly at 1.5 a.m. orders were received to move to the point of assembly and by was am this move was completed. At 3 o'clock a verbal telephone message was received from Brigade that Zero would be at 5.45 a.m. when the Barrage would come down in front of the jumping off place. At 5.40 am the Battalion moved across country in the following order:-

B Coy on the left;

C Coy on the right;

the sunken road dividing these two Coys each of which were on a one platoon front;

D Coy also on one platoon frontage was echelonned on the right rear of C Coy; and

A Coy in reserve with its left on the sunken road.

The Machine Gun Section attached to the Battalion moved with D Coy. By 5.40 a.m. jumping off trenches had been reached. At 5.45 am the barrage came down and dwelt for ten minutes in front of the old British trenches and at 5.55 crept forward. B and C Coys advanced as at once. The barrage was very weak and very wild, and C Coy sustained several casualties from it. It failed entirely to touch the front line of the HINDENBURG SYSTEM.

By 6.10 a.m. B and C Coys were held up by thick wire in front of the HINDENBURG LINE which had in no way been damaged. The section of C Coy under Corporal STAFF succeeded in penetrating the wire and entering the trench where they accounted for 13 of enemy, but when enemy reinforcements arrived they were forced to evacuate the trench and take up a position about 30 yards from the trench in shell-holes in the wire. At this time there were no troops either on the left or the right flanks of the Battalion. Shortly afterwards the 1st Royal Scots came up on the left. Subsequent investigations proved that there were 9 machine guns in the Hindenburg Trench covering the whole area attacked by the Battalion. In addition flanking fire from the far side of the HIRONDELLE Valley also covered the Battalion front. Many efforts were made to advance through the wire but it was found impossible in face of the heavy fire encountered and a line was taken up roughly as follows from U.30.d.3.2 to C.6.b.3.2 to C.6.c.4.4, that just south-west of C.6. Central being taken up by D Coy, machine gun section shooting on the extreme right of the line. OC 4 Coy finding no one on the left of D line moved his Coy over to that flank.

The enemy made several attempts at outflanking the Battalion by working down the Railway line. These were in all cases frustrated by D Coy and the machine guns on the right flank. For two and a half hours this position was maintained in spite of enemy machine gun fire. Several more or less successful attempts were made to combat this, notably Sergeant MCGREGOR who got hold of a Lewis Gun, whose section had been knocked out, and stood on a machine gun directly to his front and knocked out the team. Owing to the number of shell-holes sufficient cover was available to prevent casualties. Though had the enemy made use of artillery or trench mortars the situation would have been precarious. As it was however the only casualties suffered at this time were due to platoon commanders going forward in an endeavour to find means of breaking through the wire. Useful work was done by runners and Stretcher bearers who had to cross the open under very heavy fire. So far the remainder of the Battalion sections remained in their shell-holes and kept a sharp look out.

About 15:30 Privates McClure and Cardlish, noticing the fire from the trench had decreased, crept forward through the wire to the trench and found that at that point unoccupied. They at once brought back information that the line at that point was not held, and "C" Coy. at once pushed forward and seized that portion of the line. "D" Coy. followed their example and by 15:40 the front line of the HINDENBURG SYSTEM was in our hands. Preparations for advancing to the final objective were hurried forwards and the advance began against heavy machine gun fire both from the front and also from the direction of QUEANT. Two platoons of "D" Coy. one under Lieutenant McGlashan the other under Lieutenant Watson noticing the concentration of machine gun fire on our right flank manoeuvred their platoons into position and brought their Lewis Guns into action and inflicted heavy casualties on the enemy in that direction silencing their guns and enabling the line to advance. At 16:10 all objectives had been gained and were in process of being consolidated.

Orders had been received to push forward patrols at once into QUEANT and "A" Coy. had already detached two platoons for this duty when heavy machine gun fire from the village showed that it was still strongly occupied. These patrols were ordered to stand by for the time being. At about 9 o'clock a message was received from Brigade that a new line would be taken up from about D.2.d.9.6. along the railway to C.6.d.8.9. This was afterwards cancelled. At 9:30 pm Very lights and machine gun fire which had been prominent in QUEANT during the earlier part of the evening almost entirely ceased and patrols were pushed forward and found the place evacuated. Patrolling of this area was continued throughout the night and about 5 am the patrols of the 155th Brigade pushed through the Batln. from the north and occupied the ground about QUEANT. At 6:30 am the next morning a patrol under Lieutenant BIRD started to reconnoitre PRONVILLE but the heavy barrage of our own guns on to QUEANT held them up on our side of the village and it was not until 9.45 a.m. that they were able to enter PRONVILLE which they found to be evacuated, and no signs of the enemy were encountered. About the same time the 155 Brigade began to mop up the trenches of the HINDENBURG LINE west and south of QUEANT and the 156 Brigade assembled in and about square O.30.d. where they remained without further action until on relief at 7 a.m. on September 4th.

Casualties

	Killed	Wounded
Officers	-	7
Other Ranks	11	48
	" missing at duty	6

Attached
Chapter II

"A" Form
MESSAGES AND SIGNALS.

Army Form C. 2121 (in pads of 100).

TO 7th Scottish Rifles

Sender's Number.	Day of Month.	In reply to Number.	AAA
* BM 16	1		

The 156th Inf Bde will not carry out the attack outlined by Bde today for the present aaa 155th Inf Bde are attacking under a creeping barrage and are to gain the following line — C5D central — U.29.D.7.7. thence M in SANS SOUCI inclusive aaa Zero hour will be 17:55 aaa The 156th Infantry Bde will move up in support of 155th Inf Bde and will be located as follows aaa Front of 7 Cameronians in PELICAN AVENUE and BORDER LANE from U26.B.6.5 to U21.C.5.8. front of 4th Royal Scots in BORDER LANE and

B

"A" Form — MESSAGES AND SIGNALS.

TRIDENT LANE from U21.c.58 to U21.B.29. aaa Each Bn will be on a two company front with the remaining coys distributed in depth aaa 7" Royal Scots will move up and occupy trenches in U20 B aaa attached MG Sections will move up with Bns and occupy defensive positions on Bn fronts aaa Moves are to commence at 6.30 PM and all movement is to be by trenches aaa Units will report location of their new HQ as early as possible before move takes place aaa LTM Batty and reserve section of MG will remain in present location aaa Units

"A" Form
MESSAGES AND SIGNALS.

Army Form C. 2121 (in pads of 100).

will report completion of move by wire and will forward a note of disposition by runner as soon as possible after completion aaa Bde HQ remains at present location aaa

By Runner

From: 156th Inf Bde
Time: 3 PM

(Sgd) H Sayer
BM Capt

"A" Form
MESSAGES AND SIGNALS.

Army Form C. 2121 (in pads of 100).

OKA COPY

TO: 7th Scottish Rifles (2 copies)

Sender's Number.	Day of Month.	In reply to Number.	AAA
* BM 32	2		
Ref	Bde	order	54 aaa
4th Royal	Scots	and 7th	Scottish
Rifles	will	move	to
TANK	AVENUE	and	TANK
SUPPORT	forthwith	aaa	Both
Bns to	be	in	position by
4.45 a.m.	boundary	line	between
bns	trench	junction	U 28 B 7 3
aaa	Bns	will	report
when	in	position	aaa
SFKOB	Reserve	section	and 156
LTM	Bty	will	move to
KNUCKLE	AVENUE	in	time
to	arrive	there	by 4.30 a.m
aaa	7th Royal	Scots	
will	remain	present	position
aaa	All	units	will

From
Place
Time

The above may be forwarded as now corrected. (Z)

"A" Form
MESSAGES AND SIGNALS.

Army Form C. 2121 (in pads of 100).

TO: N 2

send	runners	to	new
Bde	HQ	to	arrive
there	by	5 am	aaa
LTM	Bty	and	SEKOB
COs	will	report	new
Bde	HQ	at	5 am
aaa	addressed	three	bns
LTM	Bty	SEKOB	repeated
SENQ	and	155	INF
BDE			

Bde HQ - THE KNUCKLE

From Place: SERU
Time: 12.10 a.m.

"A" Form
MESSAGES AND SIGNALS.

TO	Sedu	

Sender's Number.	Day of Month.	In reply to Number.
*BM 37	2	AAA

Confirming phone conversation aaa The attack will commence at 8.46 am. aaa Barrage will then come down as previously notified aaa Sedu and Sepu will at once move forward to 155 Bde advanced line and attack at hour mentioned aaa Sepu will move forward to the line U27 B40 U27 B.49. and be prepared to follow up our attack addressed Sepu Sedu reptd. SEKOB SEFU

From: Servy
Time: 8.9 a.m.

"A" Form
MESSAGES AND SIGNALS.

Army Form C. 2121 (in pads of 100).

TO: all coys

Sender's Number: JR 20

AAA

Copy of BM 56 for your information and compliance. C Coy will send out two patrols of 1 platoon each to QUEANT aaa. A plentiful supply of bombs will be taken

From / Place / Time: A/30

(Sd) J G Romanes

"A" Form
MESSAGES AND SIGNALS.

Army Form C. 2121 (in pads of 100).

Prefix ...... Code	Words	Charge	This message is on a/c of:	Recd. at ...... m
Office of Origin and Service Instructions.	Sent			Date ......
	At ...... m.		...... Service	From
	To			
	By		(Signature of "Franking Officer.")	By ......

TO: SEBV

Sender's Number.	Day of Month.	In reply to Number.	AAA
BM 56	2		

4 Royal Scots and 7 Scottish Rifles will at once push forward and obtain their final objectives aaa. 7 Royal Scots will move up at once and go through 4 Royal Scots about 30 b 99 and will up HINDENBURG suppd lines as far as V 26 a. and c central their right flank being refused to V 25 d.9.1 a.a. 4 Royal Scots and 7 Scottish Rifles on obtaining final objectives will at once push forward patrols in to QUEANT which is reported evacuated aaa. acknowledge addressed 3 Inf rptd to SEK OB

From: 156 Bn / Bde
Place:
Time:

The above may be forwarded as now corrected. (Z)

156th Infantry Brigade
Order No 57

Secret
App. III.
26th September 1918

Ref. Map 57c N.E. (1/20,000)

1. **Information**
   (a) The 52nd Division, in conjunction with the 63rd (R.N.) Division on their left, and the Guards Division on their right, are taking part in an attack on the Canal du Nord and ground East thereof, on a day and at a zero hour to be notified later.
   The Canadian Corps, further North, is attacking the Canal du Nord and Bourlon Wood on the same date.

   (b) The attack of the 52nd Division is being carried out by the 156th Inf. Bde. on the left and the 157th Inf. Bde. on the right.
   The 190th Inf. Bde. will be on the left of the 156th Inf. Bde.

   (c) The 157th Inf. Bde. are in the initial stages, clearing the right flank of 4th Royal Scots and advancing at zero plus 40 from the line E.26.b.7.4 - E.26.a.8.6 to mop up the Hindenburg Front Line, and both banks of the Canal in E.26, K.2.b and K.3.a. They are advancing at the rate of 100 yards per 5 minutes, and should reach the line K.3.a.7.7 - K.2.b.6.8 by zero plus 90 minutes. During their advance Southwards, platoons will be dropped at intervals to clear the Canal.

   (d) The 190th Inf. Brigade, with the 4th Bedfordshire Regiment on their right, are following up West of the Railway line at E.20 central to E.14.d.5.5 and are attacking the Canal and the Hindenburg Support Line with their right on the Moeuvres - Graincourt Road (exclusive).

2. **Intention** The 156th Inf. Brigade will attack and capture the Canal du Nord between E.26.d.7.7 and the Moeuvres - Graincourt Road (inclusive) and clear the area shewn in Red on attached map.

2

Intention (continued)

The first Phase of the attack will be carried out by 4th Royal Scots, and the second Phase by 7th Sco Rifles.

7th Royal Scots will be in Brigade Reserve.

3. Assembly Areas   By zero hour Battalions will assemble in the following areas:-

(a) 4th Royal Scots .. E20.c.8.2 — E20.c.90.95
                       E20.a.4.2 — E20.c.1.5

(b) 7th Sco Rifles .. E19.d.7.6 — E20.a.2.3
                      E19.b.7.7 — E19.b.2.0

(c) 7th Royal Scots .. E19.a.7.3 — E19.b.2.8
                       E13.c.7.2 — E19.a.4.7

4. March to Assembly Area

4th Royal Scots will march on Y/Z, from present location in D.14 to Assembly Area by track "156" already indicated to Battalion Commanders.

They will be clear of point D.22.b.05 by 11 p.m. on Y evening, but head of Battalion will not pass track junction at D.23.c.35 before 9.30 p.m.

Arrival in Assembly Area will be reported to Bde. HQ.

7th Sco Rifles will march via tracks to be reconnoitred by them to join "156" track in D.23.c. They will be clear of track junction at D.23.c.35 by 9.30 p.m.

5. Action of 4th Royal Scots

(a) At zero hour the leading wave of the 4th Royal Scots will be formed up on line E.20.c.8.2 — E.20.c.90.95

(b) At zero plus 10, 4th Royal Scots will advance under the barrage which at zero plus 15 moves forward from line E.26.b.2.6 — E.20.d.39 at rate of 100 yards per 3 minutes to Western bank of Canal.

(c) At zero plus 28, 4th Royal Scots will have advanced and captured Canal du Nord and by zero plus 40 have captured Leopard Avenue from the Moeuvres - Graincourt Road (inclusive) to E.27.a.2.5

5. Action of 4th Royal Scots (continued)

(d) As soon as this line has been obtained, parties will be pushed South down Leopard Avenue to its junction with Lion Trench.

(e) As soon as 7th Sco. Rifles have obtained their objective (see para 6) 4th Royal Scots will move forward and occupy and consolidate Lion Trench.

6. Action of 7th Sco. Rifles

(a) One Company 7th Sco. Rifles will move forward immediately in rear of last wave of the 4th Royal Scots and as soon as the 4th Royal Scots have secured Leopard Avenue as far South as its junction with Lion Trench, this company will pass through and push patrols as far as possible Eastwards along Lion Trench and Southwards to Kangaroo Trench and down Ley Avenue, where they will endeavour to gain touch with the 2nd Guards Brigade.

(b) At Zero plus 40, 7th Sco. Rifles (less one Coy as above) will move forward and form up immediately in rear of the 4th Royal Scots front line between the Beaucourt-Graincourt Road and E 27.a.2.5.

(c) At Zero plus 119, 1/7th Sco. Rifles will advance in f_____ with 4th Battalion Bedfordshire Regiment on their left and clear the area shaded in Red on attached map as far as the line Kangaroo Trench - Low Avenue, which will be captured and consolidated.

Zebra Trench will be captured by Zero plus 151 and Kangaroo Trench by Zero plus 192.

During this advance the left of 7th Sco. Rifles will be covered by an artillery barrage and the right by M.G. fire time.

(d) As soon as line Kangaroo Trench - Low Avenue has been captured, strong patrols will be pushed out and established in K 4 a and c

7. **Action of 7th Royal Scots**

(a) As soon as 7th Sco. Rifles move forward to form up in rear of 4th Royal Scots, 7th Royal Scots will move forward to the area vacated by 7th Sco. Rifles.

(b) As soon as 7th Sco. Rifles have obtained their final objectives 7th Royal Scots will move up to Band du Nord which they will consolidate as rapidly as possible between the Manoeuvres-Graincourt Road (incl) and E.26.b.6.6.

(c) Orders for these moves will be issued from Bde. H.Q.

8. **Artillery**

(a) A tracing shewing the artillery barrages on the front of 155 Inf. Bde. and 170th Inf. Bde. is issued herewith.

(b) In addition, Howitzers firing H.E and gas will fire on the following points at the following times:-

(1) Zero plus 30 to Zero plus 50 - Lion Trench and Sunken Road and Trench between E.27.b.5.4 and Road at E.27.d.5.8.

(2) Zero plus 50 - Zero plus 70 - Zebra Trench from E.27.c.5.0 to E.27.d.4.6.

(3) Zero plus 70 to Zero plus 90 - Kangaroo Trench from K.3.a.95.75 to E.27.d.8.1.

It should be noted that the gas shells being used are a new kind, the gas in which evaporates 1 minute after bursting.

9. **Machine Guns**

(a) One Section "B" by 52nd M.G Battalion will move immediately in rear of 4th Royal Scots and as soon as the latter have captured Leopard Avenue will come into action in Leopard Avenue about E.27.a.2.5.

(b)

9. <u>Machine Guns.</u> (continued)

(b) One Section B coy 52nd M.G. Battalion will take up defensive position on the Canal as soon as 4th Royal Scots have captured Leopard Trench.

(c) At zero plus 150, the Section mentioned in sub-para (a) above will move forward to Zebra Trench and will be replaced by Section mentioned in Sub-para (b)

(d) As soon as 7th Sco Rifles have obtained their final objective, One Section will be moved up to about K.4.a.1.8 and the remaining section will move forward with 4th Royal Scots and take up positions in Leopard Trench.

10. <u>Tanks</u> Two Tanks will probably be available to assist 7th Scottish Rifles in clearing their area. Details as regards their action will be issued later, but O.C. 4th Sco Rifles will ignore these tanks in his preparation of his plan of action.

11. <u>R.E.s.</u> O.C. 412th Field coy R.E. will detail the following parties to be attached to Battalions:-

(a) No 4th Royal Scots.-
(1) 5 tunnellers to look for mines and booby traps in the Canal Bed, or in the dug-outs situated in the Canal.
(2) 4 Sappers to assist in consolidating of Leopard Avenue, and the formation of a block in Lion Trench, if it is necessary to make one, and subsequently in the consolidation of Lyon Trench.

(b) No. 7th Royal Scots
(1) 4 Sappers to assist in the consolidation of the Canal du Nord.
(2) 2 Sappers to supervise the gas-proofing of dug-outs in the Canal. These Sappers will bring the necessary tools etc.

12. **Assistance to Flanks**

7th Scottish Rifles will be prepared to assist both the 157th and 190th Inf Brigades in the event of either of them failing to make satisfactory progress at any time. It is essential that 157th Inf Bde clear the Canal early in the operations and the Coy 7 Sco Rifles which moves South of Leopard Avenue will be prepared to assist them in every way.

157th Inf Bde will similarly assist 7 Sco Rifles in the event of their being hung up.

Great care will be taken not to fire on either troops of 63rd Division or of the 2nd Guards Brigade.

13. **Consolidation**

All ground gained will be consolidated and fought for. In the event of a serious counter attack being made, Battalions may possibly be ordered to withdraw, but it must be clearly understood that the line of the Canal du Nord must be fought for to the last.

14. **Reforming** As soon as all objectives have been gained and consolidated and other formations have advanced, the Brigade will reform in E 27 a and c. Orders for this will be issued by Brigade H.Q.

15. **Liaison** (a) In order to ensure co-operation with 190th Inf Bde, 4th Royal Scots and 7 Sco Rifles will each detail one platoon to work astride the Moeuvres-Graincourt Road, to work in conjunction with a platoon of the 190th Inf Bde similarly placed. Reports will be punched by the platoon Commander concerned on arrival at the following points:-

Cross Roads E 27 b 5 8 - E 28 a 2 1 - Kangaroo Trench at E 28 c 7 7

15. Liaison (continued)

(b) 7th Sco Rifles will send patrols to get into touch with 2nd Guards Brigade at:—
(1) Junction of Low Avenue and Bat Trench
(2) The road at K 3 d 6.9.

7th Sco Rifles will report when touch is gained.

(c) 4th Royal Scots will send a patrol westwards along Dion Trench to gain touch with 157th Inf Bde.

(d) 7th Sco Rifles will similarly send patrols down the Cambrai Road, Zebra Trench and Kangaroo Trench.

(e) Each Battalion will send a Liaison Officer to Brigade H.Q. on Y/Z night. He should report as soon as Battalions are established in their assembly areas.

(f) 52nd M.G. Battalion are sending one officer to each Battalion for Liaison purposes.

16. Headquarters. Battalion H.Q. in the assembling areas will be established at the following points:—

4th Royal Scots   E 20 c 4.9.
7th Sco Rifles   E 17 d 7.7
7th Royal Scots   E 13 c 5.3

17. Communications

(a) Lines will be laid to all Battalions in their assembly areas, and 4th Royal Scots and 7th Sco Rifles will be joined up laterally.

(b) Any line laid forward of 4th Royal Scots H.Q. will be laid down the Northern Trench of the Hindenburg Front Line.

(c) One linesman will be at 4th Royal Scots H.Q. and 3 at 7th Sco Rifles H.Q. These men will lay cables forward in the event of a move forward being made, but 7th Sco Rifles will

17. **Communications** continued

(c) will detail a carrying party of 3 men to carry cable forward of 4th Royal Scots H.Q. in event of 7th Sco. Rifles moving forward. The carrying party to report to H.Q. 4th Royal Scots before zero hour.

(d) Visual will be employed to its utmost limits. A Brigade station will be established near Morse Lane. Battalions will man their own stations, and must so place them that they can see the visual station.

(e) Pigeons. 4 pigeons will be allotted to 4th Royal Scots and 6 to 7th Sco. Rifles. They will be carried by the leading companies and will be released on attaining following objectives:-

(1) Leafort Avenue
(2) Zebra Trench
(3) Final objective of 7th Sco. Rifles.

(f) Golden Rain Rockets will be fired by the right and left flanks of the leading companies on attaining the objectives named in the sub para (e) above.

(g) Runners. 4 runners per Battalion will report at Brigade H.Q. as soon as Battalions reach their H.Q. in Assembly areas and subsequently 4 fresh runners will be sent in the event of Battalions moving their H.Q.

In the event of 7th Sco. Rifles moving their H.Q. southeast of 4th Royal Scots H.Q. messages from 7th Scottish Rifles will be sent to 4th Royal Scots H.Q. who will be responsible for sending them on either by telephone or runner.

18. **Aeroplane Flares**

The hour at which contact planes will fly over our lines will be notified to all concerned at a later date, but the necessity for the foremost troops at once lighting flares

18. <u>Aeroplane Flares</u> (continued)

flares when called upon to do so, must be impressed on all concerned.

19. <u>Prisoners of War</u>   Any prisoners of war taken by the 7th Scots Rifles will be sent to H.Q. 7th Royal Scots, who will in turn forward them to Bde P of W. collecting station.

20. <u>Administrative Instructions</u>

Separate Administrative Instructions have already been issued to all concerned.

21. <u>General</u>.   In the forthcoming fight, which the B.G.C. believes will be the last this year in which the Division will be engaged, he desires to wish every Officer and man the best of good luck. Upon the results obtained by the British Forces in the Field on this occasion, hangs the question of whether there will be a crushing defeat of the German army in the Field, and as a result of that an early and glorious peace or an indecisive battle and a long continued war.

That the 156th Bde will play its part gloriously as it has done in the past is beyond all doubt, and once again Scotland will, please God, have reason to be proud of us.

22. Brigade H.Q. will close present location at 6.30 p.m. on Y day and reopen at some hour at E.19.a.2.9.

Issued at 11.15 a.m.

Secret

Addendum to 156th Inf Brigade Order No 57
Action of Tanks

26th September 1918

1. At about zero plus 90, two tanks will cross the Canal by the Cambrai Road in E.27.c.1.3 with view to co-operating with 1/7th Sco. Rifles South of the Cambrai Road. They will under no circumstances proceed North of it except to gain touch with 1/7th Scottish Rifles as mentioned in Para 2.

2. After crossing the Canal, one Tank will move to Lion Trench at E.27.c. central to gain touch with 1/7th Sco Rifles and will move North up Lion Trench until touch is gained.
   It will then return and moving S.E. proceed to mop up Zebra Trench and Trenches running from E.27.d.40.65 to E.27.d.90.00.

3. One Tank in crossing Canal at zero plus 90 will turn South and moving along Eastern bank will turn East and mop up entire length of Kangaroo Trench.

4. Both Tanks will thereafter deal with Dig and Saw Avenues and move about in 156th Bde area dealing with all places requiring attention.

5. It is realised that the only close support we can give to tanks will be to the second Tank mentioned, which while moving Southwards along East bank of Canal should be closely followed by the Company 1/7th Sco. Rifles, operating in that area.
   Elsewhere the Tanks will be supported closely by us wherever possible.

6. The Tank Commander lays special stress on the absolute necessity of our forward infantry displaying some prearranged sign by which they can be recognised.
   This sign will be blue Signal Flags, two of which must be carried by the forward platoons of each Coy 1/7th Sco Rifles.

6. (continued)

If on the move, when tanks are seen, infantry will wave the flags. If not on the move, the flags will be stuck up as prominently as possible on a parapet or on open ground.

7. Battalions should not count on the assistance of Tanks on this occasion. If they do cross the Canal safely, they may be of great help to us, but our calculations should be based on the probability of their not being able to do so.

Issued at 1200

Secret

B.M. 26/3

9th Sea Rifles   Copy

1.   The Guards Red Line objective is modified as follows:-

(a) On North
From Pig Avenue - K.3.d.4.7. it runs across the Bear Trench, K.3.a.5.1.

(b) On East
It runs down Owen Trench as far as road in K.11.c.8.8. thence S.W. down the road to original Red Line.

2.   The Guards will put up a Red and Yellow Flag on their objectives when reached.

3.   (a) No Guards Machine Guns will be shooting into the Divl. area South of the Cambrai Road after Zero plus 30 minutes.

(b) Their protective barrage on North will lift at Zero plus 80 minutes.

26/9/18

War Diary
September
Appendix II

REPORT
on
OPERATIONS
of
156th INFANTRY BRIGADE
during period
31-8-18 – 7-9-18

Ref. Maps
1/20,000 Sheets 51b S.W. & S.E.
57c N.E. & N.W.

August 31st

1. The Brigade with "B" Coy, 52nd M.G. Battalion attached, moved at 4 p.m. from bivouac area about S.5.b. to relieve the 167th Inf. Brigade of the 57th Division, in support of the Battle Line which at that time ran through BULLECOURT.

The relief had to be carried out after dark, and was completed by 12.30 a.m. on September 1st, at which time the three Battalions were disposed as shewn in Red on the attached Map.

Septr. 1st.

2. The Brigade remained in the above position until 6.30 p.m. when, under orders received from Division, it moved up into support of the 155th Inf. Brigade who attacked from BULLECOURT at 5.55 p.m. and endeavoured to gain the line C.5.central – U.29.d.7.7.– MOULIN SANS SOUCI. The move forward commenced at 6.30 p.m. and was completed by 10 p.m. All movement was confined to trenches in order to minimise the chance of casualties from shell fire, which it was thought might be consider:able during the attack of the 155th Inf. Brigade.

On completion of the move, the Brigade was disposed as shewn in Blue on attached Map – 1/7th Cameronians in PELICAN AVENUE and BORDER LANE from U.26.b.6.5. to U.21.c.5.8./

2.

U.21.c.5.8. - 4th Royal Scots in BORDER LANE and
TRIDENT AVENUE from U.21.c.5.8. to U.21.b.2.9. - 1/7th
Royal Scots in U.20.b. with 2 Companies in BULLECOURT.
These two Companies were ordered at 6 p.m. to relieve
two Companies 5th Royal Scots Fusiliers in BULLECOURT
as soon as possible, in order to enable the latter to
be in closer support of the 155th Inf. Brigade attack.

3. Whilst the above move was taking place, 52nd
Divisional Order No 130 ordering the Brigade in certain
eventualities to pass through the 155th Inf. Brigade
and attack the HINDENBURG LINE on the morning of the
2nd instant was received. Accordingly 1/7th Cameronians
and 1/4th Royal Scots were ordered to be prepared to move
up into TANK AVENUE and TANK SUPPORT TRENCHES on receipt
of a further order from Bde. H.Q. These two Battalions
to be prepared to carry out the attack ordered any time
after 5.30 a.m. on the 2nd instant. 1/7th Royal Scots
and 156th L.T.M. Battery were similarly ordered to hold
themselves in readiness to move to GORDON RESERVE (immed-
:iately E. of BULLECOURT) on receipt of orders.

September 2nd 4. At 1.40 a.m. orders were issued for the above moves to
take place. By 4.55 a.m. all Battalions (each with one
Section Machine Guns attached) were in position as shown in
Green on attached map. Brigade H.Q. moved forward to
U.20.a.9.6., when a joint H.Q. with 155th Inf. Brigade
was established.

5. The attack to be carried out on the HINDENBURG LINE
was entrusted to the 1/7th Cameronians and 1/4th Royal
Scots. The objectives were as follows:-

  1/7th Cameronians - C.6.b.9.0. - D.1.a.5.1. - V.25.c.6.
            (Cross Roads inclusive)

  1/4th Royal Scots - V.25.c.6.2., along Road in U.30.b.
         to MOULIN SANS SOUCI.
            (inclusive)

The/

3.

The 1/7th Royal Scots (in Brigade Reserve) were instructed to hold themselves in readiness to pass through the 1/4th Royal Scots after they had obtained their ob:jective, and to advance and mop up the HINDENBURG SUPPORT LINE in V.25. and 26.a. and c., as far as the line V.26.cent. - V.26.d.0.4.

A Section of Machine Guns from "B" Company, 52nd M.G. Battalion was attached to each Battalion, the remaining Section being kept in reserve at Brigade H.Q.

The jumping off place for the attack was to have been the most forward line gained by the 155th Inf. Brigade.

The artillery barrage was to come down on the line of the road U.30.c.5.0. to U.30.b.5.7. at Zero hour and to creep forward at 100 yards per 4 minutes to the objective line.

6. At 7.45 a.m. a telephone message was received from Division saying that the attack on our left had gone very well, and that the Zero hour for our attack would therefore be 8.45 a.m.

This only allowed one hour for the message to be conveyed to the two leading Battalions, 1/7th Cameronians and 1/4th Royal Scots, for them to get the order to their leading Companies, and finally for the line to advance 1500 yards before the artillery barrage came down at 8.45. The order to advance was telephoned to the two Battalions concerned, taking in the case of 1/7th Cameronians, 5 minutes and in the case of 1/4th Royal Scots 15 minutes.

By a great effort, the 1/7th Cameronians managed to get up under the barrage in time, but the 1/4th Royal Scots were unable to get up until some 10 minutes later.

The barrage itself was weak, and somewhat wild, and the right Company of 1/7th Cameronians sustained some casualties from it in the early stages of the advance.

7. The 1/7th Cameronians attacking on a two Company front with one Company and a Machine Gun Section echeloned to their right rear, and one Company in reserve, advanced steadily/

steadily under the barrage until held up at 9.40 a.m. by the very strong wire in front of the HINDENBURG LINE, on which the artillery had failed to have any effect. Only one Section on the extreme right of this Battalion was able to penetrate this wire, which they did success:fully, and reached the front trench where they were attacked by 13 Huns, all of which they killed. However, on being attacked again by superior numbers, they were forced to withdraw to shell holes just in front of the trench.

Both on the way up to the wire and whilst lying in front of it the 1/7th Cameronians were considerably bothered by M.G. fire from both flanks.

8. The 1/4th Royal Scots (attacking on a three Company front) in spite of being some distance behind the barrage advanced up to the HINDENBURG LINE and were almost immed:iately successful in gaining their objective at MOULIN SANS SOUCI with their left Company. The remainder of the Battalion were, however, held up by the wire in a similar way to the 1/7th Cameronians.

9. Many efforts were made, both by individuals, sections and platoons, to find a way through the three belts of very strong wire (at least 200 yards wide in all) but it was not until the 1/4th Royal Scots had put in their remaining Company on the left with instructions to work down the Brigade front and the increased pressure from the North had made itself felt, that the enemy M.G. fire began to slacken. One Section M.Gs from "A" Company 52nd M.G. Batt had also been sent forward to take up a position on the high ground near MOULIN SANS SOUCI, from which place the enemy front line could be effectively dealt with.

Two Stokes Guns with half the L.T.M. Battery and as many shells as they could man-handle had also been sent forward/

5.

forward to 4th Royal Scots to assist the Company ordered
to work in on the left and to clear the Brigade front.
Immediately this happened, both Battalions went in and
the whole of the front line on the Brigade front was
in our hands by 3 p.m., but owing to difficulties of
communication between Companies and Battalion H.Q., this
was not reported to Brigade H.Q. until 4.45 p.m.

10.   Immediately the front line had been taken, 1/7th
Cameronians and 1/4th Royal Scots pressed forward to
their final objectives, all of which were in our hands
by 4.30 p.m., with touch gained with 57th Division on
our left.

    Both Battalions were ordered to send out patrols
to reconnoitre QUEANT, which was reported by the R.A.F.
to be clear of enemy.

11.   Immediately the attack by the 1/7th Cameronians and
1/4th Royal Scots had got under way, the 1/7th Royal Scots
were ordered to move up to SELBY LANE and RIPON LANE in
close support, and as soon as the 1/4th Royal Scots had
reported the capture of their final objective, this Batt-
:alion was ordered to carry out its original orders to
clear the HINDENBURG SUPPORT LINE in V.25. and V.26.a. & c.
as far as the line V.25.central - V.26.d.0.4.

    Owing to the maze of trenches and mass of wire which
had to be traversed this operation, though meeting with
no opposition, was not completed until nearly midnight,
at which hour our line was as shown in Purple on attached
Map.

12.   The patrols sent forward toward QUEANT by 1/7th
Cameronians and 1/4th Royal Scots reported that the place
was still fairly strongly held by M.Gs. However, at
9.30 p.m., the M.G. fire ceased, and patrols of 1/7th
Cameronians/

6.

Cameronians found the place clear of enemy by 11 p.m.

September 3rd.
13. Further patrols, sent out at 4.30 a.m., on September 3rd, with orders to push on to PRONVILLE, if possible, were forced to return by our own barrage.

14. At 1 a.m. orders were received to concentrate the Brigade in V.30.d. This concentration was complete by 7.30 a.m., and Brigade H.Q. moved forward to V.30.d.5.3.

15. The Brigade remained concentrated in V.30.d. until the 7th instant, when it moved back to rest in bivouacs in Corps support.

16. Attached are Appendices shewing:-
    (1). Casualties in Brigade by Units.
    (2). Prisoners of War captured by units.
    (3). War material captured by units.

HEADQUARTERS,
156TH
INFANTRY BRIGADE.
12th September 1918.

Archd E Bird
Brig. General,
Commanding 156th Inf. Brigade.

Casualties Second Phase – 1st September 1918.

Unit.	Killed O.	Killed O.R.	Wounded O.	Wounded O.R.	Wounded (Gas) O.	Wounded (Gas) O.R.	Wounded at duty O.	Wounded at duty O.R.	Missing O.	Missing O.R.	Total O.	Total O.R.
4th Royal Scots	3	1	–	7	–	–	–	–	–	–	3	8
7th Royal Scots	–	–	–	–	–	–	–	–	–	–	–	–
7th Sco. Rifles	–	11	7	48	–	–	–	6	–	–	7	65
TOTAL	3	12	7	55	–	–	–	6	–	–	10	73

NAMES OF OFFICER CASUALTIES.

4th Royal Scots.

Killed.

    Lieut. J.G. MYLNE,   ...   8th Royal Scots.
    Lieut. S. MACDONALD,   ...   8th Royal Scots.
    2/Lt. W.J. TURNER,   ...   4th Royal Scots.

7th Sco. Rifles.

Wounded.

    Lieut. G. SOUTER,   ...   7th Sco. Rifles.
    Lieut. T. HAYDOCK,   ...   7th Sco. Rifles.
    Lieut. R. BARR,   ...   7th Sco. Rifles.
    2/Lieut. A. GORDON,   ...   7th Sco. Rifles.
    2/Lieut. D. McQUEEN,   ...   7th Sco. Rifles.
    2/Lieut. C. GILLIES.   ...   7th Sco. Rifles.

PRISONERS CAPTURED 2nd PHASE, 1st to 7th September 1918

UNIT.	OFFICERS.	OTHER RANKS.
4th Royal Scots	–	4
7th Royal Scots	–	–
7th Sco. Rifles	–	7
TOTAL.	–	11

WAR MATERIAL CAPTURED SECOND PHASE 1st- 7th September 1918.

4th Royal Scots.

- Guns - 77 mm ... 3
- Machine Guns ... 8 10
- Bombs ... 140
- Range finders ... 1
- Transport Carts ... 1
- 77 mm shells ... 500
- Quantity S.A.A. & Miscellaneous material.

7th Royal Scots.

- Trench Mortars (light) 1
- Machine Guns (light) 1

7th Sco. Rifles.

- Machine Guns 8 12
- Trench Mortars (light) 12
- Quantity rifles & S.A.A.

B.M. 887.

LESSONS learned during OPERATIONS between 25/8/18 and 7/9/18, and SUGGESTIONS for IMPROVEMENT in EQUIPMENT, TRAINING etc.

1. **EQUIPMENT AND TRANSPORT.**

   PACKS. (a). It is recommended that Packs be carried instead of haversacks in "fighting order". When carrying haversacks many things, such as iron rations, and the current day's rations have to be slung on the man, or carried in a sandbag by hand. It is considered that it would be preferable to put all these things inside the pack, and thus avoid the necessity for articles of equipment etc being hung all over the man. Enquiries have been made from all Battalion Commanders and from the men themselves and all are in favour of substituting the the pack for the haversack. Apart from the change from the haversack to the pack, exactly the same equipment as at present would be carried.

   GRENADES. (b). It is recommended that in future No. 36 grenade <u>only</u> shall be issued during operations.
   Nos. 23 and 36 grenades are equally effective for throwing purposes, but when it comes to using either as a rifle grenade in open warfare, No 36 is infinitely preferable on account of its increased range. Moreover by issuing <u>only</u> No. 36 grenade the necessity for carrying two sorts of cartridges would be obviated. This would be an undoubted advantage.

   SIGNALLING EQUIPMENT. (c). It has been clearly demonstrated that something better than the present issue of enamel wire is required for use in front of Battalion H.Q.
   It is recommended that from 2 to 3 miles of D.3. cable be issued to all battalions for use in front of Battalion H.Q. This cable to be carried on two, out of the 6 pack animals with each Battalion.
   Note. It has been proved beyond doubt that in open warfare the chances of cable being cut by shell fire are small, and therefore this extra issue of cable can now be considered justifiable whereas it may not have been so considered in the Battles of the SOMME and at YPRES in 1916 and 1917.

   PACK SADDLES. (d). It is recommended that an issue of at least 50 extra pack saddles per Brigade be always made in the event of any active operations being probable.
   The pack saddles, during recent operations, proved to be of great value, and might have been absolutely invaluable had the hostile shelling been more severe, or the roads worse than they were.
   When not in use they can easily be carried on the off mules in the limbered G.S. wagons.

   TRANSPORT FOR L.T.M. BATTERY. (e). The transport (2 G.S. wagons) at present provided for L.T.M. Batteries is totally unsuited for any type of mobile warfare, as all shells have to be manhandled from at least Bn. H.Q.
   It is recommended that, if it is intended to use L.T.Ms in mobile warfare, the batteries shall be put on a pack or semi-pack basis.

2. TRAINING. /

2. TRAINING.

REPORTS. (a). Reports from Companies, and in some cases, from Battalions were not as good as they should have been or so frequent.
Extra training in this respect is required and it is recommended that more exercises without troops be carried out, and that in these exercises Adjutants and Company Commanders be made to write the actual reports and messages that they would normally write in active operations.

"SECTION BLOBS" (b). The use of Section Blobs, and consequently being able to attack on a wide front with a small number of men, has more than proved its worth. All tactical training should in future be carried out on this principle.

SECTION COMMANDERS. (c). The formations recommended above necessitate great independence of action and initiative on the part of Section Commanders and all platoon and Company Training should be designed to encourage this. The present system of training designed by I.G.T. seems to meet the case admirably.

3. ORGANIZATION.

TUMPLINE PLATOONS. (a). It is recommended that one TUMPLINE PLATOON per Battalion, and one per Brigade H.Q. be organised forthwith. In the one Battalion in this Brigade in which this has been done, the platoon proved of very great service.
The great merit of it is that the necessity for calling on the front line Companies for carrying parties, (for rations) water etc is obviated, and instead of using absolutely tired out men for carrying, comparatively fresh men are used, who can consequent:ly carry greater loads in a shorter time.
A certain amount of training is required before the best can be got out of a Tumpline platoon, but this is easily arranged for.
It is recommended that men for these tumpline platoons be not taken from the fighting strength but that they be made extra to establishment.

4. GENERAL.

Recent operations clearly prove that more time is required in which to get orders to their destin:ations. Success lately was imperilled by the late receipt of orders by Brigade.

13-9-18.

Brig. General,
Commanding 156th Inf. Brigade.

Appendix IV

SECRET.
Copy No. 12

186th INFANTRY BRIGADE ORDER No. 25.

Ref. Maps,
1/20,000, Sheets 51b. S.E. & S.W.
51c. N.E. & N.W.

14th September 1918.

1. (a). The 62nd Division is relieving the 57th Division in the Front Line of the XVII Corps Sector on the nights of 15th/16th and 16th/17th September.

   (b). The 186th and 187th Inf. Brigades are taking over the Right and Left Brigade Sections on the nights of 15th/16th and 16th/17th September respectively.

2. The 186th Inf. Brigade will relieve the 171st Inf. Brigade as under on the 16th September, and, on completion of relief, will be in Divisional Reserve.

   1/4th Royal Scots will relieve 2/7th King's Liverpool Regt.
   1/7th Royal Scots   "   "   2/5th   "   "   "
   1/7th Cameronians   "   "   2/6th   "   "   "
   186th L.T.M. Battery will not relieve the 171st L.T.M.

   Battery, but will be located in the neighbourhood of Brigade H.Q. Exact location will be pointed out on arrival.

4. All details of relief will be arranged between Battalion Commanders concerned, but the two forward Companies of the 2/6th King's Liverpool Regt. will not be relieved by two Companies of 7th Cameronians until after dark.

5. Battalions will leave present bivouac area at the following hours, and will march independently to the new area:-

   7th Cameronians (S.R.)   ...   9 a.m.
   4th Royal Scots   ...   ...   10 a.m.
   7th Royal Scots   ...   ...   12 noon
   186th L.T.M. Battery)
   Brigade H.Q.   )   ...   12.45 p.m.

   Route - CROISILLES - BULLECOURT - QUEANT.

   7th Cameronians and 4th Royal Scots may halt for an hour for a meal on the march, but must not concentrate unduly for this meal on account of Aeroplane observation.

6. Owing to the danger of gas during relief, the greatest care will be taken throughout the relief to conceal any extra movement by daylight, especially on the high ground immediately West of QUEANT.
   Platoons will march at 100 yards distance. The same distance will be maintained between every four vehicles of any description. Closing up must be specially guarded against.

7. Command of Battalion areas will pass on completion of each Battalion relief.

8. Completion of relief will be wired "Priority" to Brigade H.Q. using code "B.M. 908 noted".

9. Command of the Brigade Section passes to B.G.C., 186th Inf. Brigade, on completion of all Battalion reliefs.

10./

2.

10.   Brigade H.Q. closes at present location at 2 p.m. on 18th instant, and re-opens at the same hour at G.6.b.8.2.

11.   ACKNOWLEDGE. (Units 156th Inf. Brigade only).

H. Sayer
Captain,
Brigade Major, 156th Inf. Brigade.

Issued at 5.30 p.m.

```
Copy No 1 to 4th Royal Scots.
        2    7th Royal Scots.
        3    7th Cameronians.
        4    156th L.T.M. Battery.
        5    155th Inf. Brigade.
        6    157th Inf. Brigade.
        7    171st Inf. Brigade.
        8    Staff Captain.
        9    Bde. Transport Officer.
       10    Bde. Supply Officer.
   11 & 12   Diary.
       13    File.
```
14 Bde. Sigs.

Appendix V

SECRET.
Copy No. 13

156th INFANTRY BRIGADE.

ADMINISTRATIVE INSTRUCTIONS No. 11.

Reference 156th Inf. Brigade Order No 58.   18th September 1918.

1. **TENTS and SHELTERS** in present area will be left standing when units march out and will be taken over by 63rd Division. Each Battalion will leave two men and T.M. Battery one man in charge of camps until a representative from the 63rd Division arrives. Receipts will be obtained, and a note of all stores handed over will be forwarded to Bde. H.Q. within 24 hours of arrival in new area, together with a Certificate that bivouac areas were taken over in a clean and sanitary condition. Tents and shelters in new area will be taken over from units of 57th Division, and a note forwarded to Bde. H.Q. within 24 hours of arrival there stating the numbers in possession.

2. **SURPLUS KITS** Materials
   (i). Men's haversacks, and any kit which cannot be carried in units' baggage wagons will be dumped by 7 a.m. tomorrow at the Bde. Transport Lines, at a point which will be shown to Transport Officers by the B.T.O. at 5 p.m. today.
   (ii). What kit cannot be put in haversacks will be packed in sandbags.
   (iii). Each unit will supply a guard of 2 men to take charge of their kits, until arrival in new area.
   (iv). The B.T.O. will move these kits by motor lorry at 9 a.m. tomorrow to new Brigade Transport Lines. Units' Admin. H.Q. will take these over on arrival.

3. **TRANSPORT.**
   (i). Brigade Transport and Admin. H.Q. will take over their old quarters at U.28.central.
   (ii). The B.T.O. will be in charge of the camp.
   (iii). Train baggage wagons will join units at 6 a.m. tomorrow.
   (iv). 4th Royal Scots and 7th Royal Scots baggage normally carried on their train wagon used as Brigade Tool Wagon, will be moved by Motor Lorry. The B.T.O. will arrange details direct with Transport Officers.
   (v). Field Cookers will be kept at transport lines.

4. **SUPPLIES.** Rations will be delivered to units new Transport Lines by Train Supply Wagons by noon tomorrow, and daily thereafter by that hour.

5. **WATER.**   WATER POINTS.

LOCATION.	REMARKS.
BOISLEUX AU MONT S.9.d.7.4.	Water Cart Refilling Point. 2 Standpipes. Troughs.
BOYELLES S.16.b.5.0.	Water Cart Refilling Point. 1 Standpipe. Troughs.
CROISILLES. T.24.a.5.5.	(a) Water Cart Refilling Point. 1 Standpipe. Troughs. (b) 3 wells.
BULLECOURT. U.20.d.2.4.	Troughs.
(Factory) U.22.b.5.6.	Water Cart Refilling Point. 2 Standpipes. Troughs.
ST LEGER. T.29.c.7.5.	Water Cart refilling point. 1 Standpipe. Troughs.

QUEANT./

2.

```
        QUEANT                          Troughs.
           D.1.d.7.8.                   Troughs.
           D.8.a.2.0.                   Troughs.

        ECOUST                          Three wells with Troughs.
                                        Water cart refilling point.

        LONGATTE                        Troughs.
           C.9.b.8.7.

        NOREUIL.                        2 wells with troughs.
                                        Water cart Refilling Point.
```

6. **LOCATIONS.**

UNIT.	LOCATION	TRANSPORT LINES.
Div. Amm. Column		
(less S.A.A. Sect)	U.19.d.	
S.A.A. Section	C.4.d.2.8.	C.4.d.2.8.
412th Field Company	D.7.b.8.0.	V.25.a.5.0.
No 3 Coy Div. Train	C.1.d.8.3.	
Refilling point	C.1.d.8.3.	
1/1st Low. Fd. Amb	D.1.d.8.9.	D.1.d.8.9.
D.A.D.O.S.	C.7.a.central.	
Div. Salvage Off.	C.13.b.0.9.	
Div. Burial Officer	D.7.c.	
(with Div. Pion. Bn.)		
Div. Reception Camp	BOISLEUX AU MONT (from 18th inst)	
Div. Bulk Canteen	ECOUST	
Div. Baths Officer	ECOUST	
Adv. Clothing Exch.	C.7.a.central.	
Div. S.A.A. &		
Grenade Dump	C.8.a.	
22nd Mobile Vet.		
Section	U.6.d.9.5.	
Reinforcement		
Railhead	Boisleux au Mont (from 18th inst)	

7. **AMBULANCE.**
   (i). 1 N.C.O. & 8 men will be attached to each unit from tomorrow to act as bearer party.
   (ii). Sick and wounded will be evacuated to A.D.S., D.1.d.8.9.
   (iii). One horse ambulance will join each Battalion early tomorrow to proceed with it on the march, on completion of which it will rejoin 1/1st L.F.A.

8. **BUGLERS.** will proceed to Divisional Reception Camp, BOISLEUX, tomorrow, and they will rendezvous at Brigade Transport Lines at 9 a.m. One G.S. wagon will be provided by Divisional Train.

9. **ACKNOWLEDGE.**

                                                    Captain,
                                        Staff Captain, 156th Inf. Brigade

Issued at _____

```
                    Copy No 1 to G.O.C.
                         2    4th Royal Scots.
                         3    7th Royal Scots
                         4    7th Sco. Rifles
                         5    156th L.T.M. Battery
                         6    Brigade Major.
                         7    Sigs.
                         8    Bde. Trans. Officer
                         9    Supply Officer.
                        10    C10th Coy A.S.C.
                        11    Div. Train.
                        12    1/1st Low. Field Amb.
                    13 & 14   War Diary
                        15    
```

156th Infantry Brigade — War Diary Appx. XV

Effective Strength - September 1918

Unit	Week ending 7th		Week ending 14th		Week ending 21st		Week ending 28th	
	O	OR	O	OR	O	OR	O	OR
4 Royal Scots	36	680	42	775	42	779	37	720
7 Royal Scots	39	555	41	621	39	650	34	666
7 Scot Rifles	36	718	35	761	34	762	39	742
	111	1953	118	2157	115	2191	110	2128

156th Infantry Brigade.   War Diary Appen. XV

Casualties – September 1918

	Killed		Wounded		Wounded (Gas)		Missing		Total	
	O	OR	O	OR	O	OR	O	OR	O	OR
4 Royal Scots	7	33	12	141	1	4	–	7	20	185
7 Royal Scots	3	14	2	39	–	2	1	46	6	101
7 Cam Rifles	4	28	8	107	–	24	–	12	12	171
156th T M By	–	–	–	1	–	–	–	–	–	1
Bde HQ	–	–	1	–	–	–	–	–	1	–
Bde Sig. Sec	–	–	–	2	–	–	–	–	–	2
Total	14	75	23	290	1	30	1	65	39	460

Appendix VI

SECRET.

82nd DIVISION — XVII Corps.   Copy No. 13

RESERVE BRIGADE DEFENCE SCHEME.

Ref. Map.
1/10,000. 57C N.E.
        57B S.E.

1. The 82nd Division holds the 17th Corps front from E.30.d.0.0. to the LOCK at V.27.d.9.9. (exclusive)

2. The Divisional Front is held with two Brigades in line:-

    The RIGHT BRIGADE holds the HOUVIN SECTOR on a two Battalion Front.

    The LEFT BRIGADE holds the ENGHY SECTOR on a two-Battalion Front.

    and there is one Brigade in reserve.

3. The attached Tracing shows:-

   (a). The OUTPOST SYSTEM, in GREEN.

   (b). The MAIN LINE of RESISTANCE, in RED.

   (c). The SECOND SYSTEM, in BLUE.

   (d). BRIGADE and BATTALION HDQRS of the RESERVE BRIGADE.

   (e). DIVISIONAL and INTER-BRIGADE BOUNDARIES.

4. **DISPOSITIONS OF INFANTRY.**

   (a). The two Companies of "A" Battalion, situated in BRITISH TRENCH in D.6.b. & d. are at the disposal of O.C., ENGHY SECTOR to assist in the defence of the MAIN LINE OF RESISTANCE, but are not to be used forward of it without the sanction of Divisional Hdqrs.

   (b). "A" Battalion (less two Companies referred to above) situated in the HINDENBURG LINE in D.4.d. will be prepared to deliver an immediate counter-attack to restore the situation in any portion of the Main Line of Resistance in the ENGHY SECTOR.
   In the event of this not being possible, the two Companies must be prepared to take up positions as follows:-
   One Company in CABLE TRENCH (not named in map) from about D.4.c.8.8. to D.4.b.8.8.
   One Company in the HINDENBURG LINE in D.4.d., facing South.

   (c). "B" Battalion is responsible for the defence of that portion of the RESERVE LINE in the ENGHY SECTOR, and will hold it with three Companies in the line and one in reserve.

   (d). "C" Battalion, situated in V.27. will be prepared to counter attack to regain any portion of the Main Line of Resistance or of the Outpost System which may be lost in any portion of the Divisional Front.

5./

2.

5.   In the event of the enemy seriously penetrating any portion of the Main Line of Resistance, the Reserve Brigade may be ordered to carry out a deliberate counter-attack. Such a counter-attack would be assisted by an adequate Artillery and M.G. Barrage.

All Commanding Officers and Company Commanders will take steps to reconnoitre the ground between the RED LINE and the Main Line of Resistance.

ARMOURIES.

[signature]

Captain,
17th September 1918.   Brigade Major, 156th Inf. Brigade.

oooooooooooooooooooooooooooooooo

Copy No. 1 to 4th Royal Scots.
        2   7th Royal Scots.
        3   7th Cameronians. (S.R.)
        4   156th L.T.M. Battery.
        5   52nd Division.
        6   155th Inf. Brigade.
        7   157th Inf. Brigade.
        8   B.G.C.
        9   Brigade Major.
       10   Staff Captain.
       11   Brigade Signals.
       12   War Diary.
       13   "
       14   File.

oooooooooooooooooooooooooooooo

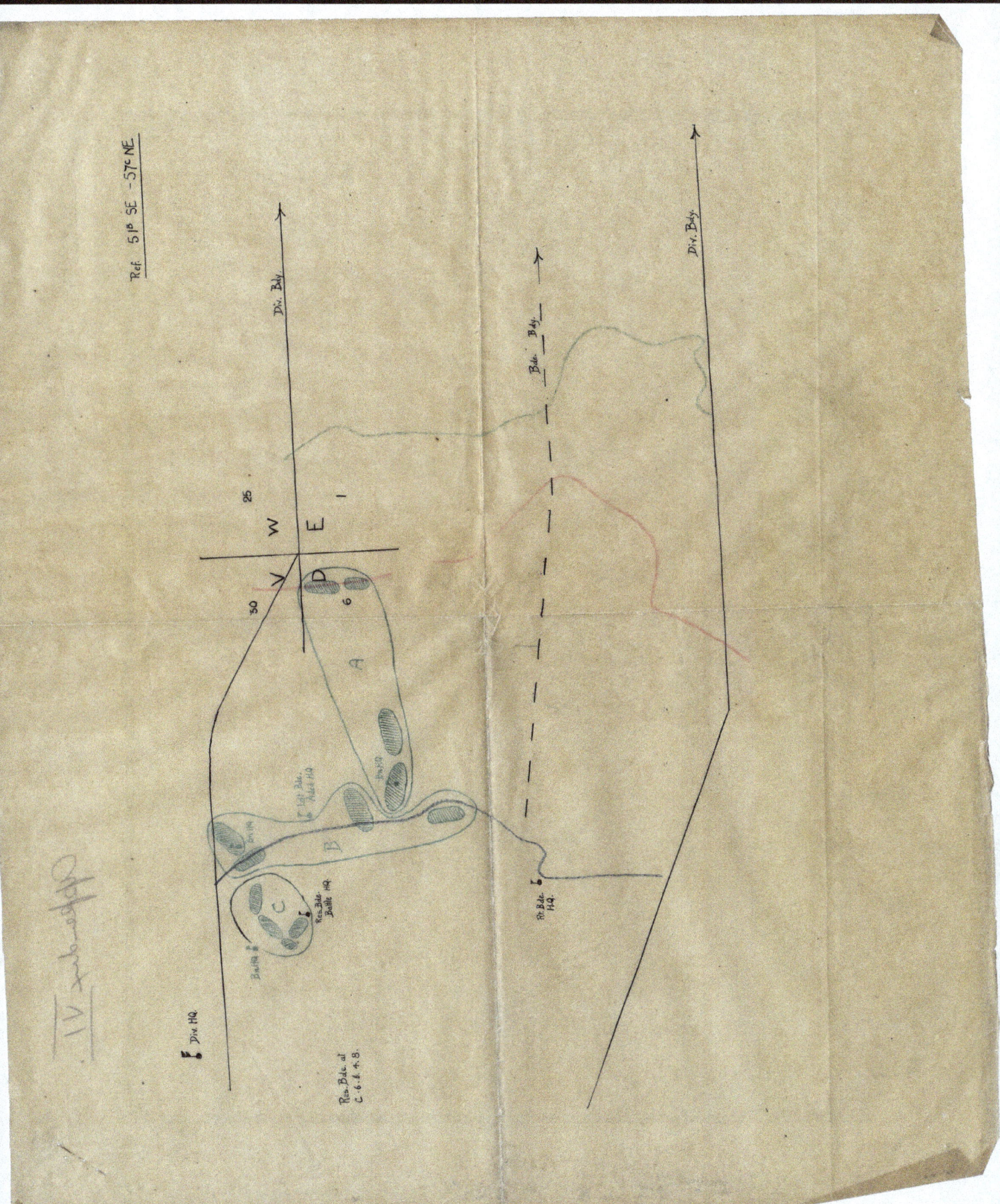

App. I

4/7 Royal Scots   'B' Coy 52nd M.G. Bttn.   SECRET
7th Royal Scots   D.T.O.   Bm 101
7th Sco. Rifles   A/Staff Captain
156th L.T.M.Bty.   O.C. Sigs.

1. The 156th Inf Bde. will march westwards to new bivouac area tomorrow (7-9-18)

2. Order of march & starting times as follows:-
   7th Royal Scots & L.T.M. By.   6.30. am.
   4th Royal Scots   6.40 am.
   7th Sco. Rifles   7   am.
   'B' Coy 52nd M.G. Battn.   7.20 am.
   156th Inf Bde HQ & Signal Section   7.15 am.

3. Starting Point - Cross Roads C.5.b.5.7.

4. Route will be via BULLECOURT - CROISILLES

5. Destination B.2.3.4.+8. Details of Bivouac Areas have been given to Assistant Adjutants who will join Coys as they pass Bde. Transport Lines

6. Transports will march with units. All arrangements for picking up Transport to be made by Battns.

(Sgd) K Sayer Capt.
                     Sta Major 156th Inf Bde

6/9/18

"A" Form.
MESSAGES AND SIGNALS.

Army Form C. 2121.
(In pads of 100.)

APPEN. VII

TO	LIZI	LIGU	LIME	
	LIVA	LIPI	QIWU	

Sender's Number.	Day of Month.	In reply to Number.	AAA
BM.2	19		

Units	L150	will	move
into	following	areas	tonight
AAA	LIZI	D18c	and
D	LIVA	D16	LIGU
and	LIPI	D14	AAA
Each	areas	are	being
pointed	out	to	representatives
AAA	Moves	of	LIZI
LIVA	and	LIPI	to
commence	at	dusk	both
LIGU	to	wait	relief
ordered	in	LIME	Order
No 142	AAA	On	arrival
new	area	LIZI	will
come	under	orders	QIWU
AAA	Completion	of	moves
to	be	wired	AAA

"A" Form.
MESSAGES AND SIGNALS.

Army Form C. 2121.
(In pads of 100.)

TO	2		
Sender's Number.	Day of Month.	In reply to Number.	**AAA**
L150	closes	present	location
5.30 pm	and	opens	D156.5.7.
same	hour	AAA	Separate
Administrative	Orders	are	being
issued	AAA	Addressed	all
Units	L150	repeated	LIME
and	QIWU		

From L150
Place
Time 1.35 pm

Sgt H Sayer
Capt

Appendix VIII Secret.
156th Inf Bde Order No 56 Copy No 17

Ref map   20th Sept. 1918
1/20000 Sheet 57c NE

1. The 156th Inf Bde will relieve the 155th
   Inf Bde in MOEUVRES SECTION on the
   20th/21st September as follows:-
   4th Royal Scots will relieve 4th R.S.F. and
      portion of 7th H.L.I. in the left sub-
      section
   7th Royal Scots will relieve 5th R.S.F. in
   the right sub section.
   7th Scot. Rifles will relieve 4th K.O.S.Bs
   in Bde reserve.
   156th L.T.M. Batty will relieve 155th
      L.T.M. Batty.
      Relief to commence at dusk
2. As far as possible dispositions of the
   155th Inf Bde units will be taken
   over by 4th Royal Scots and 7th Royal
   Scots but the following posts
   will be definitely established.
   Right Subsection:- E.20.C.8.1
                      E.20.D.35.80
                      E.20.B.4.5
                      E.20.A.4.0

   Left Subsection:/-

2.

Left Subsection — E.20.B.1.8
E.14.D.5.1
E.14.D.6.3
E.14.D.4.5
E.14.D.4.8 (approx.)
E.14.D.2.6
E.14.A.8.0
E.14.C.35.85
E.14.C.9.8

Each Bn. will be distributed in depth and will have one passive defence coy located in the RED LINE which has already been pointed out to Bn. Commanders.

3. On completion of relief 7th Scot. Rifles will be disposed as follows:—
1 Coy. in trenches between E.19.B.4.5 and E.19.A.8.9
1 Coy. in trench between E.13.D.7.3 and E.13.D.1.8
2 Coys in HOBART STREET between E.19.A.0.5 and E.13.B.3.2

The first two coys are at the disposal of O/s. C. 4th Royal Scots and 7th Royal Scots respectively for the purpose of delivering an immediate counter attack in the event of the reserves of their own Bns being insufficient to restore

3

the situation. The two last named Coys will be ready to carry out a counter attack on any portion of the front on receipt of orders from Bde HQ.

4. O.C. 156th L.T.M. Batty will detail 4 guns to O.C. 4th Royal Scots and 4 guns to 7th Royal Scots. Targets and S.O.S. lines for these guns will be indicated by Bn. Commanders concerned.

5. Each man on the way up to the relief will carry forward as many bombs and as much R.E. material as possible

6. Northern and Southern Boundaries and Inter-Bn. Boundary on completion of relief will be as follows:-
Southern Boundary An East and West line along the grid line between D.24 and D.30.
Northern Boundary E.14 central - E.14.A.0.2, E.13.A.0.2 - E.18.A.0.4
Inter Bn. Boundary. An East and West line drawn through E.19.B.7.5

7. (a) Bn. H.Q's on relief will be situated as follows:-
7th Royal Scots - E.19.A.2.9
4th Royal Scots - E.13.D.0.8

4

7th Seo. Rifles - D.18. D.5.4

(7) H.Q of 2nd Bn. Coldstream Guards on night of 7th Royal Scots is situated at D.29.C.1.5. Location of Bn on left of 7th Royal Scots will be notified later.

8. Completion of relief will be wired "PRIORITY" to Bde. H.Q by code word "CHARLES".

9. MOEUVRES is a village, which for reasons of the utmost tactical importance must at all costs be retained by us. The enemy attach to its capture and retention just as much value as we do, and it is certain that he will make vigorous and determined attempts to wrest it from us. He must and will fail before the men of this Bde. The B.G.C. calls upon all ranks for a great and determined effort during the next few days but knows that success as ever will be the result of their devotion and gallantry.

10. Bde. H.Q will remain in its present location (D.15.B.5.7)

5

11 ACKNOWLEDGE

H Stanley Smith
Captain
ffor Brigade Major 156 Inf Bde

Issued at 8.30 pm

Copy No 1 to 4th R.S.
2   7th K.S
3   7th S.R
4   156 L.T.M.B
5   1st Guards Bde.
6   5 C.I. Bde
7   155 Inf Bde
8   157 Inf Bde
9   5th Divn
10   412 Field R.E
11   1/1 L.F. Amb.
12   S.6
13   Bde Sigs
14   B.T.O
15   a/S.6
16   Bde S.O
17 & 18 Diary
19   File

APPENDIX IX

R E P O R T
on
O P E R A T I O N S
of
156th. INFANTRY BRIGADE.

20th. - 24th September 1918.
(inclusive).

Ref. Map. 57
Sheet 75c N.E. 1/20,000.

The Brigade having moved up in close support of the 155th Inf. Brigade on the 19th September, proceeded to relieve it and take over the defence of MOEUVRES on the night of the 20th/21st.

The arrangements for relief left something to be desired, as the situation in MOEUVRES was at the time somewhat obscure, and the enemy were in very close contact with its defenders. The exact location of some of the picquets of the 155th Inf. Brigade were indeed not known, and of the dispositions of 2 Companies 1/7th H.L.I., attached to, and under the orders of the B.G.C., 155th Inf. Brigade, nothing was known, except that a small party was in position at about E.14.d.central. It was decided, in view of the prevailing uncertainty, to take over all front line posts held by the 155th Inf. Brigade, but other:
-wise to adopt our own dispositions for defence.

To this end orders were issued as follows:-

Two Battalions, 1/7th Royal Scots and 1/4th Royal Scots, to be distributed in depth, and be responsible for the defence of MOEUVRES up to and inclusive of the RED LINE shewn on Map.
Dividing line between Battalions a due E. and W. line through E.20.a.central, - The 1/4th Royal Scots to be North of that line with its North boundary an E. and W. line through E.14.a.9.2., and the 1/7th Royal Scots to be South of it, with Southern boundary an E. and W. line through E.20.c.8.2.
In each Battalion, three Companies to be East of the RED LINE with most forward posts to be not less than one platoon in strength and one Company of each Battalion in position in the RED LINE, orders to improve and strengthen which were given.
The remaining Battalion of the Brigade, 1/7th Scottish Rifles, were disposed as follows:-
Two Companies in HOBART STREET to strengthen that line at once and hold it at all costs; one Company in E.13.d.central, and one Company in E.19.b.central, each Company to be ready to move at a moment's notice, with a view to counter-attacking in the event of the enemy anywhere penetrating our forward positions, and the Battalions holding the same not being able to cope with the situation unaded.
Two/

2.

Two Stokes Mortars were allotted to each forward Battalion, no personnel being available to man the remainder.

Two Companies M.G. Battalion were distributed in suitable positions between and in RED and BLUE LINES, from which fire could best be brought to bear on pro:-bable enemy lines of attack, and from which harassing fire could best be employed by night.

One Battalion 155th Inf. Brigade, after relief, was directed to take post at D.17.central and remain there for purposes of deliberate counter-attack, if required.

The relief of the 155th Inf. Brigade and adoption of fresh dispositions was reported complete by 0230 on the 21st, much annoyance, however, being occasioned during the night by heavy gas shelling. (Blue Cross).

The enemy, and not our own troops, were found to be in possession of E.14.central, and all that part of Cemetery Support Trench, which lies to the East of it.

Platoon posts, however, were taken over, or established, by the Brigade as depicted by BLUE blobs on the Map, with the exception of that one shewn at E.14.d.1.1., which was established later.

21st
September. The morning passed comparatively quietly, shelling being intermittent. Some enemy movement westwards was observed, however, taking place in E.15.central and in E.16.central.

At 1450, the enemy suddenly opened a heavy bombardment on MOEUVRES, which included all our advanced posts, the RED and BLUE LINES, and communication trenches connecting them.

It was considered to be the prelude to an attack, and counter preparation was at once called for and as promptly responded to by all available artillery.

The enemy's bombardment increased in intensity, and to it was added extremely heavy Trench Mortar fire, both heavy and light.

The Brigade "Stood-to" ready for the attack which materialized at 1530. It was directed entirely against that part of our front which lay between E.14.d.3.0. and E.20.c.2.1., the main object of the enemy apparently being to capture the spur N.E. and S.W. of E.20.central, from which MOEUVRES is "commanded" at close range, and from which uninterrupted view can be obtained of the valley in D.30.

The enemy attacked in strength and with much determination. Under Artillery and Trench Mortar Barrage his Infantry advanced up Trenches and Saps leading to our positions, and then deploying outwards endeavoured to envelop our picquets. In this he was successful, principally owing to the fact that his bombardment had caused us heavy casualties, annihilating two picquets in E.20.b.5.4. and E.20.d.3.8., and to the fact also that the dust raised by bombardment was so thick that enemy movement, until very close at hand, was obscured.

The German Infantry relied principally on hand grenades, which he used with effect.
By/

By 1600, he was reported in possession of the ridge between E.20.b.5.4. and E.20.c.8.1., with small parties some 200 yards West of that line. North of E.20.b.5.4., however, he was successfully repulsed at the outset, his attack in that quarter not being pressed with the same vigour and determination displayed elsewhere.

The German Guardsmen, however, were not to remain for long in the positions they had gained.

A Counter-attack was at once launched by the reserve Company of the 1/7th Royal Scots, together with the remnants of the garrisons who had been forced back from the ridge, and by 1645 the last Guardsman had been hunted from the field, leaving over 40 dead on the ground, and two machine guns in our hands.

At 1700, large bodies of the enemy were observed moving Eastwards and very fast along LYNX TRENCH in E.21.b., and our artillery were not slow to take advantage of the favourable target afforded them. At 2000, according to programme, two platoons of "D" Company, 1/4th Royal Scots, were launched to the attack of E.14.b.1.1., while two platoons of "C" Company of the same Battalion advanced to the attack of that part of CEMETERY SUPPORT which lies East of E.14.central. The latter attack failed in the face of superior numbers and intense Machine Gun fire, but the former succeeded, three Germans being killed, three prisoners and three Machine Guns remaining in our hands, the latter at once being taken into use and brought into action with effect.

22nd September.
At 0630, and later at 1600, very heavy enemy shelling took place, and counter-preparation was at once resorted to by us. No attack followed in either case. At 2041, however, intense shelling by the enemy again broke out, and an S.O.S. Signal went up immediately on the Right of our Brigade Sector, repeated by us and by the Canadians on our left, and our protective barrage came down promptly.

A futile attempt by the enemy against one of our picquets at E.14.d.3.0. was repulsed, and all was quiet by 2130.

23rd September.
After a fairly quiet night, shelling and trench mortar activity became pronounced just before dawn in the neighbourhood of E.14.central. This was followed by an attack on that point just as dawn was breaking. Our men were, however, ready for it, and it was easily repulsed by rifle and Lewis Gun fire.

At 1800, the enemy again heavily bombarded the MOEUVRES area, which necessitated retaliation on our part. This had the desired effect of silencing the hostile batteries and producing a calm, during which the 155th Inf. Brigade relieved the 156th Inf. Brigade, the latter withdrawing into Divisional Reserve about D.16. and 17., which area was reached about 0100, 24th September.

The period under review was one of great strain and one during which the men, as usual, responded with the utmost keenness and determination to the many calls made upon them. Contact with the enemy was always very close, the shelling endured was always very heavy exceptionally heavy, but the firm resolve to hold MOEUVRES at all costs animated every man of the Brigade and they held it. It is not unreasonable to assume that the enemy losses were considerable. In attack and our Counter-attacks, he lost/

4.

lost severely, and our harassing fire by guns and machine guns on carefully selected points and areas must also have cost him dear. An average of 80,000 rounds per night were fired by our machine guns alone.

Our losses were severe, but not out of proportion to the fire sustained, or the results achieved. They total in all approximately 220 all ranks.

Archd C Bird Lieut.
A.T.O. for Brig General
Commdg. 156 Inf Bde.

"A" Form.
MESSAGES AND SIGNALS.

Army Form C. 2121.
(In pads of 100.)

~~APPENDIX X~~

TO	LIZI	LIPI	WAR DIARY
	LIVA	QIWU	FILE
	LIGU	Staff Capt? LISO	

Sender's Number.	Day of Month.	In reply to Number.	AAA
BM64	23		

Continuation	BM 59	and	61 (Warning orders)
AAA	all	troops	of No.
LIZI	and	LIGU	16.
of	an	E.	and
W	line	drawn	through
E206.0.9	and	E.	of
SWAN	LANE	line	will
be	relieved	by	QIKI
AAA	all	troops	of
LIVA	LIZI	and	LIGU
South	of	above	line
and	E.	of	SWAN
LANE	will	be	relieved
by	QITE	AAA	all
troops	of	LIGU	in
SWAN	LANE	line	and
W	of	it	~~will~~

From

Place

Time

"A" Form.
MESSAGES AND SIGNALS.

Army Form C. 2121.

will	be	relieved	by
QIHO	AAA	LIPI	will
be	relieved	by	LITA
and	will	exchange	guns
AAA	LIVA	on	relief
will	relieve	one	Coy
QIHO	in	HINDENBURG	LINE
at	E.19.central	and	E.19.d.
AAA	LIVA	less	one
Coy	will	occupy	HOBART
STREET	and	HORSE	LANE
with	HQ	at	D.17.d.4.8
AAA	On	relief	LIGU
will	take	over	area
E.17central	with	HQ	at
D.17.a.9.4	and	will	be
at	disposal	of	QIHU

"A" Form.
MESSAGES AND SIGNALS.

Army Form C. 2121.
(In pads of 100.)
No. of Message ....

Prefix......Code......m.	Words.	Charge.	This message is on a/c of:	Recd. at......m.
Office of Origin and Service Instructions.	Sent			Date............
....	At......m.		............Service.	From............
....	To			
....	By		(Signature of "Franking Officer.")	By

TO		3		
Sender's Number.	Day of Month.	In reply to Number.		AAA

for	counter	attack	AAA
On	relief	LIZI	will
proceed	to	area	D16
with	HQ	at	D16.d.4.9
AAA	LIPI	will	go
to	old	LITA	area
in	D.14	with	HQ
at	D14.a.9.6		

From LISO
Place
Time

The above may be forwarded as now corrected. (Z)

H. Sayer Captain
Bde Major

APPENDIX XI

SECRET.

No. 10

Instructions No. 2 re attack ordered
in Divisional Order No. 150 (issued
to Battalion Commanders with map attached)
==

1. The attack will be carried out by 4th. Royal Scots and 7th. Scottish Rifles with 7th. Royal Scots in Brigade Reserve.

2. At Zero hour Battalions will be formed up in following areas:-

(a) 4th. Royal Scots ... E.20.a.8.8 - E.20.d.00.95 -
E.20.a.4.9 - E.20.c.1.5

(b) 7th. Sco. Rifles ... E.19.d.7.6 - E.20.a.2.8 -
E.19.d.7.9 - E.19.b.3.8

(c) 7th. Royal Scots ... E.19.a.7.3 - E.19.b.0.8
E.19.c.7.9 - E.19.a.3.7

Moves to these forming up areas will take place as follows:-

(a) <u>on night 26th/27th</u> - 7th. Sco. Rifles will move from
B.H.P. central to F.U.P. mentioned in
para 2 (b) above
7th. Royal Scots will withdraw one
Company from E.19.d to F.U.P. mentioned
in para 2 (c) above.

(b) <u>on night Zero - 1/Zero</u>
7th. Royal Scots less one Company will
move from present location to F.U.P.
mentioned in para 2 (c) above

4th. Royal Scots will move from present
location at F.17 to F.U.P. mentioned in
para 2 (a) above.
Move to be carried out by following
route:-
Sunken Road running South through
E.19.b and d. and E.21.b and d. thence
by "100" track to FIFTEENTH LINE in
E.19.d - northwards up trench to
E.19.b.3.7 - thence along N. front line
support trench to F.U.P.

Times for move of 4th. Royal Scots will be notified later
but reconnaissances of "100" track will be carried out forthwith
and arrangements will be made by 4th. Royal Scots to picket this
track so that there can be no possible chance of an error being
made on the night of the move.

3. At Zero hour 4th. Royal Scots will be formed up on the line
E.20.c.8.8 - E.20.d.95.95.
At Zero plus 24 4th. Royal Scots will advance under the
barrage - cross the CANAL DU NORD and capture the line of
LEOPARD AVENUE from the MOEUVRES-GRAINCOURT Road (inclusive)
to E.27.b.5.5.
As soon as this line has been obtained parties will be pushed
South down LEOPARD LANE to its junction with LION TRENCH.
On arrival there blocks will be established in LION TRENCH
100 yards West of that point and at E.27.d.4.7.
Later. As soon as 7th. Sco. Rifles have captured their final
objective 4th. Royal Scots will move forward and occupy and
consolidate LION TRENCH.

4. As /

- 2 -

ACTION OF 7TH. SCO. RIFLES.
4. As soon as 4th. Royal Scots have obtained the line of LEOPARD AVENUE 7th. Sco. Rifles will move forward and will form up immediately in rear of the 4th. Royal Scots front line between the MOEUVRES-GRAINCOURT Road and N.27.a.8.8.
At Zero plus 100 1D 7th. Sco. Rifles will advance under cover of an Artillery barrage on their left and a machine gun barrage on their right and will clear the area shaded RED on attached map as far as the line KANGAROO TRENCH - EMU AVENUE which will be captured and consolidated.
As soon as this line has been captured strong patrols will be pushed out and established in N.4.a and o.

ACTION OF 7TH. ROYAL SCOTS.
5. As soon as 7th. Sco. Rifles move forward to form up in rear of 4th. Royal Scots, 7th. Royal Scots will move forward to the area vacated by 7th. Sco. Rifles.
As soon as 7th. Sco. Rifles have obtained their final objectives 7th. Royal Scots will move up to CANAL DU NORD which they will consolidate as rapidly as possible between the MOEUVRES - GRAINCOURT Road (inclusive) and N.27.a.8.8. All possible use is to be made of existing dugouts which will be gas proofed under the supervision of an R.E. party from 417th. Field Coy. R.E. A supply of gas curtains will be taken forward by 7th. Royal Scots for this purpose.

ACTION OF M.Gs
6.(a) One section "P" Coy. 32nd. M.G. Battalion will be attached to 4th. Royal Scots. This section will advance in immediate support of the Battalion and as soon as the junction of LEOPARD AVENUE and LION TRENCH has been captured will be pushed forward to about N.27.a.3.8 where it will take up a position from which it can protect the front of the 4th. Royal Scots and assist the subsequent advance of the 7th. Sco. Rifles as far as LION TRENCH.
As soon as 7th. Sco. Rifles have obtained their final objective this section will move into LION TRENCH with 4th. Royal Scots.
Care must be taken not to shoot 52rd. Naval Division advancing down HINDENBURG SUPPORT LINE.
(b) One section "D" Coy. will

CONSOLIDATION.
7. All ground gained will be consolidated and fought for. In the event of a serious counter attack being made Battalions may be possibly ordered to withdraw, but it must be clearly understood that the line of the CANAL DU NORD is to be fought for to the last.

COMMUNICATIONS.
8. A line will be laid in the first case to all 3 battalions in the F.U.P's.
Subsequently two lines will be maintained to the leading Battalion and all Battalions moving forward must occupy the H.Q. recently occupied by the Battalion in front of them.
Note. Battalions will inform Bde. H.Q. by 6 p.m. 25/9/18 of the location of their Battalion H.Q. in their forming up areas.
Visual will be employed to its utmost limits. A Bde. station situated on the high ground in N.28.d will be manned continuously and will both receive and send messages.
Pigeons. A supply of pigeons is being obtained (probably 6 for 4th. Royal Scots and 6 for 7th. Sco. Rifles) and should be issued to the leading Companies.
Runners. Four runners per Battalion will be sent to Bde. H.Q. directly it opens at its new location and a fresh 4 runners will be sent each time a Battalion moves its H.Q. when the old 4 will be sent back.

9. Separate Administrative Instructions will be issued.
10. Bde./

- 5 -

10. Bde. H.Q. will open at D.19.a.2.0 on the night Zero - 1/Zero at an hour to be notified later.

11. ACKNOWLEDGE.

25th. September 1918.

Captain,
Brigade Major, 15th. Inf. Bde.

```
Copy No. 1 to  O.C. 4th. Royal Scots
         2     O.C. 7th. Royal Scots
         3     O.C. 7th. Sco. Rifles
         4     O.C. "B" Coy. 52nd. M.G. Battalion
         5     D.T.O.
         6     B.C. and File
         7     B.M.
         8     Bde. Sign.
     9 and 10  War Diary
```

APPENDIX XII

Copy No.

155th Infantry Brigade Administrative Instructions No .22

Issued in connection with 155th Inf. Bde. Instruction No 1
of 25/9/18.

Ref. Map 57c N.E. 1/20,000.

27th September 1918

1. Administrative H.Q. and Transport Lines will remain in their present location until after the attack. They will be prepared to move to D.30.b. to position pointed out to B.T.O. today, when the tactical situation permits.

2. SUPPLIES.
   (i). P.L. and part biscuit ration will be issued on and after Z - 1 day for all except transport personnel.
   (ii). On morning of Z day each man will have in his possession rations for that day and his iron rations.
   (iii). The Supply Wagons will continue to deliver rations before noon daily at Bde. Transport Lines.

3. WATER.
   (i). O.s.C. units will ensure that each man's water bottle is full on the morning of Z day. All petrol tins, except what are required for this purpose will be returned to units' transport lines on the night of Z - 1 day.
   (ii). Petrol tins and water carts will be filled at Brigade Transport lines by Water lorry daily at an hour to be notified to units' Admin. H.Q. by the A/Staff Captain.
   (iii). An advance Water Dump will be formed at the Brigade Dump (D.30.b.1.4.) containing the following. Application to be made to O.C. Dump:-
        500 petrol tins
        100 water bottles.
   The A/Staff Captain will be responsible for refilling this dump.
   (iv). Animal Watering. - ETONVILLE., D.9.a.0.9.
                             QUEANT., D.1.d.central.
                             HOPSHIL., G.10.c. (well).
                             (Railway-filled Troughs)
                             LONGATTE., G.9.b.
                             NOREUILES., I.6.c.

4. AMMUNITION SUPPLY.
   (i). A Brigade Dump will be formed at D.30.b.1.4. on Z - 1 day, containing:-
        55 boxes S.A.A. rifle.
        20 boxes do. M.G.
        105 boxes Grenades No 36.
        4 boxes V.P.A.
        6 Golden Rain Rockets
        45 boxes L.G. Drums. (filled)
        75 picks
        150 shovels
        10 Gas blankets.
        990 lbs Chloride of lime.
   (ii). Personnel will be as follows:-
      (a). O.C. Dump - Captain SCOTT, 155th L.T.M. Battery.
      (b). Personnel found under para 13 of Standing Orders for Battle (B.M. 028)
      (c). Lieut. Trotter and half T.M. Battery (to carry ammunition etc to 4th Royal Scots.)
      (d). Lieut. OGILVIE and half T.M. Battery (to carry ammunition not to 7th Bn. Rifles.)
            Officers detailed in (c) and (d) are responsible for keeping touch with the units to which they are attached and for getting forward their requirements from the Brigade Dump.
            The/

2.

The above personnel will live at the dump.
O.C. Dump may call on part of these parties for any urgent work required to be done. They will rendezvous at the dump at 9 p.m. on Z - 1 day. O.C. Dump will send a guide to Rear Brigade H.Q. at 8 p.m. on Z - 1 day to collect personnel detailed under (b) and take them to the dump.

(e). 24 pack mules, under Lieut. ANDERSON, Transport Officer 1/7th Sco. Rifles, will be at the dump under the orders of O.C. Dump at and after Zero plus 90 minutes. The B.T.O. will detail 2 N.C.Os and the mules from Battalions; 24 hours' forage will be carried for all animals. The B.T.O will ensure that forage goes forward daily with L.T.M. Bty rations.

All personnel living at the dump will be rationed by 180th L.T.M. Battery, Rear H.Q.

The Dump Officers and N.C.Os will reconnoitre all routes leading forward from the Dump forthwith.

(iii). Method of supply will be as follows:-
The Dump will be refilled by First Line Transport. Ammunition etc will be forwarded from the dump on pack mules or by carrying parties ((ii) (c) & (d) above).

(iv). O.C. Dump is responsible that all grenades forwarded are detonated, and L.G. Magazines full.

(v). **Emergency Dumps.** D.16.b.0.7.
D.27.D.3.8.

(vi). Divisional Dump, D.7.central, from which First Line Transport will be refilled. Application will be made through Rear Bde. H.Q.

5. **STRAGGLERS.**
(i). Bde. Stragglers Posts will be formed at a place and hour to be notified later. Any Stragglers stopped by these posts will be sent back direct to their units under a N.C.O.

(ii). D.A.P.M. will form a line of Div. Straggler Posts and establish a Straggler Station which will be under control of Div H.Q.

6. **PRISONERS OF WAR** will be sent by units to the Brigade P. of W. Cage at D.20.b.1.1. where they will be taken over by the Brigade P. of W. Guard.

The Brigade P. of W. Guard will rendezvous at Rear Bde. H.Q. at 8 p.m. on Z - 1 day. Their rations will be sent forward nightly with those of T.M. Battery.

Div. P. of W. Cage - D.1.c.5.1.
Prisoners of War will be marched back by cross-country routes. They will not use PRENVILLE - QUEANT ROAD.

7. **TRAFFIC.**
(i). Troops and empty M.T. will use cross-country tracks as far as possible. Transport Officers will reconnoitre alternative routes forthwith.

(ii). Animals proceeding to and from water will not use lorry routes. Transport Officers will cut wire or fill in trenches where necessary.

(iii). Vehicles will not halt on lorry routes; they will pull clear of the road or move down a side road.

(iv). QUEANT - PRENVILLE - MORCHIES ROAD will be used as little as possible.

(v). The following tracks are allotted to the Brigade:-
(a). Before Zero hour.
D.26.b.0.5. - D.26.d.5.5. - D.27.d.4.0. - D.30.a.5.7. - E.19.c.0.0.
(b). After Zero hour.
D.26.b.0.5. - D.26.d.6.20 - D.25.c.0.2. - D.29.b.8.5. - D.30.a.5.5. - E.25.a.0.75. - E.19.c.5.0.; thence on to the road running through E.19.c. and d.

(c)/

3.

(c) After ZERO hour the 155th Inf. Bde will use the road described in (a) but will not use that part of it which is East of the grid separating M and N.
(d). The Route described in (a) is known as "E" track and that described in (b) as "Q" track.
(e). The 156th Bde. route will be marked with 156th Bde. boards.

8. MEDICAL.
(i). Separate orders will be issued by O.C., Brigade Bearer Party.
(ii). Locations

A.D.S. (1/1st Low. Field Amb. D.1.d.5.5. techegecats
Relay Posts ... ... D.17.d.1.8.
D.18.c.1.8.
D.19.d.2.8.
M.19.a.9.9.
M.19.a.9.8.
Trolley Post ... ... D.17.a.9.9.
Horse Amb. Post ... ... D.17.b.1.6.
Motor Amb Post ... ... D.1.d.5.5.

9. VETERINARY.
Adv. Collecting Station ... D.7.d.5.5.
M.V.S. ... ... BOUZINCOURT.

10. BURIALS
(i). The Bde. Burial Party will parade at Rear Bde. H.Q. at
4 p.m. on Z - 1 day, rationed for the following day, after
which they will be rationed by 17th North'd Fusiliers. They
will report under senior N.C.O. to Div. Burial Officer at
H.Q. 17th North'd Fusiliers (D.7.a.) at 5 p.m. that day.
(ii). A new Divisional Cemetery will be selected by Div. Burial
Officer.

11. SALVAGE.
(i). The Brigade Salvage party will rendezvous at Rear Bde. H.Q.
at 8 p.m. on Z - 1 day, and will proceed to Brigade Dump, where
they will come under the orders of O.C. Dump until required as
"Carriers" for Brigade Salvage Dump.
(ii). The salvage area allotted to the Brigade is the ground in
Divisional area East, and exclusive of, CASAL DI NORD.
(iii). Salvage collected will be placed in dump near a road, leaving sufficient space for vehicles collecting it to draw clear
of the road. Bde. H.Q. will be notified of the location of
salvage dumps formed.
(iv). Every effort will be made to salve British Rifles in serviceable condition and place them in cover from rain etc.
(v). Returning transport will, as far as possible, bring back a
load of salvage which will be dumped at Div. Salvage Dump,
D.7.central.

12. BICYCLES will parade at Rear Brigade H.Q. at 2 p.m. on Z - 1 day,
and proceed to Div. Reception Camp. Transport will be arranged.
From Z day inclusive, Reinforcements and returning leave
personnel will remain at Div. Reception Camp until ordered by Div.
H.Q. to join their units.

13. COMMUNICATIONS. The B.S.O. will detail two mounted orderlies to
report at Div. Signal Office at 4 p.m. on Z - 1 day to clear
messages to Rear Brigade H.Q.

14. ACKNOWLEDGE.

Issued at 23.30

Captain,
Staff Captain, 155th Inf. Brigade.

APPENDIX XIII

SECRET.

155th Infantry Brigade.   Copy No. 19

ORDER No. 87.

Ref. Map 1/40,000 (1/20,000)   28th September 1918.

1. **INFORMATION.**
   I. (a).   The 52nd Division in conjunction with the 63rd (R.N.) Division, on their left, and the Guards' Division on their right, are taking part in an attack on the CANAL DU NORD and ground East thereof, on a day and at a Zero hour to be notified later.
              The Canadian Corps, further North, is attacking the CANAL DU NORD and BOURLON WOOD on the same date.

   (b).   The attack of the 52nd Division is being carried out by the 155th Inf. Bde., on the left, and the 157th Inf. Bde., on the right.
              The 190th Inf. Bde. will be on the left of the 155th Inf. Bde.

   (c).   The 157th Inf. Brigade are, in the initial stages, clearing the RIGHT FLANK of 4th Royal Scots and advancing at ZERO plus 40 from the line E.27.d.9.4. – E.28.a.2.8. to mop up the HINDENBURG FRONT LINE, and both banks of the CANAL in E.28., E.8.b. and E.9.a. They are advancing at the rate of 100 yards per 5 minutes, and should reach the line E.9.d.7.7. – E.3.b.8.8. by ZERO plus 90 minutes. During their advance NORTHWARDS, platoons will be dropped at intervals to clear the CANAL.

   (d).   The 190th Inf. Brigade, with the 4th Bedfordshire Regiment on their Right, are forming up West of the Railway Line at E.20.central to E.14.d.8.8., and are attacking the CANAL and the HINDENBURG SUPPORT LINE with their Right on the MOEUVRES – GRAINCOURT ROAD, (exclusive)

2. **INTENTION.**
              The 155th Inf. Brigade *and* will attack and capture the CANAL DU NORD between E.27.d.7.7. to the MOEUVRES – GRAIN-COURT ROAD (inclusive), and clear the area shown in RED on attached Map.
              The First Phase of the attack will be carried out by 4th Royal Scots, and the Second Phase by 7th Scot. Rifles.
              7th Royal Scots will be in Brigade Reserve.

3. **ASSEMBLY AREAS.**
   (a);   By ZERO hour Battalions will assemble in the following areas:-
   (a). 4th Royal Scots ...   E.20.c.9.2. – E.20.c.90.95. –
                               E.27.a.4.9. – E.27.c.1.9.
   (b). 7th Scot. Rifles ...   E.19.d.7.9. – E.20.a.8.3. –
                               E.19.b.7.7. – E.19.d.9.0.
   (c). 7th Royal Scots ...   E.13.a.7.7. – E.19.b.2.8. –
                               E.13.c.7.2. – E.19.a.4.7.

4. **MARCH TO ASSEMBLY AREA.**
              4th Royal Scots will march on Y/Z. from present location in E.14. to Assembly Area by track "100" already indicated to Battalion Commander. *point*
              They will be clear of ~~point~~ E.27.b.0.5. by 11 p.m. on Y evening, but head of Battalion will not pass track junction at E.27.a.4.5. before 9.30 p.m.
              Arrival in Assembly Area will be reported to Bde. H.Q.

   7th /

2.

4. MARCH TO   7th Sco. Rifles will march via tracks to be
   ASSEMBLY   reconnoitred by them to join "10" track in E.21.c.
   AREA (Cont'd)   They will be clear of TRACK Junction at D.23.c.8.5.
                       by 9.30 p.m.

5. ACTION of 4th   (a). At Zero hour the leading wave of the 4th Royal Scots
   ROYAL SCOTS.   will be formed up on line E.20.c.0.5.5. - E.20.c.90.95.
                   (b). At Zero plus 10 4th Royal Scots will advance under
                        the barrage which at Zero plus 15 moves forward from
                        line E.20.b.0.0. - E.20.d.0.9. at rate of 100 yards
                        per 3 minutes to Eastern Bank of CANAL.
                   (c). At Zero plus 25, 4th Royal Scots will have advanced
                        and captured CANAL DU NORD and by Zero
                        plus 45 have captured LEOPARD AVENUE from the MOEUVRES
                        - GRAINCOURT ROAD (inclusive) to E.27.c.5.5.
                   (d). As soon as this line has been obtained, parties
                        will be pushed South down LEOPARD AVENUE to its junction
                        with LION TRENCH.
                   (e). As soon as 7th Sco. Rifles have obtained their
                        objective (see para 6) 4th Royal Scots will move forward
                        and occupy and consolidate LION TRENCH.

6. ACTION OF 7TH   (a). One Company 7th Sco. Rifles will move forward immed-
   SCO. RIFLES.   iately in rear of last wave of the 4th Royal Scots and
                        as soon as the 4th Royal Scots have secured LEOPARD
                        AVENUE as far South as its junction with LION TRENCH,
                        this Company will pass through and push patrols as far
                        as possible Eastwards along LION TRENCH and Southwards
                        to KANGAROO TRENCH and down PIG AVENUE, where they will
                        endeavour to gain touch with the 2nd Guards Brigade.
                   (b). At Zero plus 45, 7th Scottish Rifles (less 1 Company
                        as above) will move forward and form up immediately
                        in rear of the 4th Royal Scots front line between the
                        MOEUVRES - GRAINCOURT ROAD, and E.27.c.5.5.
7th Sco. Rifle (c). At Zero plus 115 will advance in conformity with
                        the 4th Battalion Bedfordshire Regiment on their left
                        and clear the area shaded in RED on attached map as
                        far as the line KANGAROO TRENCH - SOW AVENUE, which
                        will be captured and consolidated.
                        ZEBRA TRENCH will be captured by Zero plus 143 and
                        KANGAROO TRENCH by Zero plus 190.
                        During this advance the left of 7th Sco. Rifles will
                        be covered by an artillery barrage and the right by
                        M.G. fire.   line KANGAROO TRENCH - SOW AVENUE
                   (d). As soon as above line has been captured, strong
                        patrols will be pushed out and established in K.4.a. &
                        c.

7. ACTION of 7th   (a). As soon as 7th Sco. Rifles move forward to form up
   ROYAL SCOTS.   in rear of 4th Royal Scots, 7th Royal Scots will move
                        forward to the area vacated by 7th Sco. Rifles.
                   (b). As soon as 7th Sco. Rifles have obtained their final
                        objectives 7th Royal Scots will move up to CANAL DU NORD which
                        they will consolidate as rapidly as possible between the MOEUVRES
                        - GRAINCOURT ROAD (inclusive) and E.26.b.6.6.
                   (c). Orders for these moves will be issued from Bde.
                        H.Q.

8. ARTILLERY.   (a). A tracing showing the Artillery Barrages on the front
                        of 154th Inf. Brigade and 190th Inf. Brigade is issued
                        herewith.
                   (b). In addition, Howitzers firing H.E. and gas will
                        fire on the following points at the following times:-
                        (1). Zero plus 30 to Zero plus 60 - LION TRENCH and
                             SUNKEN ROAD and TRENCH between E.27.b.5.5.
                             and Road at E.27.d.5.5.
                        (2). Zero plus 60 to Zero plus 70 - ZEBRA TRENCH from
                             E.27.c.5.5. to E.27.d.5.5.
                   (3)/

3.

8. ARTILLERY, Contd.
  (5) Zero plus 70 to Zero plus 90 - KANGAROO TRENCH
   from K.5.d.95.75 to E.27.d.8.1
   It should be noted that the gas shells being used
  are a new kind the gas in which evaporates one minute
  after bursting.

9. MACHINE GUNS. (a) One section "D" Coy. 32nd. M.G. Battalion will move
   immediately in rear of 4th. Royal Scots and as soon
   the latter have captured LEOPARD AVENUE will come
   into action in LEOPARD AVENUE about E.27.a.9.5.
  (b) One section "D" Coy. 32nd. M.G. Battalion will
   take up defensive position on the CANAL as soon as
   4th. Royal Scots have captured LEOPARD AVENUE.
  (c) At Zero plus 150 the section mentioned in sub-part
   (a) above will move forward to ZEBRA TRENCH and will
   be replaced by section mentioned in sub-para. (b).
  (d) As soon as 7th. Som. Rifles have obtained their
   final objective one section will be moved up to about
   K.4.d.4.4 and the remaining section will move forward
   with 4th. Royal Scots and take up positions in LION
   TRENCH.

10. TANKS. Two Tanks will probably be available to assist 7th.
  Som. Rifles in clearing their area. Details as
  regards their action will be issued later but O.C.
  7th. Som. Rifles will ignore these tanks in the
  preparation of his plan of action.

11. R.Es. O.C. 416th. Field Coy. R.E. will detail the following
  parties to be attached to Battalions:-
  (a) To 4th. Royal Scots
   (1) 2 unrollers to look for mines and booby
    traps in the CANAL bed or in the dugouts
    situated in the CANAL.
   (2) 4 sappers to assist in consolidation of
    LEOPARD AVENUE and the formation of a block
    in LION TRENCH if it is necessary to make
    one and subsequently in the consolidation
    of LION TRENCH.
  (b) To 7th. Royal Scots
   (1) 4 sappers to assist in the consolidation of
    the CANAL DU NORD.
   (2) 2 sappers to supervise the gas proofing of
    dugouts in the CANAL. These sappers will
    bring the necessary tools etc.

12. ASSISTANCE TO OTHERS. 7th. Som. Rifles will be prepared to assist both
  the 17th. and 120th. Inf. Bdes. in the event of
  either of them failing to make satisfactory progress at any time.
  It is essential that 17th. Inf. Bde. clear the
  CANAL early in the operations and the Company 7th.
  Som. Rifles which moves South of LEOPARD AVENUE
  will be prepared to assist them in every way.
  17th. Inf. Bde. will similarly assist 7th. Som.
  Rifles in the event of their being hung up.
  Great care will be taken not to fire on either
  troops of 63rd. Division or of the Purple Bde.

13. CONSOLIDATION. All ground gained will be consolidated and fought
  for.
  In the event of a serious counter attack being
  made Battalions may possibly be ordered to withdraw, but it must be clearly understood that the
  line of the CANAL DU NORD must be fought for to
  the last.

4.

14. **REFORMING.** As soon as all objectives have been gained and consolidated and other formations have advanced, the Brigade will reform in N.27.a. and c. Orders for this will be issued by Brigade H.Q.

15. **LIAISON.** (a). In order to ensure co-operation with 190th Inf. Brig. 4th Royal Scots and 7th Scot. Rifles will each detail one platoon to work astride the MOEUVRES – GRAINCOURT ROAD to work in conjunction with a platoon of the 190th Inf. Brigade similarly placed. Reports will be furnished by the platoon commander concerned on arrival at the following points – Cross Roads, N.27.b.5.8., – N.29.a.2.1. – KANGAROO TRENCH at N.29.c.7.7.
(b). 7th Sco. Rifles will send patrols to get into touch with 2nd Guards Brigade at
(1). Junction of EON AVENUE and CAT TRENCH, so
(2). The Road at N.H.d.4.9.
7th Sco.Rifles will report when touch is gained.
(c). 4th Royal Scots will send a patrol westwards along LION TRENCH to gain touch with 19th Inf. Brigade
(d). 7th Sco. Rifles will similarly send patrols down the CAMBRAI ROAD, ZEBRA T TRENCH and KANGAROO TRENCH.
(e). Each Battalion will send a Liaison Officer to Bde. H.Q. on Y/Z night. He should report as soon as Battalions are established in their Assembly Areas
(f). 2nd H.S. Battalion are sending 1 Officer to each Battalion for liaison purposes.

16. **HEADQUARTERS.** Battalion H.Q. in the Assembly Areas will be established at the following points:-
4th Royal Scots ... N.29.c.4.5.
7th Sco. Rifles ... N.19.d.7.7.
7th Royal Scots .... N.13.c.5.5.

17. **COMMUNICATIONS.**
(a). Lines will be laid to all Battalions in their Assembly Areas and 4th Royal Scots and 7th Sco Rifles will be joined up laterally.
(b). Any line laid forward of 4th Royal Scots H.Q. will be laid down the Northern trench of the HINDENBURG TRENCH LINE.
(c). One linesman will be at 4th Royal Scots H.Q. and 5 at 7th Sco. Rifles H.Q. These men will lay cable forward in the event of a move forward being made, but 7th Sco. Rifles will detail a carrying party of 5 men to carry cable forward of 4th Royal Scots Headquarters in event of 7th Sco. Rifles moving forward. This Carrying party to report to H.Q. 4th Royal Scots before Zero hour.
(d). Visual will be employed to its utmost limits. A Brigade Station will be established near HOUGH LANE. Battalions will man their own stations and must so place them that they can see Bde. Visual Station.
(e). Pigeons. 4 pigeons will be allotted to 4th Royal Scots and 6 to 7th Sco. Rifles. They will be carried by the leading Companies and will be released on attaining following objectives:-
(1). LEOPARD AVENUE.
(2). ZEBRA TRENCH.
(3). Final Objective of 7th Sco. Rifles.
(f). Golden Rain Rockets will be fired by the right and left flanks of the leading Coys on obtaining the objectives named in the sub-para (e) above.
(g)./

2.

17. COMMUNICATIONS. (c). Runners. 4 Runners per Battalion will report
    (Continued).   at Brigade H.Q. as soon as Battalions reach their
                               H.Q. in Assembly Areas, and subsequently 4 fresh
                               runners will be sent in the event of Battalions
                               moving their H.Q.
                                   In the event of 7th Scot. Rifles moving their
                               H.Q. Southeast of 4th Royal Scots H.Q., messages
                               from 7th Scot. Rifles will be sent to H.Q., 4th
                               Royal Scots who will be responsible for sending
                               them on either by telephone or runner.

18. AEROPLANE FLIGHT.   The hour at which contact planes will fly
                               over our lines will be notified to all concerned
                               at a later date, but the necessity for the
                               foremost troops at once lighting flares when
                               called upon to do so must be impressed on all
                               concerned.

19. Prisoners of War.   Any prisoners of war taken by the 7th Scot. Rifles
                               will be sent in batches to H.Q., 7th Royal Scots,
                               who will in turn forward them to Bde. P. of W.
                               Collecting Station.

20. Administrative   Separate Administrative Instructions have already
    Instructions.   been issued to all concerned.

21. GENERAL.   In the forthcoming fight, which the M.G.C.
                               believes will be the last this year in which the
                               Division will be engaged, he desires to wish every
                               Officer and man the best of good-luck. Upon the
                               results obtained by the British Forces in the
                               Field on this occasion, hangs the question of whether
                               there will be a crushing defeat of the German Army
                               in the Field, and as a result of that an early and
                               glorious peace or an indecisive battle and a
                               long continued war.
                                   That the 156th Brigade will play its part glorious-
                               ly as it has done in the past is beyond all doubt,
                               and once again Scotland will, please God, have
                               reason to be proud of us.

22. Brigade H.Q. will close present location at 5.30 p.m. on Y day and
    reopen at same hour at H.Q.,4.R.S.

23. Acknowledge by wire.

                                                    H. Sayer
                                                    Captain,
Issued at _____11.15 AM_____   Brigade Major, 156th Inf. Brigade.
            ==

            Copy No 1 to 4th Royal Scots.
                    2   7th Royal Scots.
                    3   7th Sco. Rifles.
                    4   156th L.T.M. Battery.
                    5   157th Inf. Brigade.
                    6   2nd Guards Brigade.
                    7   150th Inf. Brigade.
                    8   52nd Division.
                    9   1/1st L.F.A.
                   10   412th Field Coy R.E.
                   11   52nd M.G. Battalion.
                   12   52nd M.G. Bn. "B" Coy.
                   13   B.G.C.
                   14   B.M.
                   15   S.C.
                   16   A/S.C.
                   17   Bde. Sigs.
                 18 & 19 Diary.

SECRET.

ADDENDUM TO 156th INF. BRIGADE ORDER NO 87.   Copy No. 10

ACTION OF TANKS.

26th. September 1918.

1. At about Zero plus 90, two tanks will cross the CANAL by the CAMBRAI ROAD in E.27.c.1.3 with view to co-operating with 1/7th. Sco. Rifles South of the CAMBRAI ROAD. They will under no circumstances proceed North of it except to gain touch with 1/7th. Scottish Rifles as mentioned in para 2.

2. After crossing the CANAL, one Tank will move to LION TRENCH at E.27.c.central to gain touch with 1/7th. Sco. Rifles and will move North up LION TRENCH until touch is gained.
It will then return and moving S.E. proceed to mop up ZEBRA TRENCH and Trench running from E.27.d.40.65 to E.27.d.90.00.

3. One Tank, on crossing CANAL at Zero plus 90, will turn South and moving along Eastern bank will turn East and mop up entire length of KANGAROO TRENCH.

4. Both Tanks will thereafter deal with PIG and SOW AVENUES and move about in 156th. Bde. area dealing with all places requiring attention.

5. It is realised that the only close support we can give to tanks will be to the second tank mentioned, which, while moving Southwards along East bank of CANAL should be closely followed by the Company 1/7th. Sco. Rifles, operating in that area.
Elsewhere the Tanks will be supported closely by us whenever possible.

6. The Tank Commander lays special stress on the absolute necessity of our forward Infantry displaying some prearranged sign by which they can be recognised.
This sign will be blue Signal Flags, two of which must be carried by the forward platoons of each Company 1/7th. Scottish Rifles.
If on the move, when tanks are seen, infantry will wave the flags. If not on the move, the flags will be stuck up as prominently as possible on a parapet or on open ground.

7. Battalions should not count on the assistance of Tanks on this occasion. If they do cross the CANAL safely, they may be of great help to us, but our calculations should be based on the probability of their not being able to do so.

H. Sayer
Captain,
Brigade Major, 156th. Inf. Bde.

Issued at 1200

```
Copy No.  1 to 4th. Royal Scots
          2    7th. Royal Scots
          3    7th. Sco. Rifles
          4    52nd. M.G. Bn.
          5    52nd. Division
          6    157th. Inf. Bde.
          7    2nd. Guards Bde.
          8    B.M.
          9    File
      10 & 11  Diary
```

APPENDIX XIV

Account of Operations of 156th Infantry
Brigade from 24/9/18 to 27/9/18 (inclusive)

Ref. Map 1/20,000
Sheet 57c N.E. and 57b N.W.

September 24th.

1. After being relieved by the 155th Inf. Brigade in the MOEUVRES SECTION, on the night 23/24th September, the Brigade was situated as follows:-
   4th Royal Scots - D.15., with H.Q. at D.15.d.4.9.
   7th Royal Scots - 3 Coys in HOBART STREET and HORSE LANE and 1 Company in HINDENBURG LINE in E.19.d. H.Q. at E.17.d.4.6.
   7th Scc. Rifles - E.17.central with H.Q. at E.17.d.4.9.
   156th L.T.M. Battery. - D.14., with H.Q. at D.14.a.9.6.
   Brigade H.Q.

   The 7th Scottish Rifles were under the orders of 155th Inf. Brigade for Counter-attack purposes, and the 7th Royal Scots were under 155th Inf. Brigade in so far as they held HOBART STREET and HORSE LANE as "passive defence" and formed a defensive flank to MOEUVRES with the Company in HINDENBURG LINE in E.19.d.

24th, 25th & 26th
September. 2.   The 24th, 25th and 26th September were quiet days as far as this Brigade was concerned, and the necessity for the use of either the 7th Scottish Rifles or 7th Royal Scots did not arise.
   These days, however, were used in active preparation and reconnaissance for the attack which was to be carried out on the 27th instant, the initial orders for which attack were received on the 24th September.

3. The task assigned to the 156th Inf. Brigade for this attack was the capture of the CANAL DU NORD and LEOPARD TRENCH between the MOEUVRES - GRAINCOURT ROAD (inclusive) and E.27.a.2.5., and the clearance of the area shown in RED on the attached map.

4. The plan of attack was briefly as follows:-
(a). The 4th Royal Scots were to form up on the area E.20.c.8.3. - E.20.c.9.9. - E.20.a.4.2. - E.20.c.1.6. their jumping off line being E.20.c.8.3. - E.20.c.9.9.
   They were to attack and capture the CANAL DU NORD and LEOPARD AVENUE between the MOEUVRES - GRAINCOURT ROAD (inclusive) and E.27.a.2.5. by ZERO plus 40, and to push down LEOPARD AVENUE as far as its junction with LION TRENCH.

(b). The 7th Scottish Rifles were to send up one Coy immediately in rear of 4th Royal Scots to move down KANGAROO TRENCH (West?) and PIG AVENUE and gain touch with 2nd GUARDS DIVISION as soon as the 4th Royal Scots had gained the junction of LEOPARD AVENUE and LION TRENCH.
   As soon as 4th Royal Scots had gained LEOPARD AVENUE the/

24th, 25th & 26th
September.
(Continued)

The remainder of 7th Scottish Rifles were to form up behind them, and at ZERO + 129 were to move forward and clear the whole of the remainder of the area shown in RED on attached map.

Patrols were to be pushed out and established on the high ground in K.4.a. and c.

The whole of the attack of this Battalion was to be by the Left i.e. by the 190th Brigade of the 63rd Division, who were to clear the HINDENBURG LINE in E.15., 21, 22, and 28 and K.4.

(c). The 7th Royal Scots were assembled in following area:-

E.19.d.7.3. - E.19.b.2.8. - E.13.c.7.3. - E.19.c. 4.7., and were in Brigade Reserve.

5. 27th September.

(a). By 0200 on the 27th September all Battalions were in their assembly areas, which had been reached without any casualties, and although Battalions were crowded and the trenches were in many cases very shallow and open, no casualties were sustained from this hour until ZERO hour.

ZERO hour was at 0520, at which hour the barrage came down on the line E.26.b.2.6. - E.20.d.3.9., on which line it stayed for 15 minutes.

(b). At 0520, 4th Royal Scots advanced to get as close under the barrage as possible. This advance continued until the leading waves had proceeded about 300 yards and had got over the crest of the hill. Here they encountered unexpected and exceedingly strong wire, and this, combined with heavy Machine Gun fire from both flanks and from the Eastern bank of the CANAL, succeeded in holding them up. In addition, the Battalion suffered from heavy T.M. fire from ZERO - 1 minute onwards, and also from heavy gas shelling, which forced them to halt and put on their box respirators. This naturally caused some disorganization and loss of direction, and as a consequence the Battalion was some considerable distance behind the barrage line. Every effort was made to continue the advance over the open as had been originally intended, but it was soon realised that this was impossible on account of the amount of wire and Machine Gun fire and the consequent casualties incurred, and recourse was therefore had to advancing by bombing up the various trenches leading Eastwards to the CANAL.

The position for a long time was obscure. The first information which was received was the fact that two golden rain rockets (success signals) had been seen by Divisional Observers to be fired at 0605 from LEOPARD AVENUE, the one on the MOEUVRES - GRAINCOURT ROAD and the other from about E.27.a.2.5.

From various reports received, it became obvious that these signals must have been false, but it was not until 0830 that a definite message was received from 4th Royal Scots that they were *held* up on the West of the CANAL (Note. The first two runners who were sent were both gassed, and consequently unable to deliver their messages, and from ZERO + 20/

3.

27th September.
(Continued)

30 all forward telegraph lines were broken, taking
several hours to repair, as they were badly cut about
for lengths of 200 yards at a stretch, and the
trench had fallen in on top of them.

(c). By 0930, however, the 4th Royal Scots had, by
means of bombing attacks, forced their way across
the CANAL at E.20.d.8.5., and at once commenced to
clear LEOPARD AVENUE and the East Bank of the
CANAL, which operation was completed in spite of a
good deal of opposition by 0955.

(d). The one Company of the 7th Scottish Rifles
detailed to clear KANGAROO TRENCH (West) and PIG
AVENUE, assisted the 4th Royal Scots to cross the
CANAL at E.20.d.8.5., and as soon as LEOPARD AVENUE
was secured, started to carry out its original role
but, chiefly owing to losses in Officers (it was
reduced to one Officer), it was unable to complete
its task, and had to be reinforced by another Company,
- the two finally effecting junction with the
GUARDS DIVISION in PIG AVENUE, taking some 200
prisoners on their way down.

(e). By 10.35, the whole of the rest of the 7th Scottish
Rifles were across the CANAL, proceeding on their
original task of clearing the area marked in RED.

By 1050 LION TRENCH was in our hands, together
with between 150 and 200 prisoners, who surrendered
practically without a fight.

The advance continued successfully on the Right
to the line of ZEBRA TRENCH, but the 7th Scottish
Rifles were definitely held up on the Left, owing
to the non advance of the 4th Battn. Bedfordshire
Regiment, who were still hung up in TIGER TRENCH
and had failed to clear the high ground in E.28.a.,
b. and d., whence heavy Machine Gun Fire was ex-
:perienced.

Bombing down KANGAROO TRENCH and SOW AVENUE had
consequently to be resorted to. This was success-
:fully carried out down SOW TRENCH, and junction
was obtained with the GUARDS DIVISION at 1330, but
it was not until 1430 when the 4th Bedfords began
to advance again, that the Eastern end of KANGAROO
TRENCH (East), and consequently the whole of our
objective, was gained. Patrols were at once
sent out and established on the high ground in
K.4.a. and c. and consolidation was started.

(f). Meanwhile, as soon as the 4th Royal Scots had
gained LEOPARD AVENUE (0930), 7th Royal Scots were
moved up into the area vacated by 7th Scottish Rifles
and subsequently (1110) they were moved up into the
CANAL DU NORD, which they at once commenced to
consolidate.

As soon as the line of ZEBRA TRENCH had been gained
by 7th Scottish Rifles, the 7th Royal Scots were
ordered up to LION TRENCH between the MOEUVRES -
GRAINCOURT ROAD and E.27.a.8.1., with orders to at
once weigh in and help 7th Scottish Rifles to
obtain their objective, if called upon to do so by
O.C., 7th Scottish Rifles. This, however,
proved to be unnecessary, and consequently the
Battalion remained in LION TRENCH, which they c-
-onsolidated.

Attached

App XIV

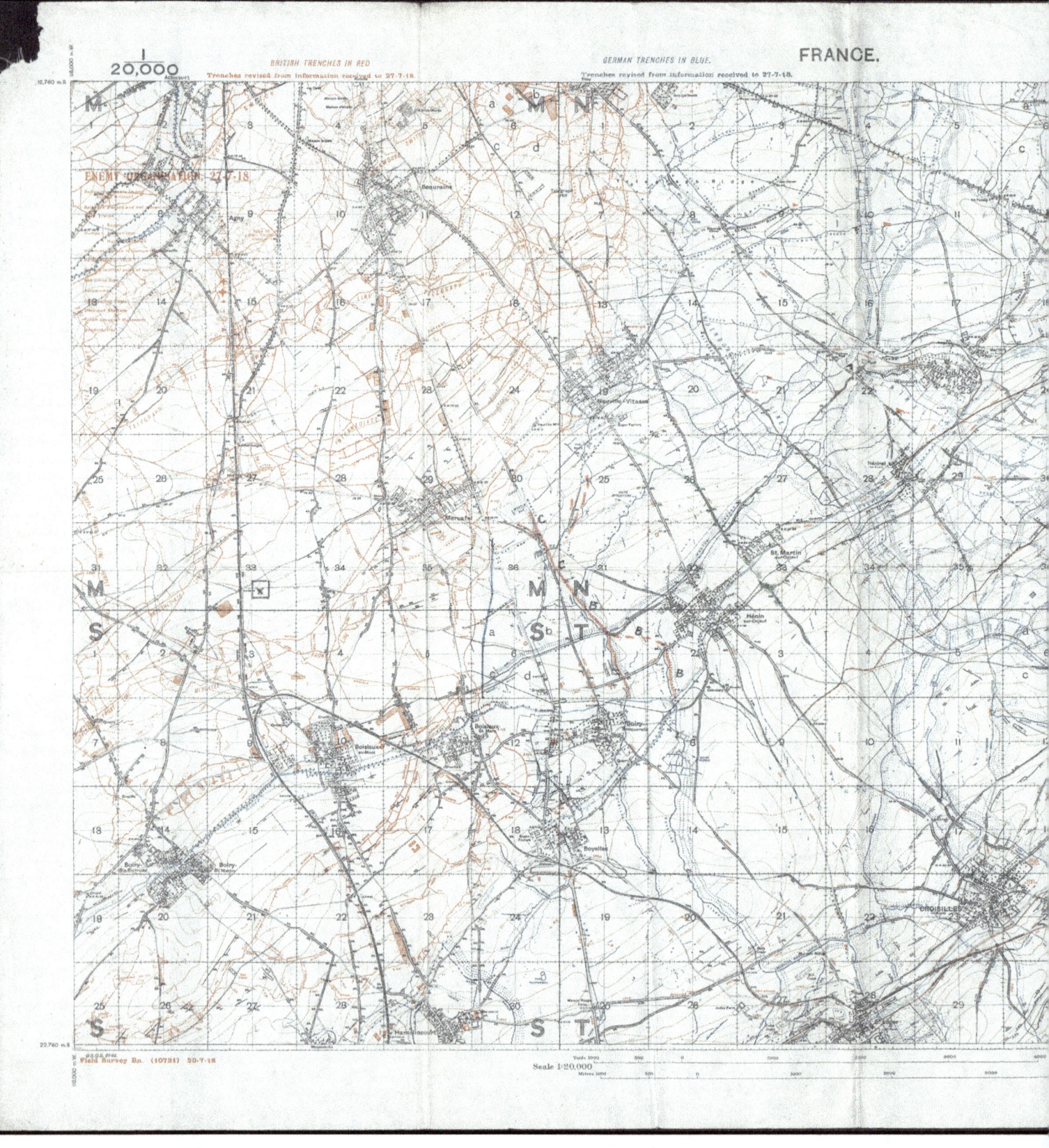

FRANCE. EDITION 8d (Local). SHEET 51B S.W.

156th Brigade

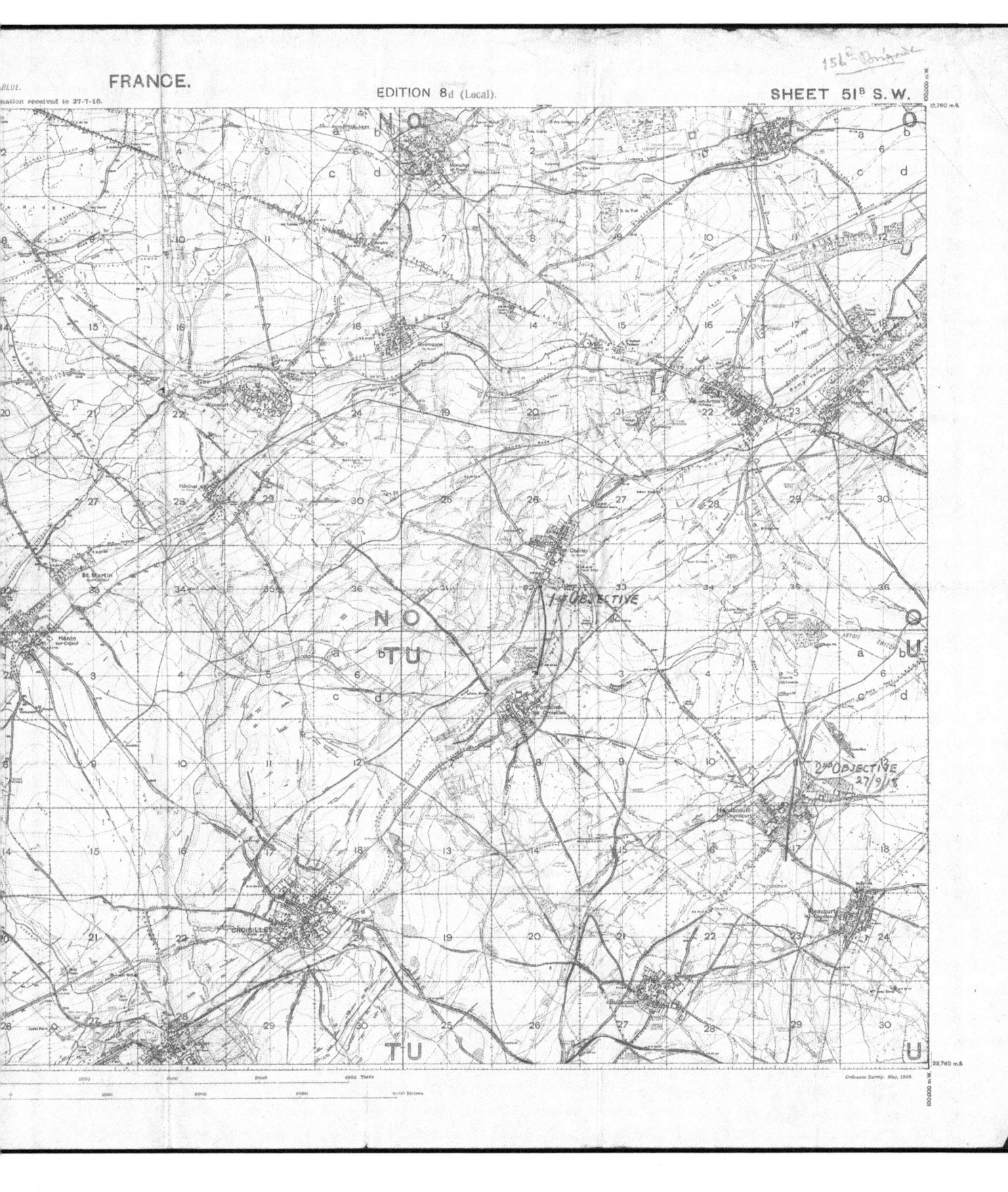

N° 7

War Diary
of
156th Infantry Brigade
1st to 31st October 1915

Volume XLIX

Army Form C. 2118.

WAR DIARY
or
INTELLIGENCE SUMMARY.
(Erase heading not required.)

Map Reference 57cNE. 57bNW. 57c.

156 Infantry Brigade. October 1918. Vol. XI

Place	Date Oct.	Hour	Summary of Events and Information	Remarks and references to Appendices
E.19.a.89.	1		Instructions received that the Division would relieve the 63rd Div(sn) in the line S. of PROVILLE.	
		4.30	The Brigade moved to Provisional reserve in L.3.w & c, W. of CANTAING. The Brigade Commander attended a Conference at Bn.H.Q. Brigade already for battle at 1500. Brigade Order No. 58 issued. (Relief of 5th Bde)	Appendix I
CANTAING	2		Brig. Gen A.H. Leggat, CMG, DSO, resumed command of the Brigade. Battalion's rested.	Appendix II
	3		The Divisional Commander visited Bde H.Q. Battalions resting and refitting.	Appendix
	4		The Brigade Commander visited Bn H.Q. 4/5 Bn reconnoitred the ground in the vicinity of SUR L'OEUVRE for a possible attack on the enemy Trench/System S. of CAMBRAI in (A28 & 29)	Appendix
	5		Instructions received that the Division was to be relieved on the 6th Oct, and would move into G.H.Q. reserve.	Appendix
	6		B.M. 13 issued. (Move to LOUVERVAL) The Brigade moved to LOUVERVAL, and arrived in bivouacs on our immediate H.Q. villages by 1800. Brigade Order No. 59 issued. (March entrainment to VAULX-VRAUCOURT)	Appendix II
LOUVERVAL	7		Brigade marched to VAULX-VRAUCOURT, and entrained, reaching TINQUES at 1800.	Appendix III

Army Form C. 2118.

WAR DIARY
or
INTELLIGENCE SUMMARY.
(Erase heading not required.)

Map Reference 51°.

156 Infantry Brigade. October 1918. Vol XII

Page 2.

Place	Date	Hour	Summary of Events and Information	Remarks and references to Appendices
	7 (cont).		Battalions detrained and marched Billets. Brigade HQ — 4th Royal Scots — 4th Royal Scots — 156 LTM.B. to IZEL-LEZ-HAMEAU 7th Cameronians PENIN (C.22).	A76.fr
IZEL-LEZ HAMEAU	8.		B.G.C. and B.M. visited Battalions who were resting. Weather broken and showery.	9/8/3.fr
	9.		B.G.C. and Bn. at Divisional Conference. Battalions resting. Instructions for training issued. (B.M. 975.)	Appendix "I" No.IV. fr A6/5.fr
	10.		Reorganisation and training commenced. B.G.C. visited training area. Weather continues broken.	
	11.		Training in the morning. Divisional Commander visited Bde. H.Q. Conference of Battalion Commanders at Bde. H.Q. Capt H. Sayer. M.C., Brigade Major, proceeded on special leave to U.K.	A76.fr
	12.		Training and bathing. R.C.V.C. visited units during parade hours. A very wet day. Lectures on 'Contact- Aeroplanes' by Col James, R.A.F. to officers and N.C.O.s of the Brigade.	A76.V

Army Form C. 2118.

WAR DIARY
or
INTELLIGENCE SUMMARY.
(Erase heading not required.)

Map Reference 57º LENS 1/100,000
15th Durham Light Brigade. October 1915 Vol XII

Page 3.

Place	Date	Hour	Summary of Events and Information	Remarks and references to Appendices
IZEL-LEZ HAMEAU	13		Church Parades in the morning.	
	14		Bathing and training in the morning. Brigade Football tournament commenced. B.G.C. visited training areas in the morning.	Appx V
	15		Training. Spots in the afternoon.	Appx V
	16		Training. B.G.C. at a Conference at Divisional H.Q.	Appx V
	17		Capt H. Sayer M.O. Brigade Major returned from U.K. B.G.C. at Divisional Conference. Training and bathing continued.	Appx V
	18		Orders received that the Division would move east on the 19th. Brigade Order No. 60 issued.	Appendix V
CHATEAU DE LA HAIE	19		The Brigade left IZEL arr at 09.00, and marched to CHATEAU DE LA HAIE, arriving about 14.00. Arrangements made in the Corps Theatre. Brigade Order No 61 issued. (March to BILLY-MONTIGNY)	Appx V Appendix VI
BILLY-MONTIGNY	20		The Brigade left CHATEAU de la HAIE at 09.00, and marched to BILLY-MONTIGNY via GIVENCHY - AVION - ROUVROY, arriving about 16.00. This was a very trying march, carried out in a downpour of rain, in consequence of which the roads were very heavy. Brigade billeted in BILLY-MONTIGNY. Brigade Order No 62 issued.	Appx V Appx VII

Army Form C. 2118.

WAR DIARY
or
INTELLIGENCE SUMMARY.
(Erase heading not required.)

Map Reference. 44A.

156 Infantry Brigade. October 1918. Vol XII

Page 4

Place	Date Oct	Hour	Summary of Events and Information	Remarks and references to Appendices
AUBY	21		Brigade marched to AUBY arriving at 13.30, no midday halt being made.	A026.J.Y.
	22	16.30	Reorganisation of "Marching Order", and "Fighting Order" dress, in a platoon from H 1st Royal Scots and 7 Cameronians respectively. B.M. 116 issued. (Dress – Marching and Fighting Order)	Appendix VIII A026.J.Y.
			Army Instructions. Battalions cleaning up and resting. Instructions received that the Division would be inspected by the Army on the 24th.	Appendix IX
			B.M. 119 issued. (Organisation of First Line Transport).	
	23		Training in the morning in the vicinity of billets.	Appendix X A026.J.Y.
		11.30	Inspection of transport by G.O.C. 52nd Division. Brigade Order No 63 issued. (Move to COUTICHES)	Appendix XI A026.J.Y.
	24		The Brigade marched from AUBY to COUTICHES (M.2.d. about 4.4), arriving about 12.45. B.M. 143 issued. (Time of Zero, expectation future).	
COUTICHES	25		Battalions engaged on road repair in the Brigade area.	
	26		B.G.C. and B.M. with representatives from Battalions reconnoitred the line on the FROUILLE area. Instructions received that the Brigade would move east on the 27th.	Appendix XII A026.J.Y.
			B.M. 164 issued. (Move to LECELLES)	

WAR DIARY
INTELLIGENCE SUMMARY

Army Form C. 2118.

Map Reference Sheet 44 1/40,000

151st Infantry Brigade

Oct 6th 1916 Vol XIV

Page 5

Place	Date Oct	Hour	Summary of Events and Information	Remarks and references to Appendices
	27		The Brigade marched to LECELLES (I.30) arriving about 1300, and billeted in this village. Instructions received that the Brigade would relieve the 36th Bde in the line on night of 28/29th. LECELLES shelled during the night — no casualties. (Relief of 36th Inf Bde) Bn. No 66 issued.	A763/1 Appendix XIII
MONT DU PROY	28		B.G.C. and Battalion Commanders reconnoitred the Brigade Sector in the morning. Relief was completed by 2200. Dispositions — 4th Royal Scots in the line, 7th Royal Scots (L) & 7th Suffolk and 6th Gordon Rifles Right Support with HQ in MAIRE de NIVELLE, FRESNOY, and MONT du PROY respectively. Bde HQ in MONT du PROY.	OCRP/1 Appendix XIV
	29		B.G.C. and Bn. visited the line. BRUILLE and NIVELLE shelled, otherwise there was little hostile activity.	A763/1
	30		Some hostile shelling of BRUILLE and CHATEAU L'ABBAYE. Patrol from 4th Royal Scots left 9.15 to examine the ground E of the E. SCAUT with a view to future operations. Patrol crossed the stream in Kl 9 r by means of a raft but found the ground E of it completely waterlogged. The ground E of the E. SCAUT was reported to be absolutely flooded.	A763/1

WAR DIARY
or
INTELLIGENCE SUMMARY.

Army Form C. 2118.

Map Reference 4 & ⅟₄₀,₀₀₀

156 Infantry Brigade

October 1918 Vol IV

Page 6

Place	Date	Hour	Summary of Events and Information	Remarks and references to Appendices
NOYELLES du PROY	31		Dull day. About noon shelling of BRUILLE and LE LONG BUHOT Farm was little hostile activity. Machine guns active at night E of the JARD CANAL. Patrol of K.O.S.B. crossed the stream in that area by means of a ladder. This patrol also reported the ground too waterlogged. Effective Strength and Casualties (Oct 1918).	Appendix XV OBBN

A. Taylor Capt.
Brigade Major, 156 Infantry Brigade.

APPENDIX I

SECRET.
Copy No. 13

188th. Infantry Brigade Order No. 18.

Ref. Man 57c. N.E. – 1/20,000.　　　　　　　　1st. October 1918.

1. (a) The 62nd. Division is relieving 63rd. Division in the line on the night 1st/2nd. October.
   (b) The 186th. Inf. Bde. is relieving the front line troops and the 187th. Inf. Bde. is to be in Divisional support in the MARCOING LINE in P.30.
   (c) The 188th. Inf. Bde. will be in Divisional reserve in L.S.a and c.

2. The 188th. Inf. Bde. will march to L.S.a. and c. in accordance with attached march table.

3. Transport will accompany units and on arrival, will be Brigaded at spot to be selected by the Brigade Transport Officer. Units will retain their field cookers with them if concealed positions near their locations can be found.

4. Men will carry greatcoats with them on the line of march.

5. Rations for consumption tomorrow will be carried by units.

6. The actual positions which units are to occupy will be indicated to units on arrival in the new area.

7. Nucleus of Battalions will be sent to Brigade Transport lines on arrival in the new area.

8. Bde. H.Q. will close at present location at 3 p.m., and will open in new area on arrival, at a place to be notified later.

9. ACKNOWLEDGE.

H. Sayer
Captain,
Brigade Major, 188th. Inf. Bde.

Issued at _____

```
Copy No. 1 to 4th. Royal Scots
        2    7th. Royal Scots
        3    7th. Scn. Rifles
        4    188th. L.T.M. Battery
        5    412th. Field Co. R.E.
        6    1/1st. S.M. Amb.
        7.   219th. Coy. A.S.C.
        8    Brigade Commander
        9    S.C.
        10   Brigade Transport Officer
        11   Bde. Sign. Officer
   12 & 13   Diary
        14   File
```

MARCH TABLE.

Serial No.	Unit	Starting Point		Route.	Remarks.
		Place	Time.		
1	Bde. H.Q. 7th. Royal Scots)	Cross Roads E.23.d.9.0	1630	URMINSTER Cross Roads, E.1.d.9.3	Bde. H.Q. will fall in in rear of 7th. Royal Scots.
2	7th. Scot. Rifles	do.	1640	do.	
3	4th. Royal Scots 106th. L.T.M. Battery)	do.	1700	do.	106th. L.T.M. Battery will fall in in rear of 4th. Royal Scots.

NOTE (a) The usual distances will be maintained on the march.
(b) In the event of hostile aircraft approaching units will halt, and take as much cover as is possible at the side of the road, and will not put their heads up to look at the aeroplane.

"A" Form
MESSAGES AND SIGNALS.

Army Form C. 2121
(In pads of 100.)

APPENDIX II

TO	L1Z1	L1P1	RIVE	
	LIVA	Bde. Seps		
	LIGU	B.T.O.		

Sender's Number.	Day of Month.	In reply to Number.	AAA
BM 13	6		

The	Bde.	will	march
to	new	bivouac	area
in	J.2.3 and	4	near
LOUVERVAL	today	AAA	starting
point	cross	Roads	L.8.B.2.7
Times	for	~~passing~~	starting
point	LIVA	0800	LIGU
0820	L1Z1	with	Bde.
H.Q.	0840	L1P1	0855
AAA	Head	of	column
to	enter	GRAINCOURT	at
0900	and	tail	to
be	clear	by	1000
AAA	Transport	will	move
with	units	and	part
will	return	for	second
journey	later	in	day AAA

"A" Form
MESSAGES AND SIGNALS.

Army Form C. 2121
(In pads of 100.)

	2.		
Advance	parties	on	bicycles
or	horses	will	meet
Staff	Captain	at	road
junction	J.5.C.9.2	at	1000
to	be	pointed	out
new	bivouac	areas	AAA
Route	to	be	followed
by	all	units	is
road	junction	E.28.A.2.0	thence
by	CAMBRAI	BAPAUME	Road
AAA	usual	distances	to
be	maintained	on	march
AAA	Bde.	HQ	closes
0845	present	location	and
reopens	in	new	area
on	arrival	AAA	An
officer	from	Bde.	H.Q.

"A" Form
MESSAGES AND SIGNALS.

Army Form C. 2121 (In pads of 100.)

will	march	at	head
of	LIVA	AAA	acknowledge
AAA	addressed	all	units
L180	repeated	RIVE	

From L180
Time 0150

APPENDIX III

SECRET.
Copy No. 16

156th INFANTRY BRIGADE ORDER No. 59.

Ref. Maps 1/20,000, Sheets 57c N.E. and 57c N.W.   6th October 1918.
and 1/100,000, LENS, Sheet.

Move of 52nd DIVISION.   1. The 52nd (Lowland) Division, less R.A. and M.G. Battn. is moving from present area to VIIIth Corps area by rail and road, on the 7th and 8th instant.

Move of 156th INF. BRIGADE.   2. (a). The dismounted portion and a proportion of the First Line transport of the 156th Inf. Bde. and attached troops will move by train to TINQUES in accordance with attached Table "A";
(b). The remainder of the transport of 156th Inf. Bde. will march to TINQUES on the 7th and 8th instants in accordance with orders which will be issued later. Probable hour of start will be 0815 on 7th instant. The whole of this transport will be under orders of Lieut. MACINTOSH, 7th Royal Scots. One N.C.O. per unit will accompany this transport.

March to Entraining Station.   3. The march of units to Entraining Station will be carried out in accordance with attached March Table marked "B".
Transport proceeding by train "B" will rendezvous under Bde. Transport Officer at Cross Roads, J.9.b.6.3. at 0900.
Transport proceeding by train "C" will rendezvous under N.C.O. to be detailed by Bde. Transport Officer at same place at 1500.

ENTRAINING.   4. (a). Entraining Officer for Units of 156th Inf. Bde. at VAULXVRAUCOURT will be Capt. C.S. SMITH, M.C., and at FREMICOURT for all units 52nd Division, will be Staff Captain, 156th Inf. Bde.
(b). Order for entraining from front to rear of train will be as follows:-
1. 4th Royal Scots, with Bde. H.Q. and L.T.M. Bty.
2. 7th Sco. Rifles.
3. 7th Royal Scots.
4. Portion Div. H.Q. (with Signal Coy).
(c). Each unit will hand a State shewing Number of personnel proceeding by train to the Entraining Officer on arrival at Entraining Station.

DETRAINING.   5. (a). Detraining Officer will be Lieut. J. AUSTIN, 7th Cameronians. He will report to the R.T.O., TINQUES Station on arrival, and will remain on duty until all troops of 52nd Division have arrived at that Station.
(b). O.C., 4th Royal Scots, will detail an unloading party of two strong platoons under an Officer. This party will report on arrival to Detraining Officer, and will remain on duty at Detraining Station until the arrival of the last train.
(c). Each unit will be held responsible for unloading its own baggage, but only minimum sized parties must be left behind to ensure that this is done.

MECHANICAL/

2.

MECHANICAL TRANSPORT.	6. (a).	One motor lorry will report to H.Q., 1/4th Royal Scots and one to 1/7th Royal Scots about 0730 tomorrow to move to entraining Station surplus stores. Officers' kits, cooking utensils, and minimum of mess stores should be sent by these lorries. 1/7th Sco. Rifles will send guide to 1/7th Royal Scots and Bde. H.Q. guide to 4th Royal Scots to conduct the lorries from the entraining Station to their respective H.Qs to move their surplus stores. 1/4th and 1/7th Royal Scots must load and despatch the lorries to entraining Station as quickly as possible.
	(b).	Two lorries for the Brigade will be available at the detraining Station to remove the above stores to new areas.
BILLETING.	7.	Billeting parties will meet their units at detraining Station to conduct them to the new areas.
TENTS, return of.	8.	All tents and shelters received today will be returned to Lieut. J; AUSTIN on the road at XVIIth Corps H.Q. at 0600 tomorrow.
SUPPLIES.	9.	The unconsumed portion of tomorrow's ration and at least a part of the ration for the 8th instant will be carried on the man.
WATER.	10.	Full water bottles will be carried, and water carts will entrain full.
SADDLES and HARNESS.	11.	Saddles and Harness will remain on the animals proceeding by tactical train, but the girths will be slackened.
AREAS.	12.	Areas occupied by units must be left scrupulously clean.
BRIGADE H.Q.	13.	Brigade H.Q. will close present location at 1030 on 7th instant, travel by train with Brigade to new area, and reopen at a place to be notified on arrival.
	14.	ACKNOWLEDGE.

Issued at 2400.

H. Sayer
Captain,
Brigade Major, 156th Inf. Bde.

```
Copy No 1 to B.G.C.           Copy No. 9 to B.T.O.
       2    4th Royal Scots         10    Lieut. J. AUSTIN.
       3    7th Royal Scots         11    52nd Division.
       4    7th Sco. Rifles         12    17th Bn; North'd Fu
       5    156th L.T.M. Battery    13    412th Field Coy R.E
       6    Brigade Major           14    1/1st L.F.Amb.
       7    Capt. G.S. SMITH.       15    O.C., Bde. Sigs.
       8    Staff Captain.       16 & 17   Diary.
                         18. File.
```

TABLE "B".

MARCH TABLE;

Issued with 155th Bde. ORDER No. 59.

A Serial No.	B Unit.	Place.	C Starting Point. Time.	D Route.	E Destination.	F Remarks.
1	4th Royal Scots, with Bde. H.Q. and 155th L.T.M. Bty in this order.	Cross Roads J.2.b.40.65	0930	Via LADNICOURT	VAULX-VRAUCOURT STATION	Transport & chargers will NOT accompany units. The whole Brigade to have reached VAULX-VRAUCOURT STATION by 1215.
2	7th Scottish Rifles	do.	0940	do.	Do;	do.
3	7th Royal Scots	do.	1000	do.	do.	do.

APPENDIX IV

O.C., 4th Royal Scots,
 7th Royal Scots,
 7th Cameronians (S.R.)

B.M. 975

1. Training on the lines stated by the Divisional Commander at the Conference today will commence on the 11th instant.

2. Tomorrow will be devoted to completing reorganization, cleaning, washing and smartening up generally.

3. The daily period of training will be limited to 4 hours of which the first 1½ hours will be devoted to specialists training especially in Lewis Gunnery and Rifle Bombing. (A supply of bombs and cartridges for this purpose have been demanded and will be issued as soon as they have been obtained).
   Training programmes will be so arranged so that all training for the day is over by 1500 at the latest. Thereafter men <u>must</u> be encouraged as much as possible to play football and other games which will give them healthy exercise.

4. Special attention must be given at once to the question of saluting and the men should be instructed to salute any motor car flying a distinguishing flag.

5. Each battalion will do one route march as a battalion every three days, the march not to be less than 6 miles and increasing up to 9 miles. Strictest march discipline will be maintained throughout these route marches.

6. Training Areas are as shown on the attached map.
   Area shown in Brown   4th Royal Scots.
    do. do.   Blue   7th Royal Scots.
    do. do.   Green   7th Sco. Rifles.
   Training can be carried out over any portion of this area and also on the stubble fields in the immediate vicinity of billets but grass land is not to be used in any area other than those marked Brown, Blue, and Green.

7. Short Ranges are shown on the attached map in Red. These ranges are not in all cases in good repair and C.O's may select others within their area but must take the usual safety precautions.
   In connection with the above it is pointed out that casualties have recently been inflicted on inhabitants, and that especial care must be taken to block side roads with flankers and Officer in charge of the firing must ensure that no inhabitants are working within the danger area behind a range.
   Standing orders for ranges in the area have been forwarded to those concerned for necessary action.
   A limited number of short range targets are being drawn by the Brigade and will be issued shortly. Battalion Commanders must be prepared to improvise targets.

8. An issue of parry sticks and sacks for bayonet fighting will be made shortly. These should be preserved as they have to be returned when the Division leaves this area.

9. C.S.M. BOWDEN, Physical Training and Bayonet Fighting Instructor is available for use within the Brigade. Battalions should notify these H.Q. by 1800 tomorrow night of the days and hours on which his services are required.

10. Battalions will submit each day by 1700 a short statement showing where the next days training is to be carried out stating times.
    In the case of route marches the route to be taken and the hour of start will be stated.

9th Octr. 1918.

J. Sayer
Captain,
Brigade Major, 156th INF. BDE

APPENDIX V

156th. Infantry Brigade Order No. 60   Copy No.

Ref. Map 1/100,000 LENS Sheet 11.   18th. October 1918.

1. The 52nd. Division is moving east by road and rail tomorrow, the 19th. October.

2. The 156th. Inf. Bde. Group consisting of the 156th. Inf. Bde. 412th. Field Coy. R.E., 219th. Coy. A.S.C., and one section 2nd. Lowland Field Ambulance will march to CHATEAU DE LA HAIE by road in accordance with attached march table.

3. Transport will march with Units.

4. Separate instructions with regard to any M.Transport that may be available will be issued later.

5. Bivouac areas will be pointed out on arrival in new area.

6. Rations for consumption on the 20th. October will be carried in the supply wagons of the Divisional Train and will be issued on arrival in the new area.

7. Bde. H.Q. will close present location at 0830, will march at the head of the column and re-open at the CHATEAU DE LA HAIE on arrival.

8. Greatcoats will be carried on the man.

9. ACKNOWLEDGE.

                                              H. Sayer
                                              Captain,
Issued at 2100   Brigade Major, 156th. Inf. Bde.

        Copy No. 1 to 4th. Royal Scots
                 2   7th. Royal Scots
                 3   7th. Sco. Rifles
                 4   156th. L.T.M. Batt.
                 5   412th. Fld. Co. R.E.
                 6   2nd. Low. Fld. Amb.
                 7   219th. Coy. A.S.C.
                 8   B.M.
                 9   S.C.
                10   Bde. Sigs.
             11 & 12 War Diary
                13   File

MARCH TABLE.

Issued with 156th. Infantry Brigade Order No. 60.

Serial No.	Units in order of march.	From. Place	Starting Point Time.	Route.	Destination	Remarks
1.	4th. Royal Scots) Bde. H.Q.)	IZEL-LEZ-HAMEAU Road Junction 1/4 mile N. of S. of St.	0900	TILLOY-LES-HERMAVILLE -Cross Road S. of L. of LA MON - AGNIERES - CAMBLAIN L'ABBE	CHATEAU DE LA HAIE	Bde. H.Q. to march in rear of 4th. Royal Scots
2.	7th. Royal Scots) L.T.M.Battery)	do.	0920	do.		L.T.M.Battery to march in rear of 7th. Royal Scots.
3.	7th. Sco. Rifles	PENIN Cross Rds. 1/2 mile N. of L. of LA MON ROUGE INN	1040	SAVY-AGNIERES-CAMBLAIN L'ABBE		To follow in rear of 7th. Royal Scots on arrival at Cross Rds.
4.	412th. Field Coy. R.E.	DENIER As for Serial No. 1	1000	LIGNEREUIL-& thence as for Serial No. 1		
5.	Sect. 2nd. Low. Field Amb.	MAVINCOURT As for Serial No. 1	1020	Via MANIN and thence as for Serial No. 1		
6.	219th. Coy.A.S.C.	DOWTINE FARM. As for Serial No. 1	1050	do.		

NOTES:-
(A) The usual distances will be maintained on the line of march.
(B) 1 Horse Ambulance wagon will follow in rear of each Battalion.

APPENDIX VI SECRET
Copy No. 12

156th. INFANTRY BRIGADE ORDER No. 61

19th. October 1918.

Ref. Maps
1/40,000 Sheets 44a and 44b.

1. The Division is continuing its march eastwards tomorrow, 20th. of October.

2. The 156th Inf. Brigade Group will march to BILLY MONTIGNY (O.32 and O.33) tomorrow in accordance with attached March Table.

3. Transport will march with units.

4. Greatcoats will be carried by Motor Transport. In the event of wet weather, waterproof sheets will be worn.

5. Separate instructions with regard to Motor Transport available and Advance Parties, will be issued later.

6. Rations for consumption on the 20th October will be carried on the man, and those for consumption on 21st instant will be carried on the Supply Wagons of Divisional Train.

7. Intelligence Officers (mounted) will meet A/Brigade Major at Brigade H.Q. at 0800, prepared to go forward to reconnoitre roads.

8. Brigade H.Q. will close present location at 0830, will march at the head of the column, and reopen in the new area at a place to be notified on arrival.

9. ACKNOWLEDGE.

H. Sayer
Captain,
Brigade Major, 156th Inf. Brigade.

Issued at 21.45

```
Copy No 1 to 4th Royal Scots.
        2    7th Royal Scots.
        3    7th Cameronians (Sco. Rifles)
        4    156th L.T.M. Bty.
        5    412th Field Coy R.E.
        6    2nd Low. Field Amb.
        7    219th Coy A.S.C.
        8    Capt. BURTON, Sect. 1/1st L.F.A.
        9    B.M.
       10    S.C.
       11    Bde. Sigs.
    12 & 13  War Diary.
       14    File.
```

SECRET

MARCH TABLE.

Issued with 156th Inf. Brigade Order No. 61.

Serial No.	Units in order of March.	STARTING POINT. Place.	Time.	ROUTE	DESTINATION.	REMARKS.
1.	4th Royal Scots.} Brigade H.Q. }	Road Junction, X.1.d.4.2.	0900	SOUCHEZ - GIVENCHY - AVION - MERICOURT - SALLAUMINES.	BILLY MONTIGNY.	Bde. H.Q. to be in rear of 4th Royal Scots.
2.	7th Royal Scots.} L.T.M. Battery }	As for Serial No. 1	0920			L.T.M. Battery to march in rear of 7th Royal Scots.
3.	7th Scottish Rifles	As for Serial No. 1	0940			
4.	412th Fd. Coy R.E.	As for Serial No. 1	1010			
5.	Sect. 2nd Low. F. Amb} Sect. 1st L.F.A. }	As for Serial No. 1	1025			
6.	219th Coy A.S.C.	As for Serial No. 1	1030			

NOTES. (1). Usual distances to be maintained on the march.

(2). One Horse Ambulance from Sect. 1/1st Low. Field Amb. will follow in rear of each Battalion.

APPENDIX VII

SECRET.

155th. Infantry Brigade Order No. 82.   Copy No. 13

Ref. Msn &m 1/11.000.   30th. October 1918.

1. 52nd. Division is continuing its march eastwards tomorrow, 31st. October.

2. 155th. Inf. Bde. Group, less 412th. Field Coy. R.E., will march to AUBY (O.3R.) tomorrow in accordance with attached march table.

3. Transport will march with units.

4. Instructions as to Mechanical Transport, Advance parties and rations etc. will be issued later.

5. A halt of 30 minutes for mid-day meal will take place on road in p.M. at about noon. Suitable ground will be pointed out by Brigade Intelligence Officer.

6. Brigade H.Q. will close at BILLY MONTIGNY at 0930 and will march at head of column opening at AUBY on arrival there.

7. ACKNOWLEDGE.

                                    Captain,
Brigade Major, 155th. Inf. Bde.

Issued at 2300

         Copy No. 1 to 4th. Royal Scots
              2   7th. Royal Scots
              3   7th. Sco. Rifles
              4   155th. L.T.M. Batt
              5   412th. Fld. Coy. R.E.
              6   2nd. Low. Fld. Amb.
              7   Captain Burton, 1/1st. L.F. Amb.
              8   219th. Coy. A.S.C.
              9   B.H.
             10   S.C.
             11   O.C., Bde. Sigs.
             12   I.O.
         13 & 14   War Diary
             15   File

MARCH TABLE

Issued with 175th. Infantry Brigade Order No. 81

Serial No.	Units in order of march.	Starting Point. Time.	Route.	Destination.	Remarks.
1.	7th. Royal Scots) Regt. H.Q.	1010	Route 4. (0.28.a.4.3) – FRESNY LIZARD – thence thro – POINT 3 and to ROUTE A to L'HOMMELET – cross roads F.20.a.9.4.	VRNY.	Bde. H.Q. to follow in rear of 7th. Royal Scots. T.M.B. Battery to follow in rear of 6th. Royal Scots.
2.	6th. Royal Scots) L.T.M. Battery)	1040			
3.	7th Bn. Fifties	1045			
4.	Bde. Lds.,)Fd. Amb) Sect. Lt.I.T., MGB.)	1110			
5.	Bgde. Coy. A.S.C.	1118			

4th Royal Scots.
7th Royal Scots.
7th Sco. Rifles.
156th L.T.M. Battery.
Brigade Signal Officer.

B.M. 118

APPENDIX VIII

1.   In accordance with the decisions arrived at at to-day's demonstrations "Marching Order" and "Fighting Order" dress will in future be as follows:-

Marching Order.
- (a). Arms as issued.
- (b). Entrenching Tool, as issued.
- (c). Box Respirator, to be carried on top of the pack, with sling attached to the front of the belt.
- (d). Accoutrements, as issued.
- (e). S.A.A., 120 rounds, all of which is to be carried in pouches.
- (f). Mess Tin which, with the unexpended portion of the day's ration in it,
- (g). is to be inside the steel helmet (which is to be carried flat on the back of the pack, retained in position by the kicking straps).

Note. Numbers 1 of Lewis Gun Sections may sling their packs, and in consequence the mess tin cannot be placed inside the helmet, which will be kept in position by the flap straps of the pack. The mess tin will, in this case, be slung on the flap straps.

- (h). Water bottle, filled.
- (i). Articles to be carried in the pack are:-
  - Greatcoat.
  - Jerkin.
  - 2 pairs sox.
  - 1 Shirt.
  - 1 Cap Comforter.
- (j). Articles to be carried in the haversack:-
  - Hold all.
  - Towel and soap.
  - Housewife.
  - Cleaning kit.
  - Iron Rations.
- (k) Waterproof sheet under flap of pack

Fighting Order.
- (a). Arms as issued.
- (b). Entrenching Tool, as issued.
- (c). Box Respirator to be slung on the right shoulder and worn on the left side.
- (d). Accoutrements, as issued.
- (e). S.A.A., 120 rounds, all of which is to be carried in pouches.
- (f). Mess tin which, with unexpended portion of day's ration in it, will be carried in the pack.
- (g). Water bottle, filled.
- (h). Steel helmet, to be worn on head.
- (i).

2.

Fighting Order. (Continued).
    (i). Articles to be carried in the pack.
        Cap Comforter.
        Towel and soap.
        Jerkin.
        Hold all.
        Balmoral.
        1 pair sox.
        1 shirt.
        Mess tin (with *unexpended portion days ration* ~~iron ration~~ inside it)
        waterproof sheet, to be carried at the top of the pack, underneath the flap.) *Iron rations*

    (j). Other articles carried:-
        (i). 2 ground flares per man (to be carried in pockets of tunic)
        (ii). 2 bombs per man (to be carried in pockets of tunic).
        (iii). 1 Very pistol and 6 cartridges to be carried either by the Platoon Commander or the Platoon Sergeant.
        (iv). 2 cup attachments for rifle grenades per platoon.
        (v). 3 sand bags per man (to be carried on top of the pack under kicking straps.)

2.   Dress for dismounted Officers both in "Marching Order" and in "Fighting Order" will in future consist of web equipment, with pack.
        Revolver
        Compass.
        Glasses.

3.   The above dress and equipment regulations will come into force forthwith, and the greatest care is to be taken to ensure that men are in future properly equipped and turned out.

4.   The extra 50 rounds of S.A.A. per man, at present in possession, will be withdrawn under orders to be issued from these H.Q.

5.   All previous orders and instructions with reference to "Fighting Order" and "Marching Order" are cancelled.

22nd October 1918.
                                    Captain,
                          Brigade Major, 156th Inf. Bde.

B.M. 119

4th Royal Scots,
7th Royal Scots,
7th Sco. Rifles,
156th L.T.M. Battery.

APPENDIX IX

First Line Transport.

Battalion First Line Transport will ~~invariably~~ in future be organised as follows:-

1. The order of vehicles in the line of march will be as follows:-
   - (i)   4 Lewis Gun Limbers, in the same order as the Coys.
   - (ii) Magazine limber.
   - (iii) S.A.A. and Grenade Limbers (2).
   - (iv) Tool limbers.(2).
   - (v)   Field Cookers in the same order as Coys.
   - (vi) Water Carts (2)
   - (vii) Mess Cart.
   - (viii) Maltese Cart.
   - (ix) Pack animals and spare Draught Horses.
   - (x)   Dismounted personnel.

2. Vehicles will be loaded in accordance with attached Table "A".

3. **Equipment to be carried by the off horse:-**
   - (1). Driver's blanket covered by driver's waterproof sheet.
   - (2). Surcingle and pad.
   - (3). 2 feeds, 1 on either side of the horse attached to the surcingle pad.
   - (4) 2 canvas buckets, 1 on either side of the horse attached to the surcingle pad. The driver's grooming kit will be carried in one of these buckets.

4. **Kit and equipment of driver.**
   - (1). Web equipment will be worn by all drivers.
   - (2). The haversack will be on the man's back and the mess tin will be slung on the haversack. Driver's sack will be carried in the fore portion of limbers and on the front of Field Cookers and water-carts.
   - (3). Greatcoats will be rolled on the front of the saddle.
   - (4). Steel helmets will be attached to the saddle on the near side of the ride horse.
   - (5). Small box respirators will be slung over the right shoulder.
   - (6). Puttees and **not** leggings will be worn.
     Note. If, and when, Field boots become an issue, puttees may be discarded.
   - (7). Driving whips will invariably be carried by the men, and will **not** be tied to the saddle.

5. **Brakesmen.** All brakesmen will wear full marching order (Steel helmets flat on the back of the pack)and will carry rifles.

6. **Lewis Gun men** marching with limbers will wear full marching order as above and will carry rifles.

7. **Cooks** marching with cookers will wear marching order less packs and will carry rifles. Packs of these cooks will be attached to the front of the cookers. All cooks will be properly dressed and will wear puttees, their cooks clothing to be disposed of elsewhere during the march.

8./

-2-

8. <u>Water duty men.</u>   2 water duty men will go as brakesmen for the 2 water carts. They will wear full marching order and carry rifles. The remainder of the water duty men, if with the transport, will march in rear.

9. <u>Sergeant Cooks</u> will march in rear of the last cooker, and will wear full marching order and carry a rifle.

10. <u>Transport Sergeant's pack</u> will be carried in the mess cart.

11. <u>Pack leaders and spare draught horse leaders</u> will march in full marching order with the rifles slung on the left shoulder.

12. <u>Personnel marching in rear of transport.</u> The number of these to be reduced to an absolute minimum. To be under the charge of a N.C.O. and strict march discipline to be insisted on.

14. <u>General.</u> More active supervision of the transport on the line of march is required. The Transport Officers and Transport N.C.Os. must exercise constant supervision by riding up and down and the 2nd in Command of Battalions should inspect the transport at least once during the march. The prevailing habit of men putting rifles and equipment in various portions of the vehicles must be checked at once.

13. <u>Hay nets</u> will be carried in the fore portion of limbers, under the cover on the rear part of the fore portion of the cookers and under the superstructure of water carts.

    The above organisation will come into force at once.

                                                H. Sayer
                                                Captain,
22nd October, 1918.   Brigade Major, 186th Inf.Bde.

TABLE "A".

Lewis Gun Limber.

Fore Portion.   Weight, lbs.
    4 guns @ 30 lbs.   120
    4 gun chests @ 10 lbs.   40
    4 spare part bags @ 10 lbs.   40
    18 mag.boxes @ 46 lbs.   828
    1 Range finder @ 15 lbs.   15
    4 gun covers.@ 1 lb.   4
                                    Total........1,047   1,047.

Rear portion.
    4 guns @ 30 lbs.   120
    1 A.A.Gun.@ 30 lbs.   30
    4 gun chests @ 10 lbs.   40
    5 spare part bags @ 10 lbs.   50
    16 mag.boxes @ 46 lbs.   736
        (2 for A.A.Gun.)
    1 A.A.Mounting @ 12 lbs.   12
    5 gun covers @ 1 lb.   5
                                    Total..........993   993

                                    Total weight..........2,040.

The limbers will be packed as follows:-

Fore portion.
    The 18 magazine cases are laid in the limber flat with lids uppermost. The 4 guns in chests are laid on top of these - 2 chests on each side, leaving a space in centre for the Range finder. A space now remains at the rear for the spare parts bags.

Rear portion.
    2 guns in chests are first placed at each side of limber. The magazine cases are packed in and between the gun chests. A space remains behind these cases for spare parts bags. A.A.Gun and mounting put on top as a top load.

    Note. As soon as pelf bag carriers are received the method of packing will be altered in accordance with the diagram which has already been circulated to battalions and copies of which will be forwarded later.

Magazine Limber.

Fore portion.   Weight lbs.
    24 mag.boxes @ 46 lbs.   1,104
Rear portion.
    24 mag.boxes @ 46 lbs.   1,104

                                    Total weight,   2,208.

    Magazine cases will be packed flat with lid uppermost.

Wol/

Tool Wagons. The following will be carried divided between the 2 wagons.-

	Weight, lbs.
110 shovels.	385
76 picks.	608
8 crowbars.	96
40 billhooks.	72
20 reaping hooks.	20
14 axes, helved.	103
16 axes, hand.	55
26 periscopes.	90
Joiners tools.	40
Tailors do.	26
Shoemakers do.	26
Saddlers do.	14
Farriers do.	29
Butchers do.	37
Signalling equipment.	150
Drum, rifle oil.	56
Drum, creosel	50
	1843

*Further orders will be issued as regards the actual equipment to be carried.

S.A.A. Wagons. Following load to be divided equally between 2 limbers:-

	Weight, lbs.
44,000 rounds, S.A.A.	3,300
24 boxes, bombs.	600
4 boxes Very Lights.	40
1 box Revolver Amn.	80
Total weight.	4,020

Field Cooker. On superstructure the bulk portion of the unexpended portion of the days ration not already issued.
    16 Dixies.
    1 Coy. Mess box (Officers)

Water cart. On superstructure 30 empty petrol tins.

Mess Carts. Transport Sergeant's pack and load as detailed by O.C., unit.

Maltese Cart.

    16 rifles (Company Stretcher bearers)
    4 stretchers.
    M.Os. equipment as ordered.
Note. The M.O's valise will be carried in the G.S. Wagon of the train.

LOAD TABLE
Light Trench Mortar Battery.

Three limbers loaded as follows:-

	Weight lbs.	
Fore portion		
Ammunition - 3" Stokes shells	1,204	1,204
28 boxes at 43 lbs.		
Rear portion		
2 Stokes Mortars at 113 lbs.	226	
Accessories at 15 lbs.	30	
1 Box S.A.A. at 75 lbs.	75	
Water, 8 gallons	80	
1 Valise at 40 lbs.	40	
3 dixies at 8 lbs.	24	
1 Mess Box at 7 lbs.	7	
Total	482	482
Total weight		1,686

In addition 1 limber carries Stationery Box at 25 lbs.

123

4. P. Sheet
5. R. Sack
6. Sea. Rifles
7. Tin Hat
8. 1. Sig. Mirror

Reference OM 118 para 1.
Marching Order add:-
(9) Waterproof sheet under
flap of Pack.

Oct 22.1918   Stanley Smith Capt.
                for Vice-Major, 156th Bn.

APPENDIX X

SECRET.
COPY NO. 14

156th Infantry Brigade Order No.63

23rd October, 1918.

Ref.Maps. Sheets 44 A 44A 1/40,000

1. 52nd Division is concentrating in the FLINES area tomorrow 24th October.

2. 156th Infantry Brigade will move by March Route tomorrow to COUTICHES and MOLINEL in accordance with attached march table.

3. Transport and baggage wagons of Train will march with units.

4. Dress - Marching Order, less Greatcoats which will be carried in Lorries.

5. Advance Parties. 1 Officer and 1 other rank per battalion and 1 officer or 1 other rank per smaller unit will report to the A/Staff Captain at 1000 at the Road Junction M.8.d.4.5. and will be allotted Billets.
   These parties will meet their units at the Road Junction N.8.a.8.4. and guide them to their billets.

6. Motor Lorries. (1) 3 Motor Lorries have been allotted to the Brigade and guides will be sent by following units to Brigade H.Q. at 0700 to collect one lorry.-
   4th Royal Scots.
   7th Royal Scots.
   The Remaining lorry will be used by Brigade H.Q. for the first trip and will then be sent to H.Q. 7th Scottish Rifles. That unit will have a guide waiting for it at present Brigade H.Q. at 0900.
   (2). No more than two trips will be made by each lorry unless absolutely necessary.

7. Supplies. (1). Rations drawn today for consumption on 25th inst., will be delivered by 219 Coy. A.S.C. Supply Wagons on arrival in COUTICHES area.
   (2). After delivering rations at units H.Q. Supply Wagons will return to H.Q. 219 Coy. A.S.C. COUTICHES.
   (3). R.P. will be at COUTICHES.

8. Div.Reception Camp. is moving tomorrow to VITRY EN ARTOIS. Leave personnel for sailing date 27th inst., should report there.

9. Billets: will be left scrupulously clean.
   Units will keep a record of the billets occupied here by them.

10. Brigade H.Qrs. will close at present location at 0900 and will move at the head of the column, opening at COUTICHES on arrival there.

11. ACKNOWLEDGE.

H. Sayer
Captain,
Brigade Major, 156th Inf. Bde.

ISSUED AT_____

Copy No; 1   to 4th Royal Scots.
         2   7th Royal Scots.
         3   7th Scottish Rifles.
         4   156th L.T.M.Bty.
         5   219th Coy. A.S.C.
         6   Capt. BURTON, 1st L.F.A.
         7   B.M.
         8.   S.C.
         9   Sigs.Officer.
        10   I.O.
        11   B.T.O.
        12   52nd M.G.Bn.
   13 & 14   War Diary.
        15   File.

————————————

LARGE TABLE.

Issued with 154th Inf.Brigade Order No.83.

Ref. Sheets 44 & 44A. 1/40,000.

Serial No.	Unit.	Starting Point.		Route.	Destination.	Name Pts.
		Place.	Time.			
1.	7th Royal Scots. Bde. H.Qrs.		0930	ROSS BARRIER — WARSDIN — LA FLAQUE — FLERS ORCHIES ROAD — COUTICHES.	COUTICHES and ROITEL AREA.	Royal March distances to be kept. Bde. H.Q. and L.T.M. Battery will move in rear of 7th Royal Scots and 7th Scottish Rifles respectively.
2.	7th Sco.Rifles. 153th L.T.M.Bty.	Cross Roads C.27.a.O.O. (Sheet 44 A.)	1000			
3.	4th Royal Scots.		1030			
4.	Sect. 1st L.F.A.		1040			
5.	219th Coy. A.S.C.		1045			

NOTE. There will be no halt for mid-day meal.

O.C.,
4th Royal Scots,
7th Royal Scots,
7th Cameronians (S.R.)
156th L.T.M.Bty.

B.M.

APPENDIX XI

1. The kind of warfare that we shall be involved in, in a very few days from now, will almost certainly, in the event of the Germans continuing their retreat as expected, take the following form – viz:-

One Inf.Brigade, two F.A. Brigades, one squadron Cavalry, two platoons of a cyclist battalion, and one M.G. Coy., will form the Divisional Advanced Guard and be responsible for clearing the whole Divisional Front which will cover a frontage of 3,500 – 4,000 yards.

2. Of the troops mentioned, the vanguard will normally consist of:-

   1 Battn; Infantry.
   4 Stokes Mortars.
   2 Batteries R.F.A. (1 from each Bde).
   1 Squadron of Cavalry.
   1 Platoon Cyclists.
   2 sections M.G.Coy.

Remaining troops form Main Guard.

3. It is now necessary to point out that while the functions of the A.G. as a whole will remain as heretofore, the methods and formations to be used will be very different to anything we have known before, particularly as regards Van Guard action and formations.

In short, what must be expected is this –
(1) The total front to be covered and swept clear of the enemy will be approximately 4,000 yds.
(2) 3 ~~squadrons~~ troops of cavalry with one in support will cover our advance, probably a mile ahead of the infantry, locate the hostile infantry, and if unable to dislodge him, make way for our Infantry.
(3) The Van Guard Infantry will be disposed as follows on the above mentioned front of 4,000 yds.
   (a) 2 Companies in front line.
   (b) 2 Companies in Support Line.

Reference to (a). Each Company will have 3 platoons in line at wide intervals and 1 in support.

Each of the 3 platoons will march in fours preceeded by scouts, until touch is obtained with the enemy when diamond or square formations will be adopted, and an attack initiated if only opposed by small hostile bodies. The supporting platoon in each case moving in fours will follow in rear of the 3 platoons of its own Company at a distance of one half – three quarter mile.

Reference (b)/ Support Companies will move in fours approximately 1,000 – 1,200 yds in rear of the supporting platoon of the leading Companies, either as one body, or by companies on different parallel roads. Probably a section R.F.A., or even a single gun, together with 2 or 4 Stokes Mortars and 1 section M.Gs will accompany these Companies.

4./ The/

-2-

4. The remaining A.C. Troops will march by one road 2,000 - 3,000 yds in rear of the Van Guard Infantry Support Companies.

5. The orders which the Van Guard Infantry Bn. Commander will receive prior to marching will be very brief.
   What is known of enemy's intentions
   (a) Strength and dispositions will be stated
   (b) The actual front he is responsible for, and the units operating on his right and left will be notified.
   (c) He will be directed to advance at a certain hour and given certain Objective lines to be made good at certain times and a final objective line. Reports to be rendered to Brigade H.Q. at head of Main Guard or wherever they may be on attainment of each objective line, beyond which advances will not be made without orders from Brigade.
   By the term "Objective line" is meant a series of tactical points of importance upon which the leading platoons will be directed. These will not necessarily be in touch with each other.

6. At night, the cavalry will withdraw and the leading platoons of the 2 leading Companies will form the outpost Line; the whole Line being therefore platoon posts holding tactical points of importance in the days final objective line or on some intermediate line if final objectives are not reached. It is probable that these platoon posts will be widely separated and not be in touch with each other.
   The support Companies will move up at night to render close support to the outpost Companies and be ready to pass through the latter and continue the Advance next day.

7. Communications will be a difficulty.
   Telephones will only be possible by night between Vanguard Infantry H.Q. and Brigade H.Q.
   The fullest use will therefore have to be made of cyclists, mounted orderlies, runners and visual signalling.

8. It is clear from what is stated above that Company Commanders generally and platoon Commanders in particular will be called upon to exercise their judgement and initiative to a very large extent, and that small fights undertaken by platoons and companies against small defended localities or posts will generally be the rule.
   Platoon and Company Commanders should therefore study particularly carefully Training Leaflet No.4, and tomorrow take every advantage of practising the formations laid down therein, explaining carefully to men beforehand the object and reason of the formations, and tell them all that we are likely to be doing when we take up the pursuit of the enemy in 3 or 4 days from now.

H. Sayer
Captain,
24th October, 1918.   Brigade Major, 156th Inf.Brigade.

APPENDIX XII

SECRET.

Copy No 13

156th Infantry Brigade Order No. 54.

28th October, 1918.

Ref. Map Sheet 44 1/40,000.

1. The 52nd Division is moving Eastwards tomorrow preparatory to relieving the 18th Division in the Left Sector of the VIIIth Corps front.

2. The 156th Infantry Brigade will move by march route to the LECELLES area (I.30) in accordance with attached march table.

3. Transport will move with units.

4. Dress - full marching order/

5. Advance parties of 1 Officer per Battalion and 1 Officer per smaller unit will meet at 7th R.S. H.Qrs. at 0830 to proceed by Motor Lorry to new area. They will bring bicycles.

6. In the event of enemy aircraft approaching, units will halt and take what cover there is at the side of the road. On no account will MEN look up at the aeroplane.

7. Billets will be left scrupulously clean.

8. Brigade H.Qrs., will close at COUTICHES at 0800 and will march at head of column opening at LECELLES on arrival.

9. ACKNOWLEDGE.

ISSUED AT

H Sayer
Captain,
Brigade Major, 156th Inf.Brigade.

Copy No. 1 to 4th Royal Scots
2. 7th Royal Scots
3. 7th Cameronians (S.R.)
4. 156th L.T.M.Bty.
5. "B" Coy. 52nd M.G.Bn.
6. 1/1st Low.Fld.Amb.
7. 412 Coy. R.E.
8. 219th Coy. A.S.C.
9. B.M.
10. S.C.
11. S.T.O.
12. I.O.
13 & 14. WAR DIARY.
15. FILE.

MARCH TABLE.

Issued with 156th Inf. Brigade Order No. 24.

Ref. Map Sheet 44. 1/40,000.

Serial No.	Unit.	Place Starting Point	Time	Route.	Destination.	Remarks
1.	7th Scot.Rif. Bde. H.Q.	Road Junction Q.32.d.3.6.	0820			Bde. H.Q. will march in rear of 7th S.R.
2.	7th Rifl. Bgde. (156th L.P.A.E.)	—do—	0838	CHOHIES – BEUVRY-LES-ORCHIES – RUE DU MOSIER (C.S.4.)		156th RB @ 1 11 each in rear of 7th P.S.
3.	4th Rpyl RBots)	—do—	0903			
4.	"B" Coy. M.G Bn.	—do—	0930			
5.	1st L.F.A.	—do—	0935			
6.	412 Fld.Coy. RE.	Junction of Road and Railway Q.30.d.5.5.	1040			

NOTE. As the road is complicated in places each unit will make itself responsible for keeping touch with the unit immediately in front of it and ensuring that it follows the same route.

APPENDIX XIII

BM 193

<u>To all Recipients of 156th. Inf. Bde. Order No. 65.</u>

Para 12 of Bde. Order No. 65 of to-day is cancelled.
156th. Inf. Bde. H.Q. will open at MONT PROY at
1500, (J.27.d.2.7.) Rear H.Q. at VIEILLE EGLISE, J.31.central.

28th. October 1918.

Stanley Smith Captain,
for Brigade Major, 156th. Inf. Bde.

[Stamp: HEADQUARTERS 156th INFANTRY BRIGADE]

SECRET.

156th. INFANTRY BRIGADE ORDER No. 68.

Copy No 19

Ref. Map Sheet 44 - 1/40,000.   28th. October 1918.

1. The 52nd. Division (less Artillery) is relieving the 12th.Division on 28th. October and the night of 28th/29th. October.

2. The 156th. Inf. Bde. will relieve the 36th. Inf. Bde. as follows in the front line of the Divisional Sector:-

   7th. Royal Scots will relieve 9th. Bn. Royal Berkshire Regt. in the front line.
   7th. Cameronians (S.R.) will relieve 7th. Bn. Royal Sussex in right support.
   4th. Royal Scots will relieve 9th. Bn. Royal Fusiliers in left support.

3. 156th. L.T.M. Battery will detail one section to be attached to 7th. Royal Scots and to come under orders of O.C. that Bn. in the front line. H.Q. and remaining 2 sections L.T.M. Battery will be located in the neighbourhood of Bde. H.Q.

4. "B" Coy. 52nd. Bn. M.G. Corps will relieve "A" Coy. 12th. Div. M.G. Corps in accordance with orders already issued.

5. 412th. Field Co. R.E. will relieve the R.E. units of the 12th. Division at present in the line. O.C., 412th. Field Coy. R.E., will call at Brigade H.Q., I.29.c.3.6 at 0815 to-day to receive instructions.

6. 1/1st. Lowland Field Ambulance is relieving 36th. Field Ambulance.

7. All details of above reliefs to be arranged between Commanders concerned.

8. All units will, as soon as possible after relief, and not later than 1500 on the 29th. inst., forward to Bde. H.Q. a statement or sketch showing their dispositions.

9. Medical arrangements are as follows:-
   Car Post J.34.a.8.5
   A.D.S. I.36.a.8.7

10. Rations will be delivered daily to Transport lines by 219th. Coy. A.S.C. Units will, as soon as possible after relief, wire Bde. H.Q. the location of Transport lines, at which place O.W. stores should also be located.

11. Completion of reliefs will be wired to Bde. H.Q. by the code "BM 90 received".

12. Bde. H.Q. will close present location at 1500 and open at J.31.central at same hour.

13. ACKNOWLEDGE. (156th Bde. Group only)

H. Sayer
Captain,
Brigade Major, 156th. Inf. Bde.

Issued at 0730

Copy No. 1 to 4th. R.S	Copy No. 8 to 219 Co. A.S.C.	No. 15 to S.C.
2 7th. R.S	9 36th. Inf. Bde.	16 I.O.
3 7th. S.R.	10 52nd. Div.	17 B.T.O.
4 156th. T.M. Bty.	11 12th. Div.	18 Bde. Sigs
5 "B" Co. 52nd. M.G.Bn	12 155th. Inf. Bde.	19 & 20 Diary
6 412th. Fld. Co. R.E.	13 157th. Inf. Bde.	21 File
7 1/1st. L.F.Amb.	14 B.M.	

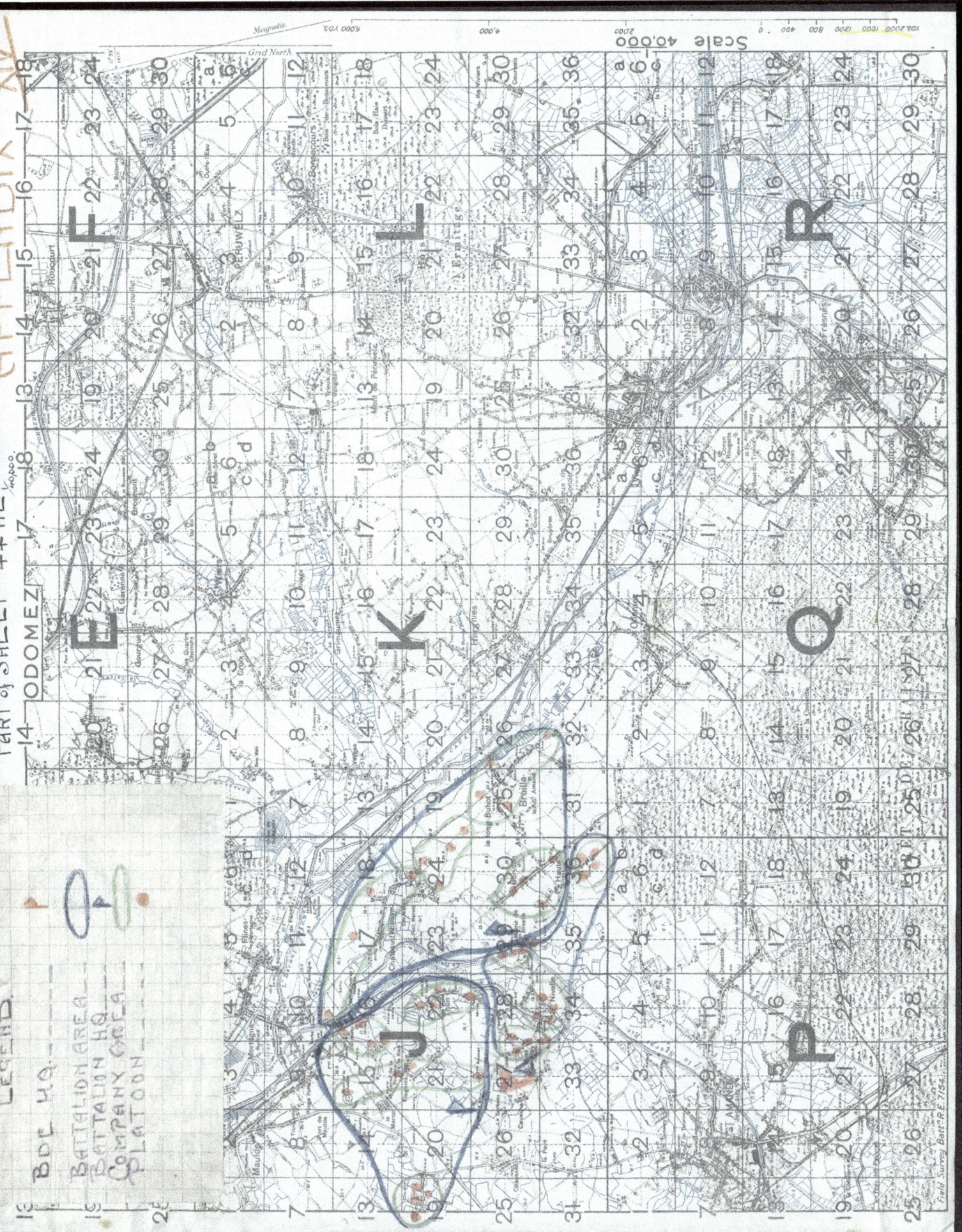

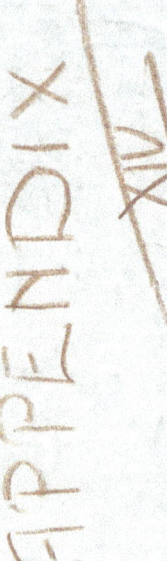

Reference Sketch on back.

To

1. My {Platoon / Company} has reached
   (Mark position on map or give map reference).
   and is consolidating.
   has consolidated.
   is ready to advance.

2. I am (not) in touch with   on right
   and (not) with   on left.

3. I am held up at   { by wire.
                                                 { by M.G. fire.
                                                 { by rifle fire.

4. Enemy's artillery is firing on
                       from

5. I have sent forward patrols to

6. I estimate { my casualties at
              { my strength at

7. I need   boxes S.A.A.
             Lewis gun drums
             Bombs
             Rifle Grenades
             Stokes Shells   (at once)
             Very Lights
             Ground Flares   (to-night)
             Stakes
             Coils wire
             Tins water
             Rations

8. I intend to

9. (General remarks on position and strength of enemy. Number of prisoners taken and identifications, if known).

Time   Name   Rank
Date   Platoon   Coy
              Battalion

Strike out all that is not applicable and forward at once to Bn. H.Q.

156th Infantry Brigade

Effective Strength - October, 1918

APPENDIX XV

Unit	Week Ending 5th		Week Ending 12th		Week Ending 19th		Week Ending 26th	
	O	OR	O	OR	O	OR	O	OR
4th Royal Scots	25	593	30	672	35	694	34	685
7th Royal Scots	34	734	39	761	40	776	41	779
7th Cam Rifles	35	667	37	660	36	678	36	684
	94	1994	106	2093	111	2148	111	2148

156th Infantry Brigade
Casualties – October, 1918

Unit	Killed		Wounded		Missing	
	O	OR	O	OR	O	OR
4th Royal Scots	-	3	-	4	-	-
7th Royal Scots	-	1	-	4	-	-
4th Sco Rifles	-	-	-	2	-	-
156 L T M Bty	-	-	-	-	-	-
	-	4	-	10	-	-

Original 1918

War Diary

of

56th Infantry Brigade

from 1st to 30th November 1918

Volume XLII

WAR DIARY
INTELLIGENCE SUMMARY

Army Form C. 2118.

Map Reference Sheet 44 1/40000
Volume XLII
November 1918.

156 Infantry Brigade

Page 1.

Place	Date Nov.	Hour	Summary of Events and Information	Remarks and references to Appendices
MONT DU PROY.	1.		Considerable hostile artillery activity during the day, BRUILLE and HAUTE RIVE receiving most attention. B.G.C. visited the line. Patrols to footbridge pt K26 A met with heavy machine gun fire. An officer and N.C.O. succeeded in crossing the bridge, but were unable to proceed any distance beyond. 9th Cameronians (S.R.) relieved 4th Royal Scots in the line. (Relief 156 Inf Bde Order No 66.) Instructions issued regarding action SPN2 RE	Appendix I (copy) O.B.83/17
	2.		Normal activity by day. The enemy is holding the JARD CANAL with machine gun posts. Some wiring has been done near FORT de FLINES, which has been shelled by our heavy artillery. Patrols in K26 A met with heavy machine gun fire. The Brigade took over piquets held by the Left Battn 2/3 Infantry Bde (2/West Yorks) relief complete by 8/30. Bde Order No 67 (Relief and dispositions)	Appendix III O.B.83/7
	3.		The B.G.C. and B.M. visited the right of the Brigade Sector. Considerable amount of hostile shelling south of BRUILLE during the afternoon. Patrols to the ESCAUT at night.	O.B.83/7
	4.		A clear day of good visibility. Considerable aerial activity on both sides. Three hostile drachen balloons observed by our aeroplanes. Patrols as usual.	O.B.83/7

Army Form C. 2118.

WAR DIARY
or
INTELLIGENCE SUMMARY.
(Erase heading not required)

Map Reference Sheet 44 49w0. Sheet 45 & 4h5 N.W.

156 Infantry Brigade.   November 1918   Page 2

Place	Date Nov	Hour	Summary of Events and Information	Remarks and references to Appendices
MONT DU PROY	5		A very wet day. Conference of Battn Commanders at Bde H.Q. in the morning. R.M. 269-260-263+264 issued (Action of Bde in the event of enemy withdrawal)	Appendix IV A96/9/1
	6		Broken weather continues. No indication of any immediate withdrawal on Brigade front, although information by Division that there prisoners taken at different parts of the front line disclose some intention of withdrawing in the night of 6/7. Night of 6/7. Slight hostile artillery and trench mortar fire above normal.	A95/9/1 C16/6/11
	7		Floods perceivably increase. Hostile artillery still active.	
	8		Patrols to bridges in K26.a met with m.g. fire until about 0700. A patrol at that hour met with no opposition, and a section immediately pushed across by means of rafts and established itself on the right bank of the JARD CANAL. Other troops crossing was a matter of considerable difficulty. By 0830 one company 7th Cameronians had crossed, and proceeded to clear HERGNIES. As patrols could not be worked at K26.a, all traffic had to be diverted to bridges at COUPURE (K.27.D). The Brigade had crossed the canal by 1500, and 7th Bn The Royal Scots were established on the line K.16 central – K.29 central by 1700. Bde H.Q. at K.29.D.9558. All roads in HERGNIES were blown up in several places. By 0 order No 69 issued (move eastwards)	A95/9/1 C16/6/11 Appendix V A95/9/1

Army Form C.2118.

WAR DIARY
or
INTELLIGENCE SUMMARY.
(Erase Heading not required.)

Map Reference Sheet 45 N.W.
15th Infantry Brigade.
November 1918.

Page 3.

Place.	Date. Nov.	Hour.	Summary of Events and Information.	Remarks and references to Appendices.
HERCHIES.	9.	0700	The head of the main body passed the starting point. Brigade proceeded via MONT DE PERUWELTZ to BONSECOURS, where the main body halted. Several towns while the ANTOING CANAL was reconnoitred. Four prisoners were taken, but the CANAL was reported clear by the evening. 1st Royal Scots took up an outpost line in G.11.17 + 23, the remainder of the Brigade being in BLATON, with H.Q. at G.15.c.6.8. Brigade Order No. 70 issued (More eastern)	
BLATON.	10		The advance was continued eastwards via COURTES-BRUYÈRES and CAVINS to SIRAULT. The Advance Guard (2nd Royal Scots), reached the line approximately C.20.D - C.26.D - I.2.B, without opposition. The enemy were reported to be holding HERCHIES and VACRESSE, and my tri was heard from the western edge of BOIS de BAUDOUR. At 1400 the 7th Cameronians passed through the 1st Royal Scots and advanced on HERCHIES. The right flank was protected by the 13th Bde working through the BOIS de BAUDOUR	Appendix VI 15Bdeg

Army Form C.2118.

WAR DIARY
OF
INTELLIGENCE SUMMARY.
(Erase Heading not required.)

Map Reference Sheet 45 N.W.
157th Infantry Brigade.

November 1918

Page 4.

Place.	Date.	Hour.	Summary of Events and Information.	Remarks and references to Appendices.
	10 (cont)		Practically no opposition was met with in HERCHIES & VACRESSE which were reported clear by 16.00. The advance was pushed on but was held up on the outskirts of ERBAUT by mg. fire. At this time HERCHIES and the SIRAULT—HERCHIES Road was subjected to harassing fire. Shoots continued intermittently until 01.00. By 01.00 ERBAUT was clear of the enemy in spite of some opposition, four dead, and seventeen prisoners being left in our hands. Our casualties were 12 O. ranks, (4 killed and 8 wounded).	O.&B. F.
HERCHIES.	11		A quiet morning, as the enemy had retired a considerable distance during the night. B.M. 11/2 issued (Relief by 155th Bde.) At 09.30 word was received by DR.LS. that hostilities would cease at 11.00. The 155th Bde. having passed through, the Brigade concentrated in HERCHIES. The Brigade rested. Some work done on the SIRAULT—HERCHIES Road. Information received that the Division would form the XXII Corps by the 15th and move to the RHINE.	(Appendix VII) O.&B. I.V. O.&B. J.

Army Form C.2118.

WAR DIARY
OF
1st Edinburgh Squadron
(Erase Heading not required).

Map Reference Sheet 45.

152 Infantry Brigade.

November 1918.

Page 5.

Place.	Date. Nov.	Hour.	Summary of Events and Information.	Remarks and references to Appendices.
HERCHIES	13.		Conference of Battalion Commanders at Bde. H.Q. Bde moved HERCHIES – SIRAULT by 7th Royal Scots. Work on roads continued by 7th Scottish Rifles.	WRK Caps
	14.		B.G.C. attended conference at Div. H.Q. SIRAULT. A representative detachment from the Bde, organised in three companies, one from each battalion, each 50 strong, marched to MONS to take part in the ceremonial Entry of First Army Commander at 1100. Major J. M. Slater DSO was in command of the 1/4th Royal Scots, J. E. P. Romanes 1/7th Scottish Rifles, commanded the whole Divisional Contingent.	WRK Caps
	15.		Work on roads continued by 1/4th Royal Scots.	WRK Caps

Army Form C. 2118.

WAR DIARY
or
INTELLIGENCE SUMMARY.
(Erase Heading not required).

Place.	Date.	Hour.	Summary of Events and Information.	Remarks and references to Appendices.
HERCHIES	16th		B.G.C. inspected 15th Line transport of the Brigade. It was only fairly fed and requires more work and more fitting. Subjects on polishing steel buckets, parts of the harness. Units have no fixed scale of rations. The wagons have also have been food.	page 6
			Bar hits carried out and steadiness of parades in the morning.	
			A very fine bright sunny day but very cold. Blankets brought up by M.T from the Dump at FLINES when they have been left on account of lack of Transport.	A.J.
"	17th		Detachment of 17th Brigade Consisting of one Coy per Bn under command of Major J.G.P. Romans B.S.O 7th Lancashires attended a Divisional Thanksgiving Service at ERISAUT at 11.00	
			A Brigade Thanksgiving Service (and ceremonial) was held at 11.30. The whole Brigade attended. The Divisional Brass Band played the Hymns. The B.G.C. was unable to attend owing to indisposition.	
			Report on strength of the Brigade for period 2/11/18 to date.	Appx VIII A.J.
			Sent to the Division.	
			A bitterly cold day with no sun.	

Army Form C.2118.

Ref Maps 1/10000 Sheet 45

WAR DIARY
OF
TRAINING SUMMARY
(Erase heading not required.)
156 Infantry Brigade

Place	Date	Summary of Event and Information	Remarks and references to Appendices
HERCHIES	18th	Another very wet day with some snow. Bns practising Ceremonial Parades and generally polishing up.	J.T.
	19th	B.G.C. inspected 4th Royal Scots and 7th Royal Scots at 1000 and 1430 respectively. Men is still room for improvement in the cleanliness of Equipment, Officers and in the bearing of the Transport. The march past in column and close column was good but the dressing still requires practice. The 7th Royal Scots had by a better a pace. B.G.C. also inspected 156' L.T.M. Batty. on Horseback Thirty Times was good, Especially their handcart which shows a noticeable improvement.	J.T.
		B.M. 3 Lig Reference Educational Training issued. (Appendix IX) Classes in English, Arithmetic, and Shorthand and French have already been started but the matter requires further pushing on a better basis	Appx IX J.T.

Army Form C.2118.

WAR DIARY
OF
156th Infantry Brigade.

(Erase heading not required).

Place.	Date.	Hour.	Summary of Events and Information.	Remarks and references to Appendices.
HERCKMES	20th	1000	B.G.C. inspected 7th Camerons (S.R.). A good parade and a good march past. Still room for improvement in steadiness and smartness in men and handout. The most noticeable thing is the bad state of the clothing. The "ration system" makes things difficult as men return from hospital and in draft tasty inadequately clothed, this system can not be replaced until the ration Requests for extra clothing has been made to the Division but so far without success.	
		1400	A riding school under the Brigade Major and B.T.O. has started. 6 Officers & N.C.Os from each Battalion are attending.	
	20th/25th		Brigade remained billeted in HERCKMES. Ceremonial parades and some tactical training has been carried out by all units. Education under the new scheme was started successfully, an average of 110 men per Battalion taking advantage of it. Sports Committee meetings are held. Inspecting football Competitions, Sports, Transport and Piping and Dancing competitions at intervals through the winter.	

Army Form C.2118.

WAR DIARY
of
(Erase heading not required). 154th Infantry Brigade

Ref Map 1/100000. TOURNAI

Place.	Date.	Hour.	Summary of Events and Information.	Remarks and references to Appendices.
LOMBISE	28		The Brigade moved to the following area – Bde Hqrs LOMBISE CHATEAU – 4th Royal Scots & 1/L.M. Batty. LES LENS – 7th Royal Scots – NEUFVILLES – 7th Cameronians LENS. Units moved in their own transit. This new area is likely to be no border quarters. All units except 4 Royal Scots are fairly comfortable. 4 Royal Scots are crowded.	A.
	29		B.G.C. went round their area. 7 Royal Scots not comfortable but remained for present. 4 Royal Scots – billeting H. & 4 Royal Scots 42 T.M.Batty to crowded L.M. Batty to known to THURICOURT, 4 R.S. are not yet fit for a Battalion if called up on. In the rooms by sounds. 7 J.R. Hq. comfortable (with four) establishing Brigade room 1st Royals returned here and Houtir. Billets again rehabed and roost hots	A.
	30		L.M. Batty moved to THURICOURT when there is ample accommodation. Gen Leggett C.M.G. F.S.O. stated for a month to Lieut K.H.R. 4 Bn. 7 J.R. RONNES pla Comm. from 7 Cameronian H Commoner to Brigade in B.G.C.'s absence. The usual States are attached.	A. Appx I

J. Larg.r.
Captain
Brigade Major
154 Infy Bde.

APPENDIX VII

156th. INFANTRY BRIGADE ORDER No. 87.

SECRET.
Copy No. 15

Ref. Map
1/40,000. Sheet 44.   2nd. November 1916.

1.   The Northern and Southern Boundaries of the Divisional Sector are being altered as shown on the attached Tracing.

2.   The 156th. Inf. Bde. will take over the increased area from the 23rd. Inf. Bde. and 174th. Inf. Bde. on the night 2nd/3rd. November and will hold the front with two Battalions in the line and one in support.

3.   The above reliefs will be carried out as follows:-
  (1) 4th. Royal Scots will relieve the two left Coys. of the 7th. Cameronians and will have two Coys in reserve, one at FLAGNIES and one at THUN. H.Q., 4th. Royal Scots will be J.27.A.5.6.
  (2) 7th. Cameronians (S.R.) will relieve 2 Coys. of 2nd. West Yorks in the new Southern Area and will have two Coys in support, one at BURIDON and one at about K.32.A.2.2.

4.   7th. Royal Scots will withdraw the Coy. at present in HAUTE RIVE and will locate it in FRESNOY or neighbourhood.

5.   O.C., "B" Coy. 52nd. Bn. M.G.C. will relieve any M.Gs. of the 8th. Division in new Southern Area.

6.   Reliefs will commence at dusk, otherwise all details will be arranged between Commanders concerned.

7.   Completion of relief will be wired to these H.Q. by following code words:-
  (1) Relief of two Coys. 7th. Cameronians (S.R.) by 4th. Royal Scots "WHISKY"
  (2) Relief of 2 Coys. 2nd. West Yorks by 7th. Cameronians (S.R.) "AND"
  (3) Completion of move of Coy., 7th. Royal Scots from HAUTE RIVE to FRESNOY "WATER"

8.   Cs.O. 4th. Royal Scots, ~~7th. Royal Scots~~, 7th. Cameronians (S.R.) and "B" Coy. 52nd. Bn. M.G.C. will forward to these H.Q. by 1200 on 3rd. inst. a tracing showing their new dispositions.

9.   Brigade H.Q. will remain in present position.

10. ACKNOWLEDGE. (Bde. units & "B" Coy. 52nd. Bn. M.G.C. only)

H. Sayer
Captain,
Issued at 1545   Brigade Major, 156th. Inf. Bde.

Copy No.		Copy No.	
1	4th. R.S.	9	174th. Inf. Bde. X
2	7th. R.S.	10	23rd. Inf. Bde. X
3	7th. S.R.	11	1/1st. Low. Fld. Amb X
4	156th. T.M. Bty.	12	S.C. X
5	58th. Bde. R.F.A.	13	S.T.O. X
6	83rd. Bde. R.F.A. X	14	Bde. Sigs.
7	"B" Co. 52nd. M.G.Bn 15)		War Diary
8	412th. Fld. Co. R.E. 16)		
		17	File

X No tracing attached

APPENDIX I

SECRET.
Copy No. 14

156th. INFANTRY BRIGADE ORDER No. 66.

Ref. Map
1/40,000, Sheet 44   31st. October 1918.

1.   7th. Bn. Cameronians (S.R.) will relieve 7th. Royal Scots in the outpost line on 1st. November and night 1st/2nd. November.

2.   In order to preserve continuity of patrols 7th. Royal Scots will leave sufficient personnel in the line on the night 1st/2nd. November to carry out the usual patrols.
      Personnel from 7th. Cameronians (S.R.) will accompany these patrols.

3.   Cookers of 7th. Royal Scots at present in the line will be left and 7th. Royal Scots will take over those of the 7th. Cameronians.

4.   After relief, 7th. Royal Scots will take over billets and Meals of 7th. Cameronians.

5.   Details of relief will be arranged between Bn. Commanders concerned.

6.   Completion of relief will be wired to these H.Q. by code word "WATER"

7.   ACKNOWLEDGE. (Bde units only)

Issued at 1800

H. Sayer
Captain,
Brigade Major, 156th. Inf. Brigade.

```
Copy No.  1  to  4th. Royal Scots
          2      7th. Royal Scots
          3      7th. Sco. Rifles
          4      156th. L.T.M. Battery
          5      83rd. Bde. R.F.A.
          6      "B" Coy. 52nd. Bn. M.G.C.
          7      412th. Fld. Co. R.E.
          8      174th. Inf. Bde.
          9      23rd. Inf. Bde.
         10      1/1st. Low. Fld. Amb.
         11      S.C.
         12      B.T.O.
         13      Bde. Sigs.
     14 & 15     War Diary
         16      File.
```

O.C.,
   7th. Sco. Rifles
   412th. Field Co. R.E.
==========================

APPENDIX II
BM 233

       With reference to paras 5 and 6 of BM 200 of the 29th. ulto.

1.   O.C., 412th. Field Co. will send 1 section to live in the forward area. This is the section that will do the bridging in the event of an advance.

2.   O.C., Front Line Battalion will detail his supporting Coy. to act as carriers of bridging material for this section. As soon as the material has been carried forward this Coy. will act as laid down in para. 4.

3.   Until the time comes to cross the Canal, the section 412th. Field Co. referred to above will be employed in strengthening cellars in the forward area for use as Coy. H.Q. etc., especially in BRUILLE and LE-LONG-BUHOT.

4.   O.C., Section, 412th. Field Co. R.E., should call at H.Q., Front Line Battalion as soon as possible in order to make the necessary arrangements for carrying out the above orders.

5.   O.C., 412th. Field Co. R.E., will report the location of section to these H.Q. as soon as they have moved.

1st. November 1918.

H. Sayer
Captain,
Brigade Major, 156th. Inf. Brigade.

Copies to:- 4th. Royal Scots
           7th. Royal Scots
           156th. L.T.M. Battery
           "B" Coy. 52nd. Bn. M.G.C.
           War Diary (2)
           File

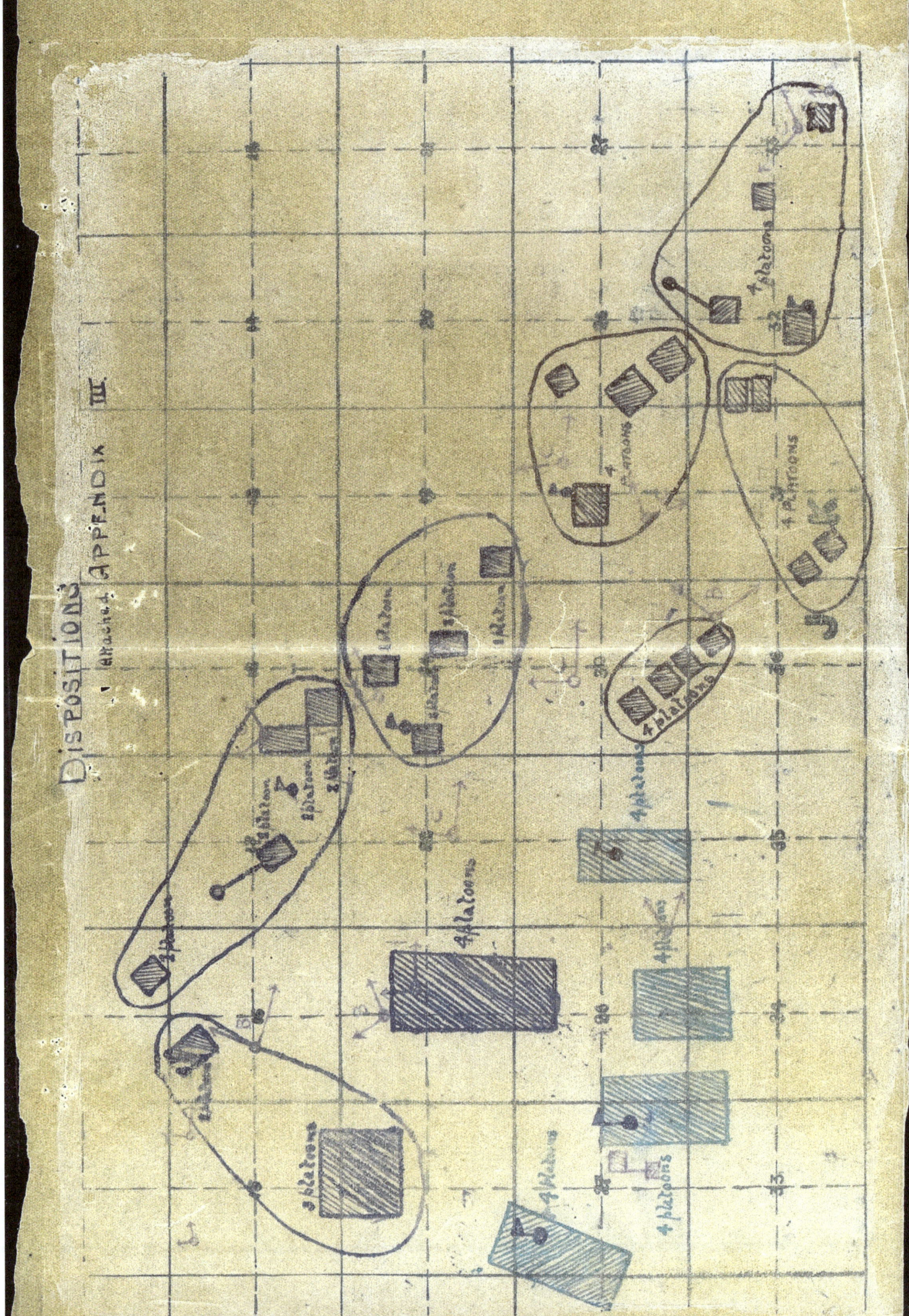

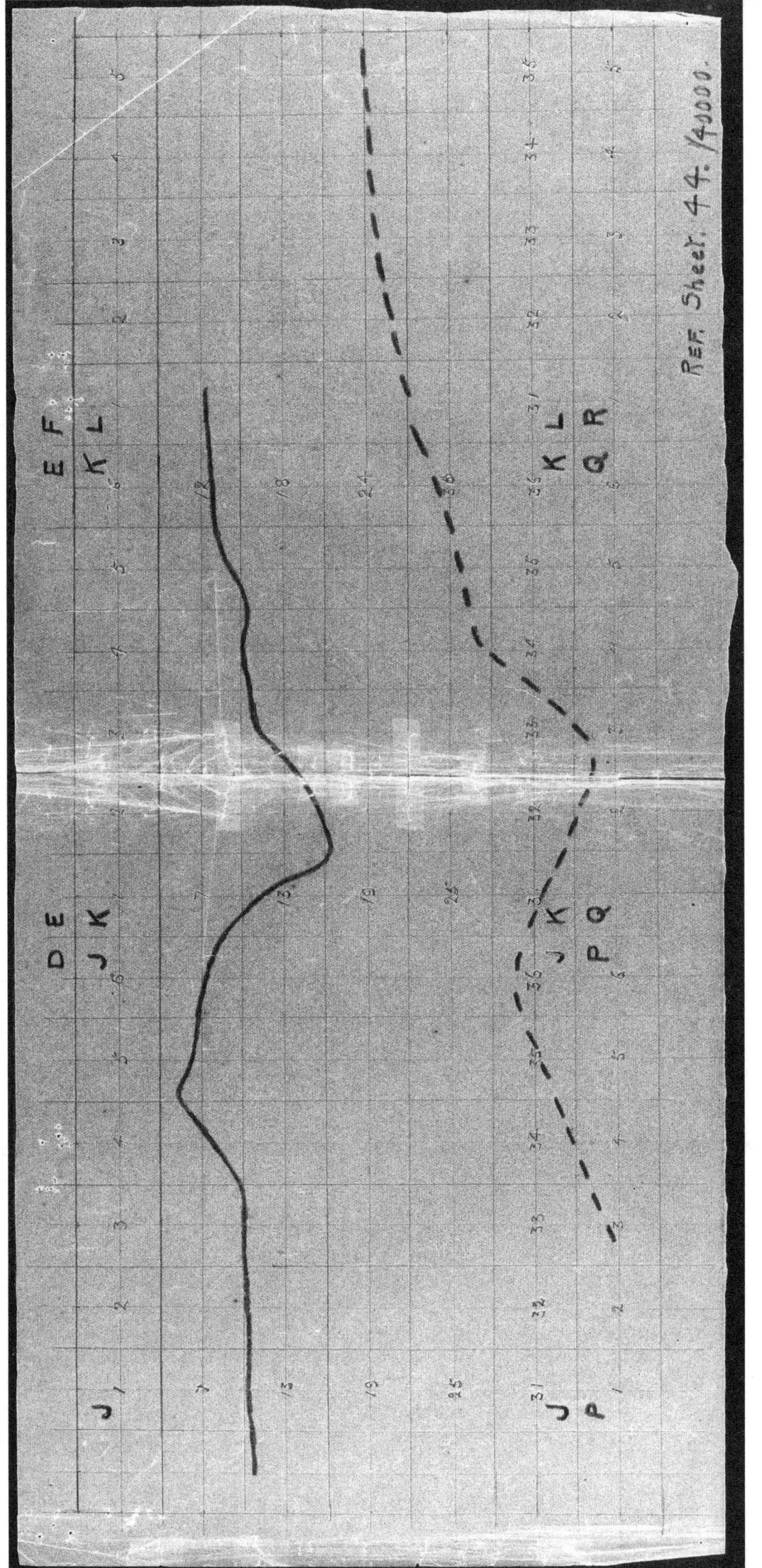

Ref. Sheet. 44./40000.

APPENDIX IV

4th. Royal Scots   412th. Field Coy. R.E.
7th. Royal Scots   "B" Coy. 52nd. Bn. M.G.C.
7th. Sco. Rifles
156th. L.T.M. Battery

==

With reference to para. 18 of BM 259 of to-day.

    Bde. H.Q., will remain in present position (J.27.D.2.3) until the line K.29.central - K.16.central has been taken up, when it will move to a position about K.21.central (exact location will be notified to all concerned).

    An officer from Bde. Staff will be at the Bridge at K.26.A.4.7 during the crossing and until Bde. H.Q. moves. All messages for Bde. H.Q. should be sent to him for transmission.

5th. November 1918.
                                                    Captain,
                      Brigade Major, 156th. Inf. Bde.

Copies to:- 157th. Inf. Bde.   B.T.O.
           155th. Inf. Bde.   O.C., Sigs.
           174th. Inf. Bde.   1/1st. L.F.Amb,
           52nd. M.G. Bn.   War Diary (2)
           B.M.   File
           S.C.

4th. Royal Scots
7th. Royal Scots
7th. Sco. Rifles
156th. L.T.M. Battery
"B" Coy. 52nd. Bn. M.G.C.
412th. Field Coy. R.E.

BM 259

Ref. Map 1/40,000 - Sheet 44 (Edition 2)

BM 200 of 29/10/18, BM 233 of 1/11/18 and BM 242 of 2/11/18 are cancelled and the following instructions are substituted:-

1. The present policy on this front is not to push any attack over the JARD CANAL too energetically or at the expense of many lives.

2. An active system of patrolling will, however, be kept up so as to ensure that the enemy does not retire without our knowledge. Patrols will, therefore, be pushed out every night and just before dawn, or after dawn if misty.

3. In the event of it being ascertained that the enemy has retired from the JARD CANAL, the Left forward Coy. of the Right Front Line Bn. will at once be sent across the footbridge at K.26.A.4.7, and if the bridge over the JARD CANAL at K.26.B.5.6 is still in existence, will cross the Canal and form a Bridgehead on the following line - K.20.A.4.4 - Road Junction, K.20.B.7.7 - Road Junction, K.21.B.0.9 - Road Junction K.21.B.8.3 - Cross Roads, K.22.C.5.1 - Road Junction, K.28.C.1.7 - K.27.D.5.2.

4. This Coy. will, as soon as possible, be followed by the support Coy. of the Front Line Bn. which will be used to strengthen the Bridgehead formed by the leading Coy.

5. In the event of the Bridge at K.26.B.5.6 being destroyed the 412th. Field Coy. R.E. will throw a footbridge across as soon as possible. The construction of this Bridge will be covered by the fire of the leading Coy. of the Front Line Bn. which, in this case, will take up a position on the Western Bank of the Canal on either side of the Bridge to be constructed.
  As soon as the Bridge has been completed this Coy. will act as laid down in para. 3.
  O.C., Right Front Line Bn. will detail his left supporting Coy. to act as carriers of bridging material for this Section. As soon as the material has been carried forward this Coy. will act as laid down in para. 4.

6. O.C., 412th. Field Coy. R.E., will arrange to have 1 Section standing by ready to proceed forward at short notice to construct the footbridge mentioned in para. 5.
  O.C., Section, 412th. Field Coy. R.E., should keep in touch with H.Q., Right Front Line Bn. in order to make the necessary arrangements for carrying out the above orders.

7. As soon as the footbridges have been constructed, and the Bridgehead mentioned in para. 3 has been formed, the support Bn. and 1 Section L.T.M. Battery will cross the ESCAUT and the JARD CANAL, pass through the Bridgehead and advance and make good the line K.29.central - K.16.central. This line will be held with 2 Coys. and the remaining 2 Coys. and H.Q., Bn. will be located in K.22.D.
  NOTE. Bn. will not be accompanied by any transport.

8. This Bn. will be followed as soon as possible by the remainder of the Right Front Bn., L.T.M. Battery less 1 Section/

- 2 -

Section and the Left Front Line Bn. in the order mentioned.
After crossing, the above units will concentrate in following areas:-

Right Front Line Bn. } K.21.D
L.T.M. Battery

Left Front Line Bn. K.21.B

9. Orders for the concentration of the left front line Bn. and the forward moves mentioned in paras. 7 and 8 will be issued from Bde. H.Q.

10. Two Coys. 52nd. Bn. M.G.C., less transport, under command of O.C., "B" Coy. will follow the support Bn. and will assist in taking up the line mentioned in para. 7 (under orders of O.C., Bn.) with 1 Coy., keeping the remaining Coy. concentrated near Bn. H.Q. in K.22.D.

11. As soon as the above mentioned line has been secured, and pontoon Bridges have been constructed,* mounted troops, consisting of 2 troops, 4th. Hussars and 1 Coy. VIII Corps Cyclist Bn. under orders of O.C., Squadron, 4th. Hussars, will cross the River and Canal, pass through the line K.29.central - K.16.central and secure the following points:-
   (a) MONT COPIEMONT
   (b) MONT DE PERUWELZ and N.W. exits from BOIS DE LERMITAGE.
   (c) BOUQUET - PERUWELZ Road

* NOTE:- Pontoon Bridges will be constructed under orders of the C.R.E. at the following points:-
(1) near COUPURE, K.27.D.3.1, to be known as Bridges A and B.
(2) near PONT DE LA VERNETTE, to be known as Bridges X and Y.

12. These mounted troops will be followed by "A" Battery, 63rd. Bde. R.F.A., who will support the mounted troops but will act independently.

13. On receipt of orders from Bde. H.Q. O.C., support Bn. will move forward with the 2 Coys. concentrated in K.22.D to support the mounted troops mentioned in para. 11 and to take over objectives from them as gained.

14. On receipt of orders from O.C., 52nd. Bn. M.G.C., the 2 Coys. M.G. Bn. mentioned in para. 10 will also move forward in support of the mounted troops.

15. The Northern and Southern Boundaries of the advance will be notified later.

16. First Line Transport will move across the Canal as soon as possible after the Pontoon Bridges have been constructed, and will be sent up to join units in their concentration areas as soon as is practicable.

18. Movements of Bde. H.Q. will be notified later.

5th. November 1918.
                          Captain,
            Brigade Major, 156th. Inf. Bde.

Copies to:- 157th. Inf. Bde.   B.T.O.
            155th. Inf. Bde.   O.C., Bde. Sigs.
            174th. Inf. Bde.   1/1st. Low. Fld. Amb.
            52nd. Bn. M.G.C.   War Diary (2)
            B.M.   File
            S.C.

156th Infantry Brigade   Appendix H

Effective Strength - December, 1918

	Week ending 7th		Week ending 14th		Week ending 21st		Week ending 28th	
	O	OR	O	OR	O	OR	O	OR
4th Royal Scots	44	841	44	849	42	845	42	847
7th Royal Scots	43	844	42	848	41	843	41	843
7th Lo Rifles	38	793	37	792	37	794	36	782
	125	2478	123	2489	120	2482	119	2472

156th Infantry Brigade   Appendix 3

Casualties – December, 1918

NIL

O.C.,
4th. Royal Scots
7th. Royal Scots
7th. Sco. Rifles
156th. L.T.M. Battery
"D" Coy. 52nd. Bn. M.G.C. (Group Commander)

SECRET.

BM 263

Continuation of BM 259 of to-day.

1. Pending the issue of further orders the Northern and Southern Boundaries referred to in para. 15 will be a continuation of the present Northern and Southern Bde. Boundaries, viz:-

    <u>Northern Boundary</u>:- K.19.B.8.9 thence along Southern Bank of VERGNE River to Railway at L.7.C.6.8.

    <u>Southern Boundary</u>:- K.35.D.6.2 – K.28.D.2.2 – Railway at L.25.A.8.9 – Road at L.21.D.5.6

2. O.C., 7th. Royal Scots will gain touch with 157th. Inf. Bde. on our right at the following points:-
    (1) K.29.central
    (2) The CONDE – PERUWELZ Railway at L.25.A.8.9.
    (3) The CONDE – BONSECOURS Road at L.21.D.5.6 in the event of an advance being made <u>through</u> the BOIS DE L'ERMITAGE.

    Definite parties will be told off for the "shaking hand" places, and reports will be sent as soon as touch has been gained.

3. As it appears unlikely that the Bde. on our left will be up in line with us for a considerable period, no actual "shaking hand" places are being laid down, but in the event of their coming into line with us touch will at once be gained by the leading troops and reports rendered to that effect.

5th. November 1918

Captain,
Brigade Major, 156th. Inf. Bde.

Copies to:-
157th. Inf. Bde.
155th. Inf. Bde.
174th. Inf. Bde.
52nd. Bn. M.G.C.
B.M.
S.C.

B.T.O.
O.C., Bde. Sigs.
412th. Field Co. R.E.
War Diary (2)
File

SECRET.

4th. Royal Scots
7th. Royal Scots   BM 264.
7th. Sco. Rifles
156th. L.T.M. Battery
"B" Coy. 52nd. Bn. M.G.C. (Group Commander)
===

Reference BM 259.

1. Reference para. 7.
    The line K.29.central – K.16.central will be continued on the right by the 157th. Inf. Bde. along the VIEUX-CONDE Road to Q.6.A.

2. The Reference para. 10.
    (a) Two Coys. 52nd. Bn. M.G.C., have been placed definitely under orders of G.O.C., 156th. Inf. Bde.
    (b) Two Sections of "C" Coy. will cross the Canal without transport and will assist in taking up the line K.16.central – K.29.central.
    (c) "B" Coy. and "C" Coy., less 2 Sections, with transport, will cross the Canal by the Pontoon Bridges after the leading Brigade R.F.A., and will concentrate near Bn. H.Q. in K.22.D.

3. Reference para. 11.
    (a) VIII Corps Cyclist Bn., less 1 Coy., are covering the whole of the Divisional front, and will pass over the Canal and River by means of foot bridges as soon as the Right Front Line Bn. has established the Bridgehead mentioned in para. 4.
    (b) O.C., Cyclist Bn. will receive his reports through O.C., Support Bn. and has been instructed to keep in close liaison with him.
    (c) Two troops, 4th. Hussars, will cross the Canal and River as soon as the Pontoon Bridges have been constructed, and will push on in support of the cyclists mentioned above.
    (d) The mounted troops as a whole will make good the following lines on the Divisional front:-

        (i)   VIEUX CONDE – PERUWELZ Railway, (R.1., L.31., L.25., L.19., L.13.)
        (ii) CONDE – MONT DE PERUWELZ – PERUWELZ Road (L.32., L.26., L.20., L.14., L.8.)
        (iii) CONDE – CHATEAU DE L'ERMITAGE – BOUQUET Road, (L.33., L.27., L.21., L.15., L.8.B. and D.)
        (iv) The line LORETTE – BONSECOURS – PERUWELZ.

4. Paras. 13 and 14 are cancelled and the following substituted:-

    On receipt of orders from Bde. H.Q., O.C. Support Bn. will move forward with the 2 Coys. concentrated in K.22.D, and H.Q. and 2 Sections "C" Coy., 52nd. Bn. M.G.C., in order to support the mounted troops mentioned in para. 11, and to take over objectives from them as gained.

5. With the above exceptions BM 259, 260 and 263 hold good.

                                                Captain,
5th. November 1918.   Brigade Major, 156th. Inf. Bde.

Copies to:- 157th. Inf. Bde.   B.M.
             155th. Inf. Bde.   S.C.
             174th. Inf. Bde.   B.T.O.
             52nd. Bn. M.G.C.   O.C., Bde. Sigs.
             412th. Field Coy. R.E. Diary (2)
             1/1st. Low. Fld. Amb.   File.

4th. Royal Scots
7th. Royal Scots
7th. Sco. Rifles
156th. L.T.M. Battery
"A" Coy. 52nd. Bn. M.G.C. (Group Commander)

SECRET.

BM 275

For your information.

With reference to this Office BM 259 of the 5th. inst:-

1. The order in which personnel of units will cross the footbridges when constructed, is as follows:-
    (1) 2 Coys. Right Front Line Bn. and 1 Section M.Gs.
    (2) VIII Corps Cyclist Bn. (less 1 Coy.)
    (3) Support Bn. and 1 Section L.T.M. Battery
    (4) 1 Section 52nd. Bn. M.G.C.
    (5) Right Front Line Bn. (less 2 Coys.)
    (6) Left Front Line Battalion.
    (7) Bde. H.Q. and L.T.M. Battery (less 1 section)

2. As soon as the Pontoon Bridges have been constructed units and transport will cross in the following order:-
    (1) Squadron 4th. Hussars
    (2) 2 Sections 52nd. Bn. M.G.C. with 12 limbers.
    (3) "A" Battery, 56th. Bde. R.F.A.
    (4) 4 Lewis gun limbers, 1 magazine limber and 2 S.A.A. limbers of support Bn. plus 1 limber L.T.M. Battery.
    (5) 56th. Bde. R.F.A. (less 1 Battery)
    (6) 1 Battery 9th. Bde. R.F.A.
    (7) 1 Coy. 52nd. Bn. M.G.C. with transport
    (8) 1/2nd. Low. Field Ambulance.
    (9) First Line Transport, 156th. Inf. Bde. in following order:-
        (a) Right Front Line Bn.
        (b) Left Front Line Bn.
        (c) Support Bn. (less fighting limbers mentioned in 4 above)
        (d) Bde. H.Q. and L.TM. Battery.

H. Sayer
Captain,
Brigade Major, 156th. Inf. Bde.

7th. November 1918.

Copies to:-
157th. Inf. Bde.
52nd. Bn. M.G.C.
56th. Bde. R.F.A. (together with copies of BM 259, 260, 263 & 264)
9th. Bde. R.F.A.
412th. Field Coy. R.E.
1/1st. Low. Fld. Amb.
1/2nd. Low. Fld. Amb.
S.C. (2)
D.T.O.
O.C. Bde. Sigs.
Spare (for Traffic officers) (6)
Diary (2)
File.

156th Infantry Brigade   War Diary Appendix X

Effective Strength - November, 1918

	Week ending 9th		Week ending 16th		Week ending 23rd		Week ending 30th	
	O	OR	O	OR	O	OR	O	OR
4th Royal Scots	43	684	42	755	43	776	43	840
7th Royal Scots	39	806	39	804	40	823	42	820
7th Scot. Rifles	36	687	36	663	37	715	35	717
	118	2177	117	2222	120	2314	120	2377

156th Infantry Brigade   War Diary Appendix X

Casualties – November, 1918

	Killed		Wounded		Missing	
	O.	OR	O.	OR	O.	OR
4th Royal Scots	–	–	–	5	–	–
7th Royal Scots	–	–	–	5	–	–
7th Sco Rifles	–	3	–	14	–	1
	–	3	–	24	–	1

APPENDIX V

Copy No. 21

156th. INFANTRY BRIGADE ORDER No. 69.

8th. November 1918.

Ref. Map
1/20,000 - Sheet 44 N.E.

1. (a)   The enemy has retired East of ANTOING POMMEROEUL CANAL and civilians report that he will not stand there but is retiring further East.
   (b)   VIII Corps Cyclist Bn. have secured the line PERUWELZ – BONSECOURS – LORETTE and met no opposition.
   (c)   157th. Inf. Bde. on right are on CONDE PERUWELZ Road.

2.   The 156th. Inf. Bde. and affiliated troops will advance tomorrow (9/11/18) and secure the line of the ANTOING POMMEROEUL CANAL between F.21.D.5.2 and G.15.C.6.5.

3. (a)   An Advance Guard consisting of 7th. Royal Scots, "C" Coy. 52nd. Bn. M.G.C., "A" Battery, 56th. Bde. R.F.A. and 1 Section 156th. L.T.M. Battery under command of Lieut. Col. W.T. EWING, D.S.O., will cover the advance of the Bde. and will make good the following lines:-
      (a) CONDE – PERUWELZ Railway between L.7.A.7.5 and L.25.A.9.6.
      (b) PERUWELZ – CONDE Road between L.3.A.2.7 and L.21.D.7.6
      (c) CADROUILLET – OUTREL'EAU – LENOUVEAU MONDE – High ground in L.12.C – L.19.central.
   (b)   Reports will be rendered when these lines have been reached and when touch has been gained on the right flank.
   (c)   In view of fact that Northern flank will probably be exposed throughout the day, Advance Guard Commander will arrange for 1 Coy. of his Main Guard to march along the FOLQUIN – PERUWELZ Road.
   (d)   The Advance Guard will move forward from present line (K.29.central – K.16.central) at 0615.
   (e)   O.C., "A" Battery, 56th. Bde. R.F.A., will report to O.C., 7th. Royal Scots (K.22.D.2.5) at 0500 to receive instructions.

4.   The Main Body will march along the HERGNIES – MONT DE PERUWELZ – BONSECOURS Road in accordance with attached march table.

5.   Advance will be pressed as rapidly as possible. If the crossing of the ANTOING CANAL is in any way possible 4th. Royal Scots will be prepared to pass through 7th. Royal Scots and make good the Eastern Bank.

6.   First Line Transport will march with units, Lewis Gun limbers in rear of Coys. remainder in rear of Battalions.

7.   Reports to head of Main Body.

8.   ACKNOWLEDGE.

Captain,
Brigade Major, 156th. Inf. Bde.

Issued at 0010

Copy No.					
1 to 4th. R.S.		No. 8 to "C" Co.52 MG Bn.		No.15 174 I.B.	
2	7th. R.S.	9	O.C. Bearer Pty.	16	175 I.B.
			1/1 L.F.A.		
3	7th. S.R.	10	1/2 L.F.A.	17	S.C.
4	156th. L.T.M.By	11	410 Fld. Co. R.E.	18	B.T.O.
5	56th. Bde. R.F.A.	12	412 Fld. Co. R.E.	19	Sigs.
6	"A" By. 56th.RFA	13	52nd. Div.	20 & 21	Diary
7	"B" Co. 52 M.G.Bn	14	157th. Inf. Bde.	22	File

MARCH TABLE.

Serial No.	Unit.	STARTING POINT.	
		Place.	Time.
1.	Bde. H.Q.	Road Junction K.23.c.5.1	0700
2.	4th. Royal Scots & 156th. L.T.M.Batt. (less 1 Section)		0700
3.	"B" Co. 52nd. Bn. M.G.C.		0720
4.	56th. Bde. R.F.A. (less 1 Battery)		0730
5.	7th. Cameronians (Sco. Rifles)		0800

APPENDIX VI SECRET.

Copy No. 18

156th. INFANTRY BRIGADE ORDER No. 70.

Ref. Map – 1/20,000 – Sheet 45 N.W. 9th. November 1918.

1. (a) Aeroplane and civilian reports indicate no enemy W. of MONS except possibly a few snipers in BOIS DE RAULOUR.
   (b) Canadian Corps have taken VILLE POMMEROEUL and are working N. and E.
   (c) 157th. Inf. Bde. are approximately in line with us on our right but 175th. Inf. Bde. are some 5 miles behind on our left.

2. 52nd. Division is continuing its advance Eastward tomorrow.

3. (a) The 156th. Inf. Bde. will advance Eastward tomorrow (10/11/18) covered by an advance Guard under command of Major J.H. SLATER, D.S.O., Commanding 1/4th. Royal Scots.
   (b) The Advance Guard will consist of –
      4th. Royal Scots
      "B" Coy. 52nd. Bn. M.G.C.
      2 platoons VIII Corps Cyclist Bn.
   (c) "B" Coy. 52nd. Bn. M.G.C. will report at H.Q., 4th. Royal Scots (G.15.A.9.1) at 0715 and the 2 platoons VIII Corps Cyclists at 0700.
   (d) The leading troops of the Advance Guard will leave the line G.23.D.9.6 – G.12.A.0.6 at 0800.

4. The Northern and Southern Bde. Boundaries for tomorrow's advance will be:–
   Northern:– An E. and W. line through G.6.central
   Southern:– An E. and W. line through G.24.central.

5. The following objectives will be made good by the Advance Guard:–
   (a) Road between PONT DU CALVAIRE and H.20.B.2.0.
   (b) The line of the Road H.4.central – H.11.A.2.3 – H.17.D.2.6 – H.23.C.8.7.
   (c) The Railway line running through I.1.B and D., I.7.B and D., I.13.B., I.20.A.
   Reports will be sent back when these lines are gained.

6. The Main Body will march in accordance with the attached March Table.

7. Lewis Gun limbers, magazine limbers, medical cart and 1 tool cart per Battalion and 3 limbers of L.T.M. Battery and fighting limbers of M.G. Coys. will march with units.
   The remainder of the First and Second Line Transport will march Brigaded under B.T.O.
   All Transport will march with units to the starting point and "B" Echelon will be assembled under orders to be issued by B.T.O. there.

8. 4th. Royal Scots will not proceed beyond the last objective mentioned in para. 5, and 7th. Sco. Rifles will be prepared to pass through them there, either to continue the advance or to take up an outpost line for the night.

9. Reports to the Head of the Column main body.

10. ACKNOWLEDGE.

Issued at 2330
Captain,
Brigade Major, 156th. Inf. Bde.

Copy Nos. 1 to 4th. Royal Scots
          5   7th. Royal Scots
          6   7th. Gord. Highrs
          7   157th. Inf.Bde. Battery
          8   59th. Bde. R.F.A.
          9   "D" Co. 52nd. Bn. M.G.C. (Group Cmdr)
          7   Bearer Party 1/1st. L.F.A.B.
          8   1/2nd. L.F. Amb.
          9   410th. Fld. Co. R.E.
         10   VIII Corps Cyclist Bn.
         11   52nd. Division
         12   157th. Inf. Bde.
         13   155th. Inf. Bde.
         14   A.A.
         15   D.A.Co.
         16   O.Co. Div. Sigs.
      17 & 18 War Diary
         19   File

MARCH TABLE.
To accompany Brigade Order No. 70.

Serial No.	Unit.	FROM	STARTING POINT Place	STARTING POINT Time.	Route.	Remarks.
1	Bde. H.Q. and 1 platoon VIII Corps Cyclists	COKE OVEN	Bridge at G.15.d.8.9	0830	G.17.D.9.8 – H.14.A.2.5 – H.11.D.5.1 – SIRAULT.	
2.	7th. Sco. Rifles	BLATON	as for Serial No. 1	0835	as for serial No.1	To be clear of Cross Roads G.14.D.9.5 by 0904
3.	"B" Co. 52nd.Bn. M.G.C. less 2 Sections. "C" Co. 52nd. Bn. M.G.C.	MONT DES GROS EILLERS	Cross Roads G.14.D.9.5	0909	Bridge at G.15.C.8.9 & thence as for serial No.1	
4.	56th. Bde. R.F.A	BONSECOURS	Cross Roads G.9.C.7.9	0925	as for serial No. 3	
5.	7th. Royal Scots 156th. L.T.M.Bty	BLATON	as for serial No. 4	1000	as for serial No. 3	No troops to use Rd. G.8.B.6.4 – G.9.C.9.7 in getting to Starting Point

"A" Form.
MESSAGES AND SIGNALS.

Army Form C. 2121.

~~APPENDIX VII~~

TO
4th N.S. L.T.M. Bty "B" Coy MG Bn
N.S. Bde Hqrs. O.T.O.
56 Bde R.F.A. 155 M. Bde

Sender's Number.	Day of Month.	In reply to Number.	AAA
M/1/2	11/11/18		

155th Infantry Bde are passing through our line this morning and taking up the pursuit AAA The head of the Advance Guard will enter HERCHIES at 0700 AAA Final objective line of JURBISE–NIMY Road AAA 56th Bde R.F.A. and "B" Coy 55th M.G. Bn. should be prepared to support this attack or to move forward on receipt of orders AAA All traffic of Bde. will be kept off the road from 0500 onwards AAA As prisoners are expected to view all men transport and animals should be placed under cover at dawn AAA Bde will communicate on receipt of orders from Bde. H.Q. AAA ACKNOWLEDGE and add all concerned

From 155th Inf Bde.
Place
Time 0345

(Z)

WAR DIARY

Appx VIII

Report on Operations of 156th Infantry Brigade for the period 2/11/18 to date.

Ref.Maps
1/20,000 Sheet 44, N.E.
1/40,000 Sheets 44 and 45.
and attached tracing.

2nd Novr.

1. The Brigade took over the left section of the 8th Divisional sector in which the Outpost Line was held by the 2nd Bn. West Yorkshire Regiment.

Relief was complete by 0150 on the 3rd inst., and on completion the Brigade was disposed as shown on the attached tracing with 7th Cameronians in the Outpost Line on the right, 4th Royal Scots in the Outpost Line on the left and 7th Royal Scots in support.

3rd Novr. to 7th Novr.

2. The Brigade remained disposed as indicated above.

A very active system of patrolling, as far as the flooded and water-logged nature of the ground in front would allow, was maintained throughout the period, as it was expected that the enemy might retire at any time.

All preparations were made for crossing the ESCAUT River and JARD CANAL as expeditiously as possible should the enemy retire. 4 rafts (JERUSALEM) were stored at LE LONG BUHOT which were to be used to ferry the leading Coy. across both the ESCAUT River and JARD CANAL. Sufficient rafts to enable foot bridges to be made over both the River and the canal were located at HAUTE RIVE and a supporting company of 7th Cameronians was told off to assist the R.E. in carrying these down to the waters edge.

8th Novr.

3. (A). The patrols sent out during the night 7/8th November drew the usual M.G. fire as did also the dawn patrol to the broken bridge at K.26.A.4.7.

Immediately after dawn all enemy fire ceased and a further daylight patrol was therefore sent down to the bridge at K.26.A.4.7. This patrol was unable to draw any enemy fire and it was therefore concluded that the enemy had withdrawn and a report sent to Division (timed 0810) accordingly.

(B) Immediately the daylight patrol returned with the above information the forward company 7th Cameronians proceeded to carry down the 4 rafts at LE LONG BUHOT and to cross the river at K.26.A.4.7.

This they did successfully but owing to the river having overflowed its banks and flooded the country between the ESCAUT River and the JARD CANAL (280-300 yds) to a depth of 3 feet in places it was impossible to carry the rafts across to the JARD CANAL. They were therefore paddled across, a slow and laborious process, and it was not until 1130 (at which time the footbridge over the JARD CANAL was completed) that a whole company was across the CANAL.

After this the crossing was slightly accelerated as a proper ferry service of rafts and pontoons had been organized across the flooded area but even then only 44 men could be put across every 20 minutes.

The first coy. of 7th Cameronians to cross the JARD CANAL took up a position covering the Bridgehead and the second company, which had completed its crossing by 1225 was directed to move southwards to clear HERGNIES of snipers who were reported to be firing on the R.E. Bridging party at COUPURE (K.27.D.) This was done and the two companies had taken up the line K.27.D.5.2./

-2-

K.27.D.5.2.-K.27.C.1.7. -K.22.C.5.1.- K.21.B.8.3.-
K.21.B.7.7.-K.20.A.4.8.by 1400.

(C) Owing to the length of time taken to cross the flooded area, it was decided to cross only the remainder of the 7th Cameronians and the Coy.VIII Corps Cyclist Bn., by the footbridges and to direct the remainder of the Brigade to the pontoon bridges at COUPURE which by this time (1400) had been completed.

The 7th Royal Scots accordingly crossed by these bridges and moved on to take up the line K.29 central - K.18.central which was reached at 1615.

(D) As it was then nearly dark and my communications were none too good I decided to halt on the above line for the night and to continue my advance at dawn the following morning.

All troops except the two outpost companies of the 7th Royal Scots and 2 platoon posts from the 7th Cameronians to protect my northern flank, were therefore billeted and ordered to be ready to start at dawn.

(E) Reports having been received from Civilians and an officers patrol to the effect that there was a small party of Huns with signalling apparatus in WIERS(K.7.B.), one platoon was sent from 4th Royal Scots to round them up. The platoon arrived there at midnight to find that the enemy had left an hour before.

9th November.4. (A) At 0615 the Brigade covered by an Advance Guard consisting of 7th Royal Scots, "C" Coy.52nd M.G.Bn., A/56th Bde.R.F.A. and 1 section 156th L.T.M.Bty. advanced to make good the line of the ANTOING-POMMEROEUL Canal, the main body marching along the HERGNIES MONT DE PERUWELZ- BONSECOURS Road. Two companies 7th Royal Scots acted as Vanguard and 1 coy. acting as left flank guard moved along the POLQUIN -PERUWELZ.

No opposition was met with and by 0930 the line of the Canal between G.15.C. and F.21.D. was reached by the vanguard.

The VIII Corps Cyclist Bn., who were acting as a screen to the Advance Guard reported that a bridges fit for infantry had been left at F.21D/.5.0. G.9.A.9.6. and G.15.C.9.7. These reports were confirmed and by the aid of the inhabitants who worked extraordinarily well they were all very soon repaired sufficient to allow M.T. to pass across.

(B) Whilst this repair work was being done Bridgeheads were formed at the two last named places by 7th Royal Scots and at 1400 4th Royal Scots were passed through 7th Royal Scots and moved forward to take up the line G.12.A.0.7.-G.24.C.1.5. which they reached at about 1500. It was decided to halt on this line for the night and the remainder of the Brigade were accordingly billetted in and around BLATON.

(C) Though no opposition was met with throughout the advance I considered it very likely indeed that the enemy would hold the line of the ANTOING CANAL and accordingly advanced on a wide front with my left flank extended as far as GADROUILLET so as to ensure that if either of the 3 bridges mentioned were

intact I might be able to get across the Canal at one point. Moreover/

Moreover the Division on our left was then, as throughout the advance, some five miles behind, and I considered it very necessary to secure the high ground to the North so as to prevent my line being enfiladed in the event of the passage of the Canal having to be forced.

Touch was gained with the enemy by VIII Corps Cyclists Bn. late that evening as they encountered a post with M.Gs. at LE PIQUET (A.11.B.) thus showing that we were close on the heels of the enemy.

10th Novr. 5. (A) The advance was continued at 0730 with an advance guard consisting of 4th Royal Scots and "B" Coy. 82nd M.G.Bn. The objective assigned to the Brigade was the capture of the village of ERBAUT.

The advance was continued as far as the TERTRE-NEUFMAISON Road when it was reported by the VIII Corps Cyclist Bn. that the enemy was holding the western outskirts of HERCHIES with M.Gs. and that they could not get on.

The advance of the main body as far as SIRAULT was somewhat delayed owing to the bad state of the roads through the BOIS DE VILLE which necessitated the diverting of 55th Bde.R.F.A. 7th Royal Scots and "B" Echelon Brigade 1st Line Transport down to HAUTRAGE.

(B) 4th Royal Scots were accordingly halted on the approximate line C.20.D.-C.26.D.-I.2.B. whilst arrangements were made to drive the enemy out of HERCHIES and continue the advance on the final objective.

The task was assigned to 1/7th Cameronians assisted by "A" Battery 9th Bde.R.F.A. and "B" Coy 82nd M.G.Bn.

The advance commenced at 1420 with 1 coy. very widely deployed on the Brigade front and 1 coy. protecting the exposed N.flank of the advance. It had also been arranged that the 157th Inf.Bde. should advance along the northern edge of BOIS DE BAUDOUR and endeavour to turn the HERCHIES position from the South, but it is not known how this move progressed as touch was not gained with that Brigade by our front line troops. Good progress was made in spite of some M.G.fire from HERCHIES itself and from VACRESSE, and HERCHIES was entered and passed by 1620.

(C) The advance continued for 1200 yards beyond HERCHIES at which point it was definately held up by heavy M.G.fire from the front. The enemy was also shelling HERCHIES and the SIRAULT-HERCHIES Road at this time with 77mm guns which it was thought were firing at about 5000 yds range.

(D) O.C., 7th Cameronians was ordered to continue his advance and gain the final objective. Accordingly he reinforced his leading companies and put in a further company on the South with the road in D.20.B. and D. as their objective with the idea of turning the position.

This second advance commenced at 2015. Progress at first was slow, partly on account of M.G.fire which prevented roads being used but mainly on account of the extreme darkness difficulty of the country.

By means largely of in...

-4-

good leadership the advance was continued and at 0100 THULIN had been cleared of the enemy and a position had been taken up on the high ground between that place and JURBISE.

(E) 2 M.Gs. and 17 prisoners were taken in this advance, which it is considered reflects the greatest credit on the 7th Cameronians.

11th Novr. 6.(A) As soon as our final objective had been taken all units, with the exception of the leading companies and 2 companies of 7th Royal Scots kept as inlying picquet and 3 platoon posts put out to protect my Northern flank, were billeted for the night.

(B) At dawn patrols of the 7th Cameronians were pushed forward, and by 7 am were able to report JURBISE clear of the enemy.

(C) At 0700 the 155th Inf.Bde. passed through HERCHIES to take up the pursuit and advanced to secure the line of the NIMY-JURBISE road.

(D) As soon as this line had been secured the whole of my Brigade was concentrated in HERCHIES and went into billets.

12th Novr. 7. The Brigade remained in billets in HERCHIES.
to
Date.

Brig.General,
Commanding, 156th Inf.Brigade.

17th November, 1918.

4th Royal Scots, (5)
7th Royal Scots, (5)
7th Cameronians (S.R.) (5)
15th T. Battery. (2)

Appendix IX

Subject: Educational Training.

1. The B.G.C., wishes that all Officers, N.C.Os and men shall do their utmost to make the Educational Training Scheme which has been set on foot, a success.

2. The general idea of future training is that the mornings shall be given up to Military Training, cleaning up, etc., and that the afternoons and evenings be devoted to Education, Sports and Amusement.

3. The hour 1630 - 1730 each day will be definitely set aside for educational purposes, and extra hours should be allotted as opportunity offers.
   (Note) An extra supply of candles for lighting class rooms, is being demanded)

4. All Officers must display interest and enthusiasm and give every possible assistance to Education Officers and Instructors.
   There must be a driving force. While the training is voluntary, it is necessary that men be compelled to understand the benefits of it and urged to take up some subject or other that may be of benefit to them.

5. Each N.C.O. and man should be individually interrogated by his Platoon Commander as to:-

   (a) The Trade or calling he desires to follow after Demobilization.
   (b) The kind of Instruction he thinks would improve his chances of success in that trade or calling.
   (c) Whether he has any desire for general education or for technical training, and if so, of what sort.

   Complete lists should be compiled, showing the kind of tuition (if any) required by each man in the Unit.

6. Each Unit has competent Instructors in many subjects, and the needs of many will therefore be able to be met within the unit. In the event of outside help being required for any particular subject, application should be made to Brigade H.Q.

7. The Scheme should be started here and now. Classes in Elementary English, Arithmetic, Shorthand, French, etc., should be formed at once and fresh subjects should be taken in hand as soon as practicable.

8. Divisional and Brigade Educational Officers will correspond direct with Bn. Educational Officers over matters of detail.
   Bn. Educational Officers should keep in close touch with one another and will meet at Brigade H.Q. each Tuesday at 1600 to exchange views and state their wants.

19th November, 1918.

H. Sayer
Captain,
Brigade Major, 156th Inf. Bde.

Original

959

War Diary
of
156th Infantry Brigade
From 1st to 31st December 1918.

Confidential

Volume XLIII

WAR DIARY / INTELLIGENCE SUMMARY

Army Form C. 2118.

R.H.Map 1/40,000 Sheet 38

156th Infantry Brigade Vol XLIII

DEC. 1918

Place	Date	Hour	Summary of Events and Information	Remarks and references to Appendices
L.OM.13.1.S.E.	DEC 1918 1st to 12th		**Page ONE** The Brigade remained in billets as follows:— B.H.Q. L.OM.13.1.S.E. — 4 Royal Scots MONTIGNIES — 7th Royal Scots NEUFVILLES — 7th Camerons — LENS 3 hours training either military or educational per man daily, the military training consisting of platoon tactical exercises, practice in wiring and entrenching, Lewis Gun Drill, Gas Drill and command, what an equal amount of time being given to Sport. Education was proceeded with as energetically as the supply of books and material would allow. Yet the necessary books and material came to supply them is to be built the scheme could be a success but at present it can [fall] a bit flat or that account. Although every encouragement they can transfer them into employ and the education officers ones my yours, the supply of material is the controlling factor and is at present poor. An interesting football competition is being played and other been arranged. Bn [starts] a Platoon league, each Platoon turning 2 teams so as they get all ranks to take the necessary amount of exercise. A Harriers club has been started and much interest taken in well, so many members in the activity and indeed Norwich a success	

Ref. Map Sheet 38 1/40000

WAR DIARY
or
INTELLIGENCE SUMMARY

DECEMBER 1916
156th Infantry Brigade.
Vol XLIII

Place	Date	Hour	Summary of Events and Information PAGE TWO	Remarks and references to Appendices
LOMBISE	Dec 13th		The Divisional Commander inspected the units of the Brigade. Bns. paraded with one coy. in marching order, two coys in fighting order and one coy in drill order. Companies were inspected first as a whole and then each coy was inspected either in company drill, rapid wiring, siting trenches, intensive or tactical training. The chief fault was lack of cleanliness, due to the great difficulty in getting cleaning material. Divisional Commanders remarks and those of the B.G.C. are shown as an appendix.	(Appendix I)
			Capt. H. SAYER, M.C. Bde major proceeded on 14 days leave to U.K on 16th Dec and his duties were taken over by Capt. G.S. SMITH, MC at 7h 800 After.	
	18th		Capt. D.B. ALLAN M.C. resumed duties of Staff Captain on his return from U.K. leave.	
			Weather from 13th to 16th was wet and made training in the open almost impossible on most days.	

WAR DIARY
INTELLIGENCE SUMMARY.

156th Inf. Bde.

DECEMBER 1918

PAGE THREE

Place	Date	Hour	Summary of Events and Information	Remarks and references to Appendices
LOMBRISE	19th		Headqrs of 156th L.T.M. Battery moved to W. Brigade Commander held a conference of Commdg. Officers re. Sadng Area Competition, and various points were drawn attention to.	(Appendix II.)
	20th		Area Competition started. Brigade Group for purposes of this Competition includes 4 Bde units also 52nd M.G. Bn. 410th and 412th Field Coys. 1st L.J.A. 1 sect. 3rd L.J.A.	
	21st		Team from No 1 Coy. 7th Royal Scots won the Divisional Association Football Competition.	
	22nd		Meeting of Brigade Sports Committee held at Hdqrs. 4th Royal Scots.	
	23rd		Bde Commander inspected Bcoy of 7th Royal Scots and thereafter visited the Company's billets. Heavy rainstorm during forenoon.	
	24th		Bde Commander inspected B Coy 7th Scot. Rifles and thereafter visited the Company's billets. Bde Commander rode through parts of area daily and minor matters were noted against certain units. Weather during 19th - 24th was dull, but generally fair.	

Army Form C. 2118.

WAR DIARY
or
INTELLIGENCE SUMMARY.

(Erase heading not required.)

1/40,000. M.Map. Sheet 38. 156th Inf. Bde.

Instructions regarding War Diaries and Intelligence Summaries are contained in F.S. Regs. Part II. and the Staff Manual respectively. Title pages will be prepared in manuscript.

DECEMBER 1918   Vol XLIII

Place	Date	Hour	Summary of Events and Information	Remarks and references to Appendices
LOMBISE	Dec 25		PAGE FOUR. Christmas Day was observed as a holiday. Divisional Commander visited Bde. Hdqrs. Weather fine and slight frost. Series of gatherings were held by various units in the evening. Lieut. Genl. Sir A.J. GODLEY, K.C.B. K.C.M.G. Commdg XXII Corps visited Bde. Hdqrs. and Hdqrs. of 4th Royal Scots and 7th Royal Scots on 28th Dec. Training during this period much suffered from continual wet weather, but education progressed, and there are now over 600 regular students, in addition to the large numbers of men attending special lectures. Further supplies of sports equipment were received and issued to units. Brigade Officers Riding School was discontinued owing to the weather and the state of the ground. Brigade Commander visited areas of different units and in several cases inspected the billeting arrangements. Casualty Return. Strength Return.	(Appendices III, IV)
	31			

[signature] Lt. Col. [signature] Capt. a/Bde. Major.

BM 112

4th Royal Scots,
7th Royal Scots,
8th Cameronians,
156th L.T.M. Battery.
----

1. The attached letter giving the comments of the Divisional Commander on yesterdays inspection, is forwarded for information and necessary action.

2. Every effort is to be made to improve the cleanliness throughout the Brigade. Equipment must be scrubbed and washed until it actually _is_ clean and men must be made to take every care when in their billets that the kit is put down in some clean spot, or properly hung up.

3. Reference para.(b) of attached letter. One of the points especially noted was that no steps had been taken to repair the covers to waterbottles before they had gone too far.

4. Reference para.(e) in many cases N.C.Os and men and even Platoon Commanders did not appear to know what the contents of a pack should be. There can be no excuse for this as it has been clearly laid down in BM 118 and 123 both of 22/10/18 both for Fighting and Marching Order.

5. It was noticed that many small details with regard to kit and equipment such as:- which kicking strap should be crossed over the other - the position of the gas helmet in fighting order (whether in front or behind the hip) require laying down by unit commanders.

6. All the above points, and those mentioned in attached letter must be given immediate attention. Most of the points show the necessity for careful and frequent inspections. Unit commanders should hold frequent inspections themselves and should instruct Junior officers _how_ to Inspect. Too much notice should not be given to Companies before an inspection by a Battn. Commander.

14th December, 1918.

sgd. H. SAYER, Captain,
Brigade Major, 156th Inf. Bde.

G. 3/11.

G.O.C.,
156th Inf.Bde.

    The Divisional Commander was pleased to note at his Inspection today that the Platoon and Section organization is adhered to, that the methods of instruction adopted in the Brigade are sound, most officers knowing how to set promptly to work, and that the standard of tactical training in the Brigade is good. The favourable impression produced by these matters was, however, spoilt by the great lack of cleanliness in most companies.

    In addition to the necessity for cleanliness, the following points require more attention:-

(a) Unsteadiness in the ranks.
(b) Minor repairs to clothes and kit. A man should be ashamed to appear with a hole in his clothes or some small article of equipment missing which he could mend or improvise himself.
(c) Fitting and putting on equipment.
(d) Close order drill. - Failure to check and point out mistakes. Talking.
(e) Incomplete and dirty kit in packs. In one Company a man was carrying a mess orderly's kit because his own was being kept ready to go on guard. The Divnl.Commander strongly objects to such practices. Incidentally the kit shown was not creditable to the man to whom it belonged.
(f) Some officers were slow in grasping verbal orders, and require to use more imagination and intelligence in carrying them out.
(g) Sections should be numbered 1 to 16 in the Company, vide O.B.1919, dated September 1918, para.3.
(h) Before giving the general salute the Officer Commanding should wait until the General is approaching in front of the centre of the battalion.
(i) Light mortar Battery. - The practice of kneeling on one knee when firing the mortar unmounted is to be discontinued forthwith.
The white line down the centre of the mortar must be maintained in a serviceable condition.
The Divisional Commander was pleased to see that the equipment worn by the battery was well cleaned.

13th Decr.1918.
                        sgd. A.G.Thomson, Lieut-Colonel,
                        General Staff,52nd Division.

		BM 167
4th. Royal Scots	Area Commandant, LLWS	
7th. Royal Scots	410th. Field Co. R.E.	
7th. Sco. Rifles	412th. Field Co. R.E.	
156th. L.T.M. Batt.	52nd. M.G. Bn.	
Lieut. Austin, Bde. H.Q.	1/1st. Lowland Field Amb.	
Section, 3rd. Lowland Field Amb.		

1. Reference 52nd. Division Memo. G.4/29 of 18/12/18.

    Brigade Commander, 156th. Inf. Bde. hopes that every effort will be made by units of the 156th. Inf. Bde. Group to win the above competition.

2. The following are suggested as means by which this end may be attained:—

    (a) Each unit to appoint a Works Officer, who will be responsible for prospecting for possible improvements and supervizing all constructional work. He should also ascertain from civilians what assistance they require and arrange for complying as far as possible with their requests, co-ordinating all the work in a definite programme for approval by his unit commander.

    (b) Each unit to keep a logbook, showing all work done and time in "man hours" since coming into this area, all assistance given to farmers, improvements to billets, carting done, etc. etc.

    (c) It is considered most important that all ranks should be made familiar with the terms of the competition, and everything should be done to stimulate interest among the men.

3. As the areas concerned are the actual billetting areas, it is essential that the necessary notice boards (Belts to be worn") be placed on all roads leading out of billetting areas, and such boards should have "Billetting Area LIMIT" on the back or facing the opposite direction so that G.O.C. or his Staff will know when they have reached any given area.

4. The Area Commandant will assist in every possible way, and will take necessary steps in conjunction with units to ensure the co-operation of the civilian inhabitants in the matter of cleanliness of streets and farmyards.

5. It is impossible to attach too much importance to the turnout and appearance of the men on and off parade. Within billetting areas where belts are not compulsory there is often a tendency to slackness especially in saluting. Much can be done by the example of N.C.Os. to raise the standard in this respect.

6. A Competition will be held concurrently within the Brigade Group on exactly the same lines as the Divisional Competition.

7. In order to arrive at the results for this, the Brigade Commander and his Staff will visit areas of units to allocate marks. If about to enter any billets the Brigade Commander or other officer will first call at H.Q. of unit concerned, but will not do so if only passing through billetting area. On conclusion of visit he will inform units of any points which he considers might be improved.

8. Communications regarding any doubtful point in connection with the Competition should be addressed to the Brigade Commander, 156th. Inf. Bde.

21st. December 1918.

Captain,
A/Brigade Major, 156th. Inf. Bde.

Confidential.

No 10

War Diary
of
156th Infantry Brigade
From 1st to 31st January 1917

Original

Volume. XLIV

WAR DIARY
or
INTELLIGENCE SUMMARY.

(Erase heading not required.)

138th Infantry Brigade

Army Form C. 2118.

Place	Date	Hour	Summary of Events and Information	Remarks and references to Appendices
LONG/SE	27th 15		Being New Years day the Brigade was given a holiday. The 7 Royal Lincs held an Inter Coy. Cross Country Run in which teams K Co. 5's represented the Bryan area and kept Gen. in Hunts Coats. Kits 5's were the Bryan area and held all men who served with them in Gallipoli.	
	5th		Training is much confined but the weather for the most part had detained the Country. Games and two points.	
	6th		7Bde (Brig Gen Riggall and G.S.O. (Capt F Bryan [illegible]) returned from leave. L.t. Col Mackenzie 7/8th Infantry Bryan that the 2nd of The son inpatched during to 7/8th Infantry Bryan that the 2nd of The as [illegible] with acted. & week he knit should any to find. The is looking very satisfactory. The scheme has been approved and [illegible] have been thoroughly entered in the stamp of the ambulation	
	7th	11.30	A [illegible] of the ceremonial [illegible] of the presentation [illegible] by [illegible] General Maxwell [illegible] ourself took very and [illegible]	

Army Form C. 2118.

WAR DIARY
or
INTELLIGENCE SUMMARY.
(Erase heading not required.)

[3rd Infantry Brigade] [page 2]

Place	Date	Hour	Summary of Events and Information	Remarks and references to Appendices
NIMBLE	Tues 8th	1100	The G.O.C. inspected the Brigade staff officers and presented 61 MMs. He paraded on arrival of the Brigade, A.D., 2 Lay R.E., Signallers and the remainder of the Brunswanne horse drawn up in a hollow square. After inspection and presentation of medals the whole paraded and marched past in close column. The G.O.C. Division expressed himself as pleased with the French parade, especially in marching with extreme steadiness. Afterwards the G.O.C. March Past. Units of the B.B. carried out round training so far as master permits. Athletics including preliminary ties for Divisional and B.B. competitions are going strong and seem to keep officers and men happy and contented. G.O.C. addressed the officers of each Battalion, pointing out the difficulties of the moment and they entail a measure of frankly taking them into our confidence. He also urged strenuous importance of education & athletics as general employment with a view to keep the men employed permanently.	
	9th 10th			

WAR DIARY or INTELLIGENCE SUMMARY

Army Form C. 2118.

Place: LUMBRES
Date: July 1918

Date	Hour	Summary of Events and Information	Remarks
17th	10.30	A parade for General Bruneval handed to Colonel entrusted not having arrived. Men Parade formed by 2nd Royal Irish at Moulton. The Regiments. The canvas huts and the station at Mouton to be empty used. A good parade.	
18th		General handed on the Drill Ground NE 4 months for inspection by the G.O.C. Commander. Parade hours at 10.30 which necessitates the units turning out by 7.30. A good parade. One cold as the men had stand for an hour and a half. Think took them rather over one meal entertainment returning about 16.00. A long day and not carefully helped with them. They the Short Royal Bruneval handed but not their long Bruneval was not known so much standing about.	
19th 20th		Cold bright days. Usual handouts etc and football competition and Try Horse Launched. Official in both days of Royal Irish won both. Tonight (under Westen) and Catering Staff Inspection. A good game and will continue.	

Army Form C. 2118.

WAR DIARY
or
INTELLIGENCE SUMMARY.
(Erase heading not required.)

156" Infantry Brigade

Place	Date	Hour	Summary of Events and Information	Remarks and references to Appendices
LMB/S/E	21st 25 26		hand having parades and games and sports. heather very cold with hard frost. This latter necessitates the cancelling of the Brigade Transport Sports which were then taken place on 24th.	
	27th		Officers 1/the Brigade front gave a very successful dance at MONS own 200 people attended including May Gen EG Sinclair Scott 74th Division who at one time commanded this Brigade	
	28 to 31		Bicycle matches with good fun were making training and sports difficult. the roads being bad for Horse Transport. General Investigation has for a close this month. the present G.O.C. Brigade is Brigadier (J?) King reached on the last day of the month. They have are him returned to about 1520 fighting strength, thoroughly happy and entirely among to the way they are looked after by Bros and Lt Col concerned of Amusement provided. Moral Strength Returns an attachment.	

A Scott Capt
Brigade Major
156 Inf Bde

156 Infantry Brigade — War Diary

Strength – January 1919

	Week Ending 4th		Week Ending 11th		Week Ending 18th		Week Ending 25th	
	O	OR	O	OR	O	OR	O	OR
4th Royal Scots	42	851	42	866	42	868	42	867
7th Royal Scots	41	846	41	862	40	861	40	827
Sco Rifles	36	777	36	804	34	800	34	791
	119	2474	119	2532	116	2529	116	2485

Original

9811

Confidential

War Diary

of

156th Infantry Brigade

1st to 28th February 1919.

Volume XLV

Army Form C. 2118.

WAR DIARY
or
INTELLIGENCE SUMMARY.

(Erase heading not required.) 136 Infantry Brigade

Instructions regarding War Diaries and Intelligence Summaries are contained in F. S. Regs., Part II. and the Staff Manual respectively. Title pages will be prepared in manuscript.

Place	Date	Hour	Summary of Events and Information	Remarks and references to Appendices
LOMBISE BELGIUM.	February 1st to February 28th 1919.		The position of the month has been the increased rate of Demobilization. During the month 18 officers and 1081 other ranks were Demobilized. A draft of 10 officers and 163 other ranks from 7th Scottish Rifles proceeded from the 5/6 Scottish Rifles at ROUEN on the 16th inst. and 10 officers and Drafts of 1 2.30 p.m. 7th Royal Scots and 10 officers and 190 O/Rs from 2nd Royal Scots an motor o/ors proceeded to the Army N°Repôts at short notice. Employment with arms other than has been very little not having this month though Education has proceeded fairly successfully and the men have been kept Happily fit and will by arranging games etc. The Brigade Sports and Transport Competition which should have come off on the 8th instant has been abandoned on account of the Shortage of numbers. The 7 Royal Scots has been the Divisional Sports chiefs by winning	

Army Form C. 2118.

WAR DIARY
or
INTELLIGENCE SUMMARY.
(Erase heading not required.)

Place	Date	Hour	Summary of Events and Information	Remarks and references to Appendices

At the Cartwright and Entry 100 Stone Tug of War Competition
Their Royal Scots won in the final of the Divisional Association Cup
and were beaten by 4th R.S.F.

The Brigade won the Arms Competition for shortness, excellent Rifle
and won the Anna Competition grove a success and enjoyed by all ranks took
day a great margin.
an interest in it.

I forward herewith returns an appendix)

A Hyden
Captain
Brigade Major
156 Infantry Brigade

War Diary Jany 1919　　　　　　　　　Appendix

Effective Strength of 156th Infantry Brigade
February 1919

Unit	Week ending 7th		Week ending 14th		Week ending 21st		Week ending 28th	
	O	OR	O	OR	O	OR	O	OR
4th Royal Scots	34	617	29	517	29	394	27	299
7th Royal Scots	31	606	29	510	28	435	27	381
7th Sco Rifles	26	541	23	442	15	207	14	116
	91	1764	81	1469	72	1036	68	796

Original

Vol 12

Confidential

War Diary
of
156th Infantry Brigade

From 1st to 6th March, 1919.

Volume XLVI

Army Form C. 2118.

WAR DIARY
or
INTELLIGENCE SUMMARY.
(Erase heading not required.)

137th Infantry Brigade

Place	Date	Hour	Summary of Events and Information	Remarks and references to Appendices
LOMPRET BELGIUM	MARCH 15th		The Brigade returned to this area — LENS — MONTIGNY LEZ LENS — NEUVILLES	
	15th	6 a.m.	On the 5th Major Brigden joined BM LEGGETT CMG DSO proceeded to UK on leave	
	17th	5 p.m.	Lieuty Bruce Wilson ask of the interior report of the whole Brigade who during his 18 months command of the Brigade has been known to him and noted him to a very high degree. There was not a man in the Brigade who would not have gone anywhere for him.	
	11th		Drafts of 9 officers and 189 other ranks 4/Royal Scots and 30 other ranks 7 Royal Scots went to 11th Bn Royal Scots in the RHINE army	
	16th		Draft of 4 officers and 200 other ranks 7/Royal Scots proceeded to 11th Bn Ir Royal Scots. The arrangements for the transfer of the above has passed and all ranks seemed very happy and contented	
	17th		The Brigade moved into Billets in SOIGNIES (Bde order No 71) Billets were not too busy to train but eventually everyone was settled in comfortably. All which could not proceed there was sent to the rail head by a railway transport.	Appendix I

Army Form C.2118.

WAR DIARY
or
INTELLIGENCE SUMMARY.
(Erase Heading not required.) 136th Infantry Brigade

Place.	Date.	Hour.	Summary of Events and Information.	Remarks and references to Appendices.
SOIGNIES BELGIUM.	March 17th to 31st.		The Brigade remained billeted in SOIGNIES during this period. Demobilization of men and horses was finally completed and all units were reduced to a Cadre with the exception of a few retained men who are to be sent on to its Regular Cadre as soon as they can stand. Rehearse strength return is attached	Appendix II

A. Taylor
Captain
Brigade Major

SECRET.

156th. INFANTRY BRIGADE ORDER NO. 71.   COPY NO. 7

Map. Ref: BELGIUM 1/100,000 Sheet 5.   15th. March 1919.

         1.   The 52nd. Division is concentrating at SOIGNIES as soon as possible.

MOVE. 2.   The 156th. Infantry Brigade will move to SOIGNIES by March Route on the 17th., instant. Battalions will move independently but will arrive there before 1500.

BILLETS. 3. Billets at SOIGNIES have already been pointed out to Battalions. Advance parties, may if desired, be sent on to SOIGNIES on the 16th. instant.

VEHICLES. 4. (a). Draft teams as under will report to Battalion H.Q., at 0800 on 17th. inst., to assist in moving all vehicles to the new area.

        Brigade Headquarters............. 3
        4th. Royal Scots................. 18
        7th. Royal Scots................. 17
        7th. Scottish Rifles............. 15

(b) On arrival in the new area, all vehicles will be unloaded, and with the exception of 2 Limbered G.S. Waggons, 1 Cooker, and 1 Water Cart per Battalion will be sent to Vehicle Park near the Station, the exact location of which has already been pointed out to Billeting Officers.

(c) Lieut. Mackintosh, Transport Officer, 7th. Royal Scots, will be in charge of the Vehicle Park, and all waggons will report to him at 1500 on the 17th. inst., at the entrance to the Park.

    Lieut. Mackintosh will report to the Brigade Major, at the Town Major's Office, SOIGNIES, at 1400 on the 17th. inst, to receive his instructions.

(d). A Guard of 1 N.C.O., and 3 men, 7th. Royal Scots, for protection of the Vehicle Park, will report to Lieut. Mackintosh outside the Town Major's office at 1600 on the 17th. inst. Lieut Mackintosh will arrange billets for a guard room at a suitable place.

LORRIES. 5. Lorries for the transport of extra stores etc., will report to Units as under, at 0830:-

        Brigade Headquarters............. 1
        4th. Royal Scots................. 2/1
        7th. Royal Scots................. 2/1
        7th. Scottish Rifles............. 2/1

Each Lorry may do 2 journeys in the day if necessary.

SUPPLIES. 6. (a). Rations for consumption on the 18th. instant will be drawn at present R.P.

(b). Rations for consumption on the 19th. instant, will be drawn at SOIGNIES in shed between Billets Nos. 58 and 60, CHAUSSEE DE ROEULX, SOIGNIES, at 1400 on 17th. instant.

(c). Refilling after 17th. inst., will be at 0900 at above-quoted shed in CHAUSSEE DE ROEULX.

VACATION/

2.

VACATION OF PRESENT AREA.	7. Steps will be taken to leave all Billets in present area scrupulously clean. Clearance Certificates will be obtained in all cases and a copy forwarded to Brigade H.Q.
MEDICAL.	8. All sick after arrival in new area will be evacuated through 1/1st. Lowland Field Ambulance. Location later.
POSTAL.	9. Changes in postal arrangements will be notified later.
ENTERIC FEVER.	10. Attention is drawn to D.R.O. 393 of 10th. instant, the provisions of which are to be rigorously enforced.
COMMUNICATIONS	11. No Telephone lines will be laid between Brigade H.Q., and Battalions on arrival in the new area in the first instance.
BRIGADE H.Q.	12. Brigade H.Q., will close at LOMBISE at 1000 on 17th. inst, and re-open at No. 61 RUE DE LA STATION, SOIGNIES, at 1400 on the same date.

13. ACKNOWLEDGE, by Wire.

H. Sayer
Captain,
Brigade Major, 156th. Infantry Brigade.

COPIES TO:-

1. 4th. Royal Scots.
2. 7th. Royal Scots.
3. 7th. Sco. Rifles.
4. Brigade Commander.
5. Brigade Major.
6. O.C., Brigade Signals.
7 &8. War Diary.
9. File.

www.ingramcontent.com/pod-product-compliance
Lightning Source LLC
Chambersburg PA
CBHW081424300426
44108CB00016BA/2292